GRADES 2–3

The Education Center®

The MAILBOX®

IDEA MAGAZINE FOR TEACHERS®

2011–2012 YEARBOOK

The Education Center, Inc.
Greensboro, North Carolina

The Mailbox® 2011–2012 Grades 2–3 Yearbook

Managing Editor, *The Mailbox* Magazine: Jennifer Bragg

Editorial Team: Becky S. Andrews, Diane Badden, Kimberley Bruck, Karen A. Brudnak, Pam Crane, Chris Curry, Tazmen Hansen, Marsha Heim, Lori Z. Henry, Troy Lawrence, Kitty Lowrance, Gary Phillips (COVER ARTIST), Mark Rainey, Greg D. Rieves, Hope Rodgers-Medina, Rebecca Saunders, Donna K. Teal, Sharon M. Tresino, Zane Williard

ISBN13 978-1-61276-244-9
ISSN 1088-5544

Printed in the United States of America.

The Mailbox® Yearbook
PO Box 6189
Harlan, IA 51593-1689

HPS242165

Contents

Language Arts

to
inform
to
persuade
to
entertain

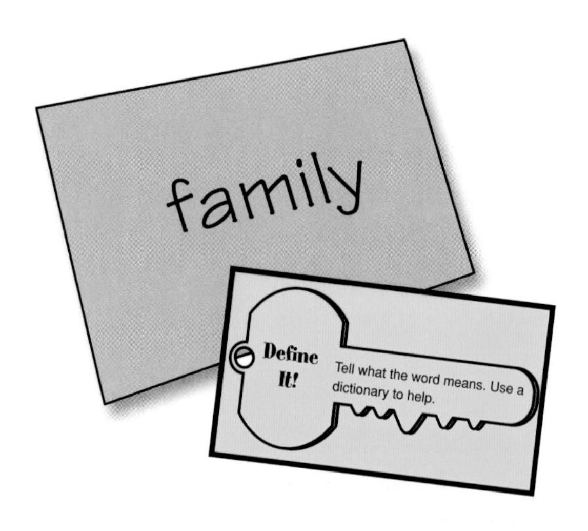
family
Define
It!
Tell what the word means. Use a dictionary to help.

Top This!

Author's purpose

Provide visual reminders to keep purposes for reading at the top of students' minds! First, gather three hats. Write each purpose for reading on an adhesive label and place each label on a hat. Then display the hats in an easy-to-see location. As students read texts throughout the day, have them identify which hat or hats match the purpose of the text. Reinforce the skill by wearing the corresponding hat or hats while you're reading aloud.

Beth Pallotta, Eden Christian Academy, Pittsburgh, PA

tip

Put your class mascot to work! Invite a student to place the matching hat or hats on the stuffed animal's head.

Keyed In

Content vocabulary, high-frequency words

Just right for small-group instruction, this activity unlocks and opens doors to new words! In advance, write words on a supply of index cards. Next, cut out the key cards from a copy of page 18 and hole-punch each one. Remove any cards with directions that don't apply to the words being practiced and store them on a metal ring. Stack the remaining cards facedown. To start the activity, show students a word card. Choose a student to take the top key card and read the directions aloud. Instruct the child to complete the task and then return the card to the bottom of the stack. Repeat with different word cards and different students.

Carolyn Burant, St. John Vianney School, Brookfield, WI

READING

tips & tools

Say, See, Me

Previewing, making predictions

Steer students through an upcoming reading with three little words. Copy and display the mini poster on page 19 in your reading area. Point out the three words featured on the poster and tell students to recite the words to themselves before they read a book. Explain that each word should remind them of a different prereading task: *say* reminds them to note important words on the cover and throughout the book; *see* directs them to the illustrations; and *me* reminds them to make connections to the content of the illustrations. Review the questions listed on the poster and encourage each student to ask himself these questions as he previews the story.

Christine A. Clemenson, Weymouth Township Elementary, Dorothy, NJ

Steer Your Reading!
SAY Look at words on the cover and in the book.
Is the story title a question? Can I answer it?
What important words give me clues about the story?
Are any words shown in bold print, italics, or in a different font? Why might they be important to the story?
SEE Look at the pictures.
How do the pictures give clues about where or when the story takes place?
What people, places, or things are shown?
What actions are happening in the pictures?
ME Look at the pictures.
Have I ever seen something like this? When?
Have I ever been anywhere like this? Where?
Have I ever done anything like this? What?

Mystery Words

Context clues

Instead of *whodunit*, students will ask, "What is it?" during this whole-group activity. To prepare, cut out a short article and a headline from the newspaper; then cover one word of the headline with a sticky note. After reading the article and any captions aloud, share any photos. Based on what they heard, guide students to determine the covered word. Remind students that when they read on their own and come to a mystery word, they should continue reading and use text features to help determine what the word means. **As an alternative**, post the partially covered clipping. Invite each child to review the clipping during her free time and write what she thinks the mystery word is in her reading-response journal. Then reveal the word at the end of the day.

Stephanie McHugh, Bristol Bay Elementary, Yorkville, IL

New School Opens
Without a

This Won't Hurt a Bit!

Contractions

Make an appointment for your doctors-in-training to provide some hands-on help. Give each child a copy of a card from page 20 and tell her to "prepare for surgery" by putting on imaginary surgical gloves (or provide her with a pair of plastic gloves) and taking out a scalpel (scissors). Direct each student to cut out the letter that isn't needed to make a contraction, flip over that letter, and write an apostrophe. If she has a *not* contraction, also instruct her to cut out the extra space between words. Guide the child to pantomime stitching the apostrophe to the word; then have her secure the pieces with a strip of tape. Finally, have each student share her original words and the newly formed contraction.

Tara Durning, Mother Teresa Academy, Clifton Park, NY

they are
they're
a

Greetings from...
the forest
Oct. 25, 2011
Dear friend,
I had a problem.
I was able to solve my problem by
Your pal,
Stellaluna

All in One

Story elements

Setting, characters, problem, and solution—this postcard activity covers them all! Copy the sentence starters, as shown, on the board; then give each child a large index card. On one side, the student draws and labels a picture that shows a story's main setting. On the other side, he writes a short letter from the story's main character's point of view, using the sentence starters to guide his writing.

Beth Pallotta, Eden Christian Academy, Pittsburgh, PA

Word	Our Meaning
zimulis	pencil
deski	desk
torakku	vehicle
szkola	school

Out of This World!

Context clues

Take students on a trip in space and introduce them to the meanings of new words all in the comfort of your own classroom! Before reading aloud *Baloney (Henry P.)* by Jon Scieszka, tell students that they may hear some words they do not know. Challenge them to use the text before and after the word, along with the illustrations, to determine the word's meaning. Reread the story, this time keeping a list on chart paper of the featured words (set off in colored text in the book) and your class-determined meanings. Then refer to the glossary in the back of the book to check students' work. If time allows, reread the story a third time, replacing the featured words with their actual meanings.

Stephanie McHugh, Bristol Bay Elementary, Yorkville, IL

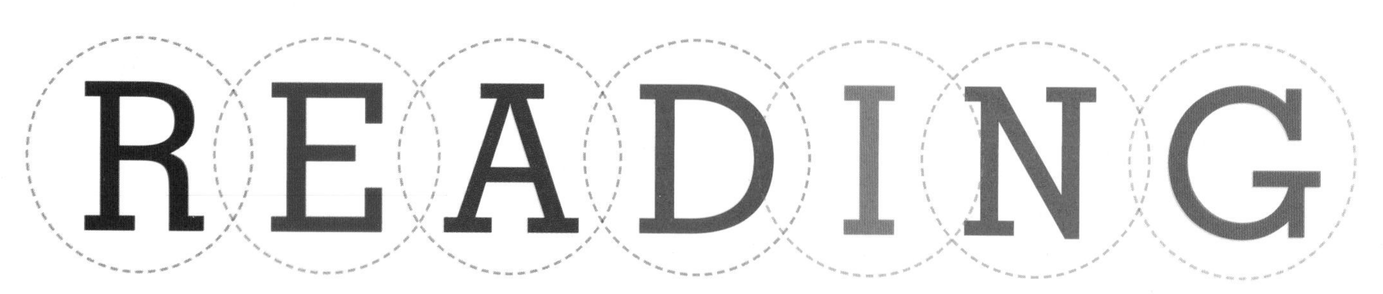
READING
tips & tools

Starring...
Character traits

Bring fictional characters to center stage with this star-studded idea. After reading a story, direct each child to write its title and author's name on a copy of page 21. Instruct her to write the name of a character in the middle of the star; then, at each point of the star, have her write to describe a different trait. If desired, have the student list evidence from the story that supports each trait. Use the student-made organizers to guide your reading discussion.

Gina Bittner, Dawson, NE

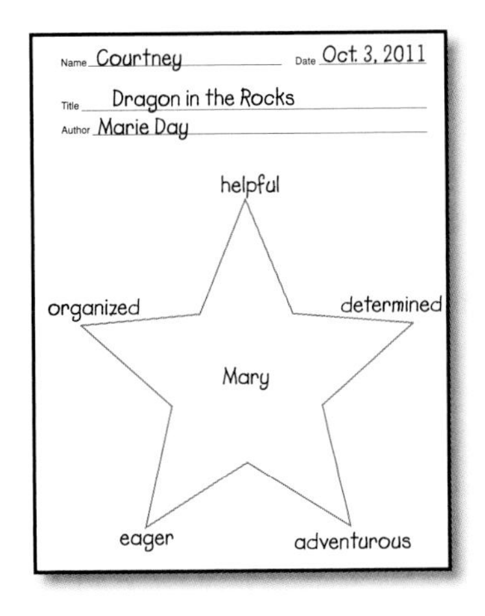
Name Courtney Date Oct. 3, 2011
Title Dragon in the Rocks
Author Marie Day

Mary: helpful, determined, adventurous, eager, organized

Help at Hand
Nonfiction text features

Have each child personalize a copy of a wristband pattern from page 22 and cut it out. Laminate each wristband for durability; then help each child secure the ends of his wristband with tape. Before reading a nonfiction selection, instruct each student to slip on his wristband and review the checklist, turning the band as needed. Encourage students to look at their wristbands after reading to verify the features found and to summarize what was read.

Leanne Baur, Hall's Cross Roads Elementary, Aberdeen, MD

Reading Nonfiction
Look for the title.
It will quickly tell you the topic you will read about.
Look for subtitles.
These are titles within the reading. They split the main topic into smaller parts.
Look for bold words.

An Attentive Audience
Fluency

Help students read expressively by designating a few minutes each week for buddy reading. During this time have each child read aloud to one friend. For students who prefer to practice independently or when there's an odd number of students, a stuffed toy animal can serve as the read-aloud buddy. Either way, students will benefit from the extra practice!

Bonnie Kinniff, St. Agatha School, Columbus, OH

PUFFIN CHAPTERS
Cam Jansen and the Mystery of the Stolen Diamonds
David A. Adler
Illustrated by Susanna Natti

Check out the main idea and details mini poster on page 23!

Perfectly sized for small-group instruction, this visual aid makes a handy reference! Copy the mini poster on page 23 and put it in a plastic page protector. Then copy a class supply of the desk tag patterns on page 24. Refer to the poster during guided reading lessons; then give each child a desk tag to use when reading independently. After the lesson, store the mini poster and pattern page in a binder or with your reading files.

Main Idea and Details
The main idea is the big message the author wants to share. It's the most important idea from the reading.
Farm Jigsaw Puzzle
Details are small pieces of information about the main idea.
Hint: Put all the details together to better understand the main idea.

All classified ads are nonrefundable!

• Please complete all information. • Fill in one word per space. • Print clearly. •

Name Travis
Date January 9, 2012
Title Mr. Popper's Penguins
Pages Chapter 15: "Popper's Performing Penguins"

Payment Information
25¢ per word
Total Ad Cost $9.75
(After writing your summary, count the total number of words you wrote. Use a calculator to multiply that number by $0.25.)

Summary (Write only one word in each space.)

The	manager	was	unhappy	because
the	Marcos	didn't	come.	Something
was	wrong.	The	Poppers	needed
money	so	they	did	a
show	called	Popper	Performing	Penguins.
It	was	a	hit!	The
Poppers	signed	a	contract	to
perform	around	the	country.	

It's All in the Ad

Summarizing

Extra! Extra! Read all about this great idea that helps students see the value in identifying the main points of a story. To start, model how to complete a copy of page 25, writing a very long and drawn-out advertisement for a previously read story. Determine the cost of the advertisement and explain to students that when summarizing text, it's better to address the main points. With students' help, omit unneeded details and recalculate the cost of the ad. Then give each child his own copy of page 25 and challenge him to write a summary of a current story that stays below a predetermined cost, such as $10.

Jodi Tuskowski, Washington Elementary, Stevens Point, WI

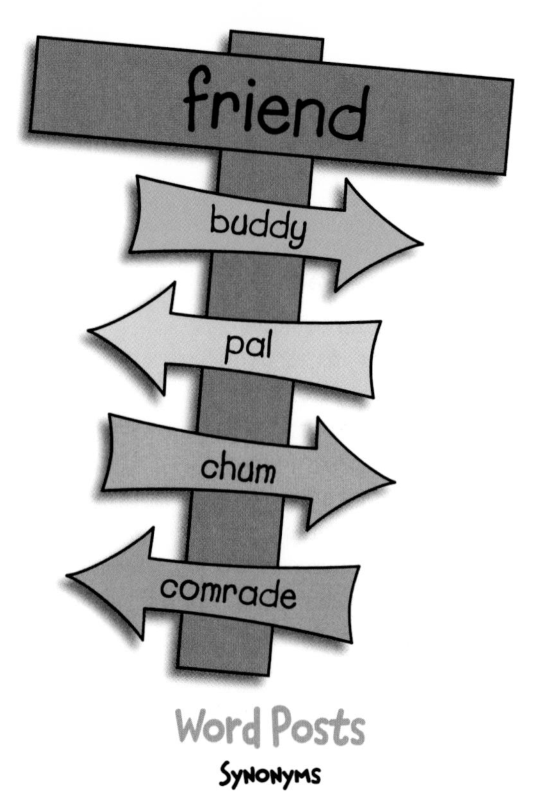
friend
buddy
pal
chum
comrade

Word Posts

Synonyms

Lead students to recognize words with similar meanings. To start, give each small group of students a 3" x 12" strip (sign) and a 3" x 15" strip (post) of light brown paper. Assign each group a word and instruct one child to write it on the sign. Next, give each group a copy of page 26. Direct students to cut out the arrow patterns and have each child write a different synonym for the assigned word on an arrow. (Guide students to use a thesaurus if needed.) Then have each student lightly color her arrow. Instruct each group to glue its sign and arrows to the post; then display the projects around the room for easy reference.

Lou Smeja, Emerson School, Elmhurst, IL

READING

tips & tools

READING

tips & tools

Step by Step

Fact and opinion

This idea gets students moving toward a better understanding of statements that are known to be true and statements that reflect a personal view. Have students walk around the room in a large circle and, as they do, announce several statements. If you announce a fact, they continue walking; but if you announce an opinion, they stop walking. If you notice students having trouble with certain statements, stop and discuss them.

Jessica Pinegar, Columbia Elementary
Madison, AL

tip

If space is limited, have students march in place at their desks.

It is cold in our classroom today.

That is Ms. Pinegar's personal view. I better stop walking.

Qualities From A to Z

Character traits

Discuss with students words that describe their personal qualities. Explain that these same qualities, or traits, can be used to describe and better understand story characters. Next, have each child list the alphabet on a 4″ x 11″ paper strip (bookmark) and then, for each letter, list as many character traits as possible. Encourage students to reference their bookmarks when describing characters they read about.

Mandy Wallace, Moraine Elementary
Prospect, PA

a: annoyed, assertive
b: brave, bossy
c: calm
d: determined
e: energetic
f: fearless
g: greedy, good
h: hopeful, helpful
i: independent
j: jolly
k: kind
l: lovable
m: mean
n: nervous
o: odd
p: proper
q: quiet
r: rowdy
s: shy, smart
t: talented
u: unfriendly
v: vain
w: worrisome
x: X-ray
y: young
z: zealous

Jot Your Thoughts

Documenting reading progress

Inform parents of their children's reading progress with this simple tip. Keep a supply of prepared notes home, like the one shown, at your guided-reading table. When you see a reading behavior to celebrate or one that needs extra attention, jot it down on a note. Make a copy of the note before sending it home. **As an alternative**, use the information to send a quick email and then file a note with the child's other running records and observations.

Lynn Sanders, Sope Creek Elementary
Marietta, GA

To the family of Jalil: 1-20-12 date

I read with your child today and noticed Jalil rereading text to make sure he understood what he was reading. I was impressed to see him being so careful! Please encourage him to keep it up.

Ms. Sanders

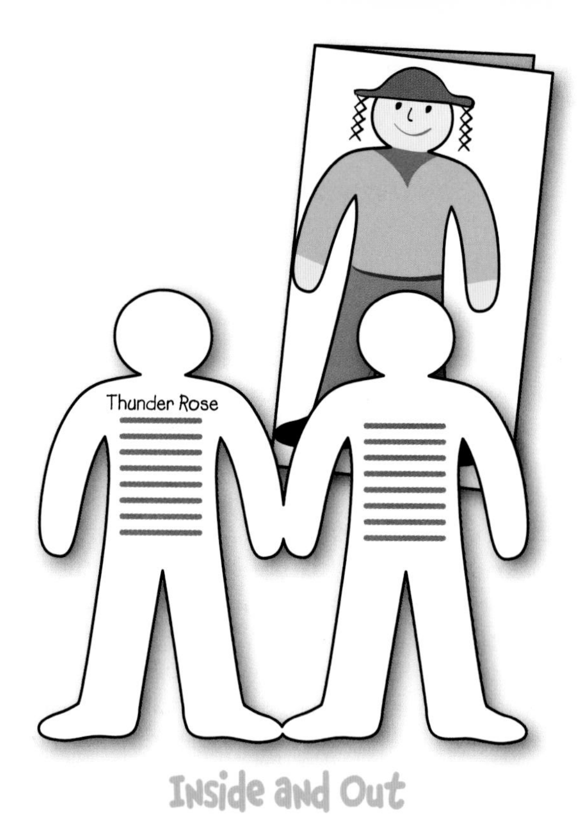
Thunder Rose

Inside and Out

Character traits

Introduce students to this fun activity, and they'll better understand a story's character. After reading a fictional text, have a child fold a sheet of paper in half and trace a copy of the character pattern from page 27 so that one arm rests along the fold, as shown. The student uses descriptions from the reading to draw a character's physical traits on the tracing. Then he cuts out the character, cutting through both layers of paper and keeping the fold intact. He opens the cutout and writes the character's name, along with a description of the character's personal qualities and feelings. If desired, post the completed projects on a display titled "We Know These Characters Inside and Out."

Beth Pallotta, Eden Christian Academy, Pittsburgh, PA

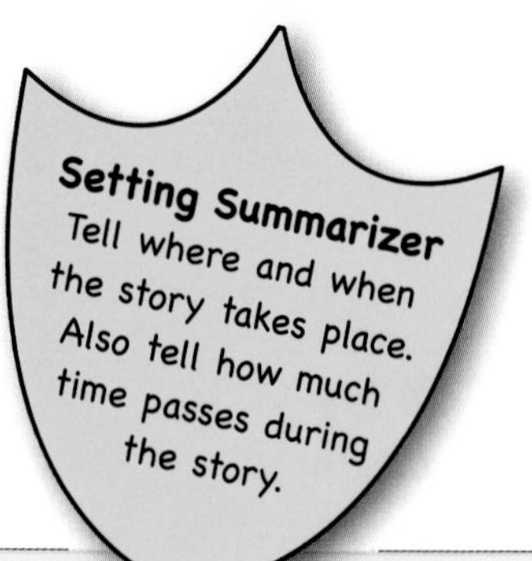
Setting Summarizer
Tell where and when the story takes place. Also tell how much time passes during the story.

Setting Summarizer
Tell where and when the story takes place. Also tell how much time passes during the story.

Character Quizzer
Write and answer three questions about one of the story's characters. Use the questions to quiz your group.

Problem Provider
Tell the main problem and how the character(s) tries to solve it.

Solution Server
Tell the group how the problem is solved in the reading. Then tell why you do or do not think this is a good solution.

Ready to Review

Story elements

Students talk story basics with this twist on literature circle roles. Prepare a supply of paper cutouts and write on each a different task, such as those shown. Laminate the cutouts for durability. Give each member of a small group a cutout and tell her she is responsible for completing the task on a sheet of notebook paper and then sharing her results with the group. Afterward, collect the cutouts to use another time. **To vary the activity**, simply write a question related to a different story element on each cutout. Tell each child she is responsible for providing the answer and must prepare evidence from the text to support it.

Karen Almond, Royston Elementary, Royston, GA

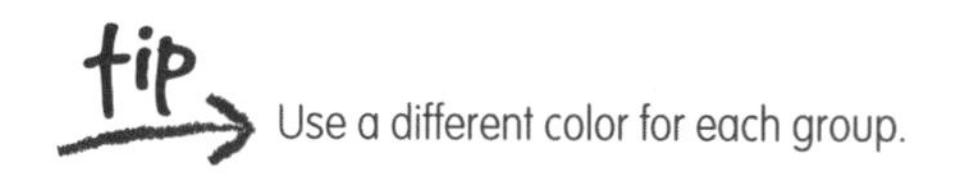
tip
Use a different color for each group.

READING

tips & tools

Picturing Words

Visualizing

To start, remind students that to visualize text is to a make a picture in their heads of what is being read. Also explain that when they can each create a picture, they better understand the text. Next, instruct each child to draw on a portable dry-erase board a large thought bubble. Read a selection aloud while students follow along silently. Then invite each child to draw in his thought bubble what he pictures in his head. When he is finished, direct him to hold his board next to his head. Then pair him with another child who is also done drawing. Instruct each partner to explain his drawing and how it matches the text.

Karen Almond, Royston Elementary, Royston, GA

Along the Line

Sequencing plot

Help students organize a story's most important events with this straightforward technique! After a student reads a story, have her complete a copy of the timeline organizer from page 27. Then have her refer to the organizer to write a summary or to provide an oral retelling. **As an alternative**, have each child complete a timeline organizer for each chapter she reads instead.

Beth Pallotta, Eden Christian Academy
Pittsburgh, PA

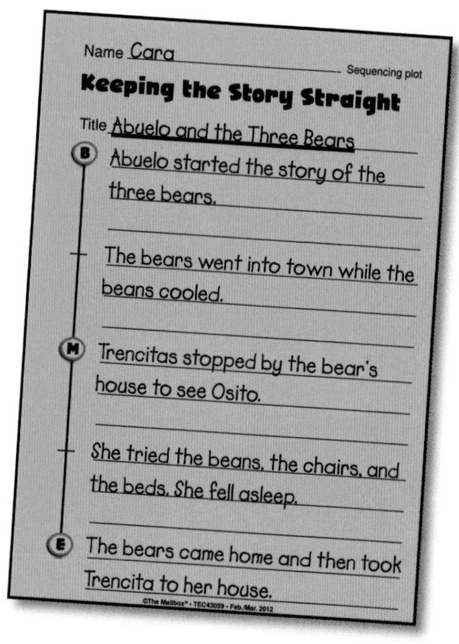
Name Cara — Sequencing plot
Keeping the Story Straight
Title Abuelo and the Three Bears
B Abuelo started the story of the three bears.
The bears went into town while the beans cooled.
M Trencitas stopped by the bear's house to see Osito.
She tried the beans, the chairs, and the beds. She fell asleep.
E The bears came home and then took Trencita to her house.

Come Out on Top

Test vocabulary

Prepare students for standardized test vocabulary with this simple routine. Title a display as shown and label each card in a supply of index cards with a different testing term. Post the cards in a triangular arrangement. On the first day of review, read aloud a word from the bottom row and discuss its meaning. Then write a student-friendly definition on the card. On the following day, review the previous day's word and its meaning before reviewing the next term on the same row. Continue each day, moving from the bottom of the display to the top until all the cards have been reviewed.

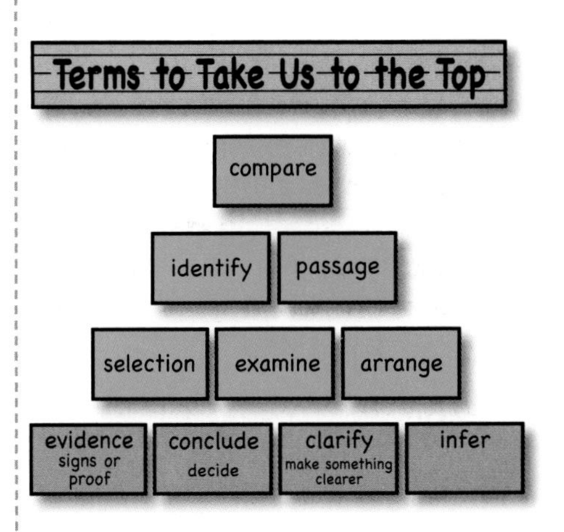
Terms to Take Us to the Top
compare
identify
passage
selection
examine
arrange
evidence
signs or proof
conclude
decide
clarify
make something clearer
infer

Check out the making inferences mini poster on page 28!

Help students dig up information from their reading with this handy visual aid! Copy the mini poster on page 28 and make a class supply of the graphic organizer on page 29. Place the poster and organizer back-to-back in a plastic page protector. Refer to the poster during your guided reading lessons. Then flip the poster over, pull out a dry-erase marker, and model how to use the graphic organizer. Ask a question about a recent reading and have each child write it at the top of a copy of the organizer; then have him complete the organizer independently. After the lesson, store the combination poster and reproducible in a binder or with your reading files.

Making Inferences
Sometimes authors don't tell you everything with their words. To dig into their meaning, act like a scientist. Use clues from the reading and add them to facts you already know. This is called inferring.

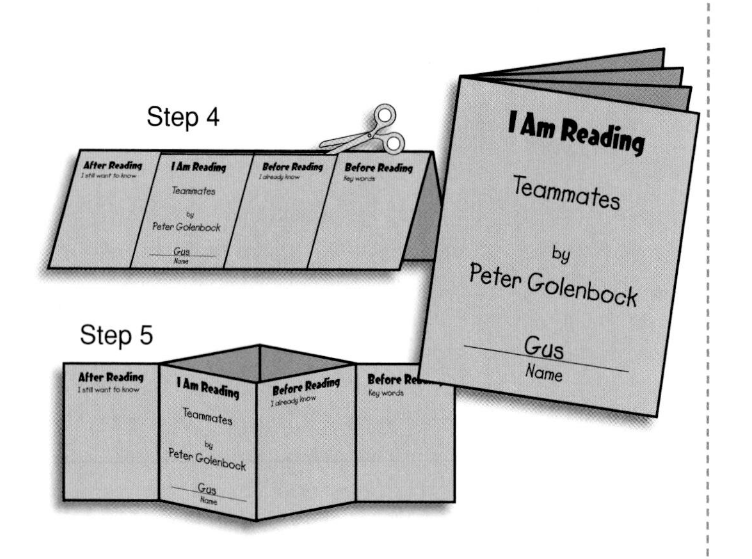
Step 4
After Reading
I still want to know
I Am Reading
Teammates
by
Peter Golenbock
Gus
Name
Before Reading
I already know
Before Reading
Key words
Step 5
I Am Reading
Teammates
by
Peter Golenbock
Gus
Name

Little Learning Log

Monitoring comprehension

Not only is this mini booklet a great way to help students organize important ideas from nonfiction text, but it's a space saver as well. Have each child follow the steps below.

1. Hold a cutout copy of page 30 vertically and fold it from top to bottom.
2. Unfold the paper, rotate it to a horizontal position, and fold it from top to bottom.
3. Fold the paper from left to right two more times.
4. Unfold the paper, poke a hole in the center, and cut along the bold middle line.
5. Press the ends towards the center until the middle expands outward.
6. Fold the pages to make a booklet and then complete each page.

Barclay Marcell, Roosevelt School, Park Ridge, IL

Magic Tree House: Lions at Lunchtime
by Mary Pope Osborne
Jay
Like the other Magic Tree House books, this one starts and ends in Frog Creek, Pennsylvania. Most of the story takes place on the plains of Africa.
Jack and Annie had to solve a riddle. A gray bird led them to the answer: honey!

A "Can-Do" Project

Book reports

To begin, a child covers a large can with construction paper. He writes the book's title and author's name on a piece of paper; then he writes his name and, if desired, adds an illustration. The student glues the paper to the can. Next, he collects three or more objects or pictures that relate to the story. For each object or picture, he writes an explanation of how it relates to the story and attaches it as shown. If desired, direct the student to include one item related to the main character, one related to the setting, and one related to the plot. The child places the objects or pictures in the can to later share aloud with his classmates.

Tanya Hampton
Creative Frontiers School
Citrus Heights, CA

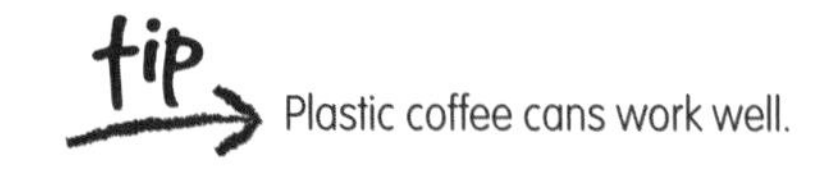
tip
Plastic coffee cans work well.

READING

tips & tools

READING

tips & tools

Quiet Comments

Reading response

This small-group activity encourages students to share ideas without uttering a single word! Give each group a large sheet of paper; then pose a question about a recent reading. Direct each child to write his response on his group's paper. Then encourage students within each group to read each other's responses and add drawings such as a smiley face for agreement and a question mark for responses that need clarification. If time allows, direct students to move from paper to paper, reading other groups' work.

Michelle VanAusdall, Centennial Elementary
Evans, CO

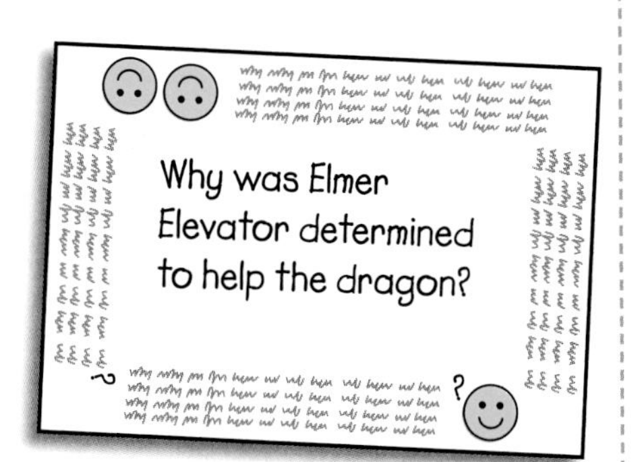
Why was Elmer Elevator determined to help the dragon?

Reading Wrap-Up

Independent reading motivation

Have students log their at-home reading with summary cards. As part of morning work or to start reading time, instruct each child to write on an index card a brief summary of her reading from the night before. If desired, direct her to include a personal opinion of the reading as well; then have the student drop her card into a designated container. Later in the day, gather students together and select two cards. Share the summaries aloud and ask students to clarify their remarks, or encourage their classmates to ask questions about the readings. Reward each of the two students with a special privilege or small prize; then remove the rest of the cards for review.

Sarah Leahy, Seven Oaks Elementary, Wesley Chapel, FL

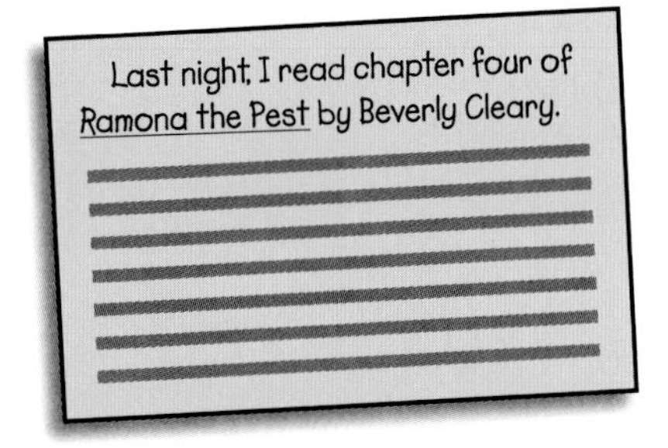
Last night, I read chapter four of Ramona the Pest by Beverly Cleary.

Everyone's Favorite Housekeeper

Multiple-meaning words

Send your students to work with Amelia Bedelia and expose them to homonyms. Read aloud *Amelia Bedelia* by Peggy Parish and then discuss with students some of the tasks that Amelia Bedelia did incorrectly. List the tasks and underline the confusing verbs. Next, have student pairs use the dictionary to find the meaning Amelia Bedelia used and the one the Rogers expected her to use. Display the definitions on a chart like the one shown. **To extend the activity**, set up a similar chart, replacing "task" with "word." As they read other texts, challenge students to find words with more than one meaning that might confuse Amelia Bedelia if she read them.

Christy Bentley-Dye, Eastminster School
Conyers, GA

Task	Amelia Bedelia	The Rogers
change the towels	make different	replace
dust the furniture	make dusty	make free of dust
draw the drapes	make a picture of	move to one side
trim the fat	to add ribbons and lace	cut or clip
dress the chicken	put on clothes	prepare for cooking

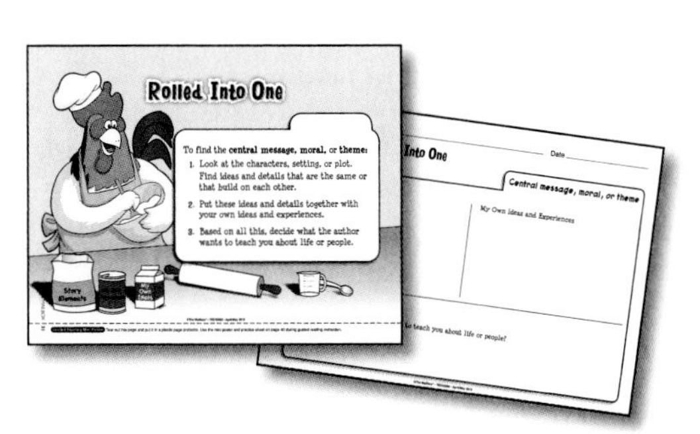
Rolled Into One

Use the mini poster and organizer (pages 31–32) to help students identify a **central message**, **moral**, or **theme**.

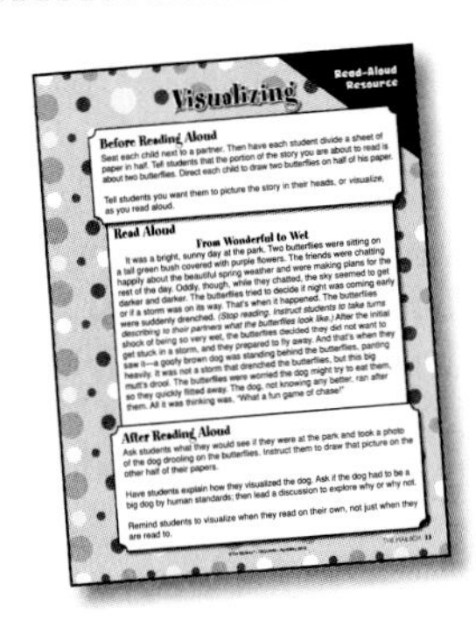
Visualizing

Provide practice with **visualizing**. Find a ready-to-use passage on page 33.

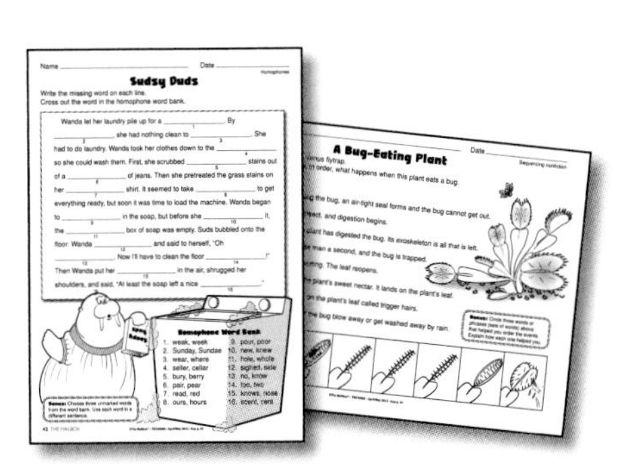
Sudsy Duds
A Bug-Eating Plant

Check out the practice pages for **homophones** (page 42) and **sequencing nonfiction** (page 51).

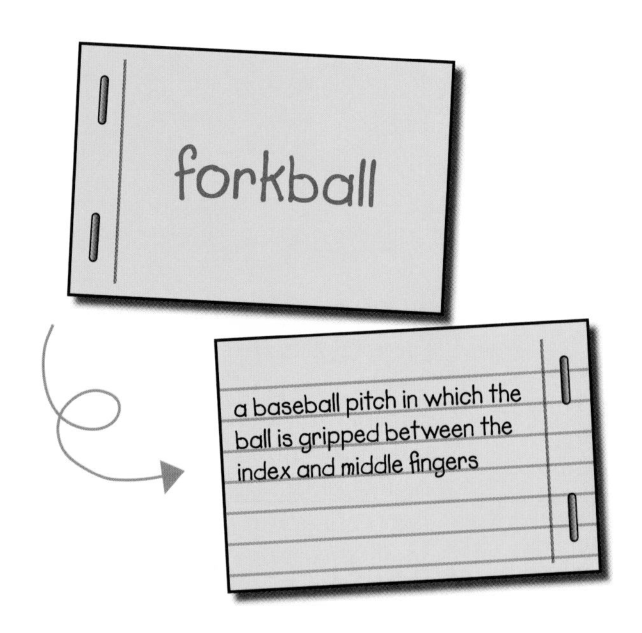
forkball
a baseball pitch in which the ball is gripped between the index and middle fingers

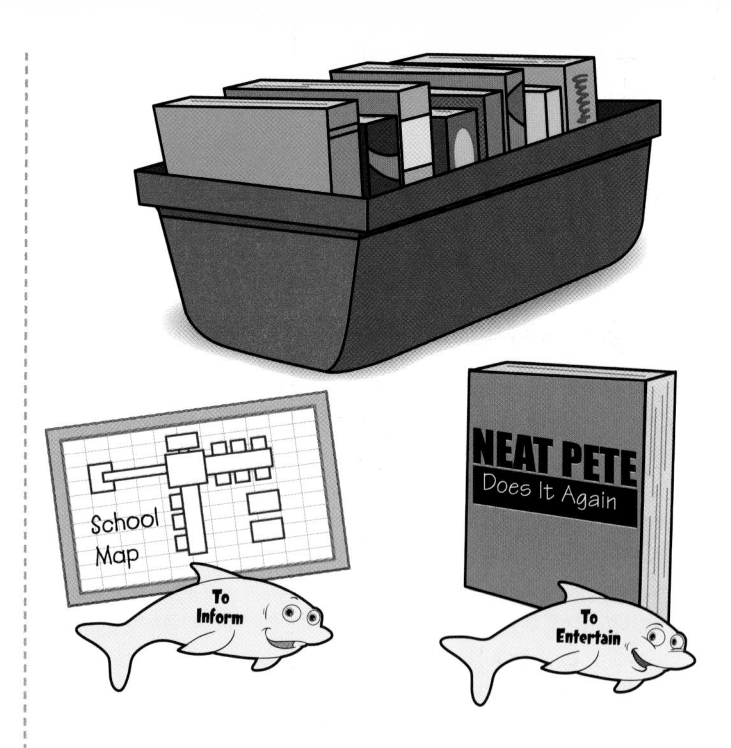
School Map
To Inform
NEAT PETE
Does It Again
To Entertain

Word of the Day

Vocabulary, dictionary

Task students with introducing new words, and everyone will benefit! Each day, choose a different child to find an interesting word in the dictionary. After approving the word, direct the student to write it on the front of an index card and its definition on the back, leaving a small margin on the right side of the card's back. Next, have him write the word on the board and share its meaning with the class. Instruct the rest of the class to copy the word on a designated page of their reading journals. Staple the card to a display, as shown, for future reference.

Brenda Wilke, Davison Elementary, Detroit, MI

On "Porpoise"

Purpose for reading

To set up this center, cut out a copy of the porpoise patterns on page 34. Select ten different texts, ensuring that each text matches one of the purposes shown. After the books are selected, laminate each cutout and use a wipe-off marker to write the matching book titles on the back of each cutout to make answer keys. Put the cutouts and books at a center. A child lays the cutouts purpose-side up and then skims each text. He stacks each text in front of the matching cutout and, when he has all of them sorted, he turns over each cutout to check his work. Periodically replace the texts with different ones and update the answer keys.

Christine A. Clemenson, Weymouth Township Elementary, Dorothy, NJ

READING

tips & tools

On Your Mark...
Reading motivation, fluency

This simple idea makes for a fun one-person reading race! To prepare, make a class supply of double-sided copies of the letter on page 35 and a poem like the one on page 262. Encourage each child to keep his copy with him so he can read the poem to ten different staff members, family members, or students. Each time he reads the poem, have the child get the listener's signature. When the student has read to ten different people, he turns in the paper for a small reward and a new paper with a different poem.

Dody Denault, Caswell County Schools
Yanceyville, NC

Dear Friend,

My classmates and I are racing to become better readers. Please sign your name after I read the selection on the back of this letter aloud to you. Thanks for your help and involvement!

1. Ms. Knight
2. Justin
3.
4.
5.
6.
7.
8.
9.
10.

When you have 10 different names, take this form to your teacher.

Arm Wrestling

Ollie was the wrestling champ
And proudly wore his crown.
Each time he faced **opponents**,
He quickly pinned them down.

He didn't win his **bouts** by wit
Or due to good-luck charms.
He was the wrestling **champion**
Because he had eight arms!

Tracking the Evidence
Character analysis

Put your reading detectives on the case with this post-reading activity. Give each child a copy of page 36 and have her write the title and author's name of a recently read story. Next, instruct the child to list in the left column the names of up to four important characters. Then the student writes five different adjectives to complete the top row. For each character, the student refers to the text to determine if there is evidence of the trait and uses the code to record a response. **To extend the activity**, the child includes a page number below each plus symbol to indicate where the text evidence was found.

April Lotempio, Ben Franklin Elementary
Kenmore, NY

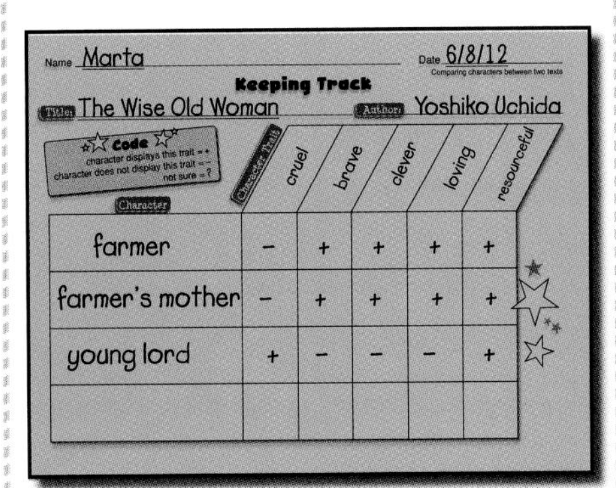

Name Marta Date 6/8/12

Keeping Track

Comparing characters between two texts

Title: The Wise Old Woman Author: Yoshiko Uchida

Code: character displays this trait = +, character does not display this trait = –, not sure = ?

Character	cruel	brave	clever	loving	resourceful
farmer	–	+	+	+	+
farmer's mother	–	+	+	+	+
young lord	+	–	–	–	+

Happily Ever After
Fairy tales

Sprinkle some magic into your fairy-tale genre study with these charming ideas!

- To signal that reading instruction is about to begin, tell students that it's time to take a magic-carpet ride. When students hear this, they report to the carpet or reading area with their materials.

- Tape a glittery star to the top of an unsharpened pencil to make a magic wand. Loan the wand to a student who exhibits exceptional behavior. Encourage him to use the magic wand to help you select students for reading aloud or contributing responses to a reading discussion.

Linda Hill, Robert Wilson Elementary
Corpus Christi, TX

Check out the reading **practice sheets** on pages 37–51.

Key Cards

Use with "Keyed In" on page 6.

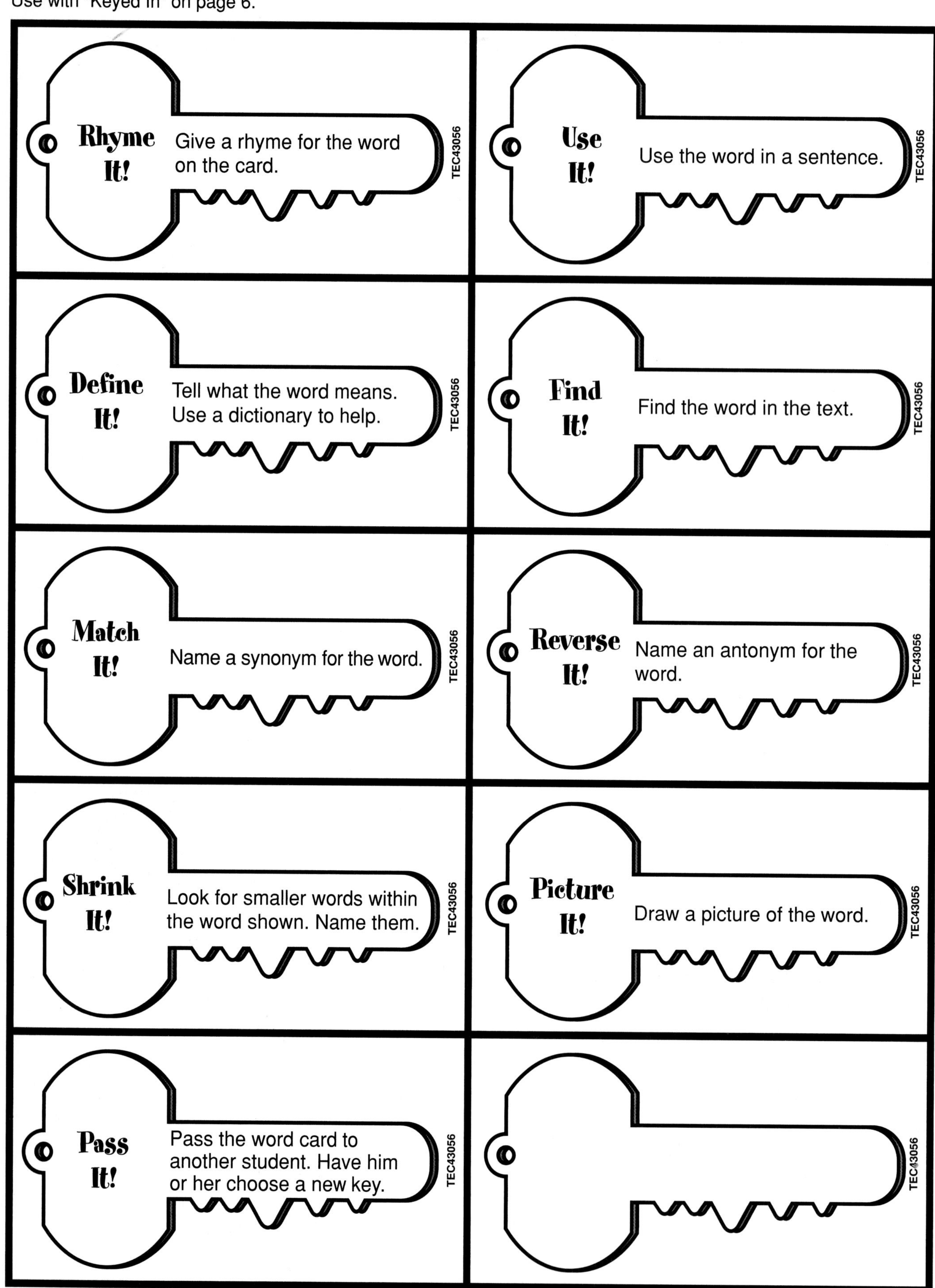

Rhyme It!
Give a rhyme for the word on the card.
TEC43056
Use It!
Use the word in a sentence.
TEC43056
Define It!
Tell what the word means. Use a dictionary to help.
TEC43056
Find It!
Find the word in the text.
TEC43056
Match It!
Name a synonym for the word.
TEC43056
Reverse It!
Name an antonym for the word.
TEC43056
Shrink It!
Look for smaller words within the word shown. Name them.
TEC43056
Picture It!
Draw a picture of the word.
TEC43056
Pass It!
Pass the word card to another student. Have him or her choose a new key.
TEC43056
TEC43056

Steer Your Reading!

SAY Look at words on the cover and in the book.

- ☐ Is the story title a question? Can I answer it?
- ☐ What important words give me clues about the story?
- ☐ Are any words shown in **bold print**, *italics*, or in a different font? Why might they be important to the story?

SEE Look at the pictures.

- ☐ How do the pictures give clues about where or when the story takes place?
- ☐ What people, places, or things are shown?
- ☐ What actions are happening in the pictures?

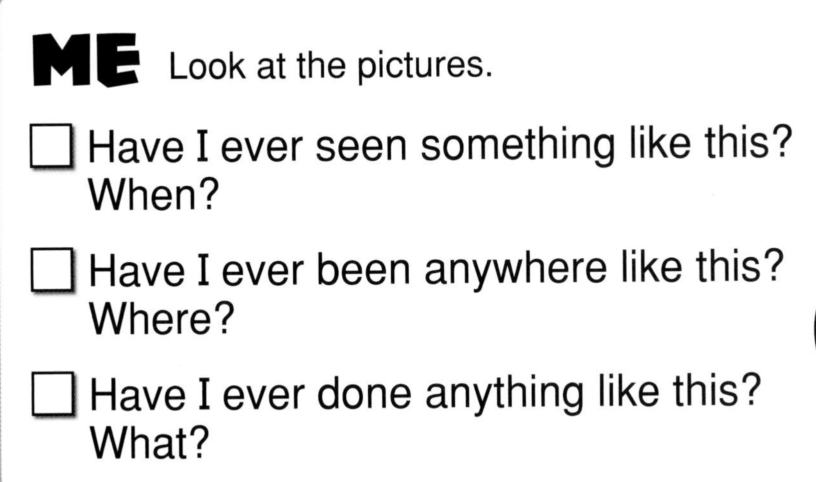

ME Look at the pictures.

- ☐ Have I ever seen something like this? When?
- ☐ Have I ever been anywhere like this? Where?
- ☐ Have I ever done anything like this? What?

SAY
SEE
ME

Note to the teacher: Use with “Say, See, Me” on page 7.

Word Cards

Use with "This Won't Hurt a Bit!" on page 7.

I am	TEC43056	he is	TEC43056
it is	TEC43056	she is	TEC43056
they are	TEC43056	we are	TEC43056
you are	TEC43056	are not	TEC43056
could not	TEC43056	did not	TEC43056
do not	TEC43056	does not	TEC43056
had not	TEC43056	has not	TEC43056
have not	TEC43056	is not	TEC43056
should not	TEC43056	was not	TEC43056
were not	TEC43056	would not	TEC43056

Name ____________________ Date ____________

Title ______________________________

Author ______________________________

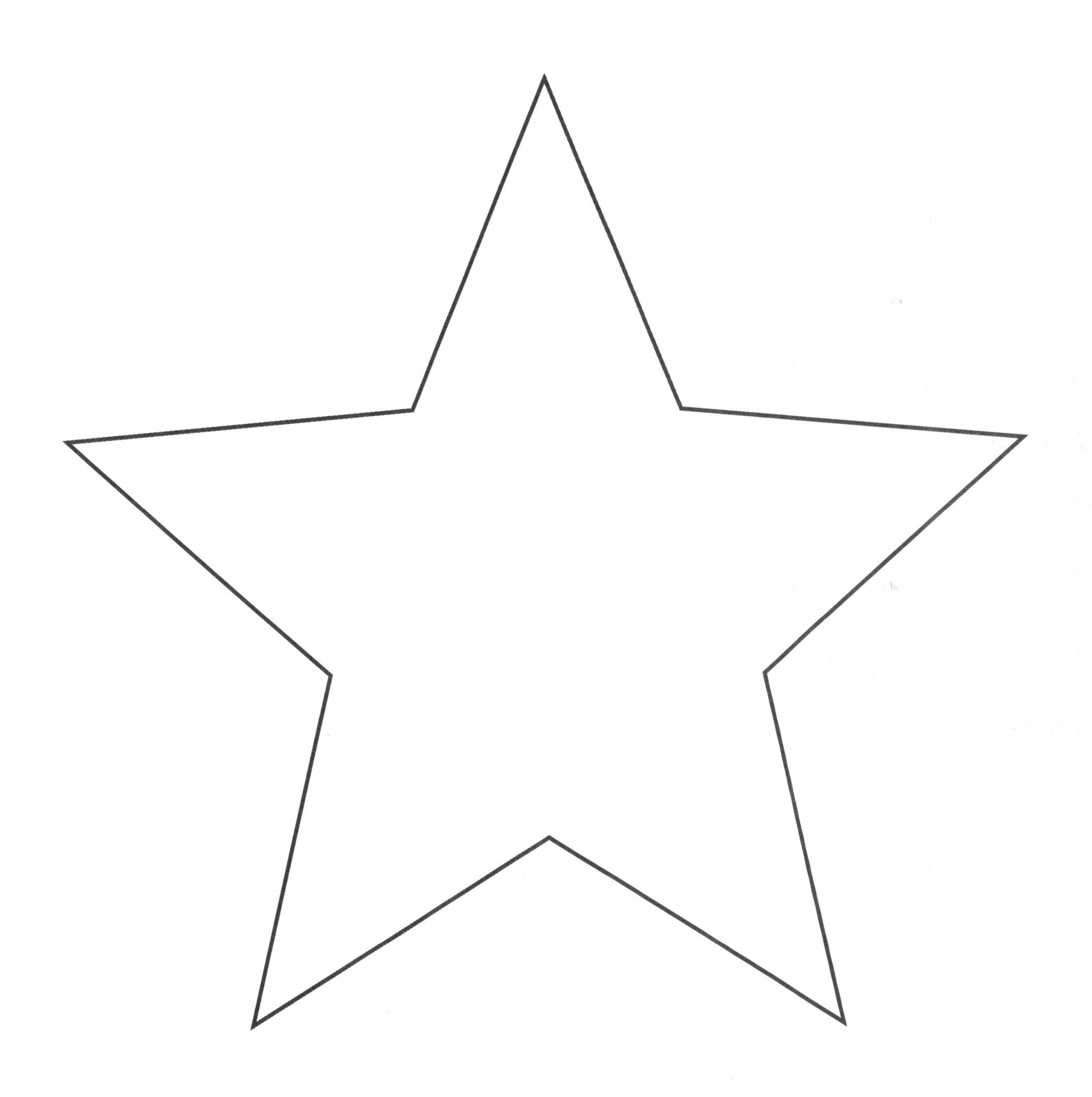

Note to the teacher: Use with "Starring..." on page 9.

Wristband Patterns

Use with "Help at Hand" on page 9.

Reading Nonfiction

☐ Look for the **title**.

It will quickly tell you the topic you will read about.

☐ Look for **subtitles**.

These are titles within the reading. They split the main topic into smaller parts.

☐ Look for **bold words**.

They are important words to know about the topic.

☐ Look for **pictures and captions**.

They show an important idea or object from the reading.

☐ Look for **maps**.

They show a place related to the reading.

TEC43057

Reading Nonfiction

☐ Look for the **title**.

It will quickly tell you the topic you will read about.

☐ Look for **subtitles**.

These are titles within the reading. They split the main topic into smaller parts.

☐ Look for **bold words**.

They are important words to know about the topic.

☐ Look for **pictures and captions**.

They show an important idea or object from the reading.

☐ Look for **maps**.

They show a place related to the reading.

TEC43057

Main Idea and Details

The **main idea** is the big message the author wants to share. It's the most important idea from the reading.
Farm Jigsaw Puzzle
Details are small pieces of information about the main idea.
Hint: Put all the details together to better understand the main idea.

See page 9 for ideas on how to store and use the poster.

Desk Tags

Use with the mini poster on page 9.

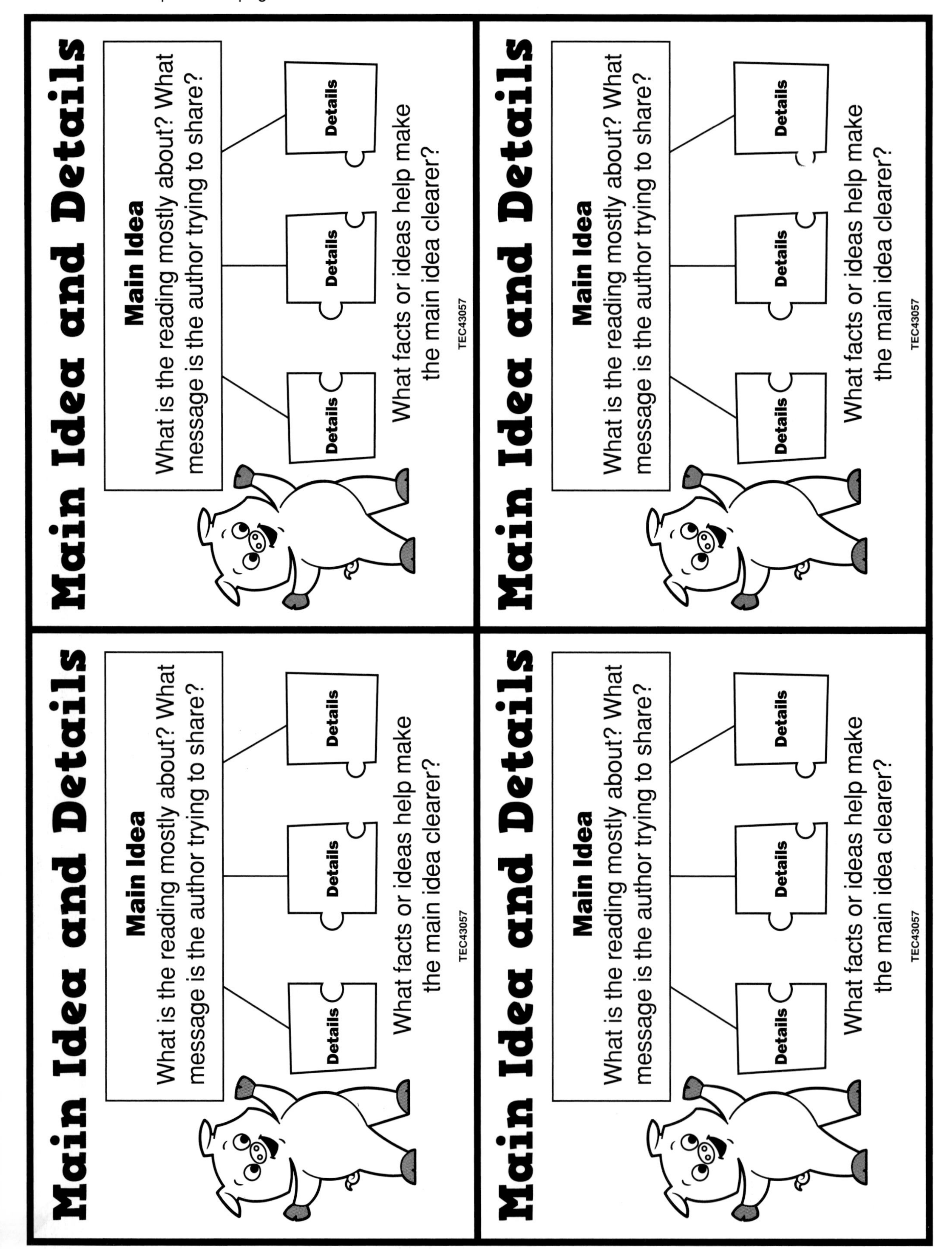

Main Idea and Details
Main Idea
What is the reading mostly about? What message is the author trying to share?
Details
Details
Details
What facts or ideas help make the main idea clearer?
TEC43057

All classified ads are nonrefundable!

• Please complete all information. • Fill in one word per space. • Print clearly. •

Name________________________________

Date________________________________

Title________________________________

Pages________________________________

Payment Information

25¢ per word

Total Ad Cost $________

(After writing your summary, count the total number of words you wrote. Use a calculator to multiply that number by $0.25.)

Summary (Write only one word in each space.)

Note to the teacher: Use with "It's All in the Ad" on page 10.

Arrow Patterns

Use with "Word Posts" on page 10.

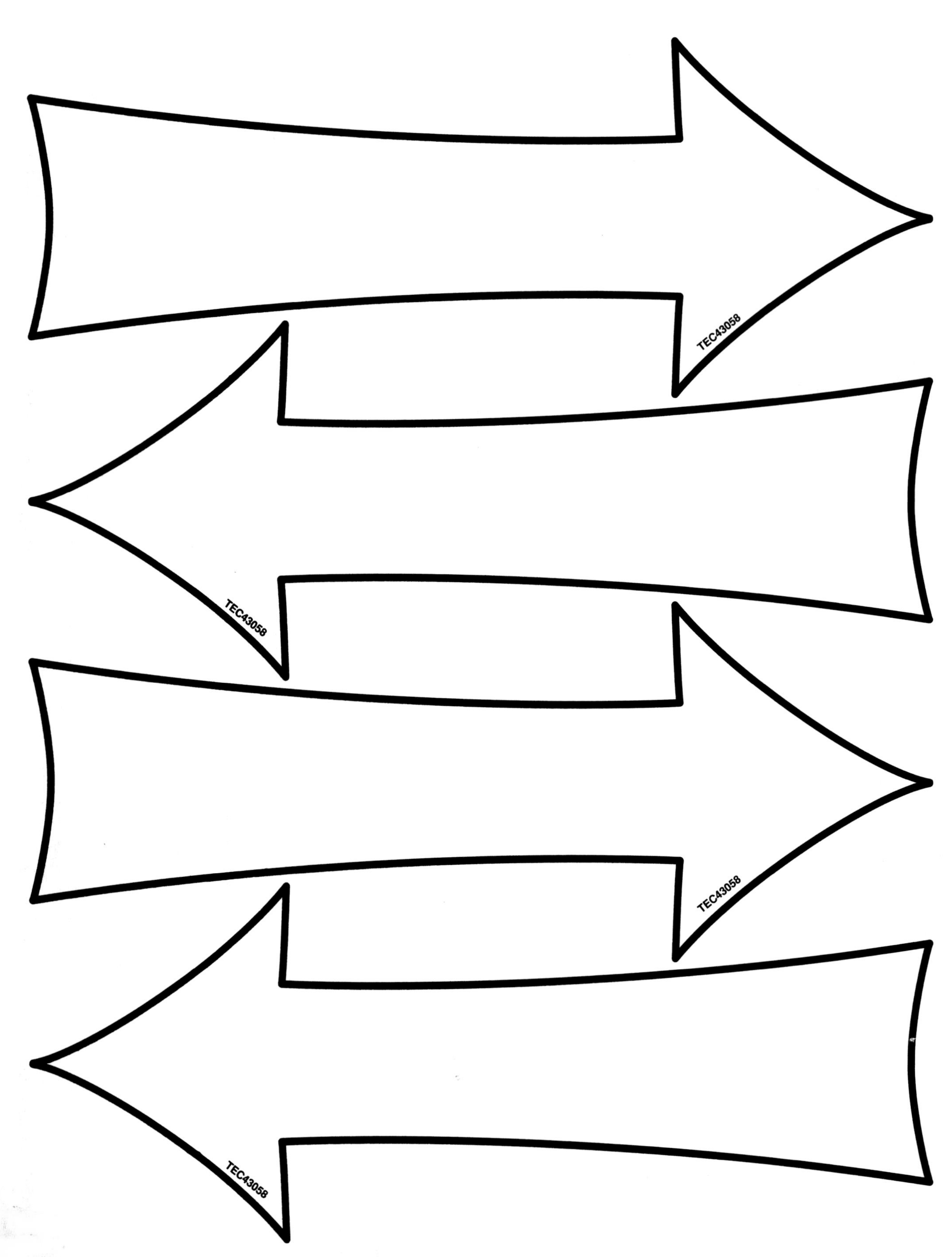
TEC43058
TEC43058
TEC43058
TEC43058

Name
Sequencing plot
Keeping the Story Straight
Title
B
M
E
©The Mailbox® • TEC43059 • Feb./Mar. 2012
TEC43059

Note to the teacher: Use with "Along the Line" on page 13.

Character Pattern

Use with "Inside and Out" on page 12.

Making Inferences

Sometimes authors don't tell you everything with their words. To dig into their meaning, act like a scientist. Use clues from the reading and add them to facts you already know. This is called *inferring*.

©The Mailbox® • TEC43059 • Feb./Mar. 2012

 See page 13 for ideas on how to store and use this page.

Name ______ Date ______

Making inferences

Dig Into Meaning

Question ______

______

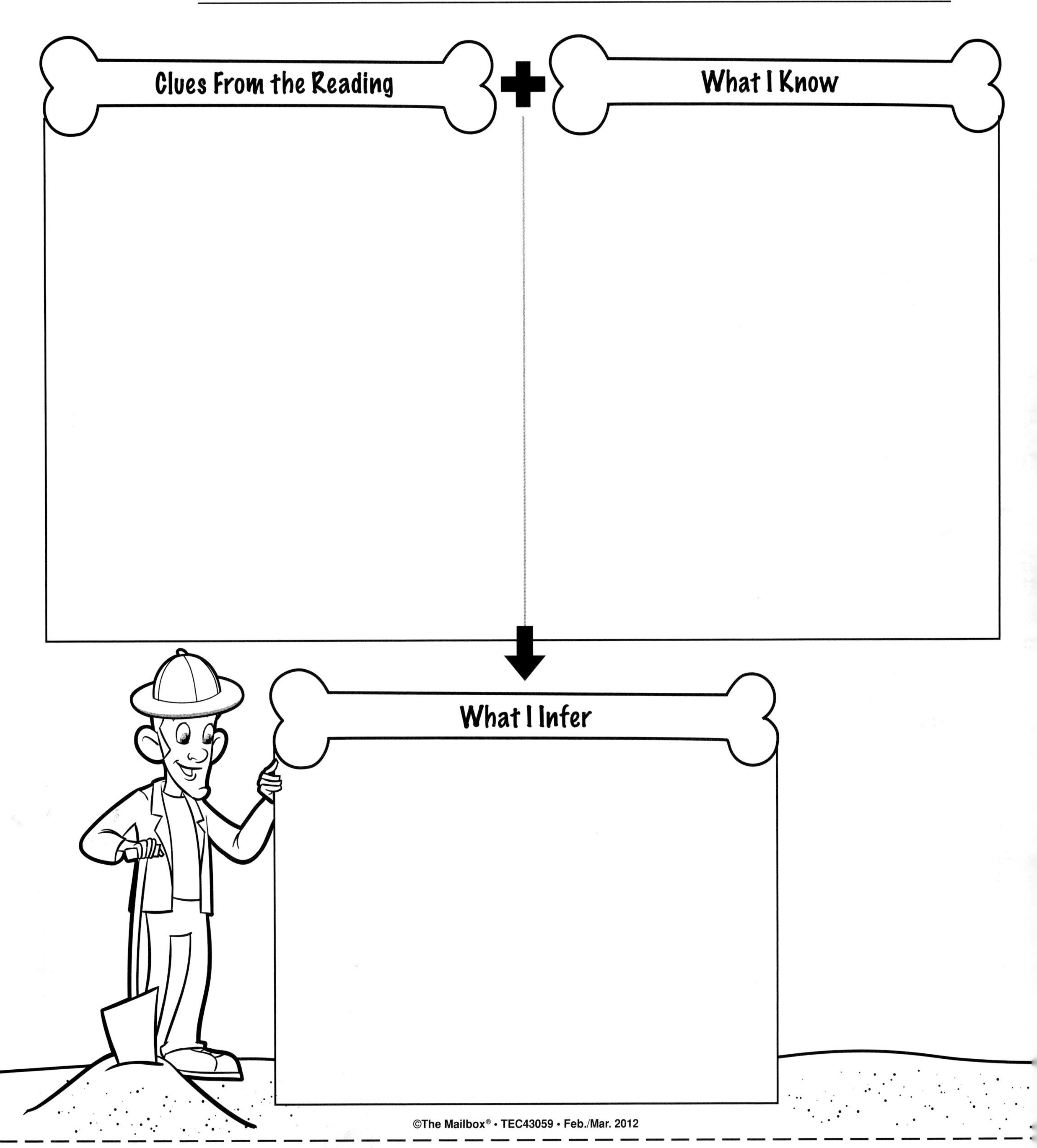
Clues From the Reading
What I Know
What I Infer

Note to the teacher: Use with the mini poster on page 28.

I Am Reading

by

Name

Before Reading

Key words

Before Reading

I already know

After Reading

I still want to know

While Reading

Questions and connections I made:

After Reading

I learned

After Reading

This is my most vivid visualization. (Draw and write.)

 Note to the teacher: Use with “Little Learning Log” on page 14.

Rolled Into One

To find the **central message, moral,** or **theme:**

1. Look at the characters, setting, or plot. Find ideas and details that are the same or that build on each other.
2. Put these ideas and details together with your own ideas and experiences.
3. Based on all this, decide what the author wants to teach you about life or people.

Story Elements

My Own Experiences

My Own Ideas

Guided Reading Mini Poster Tear out this page and put it in a plastic page protector. Use the mini poster and practice sheet on page 32 during guided reading instruction.

Name ____________________ Date ____________

Rolled Into One

Central message, moral, or theme

Ingredients:

Story Details

My Own Ideas and Experiences

Directions:

Combine the ingredients.

What do you think the author wants to teach you about life or people?

Note to the teacher: Use with the mini poster on page 31.

Visualizing

Before Reading Aloud

Seat each child next to a partner. Then have each student divide a sheet of paper in half. Tell students that the portion of the story you are about to read is about two butterflies. Direct each child to draw two butterflies on half of his paper.

Tell students you want them to picture the story in their heads, or *visualize*, as you read aloud.

Read Aloud

From Wonderful to Wet

It was a bright, sunny day at the park. Two butterflies were sitting on a tall green bush covered with purple flowers. The friends were chatting happily about the beautiful spring weather and were making plans for the rest of the day. Oddly, though, while they chatted, the sky seemed to get darker and darker. The butterflies tried to decide if night was coming early or if a storm was on its way. That's when it happened. The butterflies were suddenly drenched. *(Stop reading. Instruct students to take turns describing to their partners what the butterflies look like.)* After the initial shock of being so very wet, the butterflies decided they did not want to get stuck in a storm, and they prepared to fly away. And that's when they saw it—a goofy brown dog was standing behind the butterflies, panting heavily. It was not a storm that drenched the butterflies, but this big mutt's drool. The butterflies were worried the dog might try to eat them, so they quickly flitted away. The dog, not knowing any better, ran after them. All it was thinking was, "What a fun game of chase!"

After Reading Aloud

Ask students what they would see if they were at the park and took a photo of the dog drooling on the butterflies. Instruct them to draw that picture on the other half of their papers.

Have students explain how they visualized the dog. Ask if the dog had to be a big dog by human standards; then lead a discussion to explore why or why not.

Remind students to visualize when they read on their own, not just when they are read to.

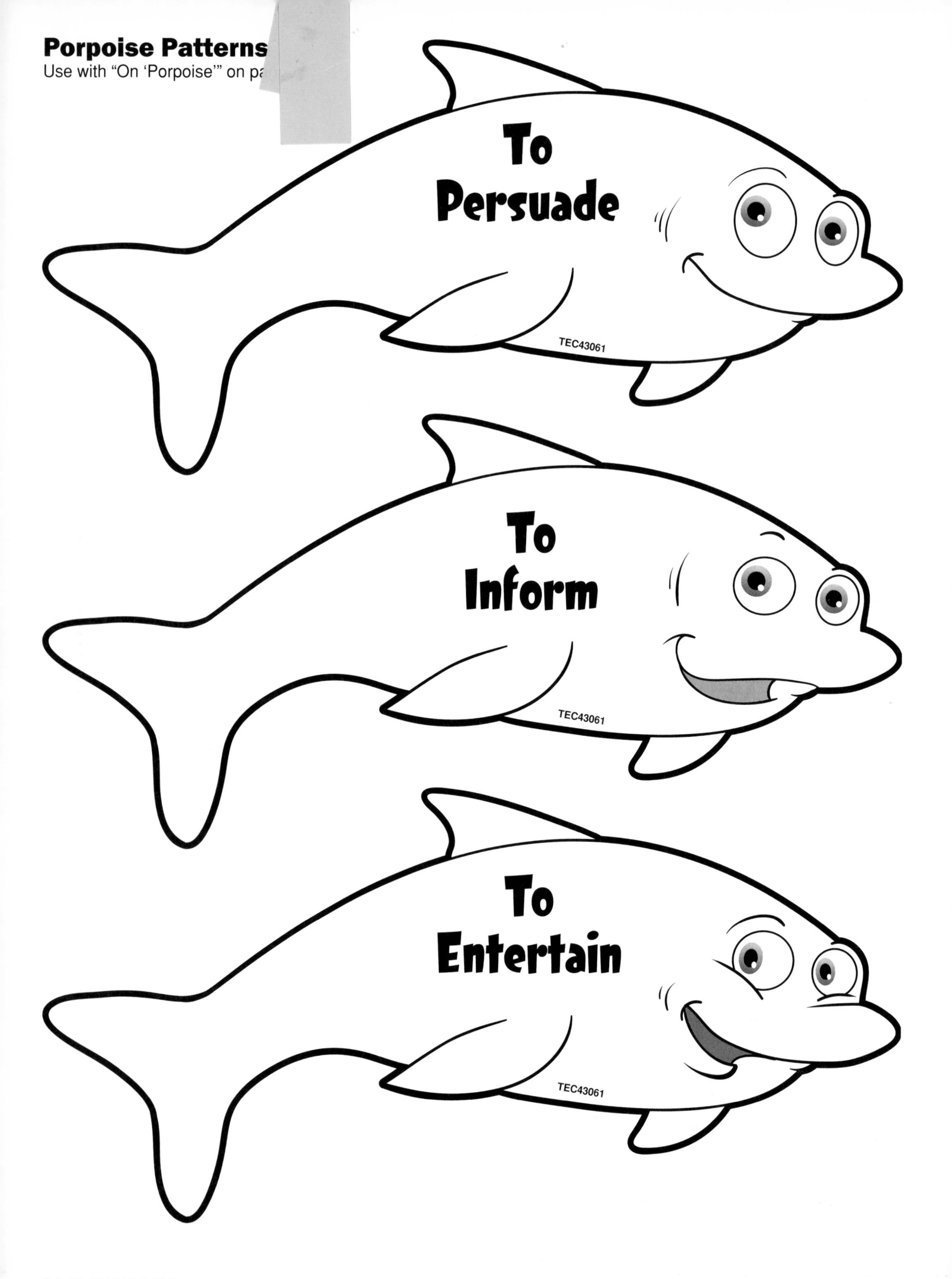
Porpoise Patterns
Use with "On 'Porpoise'" on pa
To
Persuade
TEC43061
To
Inform
TEC43061
To
Entertain
TEC43061

Dear Friend,

My classmates and I are racing to become better readers. Please sign your name after I read the selection on the back of this letter aloud to you. Thanks for your help and involvement!

1. ____________________

2. ____________________

3. ____________________

4. ____________________

5. ____________________

6. ____________________

7. ____________________

8. ____________________

9. ____________________

10. ____________________

When you have 10 different names, take this form to your teacher.

Note to the teacher: Use with "On Your Mark…" on page 17.

Name ____________________ Date ____________

Comparing characters between two texts

Keeping Track

Title: ____________________ **Author:** ____________________

Code
character displays this trait = +
character does not display this trait = –
not sure = ?

Character	Character Trait				

Note to the teacher: Use with "Tracking the Evidence" on page 17.

Name ____________________ Date ____________________

Graphic organizer: making predictions

On the Ball

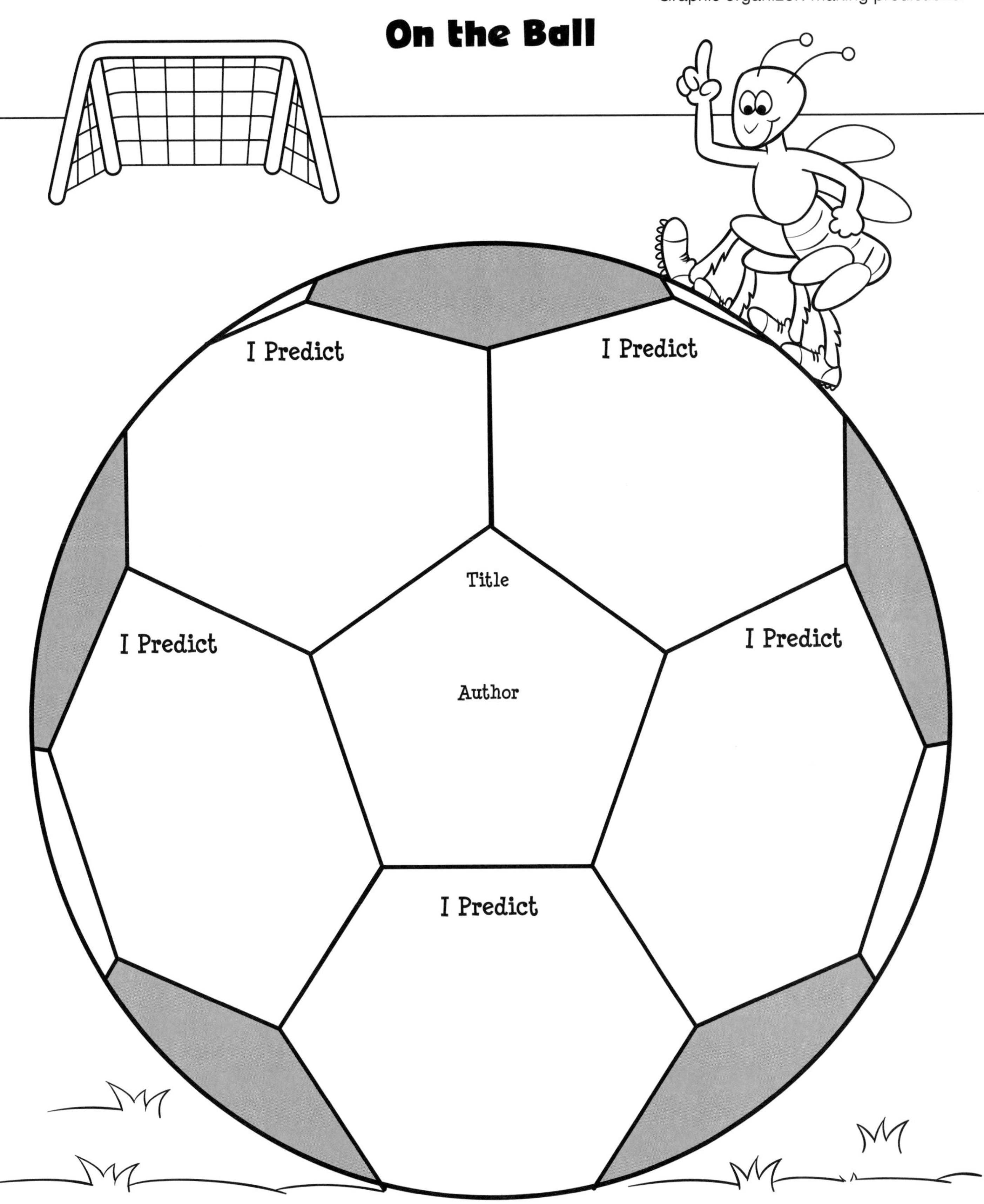
I Predict
I Predict
Title
Author
I Predict
I Predict
I Predict

How to use Before reading a selection, give each child a copy of this page. Instruct the student to record predictions about the selection before he starts reading and as he reads.

Name____________________ Date__________

A Cute Contest

Circle the *y* in each word on the word bank. Write each word under the matching bear.

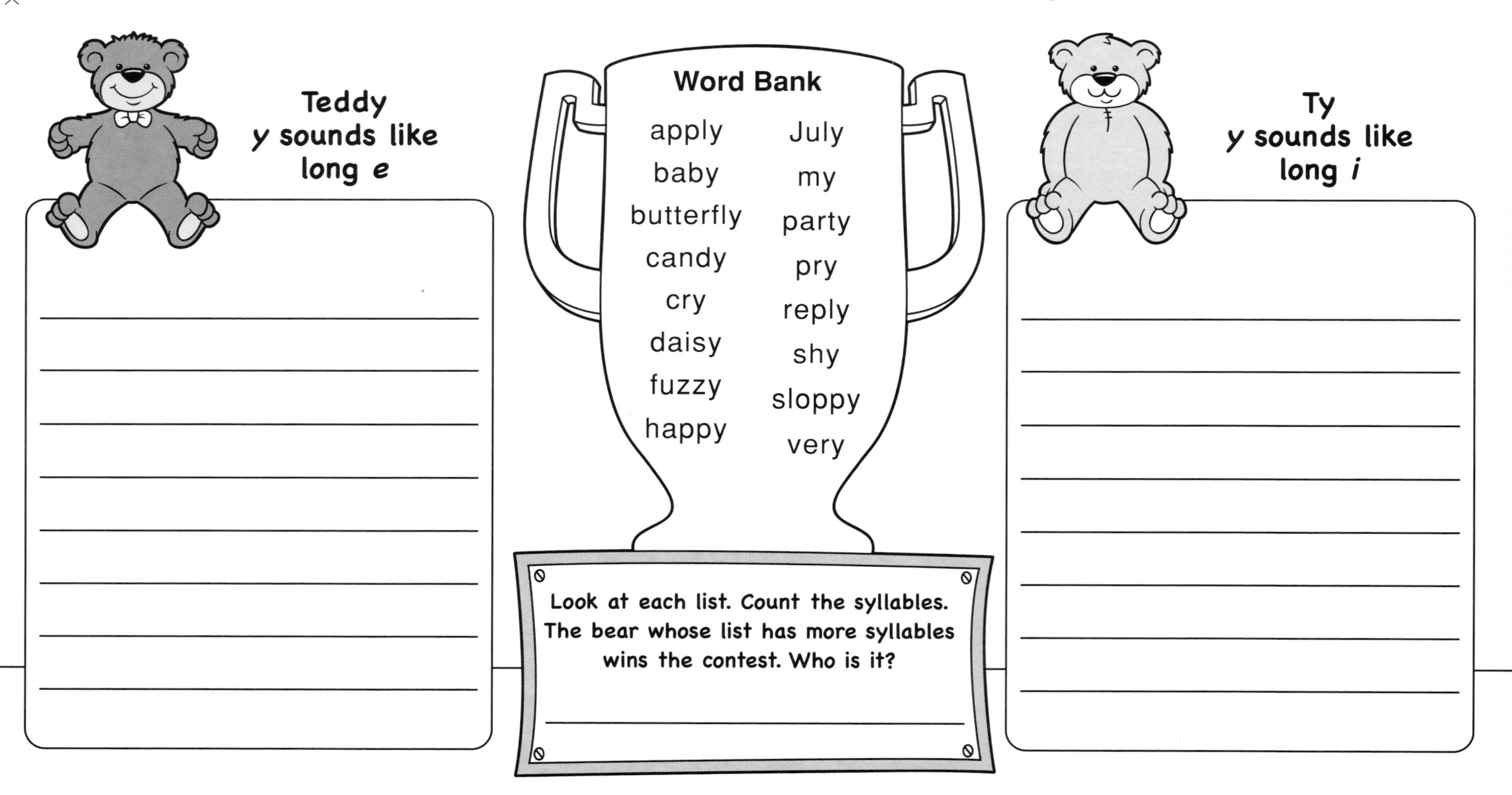
Teddy
y sounds like
long *e*
Word Bank
apply
baby
butterfly
candy
cry
daisy
fuzzy
happy
July
my
party
pry
reply
shy
sloppy
very
Ty
y sounds like
long *i*
Look at each list. Count the syllables.
The bear whose list has more syllables
wins the contest. Who is it?

Bonus: Write four adjectives (describing words) that end with *y*. What sound does each *y* make?

Name ______________________ Date ______________

Silent consonants: *k, w*

A Character at the Castle

Circle each word spelled with a silent *k* or *w*.
Write each circled word on the matching tower.

Silent *k*

Silent *w*

Sir Oddalot is a very strange knight. You might even say he lives in his own world. He knocks with his toes, not his knuckles. He also turns knobs with his knees instead of his hands, and he keeps a watch around his ankle, not his wrist. When he wraps gifts, he ties knots instead of bows in the ribbons. "What a wreck," his royal highness, the king, says.

However, Sir Oddalot knows how to rescue a princess and wrestle a dragon. He even has a knack for writing poetry. Sir Oddalot is wrong about many things, but he's right when it really matters.

Bonus: List five or more other words spelled with a silent *k*. Use a dictionary to help you.

Name ______________________________ Date ______________

Brushing at Bedtime

Underline the contraction in each sentence.
Write the meaning of each contraction.

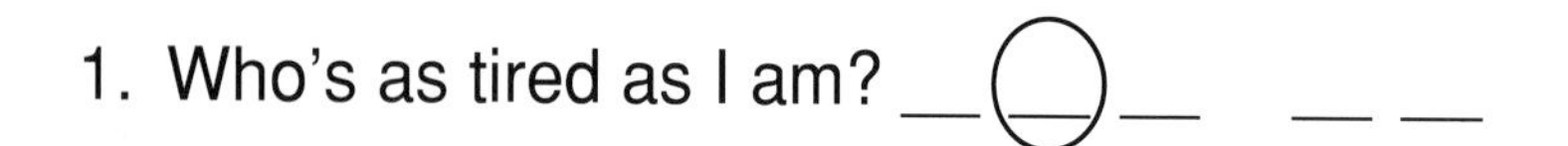
1. Who's as tired as I am? _ (_) _   _ _

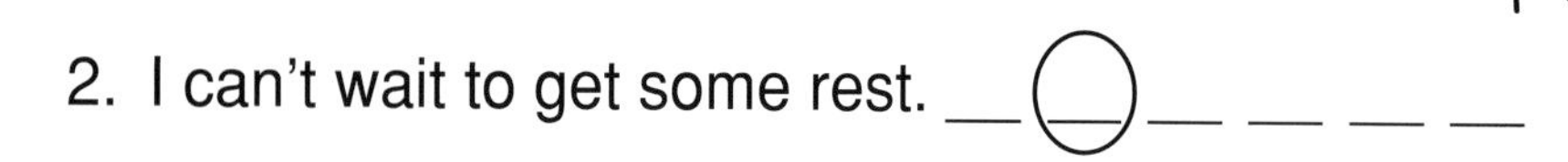
2. I can't wait to get some rest. _ (_) _ _ _ _

3. I didn't think I would be so tired from flying around all night. _ _ _   _ _ (_)

4. I could've sprained a wing from all that flying! _ _ _ _ _   (_) _ _ _

5. Note to self—don't overdo it again! (_) _   _ _ _

6. At least finding food wasn't a problem. _ (_) _   _ _ _

7. The bugs weren't able to hide from me! _ _ (_) _   _ _ _

8. I'm so full! _   (_) _

9. I must've eaten over 100 bugs. _ _ _ (_)   _ _ _ _

10. You couldn't pay me to eat another one. _ _ _ _ _   _ _ (_)

11. I'll need to brush my teeth soon. (_)   _ _ _ _

12. Now, where's my toothpaste? _ _ (_) _ _   _ _

Why did the bat need to brush its teeth?

To find out, write each circled letter from above on its matching numbered line below.

__ __   __ __ __   "b__ __"   b__ __ __ __ __.
11 10   4 2 5   6 3   7 12 8 9 1

Bonus: Write five or more contractions that are not listed above. Write the meaning of each contraction.

Name________________________________ Date ______________

Get in Gear!

Read.

Ready to Ski

Glossary

basket: a part of the pole, it is a round or star-shaped piece of plastic secured about three inches above the point; it keeps the pole from sinking too much in soft snow

bindings: attach the boots to the skis; if a skier falls, they release the boot from the ski to keep the skier from getting hurt

boots: keep a skier warm and supported; usually fastened by buckles

24

grip: the handle at the top of the pole

midbody: center part of a ski

poles: used for pushing off in snow

skis: narrow runners that skiers use to move across snow

tail: the back part of a ski

tip: front part of a ski

25

Use the glossary page to answer the questions.

1. What is another word for **skis**? ______________
2. What are the three parts of a ski? Write them in order from front to back.

   ______________ ______________ ______________
3. What does a skier use to push off in snow? ______________
4. Are ski boots fastened by laces or buckles? ______________
   Circle the part of the glossary entry that tells you so.
5. How do bindings keep a skier safe? ______________

   ____
6. What part of the pole keeps the pole from sinking in snow? ______________
7. How is the glossary arranged? ______________
8. If the author added text about **safety helmets**, where would this entry be placed on the glossary page? ______________

   ____

Bonus: Would you expect to read about ice skating in this book? Why or why not?

Name ______________________________ Date ____________________

Homophones

Sudsy Duds

Write the missing word on each line.
Cross out the word in the homophone word bank.

Wanda let her laundry pile up for a ____________ (1). By ____________ (2), she had nothing clean to ____________ (3). She had to do laundry. Wanda took her clothes down to the ____________ (4) so she could wash them. First, she scrubbed ____________ (5) stains out of a ____________ (6) of jeans. Then she pretreated the grass stains on her ____________ (7) shirt. It seemed to take ____________ (8) to get everything ready, but soon it was time to load the machine. Wanda began to ____________ (9) in the soap, but before she ____________ (10) it, the ____________ (11) box of soap was empty. Suds bubbled onto the floor. Wanda ____________ (12) and said to herself, “Oh ____________ (13). Now I’ll have to clean the floor ____________ (14)!” Then Wanda put her ____________ (15) in the air, shrugged her shoulders, and said, “At least the soap left a nice ____________ (16).”

Bonus: Choose three unmarked words from the word bank. Use each word in a different sentence.

Homophone Word Bank

1. weak, week
2. Sunday, Sundae
3. wear, where
4. seller, cellar
5. bury, berry
6. pair, pear
7. read, red
8. ours, hours
9. pour, poor
10. new, knew
11. hole, whole
12. sighed, side
13. no, know
14. too, two
15. knows, nose
16. scent, cent

Name ______________________ Date ______________

Prefixes and suffixes

Choosing Just the Right Color

Read each word in the word bank.
Draw a red circle around each prefix.
Draw a blue circle around each suffix.
Then write each word below its meaning.

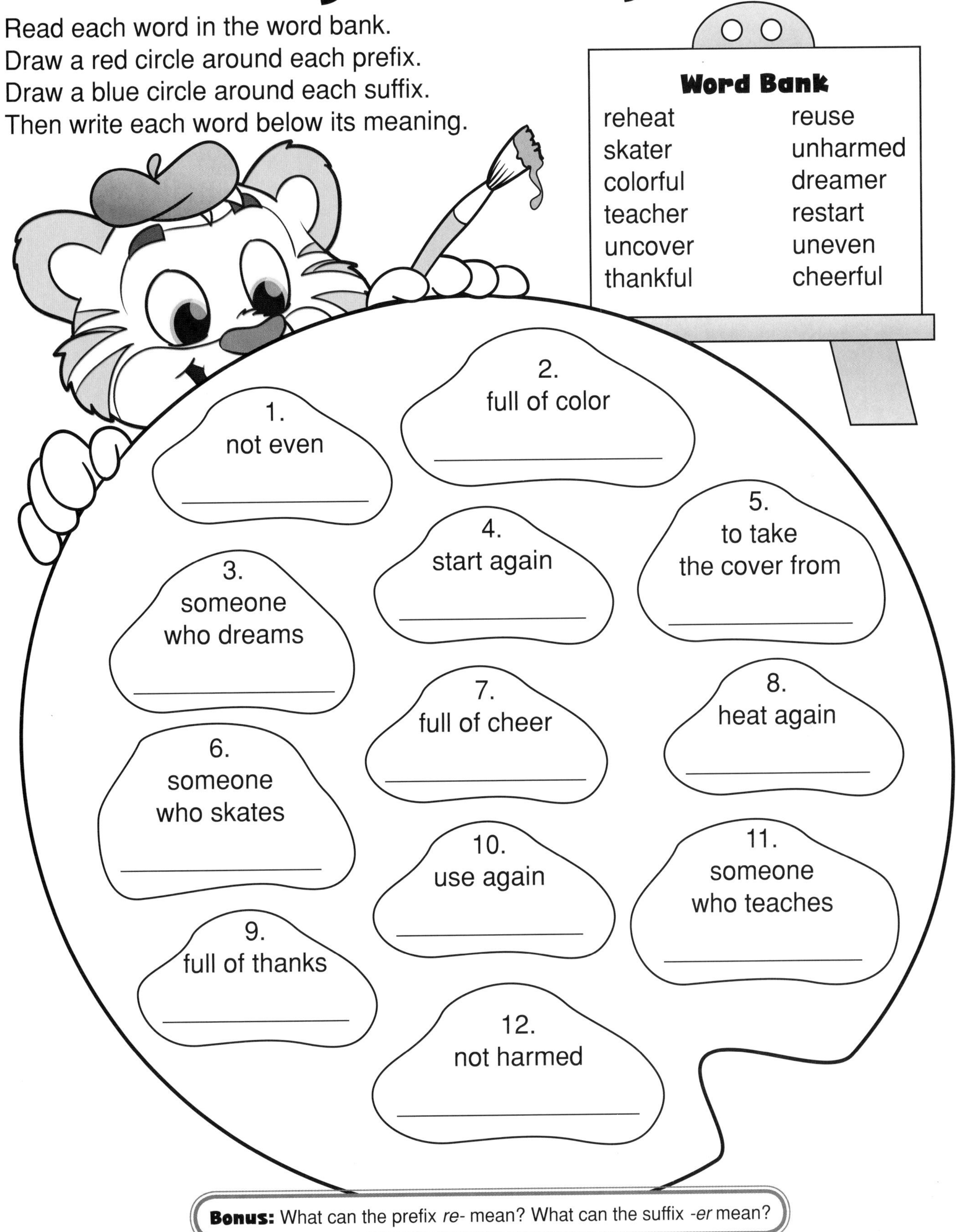

Word Bank
reheat
skater
colorful
teacher
uncover
thankful
reuse
unharmed
dreamer
restart
uneven
cheerful
1. not even
2. full of color
3. someone who dreams
4. start again
5. to take the cover from
6. someone who skates
7. full of cheer
8. heat again
9. full of thanks
10. use again
11. someone who teaches
12. not harmed

Bonus: What can the prefix *re-* mean? What can the suffix *-er* mean?

Name ____________________ Date ____________

Figurative language

The Barks and Bubbles Salon

If the sentence has a simile, write *S* on the line.
If the sentence has a metaphor, write *M* on the line.

A **simile** compares two things using *like* or *as*.

A **metaphor** also compares two things, often stating that one thing *is* another.

1. Washing this dog should be as easy as pie. ______
2. But his fur is as stinky as rotten eggs! ______
3. At least the soap is a bouquet of roses. ______
4. Time is money, so let's get started! ______
5. Can you believe he is as light as a feather? ______
6. His paws are wrinkled raisins from standing in the water. ______
7. The water has become as cold as ice. ______
8. This dog is a trooper! ______
9. His fur is now as white as snow. ______
10. He is a fluffy pile of cotton. ______
11. You were right—washing this dog was a breeze! ______
12. True, but I didn't expect him to run like the wind when we were done! ______

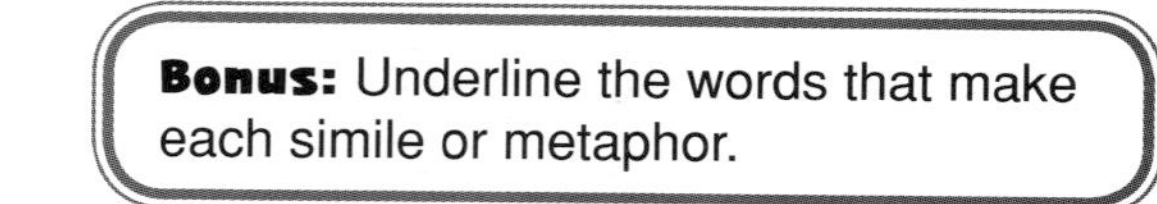

Bonus: Underline the words that make each simile or metaphor.

Name ______________________ Date ______________

Fairy tales

Once Upon a Time...

Pick and Practice Skill Review

Pick _____ activities to do.
When you finish an activity, color its number.

1 What common elements are found in most fairy tales? Write a paragraph that names and describes these elements.

2 Predict what happens next to an evil character. Write a paragraph or more telling where this character is and what he or she may be doing. Use the fairy tale to support your idea.

3 Pretend you are a main character from a fairy tale. Create a photo album that has four pictures of this character at different points in the story. Write a caption to describe each one.

4 Write a new version of your favorite fairy tale. You might change some of the story elements or you might change the plot.

5 Make a Venn diagram to compare and contrast the settings of two fairy tales. Label each circle with the title of each fairy tale.

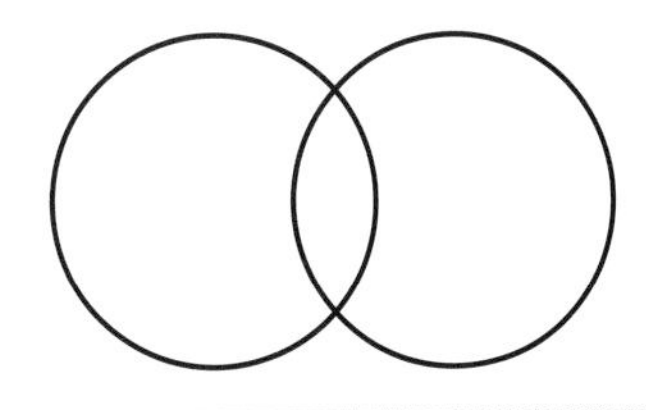

6 Pretend you have been asked to design the stage for a production of your favorite fairy tale. Choose one setting from this story. Draw and label the stage as you see it from the fairy tale's description.

7 Pretend you are one of the main characters from a fairy tale. Retell the fairy tale from this character's point of view.

8 Describe how you are like a character from a fairy tale. Include examples from the story and your personal life.

9 Write a book review of one of the fairy tales you read. State your opinion and then tell why you liked or disliked the story.

How to Use Program the student directions on a copy of this page with the number of activities to be completed. Then copy the page for each student.

Name ______________________ Date ____________

Cause and effect

One Soggy Saturday

Read each cause statement.
Write the letter of a matching effect.

1. It is a rainy day. _____
2. Max and Morty cannot agree about what to do. _____
3. Morty loves art. _____
4. Paint gets all over the table. _____
5. Max loves games. _____
6. A deck of cards is missing cards. _____
7. Max's favorite game is on a high shelf. _____
8. Mom is making cookies downstairs. _____
9. Max and Morty are getting hungry. _____
10. The mice are thirsty. _____

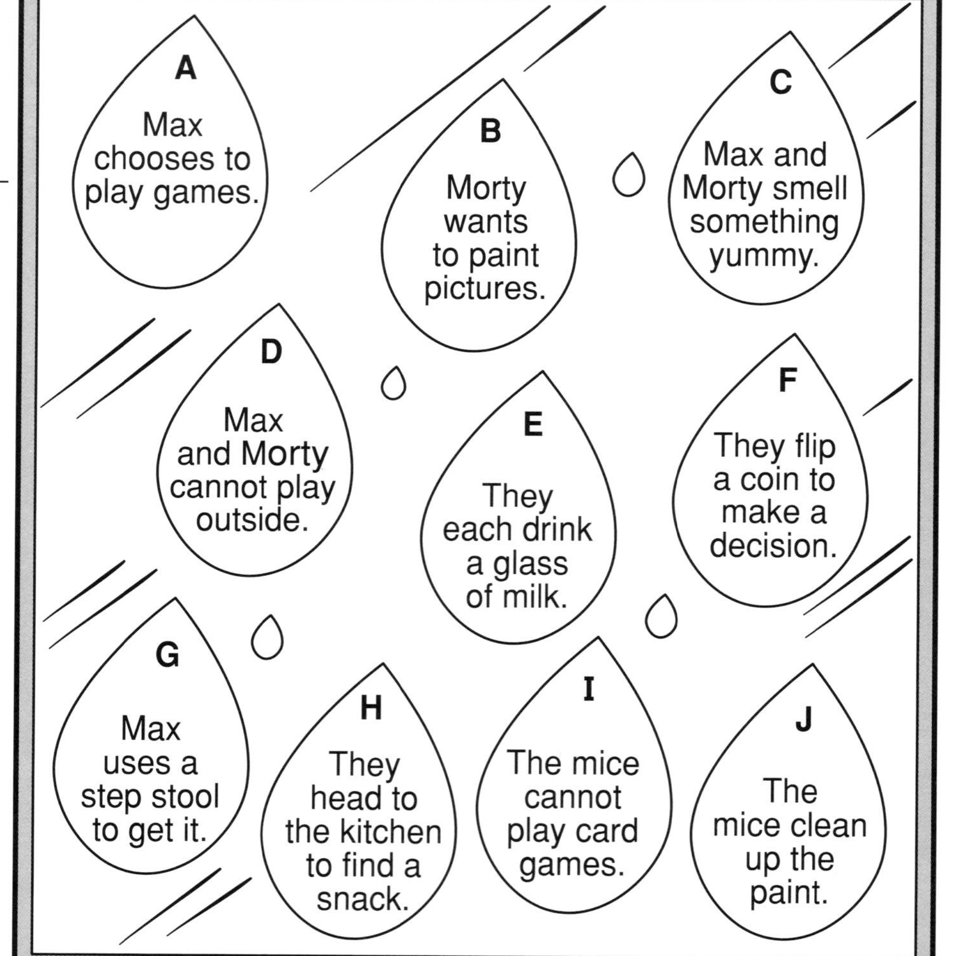
A Max chooses to play games.
B Morty wants to paint pictures.
C Max and Morty smell something yummy.
D Max and Morty cannot play outside.
E They each drink a glass of milk.
F They flip a coin to make a decision.
G Max uses a step stool to get it.
H They head to the kitchen to find a snack.
I The mice cannot play card games.
J The mice clean up the paint.

Bonus: Choose two effect statements from the raindrops. Write a new sentence with each one, but make it the cause statement.

Name______________________________ Date ______________

Asking and answering questions

Working Around the "Cluck"

Read.

Every Saturday, it's the same routine. A rooster crows. Parker and Penny yawn and stretch. "Rise and shine!" Grandma Pearl shouts. It's time for the Pollo family to do their chores!

Everyone has a chore to do, and Grandma Pearl makes sure all the chores get done. First, she watches Parker tidy the nests. Then she checks in on Penny sweeping the floor. Later, she heads outside to the coop to inspect Pa's work in the eggplant garden.

When the chores are done, the younger family members like to go *eggs-ploring*, but Grandma Pearl is too *eggs-hausted* to move. After a day of working around the clock, she curls up on a freshly made nest and takes a nap.

Write an answer for each question.
Write a question for each answer.

1. What happens every Saturday morning after a rooster crows? ______________

   ____

2. Who makes sure all the chores get done? ______________________

3. ______________________________

   Parker.

4. What's growing in the garden? ______________________

5. ______________________________

   ______________ They go *eggs-ploring.*

6. ______________________________

   ______________ She takes a nap.

Bonus: Write another question about the reading. Then write its answer.

Name ______________________________ Date ______________

Character traits

A Treetop Diner

Read.

The Squirrel family arrives at its favorite treetop diner for dinner. Dad chats with the hostess as she leads the family to a table. Mom keeps her eyes on the kids, Scarlett and Scout. Once seated, each family member looks at a menu. Scout knows right away what he wants to eat, so he passes the time by making faces at his sister, Scarlett. Scarlett wants to take her time reading the menu. She gets annoyed when Scout disturbs her.

Nut Hut

Soon the server comes to take their orders. Scout gives his order in a loud, clear voice. Dad smiles at Scout and makes a joke before placing his order. The server laughs until he cries. Mom prompts Scarlett to tell her order to the server. Scarlett whispers it to her mom instead. Mom orders for Scarlett and then herself.

Word Bank

caring	confident
friendly	funny
pesky	selfless
serious	shy

Write two words to describe each character. Use the word bank. Then use the story to explain your choices.

1. Dad is ______________ and ______________. ______________

2. Mom is ______________ and ______________. ______________

3. Scarlett is ______________ and ______________. ______________

4. Scout is ______________ and ______________. ______________

Bonus: Choose a character from the story. Write another word that describes him or her. Explain your choice.

Name ______________________ Date ______________

Character traits

Choosing His Own Path

Leon is the son of Leo. Leo is the king. The other animals know Leon will grow up big and strong like his dad. They know Leon will be their leader one day, so they give him a lot of respect. The animals stop to watch Leon when he struts by. They go to him when they have small problems. Leon likes to help, and he likes making others happy.

One day, the animals notice that Leon isn't quite the same. They see him sneaking through the grass. He seems to be avoiding them. What the animals do not know is that Leon is in a hurry to get home and does not want to explain why. You see, Leon does not want to be the next king. He wants to be a baker instead. He likes making cupcakes and cookies more than he likes the idea of being in charge. By moving quickly and quietly through the jungle, Leon thinks there is less of a chance the other animals will learn his secret.

Answer the questions. Use the passage.

1. Look at the first paragraph. Which word describes Leon? (Circle.)

   sad brave helpful

   Underline the words in the paragraph that make you think so.
2. Circle the word that describes how Leon moves in the first paragraph. Do you think that means Leon is proud or ashamed? ______________
3. Look at the second paragraph. What word do you think the animals would use to describe Leon? ______________ Explain your choice. ______________

   ____
4. What is Leon's secret? ______________

   ____
5. Based on what you know about Leon and his secret, how would you describe him? ______________ Explain.

   ____

   ____

Name________________________________ Date ______________

Nonfiction text, map

What a Cool Place!

Read.

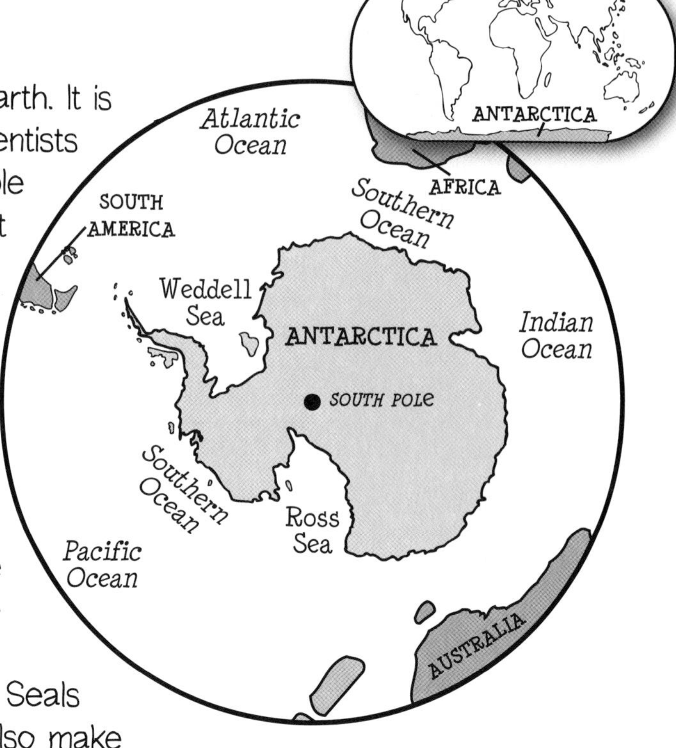
ANTARCTICA
Atlantic Ocean
AFRICA
SOUTH AMERICA
Southern Ocean
Weddell Sea
ANTARCTICA
Indian Ocean
SOUTH POLE
Southern Ocean
Ross Sea
Pacific Ocean
AUSTRALIA

Antarctica is one of seven continents on Earth. It is bigger than Europe and Australia, yet only scientists live there. With all that land, what keeps people away? This cold and dry land mass is found at the South Pole. Temperatures there almost never get above freezing. The land is mostly covered by ice and snow. It is also the windiest continent.

People may not have settled here, but some animals have. They tend to live at the edges of the land mass or in the seas that surround Antarctica. Krill live in these waters. These small, shrimp-like animals serve as food for many other animals in the seas. Whales migrate to these waters each summer. Seals can be found nesting on the coast. Penguins also make Antarctica their home.

Respond.

1. What is Antarctica? ______________________________
2. Describe Antarctica's land. ______________________________

   ____
3. What do the maps tell you about Antarctica that the reading does not? ______________________________

   ____
4. Name two seas found near Antarctica. ______________________________

   ____
5. What animals are found near Antarctica? ______________________________

   ____

   What do they all have in common? ______________________________

   ____

Bonus: Why don't more people live in Antarctica?

Name ________________________ Date ____________

Sequencing nonfiction

A Bug-Eating Plant

Read the sentences about the Venus flytrap.
Number the sentences to show, in order, what happens when this plant eats a bug.
Use the pictures to help you.

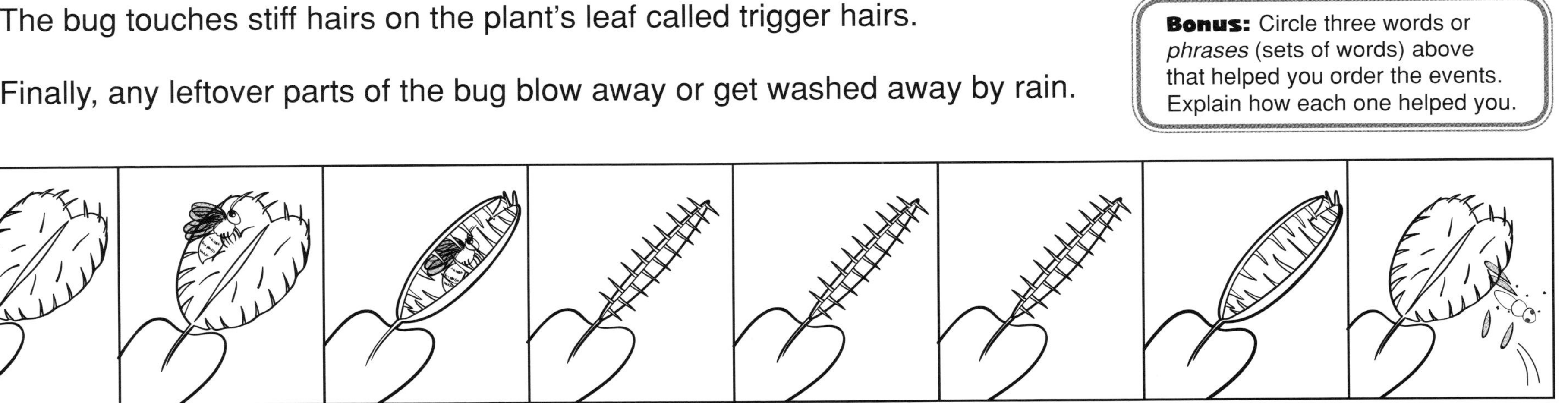

_______ Within minutes of trapping the bug, an air-tight seal forms and the bug cannot get out.

_______ The trap squeezes the insect, and digestion begins.

_______ After five to 12 days, the plant has digested the bug. Its exoskeleton is all that is left.

_______ The leaf snaps shut in less than a second, and the bug is trapped.

_______ Now the plant is finished eating. The leaf reopens.

_______ First, a small bug smells the plant's sweet nectar. It lands on the plant's leaf.

_______ The bug touches stiff hairs on the plant's leaf called trigger hairs.

_______ Finally, any leftover parts of the bug blow away or get washed away by rain.

Bonus: Circle three words or *phrases* (sets of words) above that helped you order the events. Explain how each one helped you.

Language Arts

Brain Boosters

Brain Booster 1

Rewrite the riddles.
Circle each end mark you add.

When is the moon heaviest
It is heaviest when it is full

How are false teeth like stars
They both come out at night

TEC43056

Brain Booster 2

Think of words about school.
List only the compound words.

bookcase
backpack

TEC43056

Brain Booster 3

For each word, make a list of five or more rhyming words.

school
pen
chair

TEC43056

Brain Booster 4

Add a different subject to each phrase.
Write the sentences to make a short story.

are playing a game outside
kicks the ball
knocks it out of bounds
runs down the field
scores the winning goal

TEC43056

Brain Booster 5

How many two-syllable healthy snacks can you name?
List them.

TEC43056

Brain Booster 6

For each word, change one letter.
Reorder the letters to name a pet.

tan = cat

nod
bakes
shin
dirt

TEC43056

Brain Booster 7

Rewrite each city and state pair.
Hint: Include commas and capital letters.

oatmeal texas
toast north carolina
buttermilk kansas
milkwater arizona
cheeseville wisconsin

TEC43056

Brain Booster 8

The answer is *coach.*
What are all the questions you can think of that could have this answer?

TEC43056

How to use Give each student a copy of this page (or one card at a time) to work on during free time.

Brain Boosters

Brain Booster 1

How are the words alike? How are they different?

fall spring

TEC43057

Brain Booster 2

Write a sentence with *bob*.

Write another sentence with *Bob*.

TEC43057

Brain Booster 3

Write a list of nouns related to *leaf*.

tree

pile

TEC43057

Brain Booster 4

Copy. Write a cause or effect.

I screamed!

I ate way too much turkey.

There were leaves everywhere.

Circle each cause you write.
Underline each effect you write.

TEC43057

Brain Booster 5

Answer the questions.

Would you like to hold a bat? Why or why not?

Draw two pictures to show different meanings for *bat*.
Circle the meaning you thought about to answer the questions.

TEC43057

Brain Booster 6

Add prefixes and suffixes to make a list of real words.

treat

TEC43057

Brain Booster 7

For each word, write a synonym and an antonym.

brave friendly

dangerous wicked

TEC43057

Brain Booster 8

Copy the letters. For each shape, write a matching letter.
(Hint: You should make a riddle and its punch line.)

Wh◆t ki★d of □◆O

go↑s bow♥i★g?

◆★ ◆♥♥↑y □◆O

TEC43057

How to use Give each student a copy of this page (or one card at a time) to work on during free time.

Language Arts

Brain Boosters

Brain Booster 1

Describe a sheet of writing paper without using the words *lines* or *rectangle*.

TEC43058

Brain Booster 2

Sort the words into two groups.

give	ginger	region
gather	gel	golden
gap	gym	tag
goal	giraffe	large
giant		anger

TEC43058

Brain Booster 3

Copy each sentence.
Circle the winter clothing word hidden in each.

I ate a taco at the game.
We got Mom's car fixed.
Meg loves winter!
He speaks Spanish at home.
This ticket will admit ten friends to the show.

TEC43058

Brain Booster 4

How are these words alike? How are they different?

book	roof
cooks	scoot
foot	shook
moose	woods
pooch	wool

TEC43058

Brain Booster 5

List five or more verbs that have only four letters and end with *ow*.

know

TEC43058

Brain Booster 6

The answer is *peace*.
Write three or more questions.

TEC43058

Brain Booster 7

Use each set of number and letter clues to write a fact.

7 d. in a wk. = 7 days in a week
26 l. in the a. =
an h. has 60 m. =
100 p. is the same amount as 1 d.=
2 rhyming l. in a c. =

TEC43058

Brain Booster 8

Copy the guide words.
List ten or more words that might be found on this dictionary page.

happy–holidays

TEC43058

How to use: Give each student a copy of this page (or one card at a time) to work on during free time.

Brain Boosters

Brain Booster 1

Which word doesn't belong? Explain.

break neat

male rain

TEC43059

Brain Booster 2

Read each predicate. What subject could be used for all three?

____ is a favorite pet around the world.

____ likes to climb.

____ purrs loudly.

TEC43059

Brain Booster 3

Write a riddle that gives clues about your favorite color.

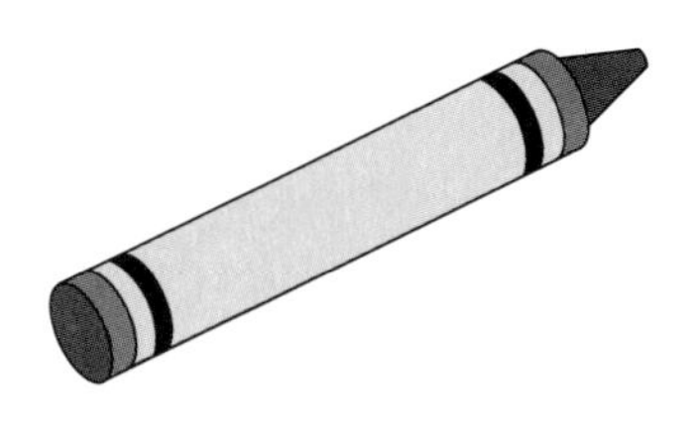

TEC43059

Brain Booster 4

How many verbs can you spell using only the letters in **Washington**? List them.

TEC43059

Brain Booster 5

List four or more plural words that do not end in *s*.

women

teeth

TEC43059

Brain Booster 6

Write two declarative sentences about your favorite snack.

TEC43059

Brain Booster 7

List three or more compound words that use the word *wind*.

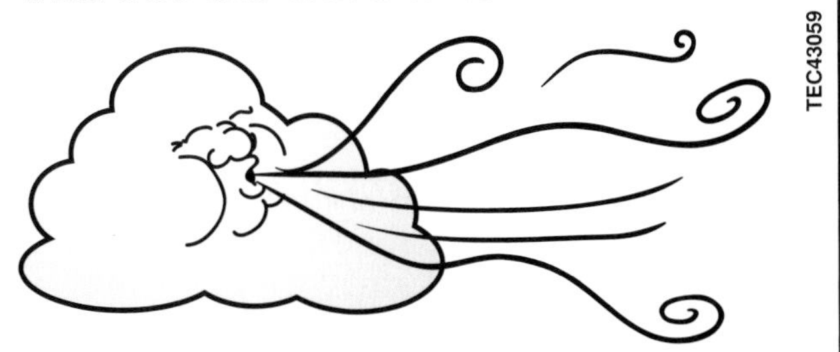

TEC43059

Brain Booster 8

The answer is *spaghetti*. Write a list of matching questions.

TEC43059

How to use: Give each student a copy of this page (or one card at a time) to work on during free time.

Brain Boosters

Brain Booster 1

Write an antonym for each word.

A. always	D. hungry	G. subtract
B. follow	E. north	H. true
C. frown	F. question	I. wet

TEC43060

Brain Booster 2

A. Which insect has another insect spelled in its name?

B. How is the letter *A* like a flower?

(Hint: Both answers use the same insect.)

TEC43060

Brain Booster 3

Write two sentences.
In one, use *bat* as the subject.
In the other, use *bat* as the predicate.

TEC43060

Brain Booster 4

List five or more adverbs that describe how a person might run.

slowly

List five or more adverbs that tell when a person might run.

today

TEC43060

Brain Booster 5

Are these words **singular** (showing one) or **plural** (showing more than one)? Explain.

team **group** **class**

TEC43060

Brain Booster 6

You are planning a class picnic.
Write a shopping list.
List each letter from *A* through *Z*.
Write one item for each letter.

TEC43060

Brain Booster 7

Choose something you know how to do well, such as tie a shoe or make a phone call.
Write the steps in reverse.
(Hint: Start with the last step and work backward.)

TEC43060

Brain Booster 8

The suffix -*ship* means the *state* or *quality of*. List all the words you know with this suffix.

friendship

TEC43060

How to Use Give each student a copy of this page (or one card at a time) to work on during free time.

Brain Booster 1

pat

Write a sentence using this word as a *common noun*.
Write a sentence using this word as a *proper noun*.

TEC43061

Brain Booster 2

Describe your favorite game to play with a friend.
Do not use the words *and* or *favorite* in your writing.

TEC43061

Brain Booster 3

Name 3 things you might put *on* ice cream.
Name 3 things you put *in* ice cream.
Name 3 things you might put *under* ice cream.

TEC43061

Brain Booster 4

If you place the words on the grid in a certain order, you will reveal in the left column a place you might go this summer. What is it?

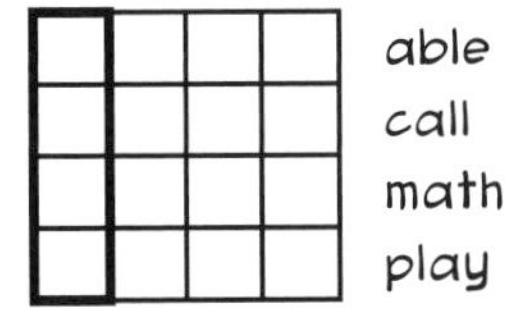
able
call
math
play

TEC43061

Brain Booster 5

Continue the chain as long as you can without repeating animals. Start each word with the last letter of the word before it.

dog → goat → toad

TEC43061

Brain Booster 6

Copy the diagram. Add four effects of a hot day.

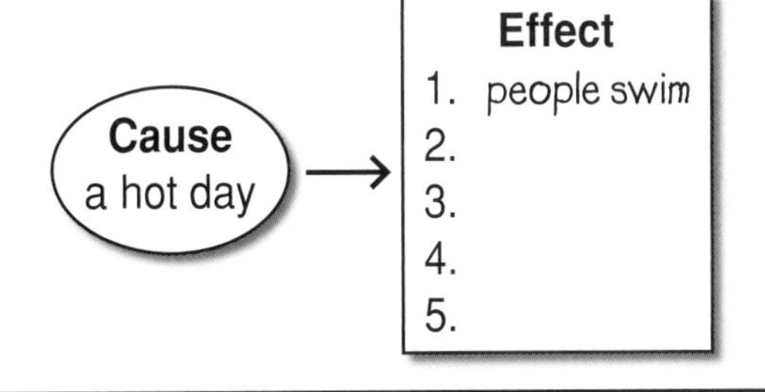
Cause
a hot day
Effect
1. people swim
2.
3.
4.
5.

TEC43061

Brain Booster 7

Write a letter on each row to make a word. Then read down the middle column to find a word that means the same as the verb "splash."

a		k
i		l
d		t
u		e
w		o

TEC43061

Brain Booster 8

Write three different words that use the base word *melt*.

For 1 word, add a prefix.
For 1 word, add a suffix.
For 1 word, add a prefix and a suffix.

TEC43061

How to Use Give each student a copy of this page (or one card at a time) to work on during free time.

Writing Tips & Tools

The Right Direction

Precise verbs

Set students on the path to stronger word choices. Discuss words that describe movement (*crawl, stroll, walk, fly, zoom*, etc.) and list the words on the board. Provide time for student volunteers to act out a race by using word pairs. For example, have one student stroll toward a designated finish line while another child walks. Then challenge students to order the words in the list from slowest to fastest. To do this, have each student pair write a word on a card; then arrange the cards on a display as shown. Encourage students to refer to the display when writing.

stroll
saunter
mosey
march
walk
run
gallop
sprint
fly
zoom

Dan Nale, Howard L. Emmons Elementary, Pemberton, NJ

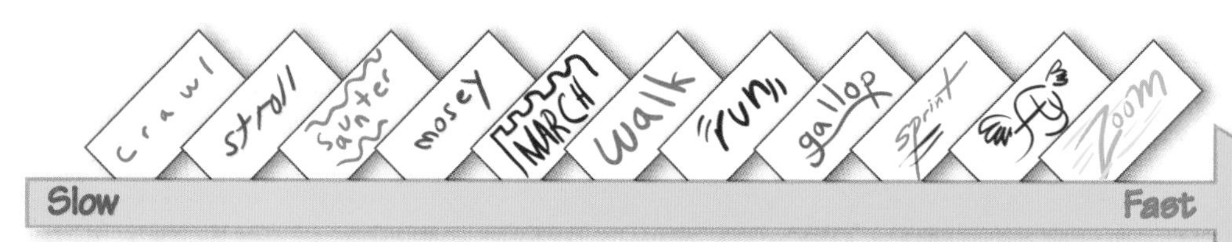

crawl
stroll
saunter
mosey
MARCH
walk
run
gallop
sprint
fly
zoom
Slow
Fast

Boning Up

Expository writing

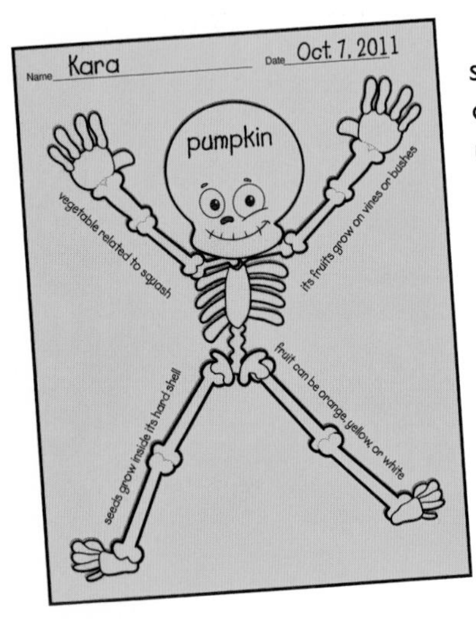

Name Kara
Date Oct. 7, 2011
pumpkin
vegetable related to squash
its fruits grow on vines or bushes
fruit can be orange, yellow, or white
seeds grow inside its hard shell

Just as skeletons shape and hold up our bodies, students use this silly skeleton planner to form and shape expository writing ideas. Guide each student to label the skull on a copy of page 67 with her main idea. Then have her record supporting details along the arm and leg bones. **For students writing multiparagraph reports,** direct them to list separate paragraph topics on each arm and leg and then plan details for each paragraph near the corresponding fingers or toes.

Susan Hass, Shields Elementary, Saginaw, MI

On the Scene

Sensory details

Hire your student writers to work as imaginary reporters. First, post a list of events like the one shown. Tell students that they will act as news reporters at one of these scenes. Explain that their job is to use strong sensory details to make television viewers (their classmates) feel as though they are there too. Then have each student write one of the events on an index card. Direct him to turn the card over and use his senses to list what he might see, hear, smell, feel, and taste at this event. Provide time for students to share their lists with a small group and have those classmates guess the scene. Follow the activity by having students share with the rest of the class which sensory details were most helpful when determining the scene.

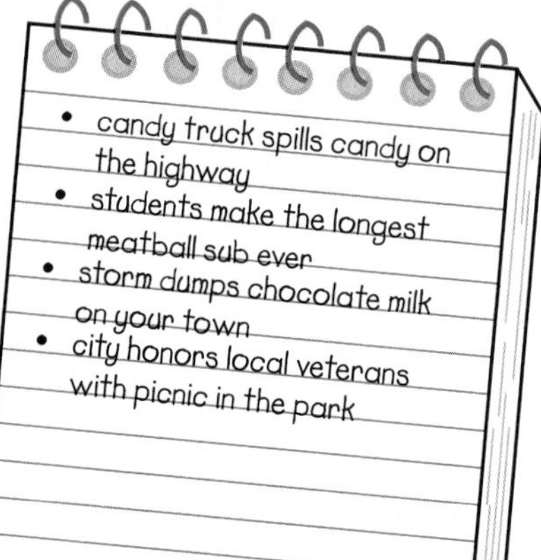

• candy truck spills candy on the highway
• students make the longest meatball sub ever
• storm dumps chocolate milk on your town
• city honors local veterans with picnic in the park

Jackie Beaudry
Getzville, NY

Name Alison
Date Nov. 18, 2011
Editing for capitalization
My Thanksgiving Plans
Did you draw 20 sets of lines?
Congratulations!
Alison
is a member of
the John Hancock Club

Join the Club!

Cursive handwriting

Get students excited about handwriting while sneaking in a little US history at the same time! Read aloud *The John Hancock Club* by Louise Borden. Tell students they have been invited to join the John Hancock Club but that official membership will not take place until they have mastered cursive writing. As the year progresses, remind students of the club. At the end of the year, award students with a certificate to welcome them to the club.

Steph McHugh, Bristol Bay Elementary, Yorkville, IL

On the Lookout

Linking words

To begin, write each word shown on a different-color paper strip and put the strips in a bag. Draw a strip from the bag and share the word with students. Next, write on the board a few sample sentences that use the word; then invite students to do the same on a sheet of paper. Direct each child to make a linking word key by titling a journal page as shown, writing the word, and then drawing a dot in the matching color. When each student writes an opinion piece, encourage him to use the word or phrase and underline it with a matching-color crayon. When students can confidently use this linking word, draw a new strip from the bag and repeat the process, instructing students to underline the new word as well as any previously practiced linking words.

Linking Words
because
and
also
therefore
since
I think fall sports are better than spring sports. One reason is because football is played in the fall and I love football! Since football is not played in spring, that makes fall sports better.
since

Around Town
October Prompts
November Prompts
Get Cooking!

Provide practice with **writing a paragraph**. Simply copy the **ready-to-use mat** on page 68!

Find 12 **writing prompts** for your student authors on page 81.

Guide students through **writing directions** with the **graphic organizer** on page 87.

Writing Tips & Tools

Add a Little Flavor

Adding descriptive details

In advance, gather a variety of clean, empty condiment containers (such as ketchup, mustard, mayonnaise, and pickles) and cover each product's sticker with a plain adhesive label. Then set the containers together. To start the activity, ask students how people add flavor to foods such as hot dogs and hamburgers. Lead students to understand that condiments are often added to make the foods taste more interesting. Then ask students to name ways they can make their writing more interesting. Write each suggestion on a different adhesive label. Display the containers and refer to them when you want students to add a little flavor to their writing.

Beth Pallotta, Eden Christian Academy, Pittsburgh, PA

Tell who, what, when, where, and why.
Explain with your senses.
Make a picture with your words.
Use specific words.
Make a comparison.

Q & A

Writing dialogue

Find out what's on your students' minds with this quick and easy activity. Instruct each child to write on a sentence strip a question a classmate could answer; then have him add quotation marks, his name, and a dialogue tag. Collect the strips and hand a different one to each student. Instruct each child to write her response on a different sentence strip; then display each pair of strips together.

Lori Rosenberg, Imagine Charter School at Broward, Coral Springs, FL

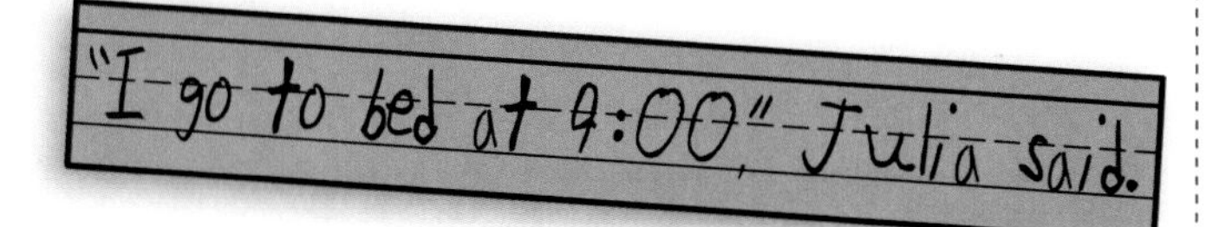
"What time do you go to bed?" Jonathan asked.
"I go to bed at 9:00." Julia said.

Help at Hand

Revising a draft

Give students the tools they need to build better writing projects. After a child completes a draft, have him read a copy of page 69. He refers to each task as he checks his draft; then he makes changes as needed. He colors the corresponding tool to show that he has addressed the task and staples the paper to his draft. As an alternative, have each child cut out a copy of the tools and glue them to a 2" x 12" paper strip (tool belt). Instruct the student to refer to the tasks on the tool belt each time he revises a draft.

Beth Pallotta

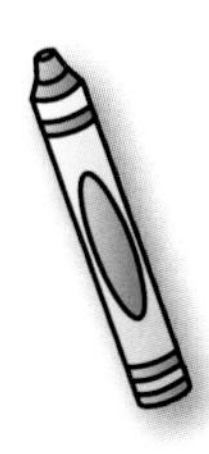

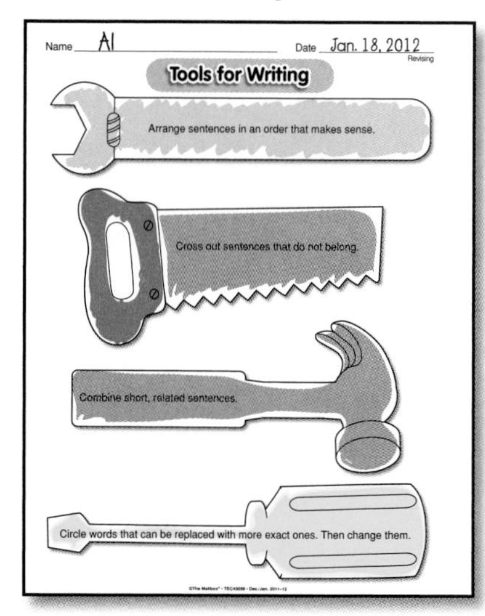

Name Al Date Jan. 18, 2012

Revising

Tools for Writing

Arrange sentences in an order that makes sense.

Cross out sentences that do not belong.

Combine short, related sentences.

Circle words that can be replaced with more exact ones. Then change them.

Countdown to Winter Break

Writing a paragraph

This idea doubles as a decorative seasonal display! First, request that each child bring in a holiday card. (Have some on hand for students who don't bring one.) List on the board prompts, such as those shown, and have each child write a paragraph on a large index card. After editing, have the child glue the index card to the back of the holiday card's cover and then cut off the remaining card. To display the cards, start at the day before break and count back days equal to your number of students; then post one card in a calendar arrangement for each date. Each day, read a paragraph aloud; then place it in a basket for students to read in their spare time. (Read Saturday cards on Friday afternoon and Sunday cards on Monday morning.) Not only will students have a visual reminder of how many days are left before vacation, but they'll also be exposed to some entertaining paragraphs!

Tammie Granger, Memminger Elementary
Charleston, SC

My Favorite Holiday Tradition
The Perfect Winter Vacation
Winter Fun With Loved Ones
The Best Gift I Ever Gave

Countdown to Winter Break

Happy Holidays

Taco Time!

Main idea and details

In this mouthwatering idea, students learn that a taco and a paragraph have a lot in common! Explain that the outer shell is like the main idea: it holds the filling, or details, together. Also explain that the main idea, which can be found in the topic sentences and conclusion, wraps around either side of the details, just as a shell wraps around the filling. Next, have each child cut out a copy of the taco shell pattern on page 70. She writes a topic sentence on one side of the shell and then labels three 1" x 8" paper strips, each with a different detail sentence. The student turns the shell over and writes a conclusion on the other side before gluing the strips inside the shell. Voila! Her taco-shaped organizer is served!

Lynette Prinz, Jefferson Elementary, Wyandotte, MI

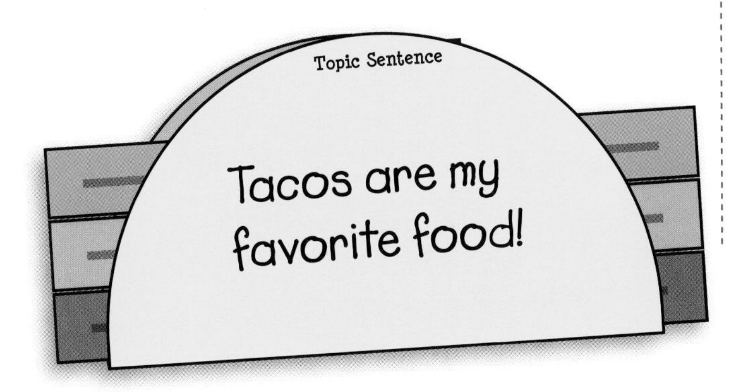
Topic Sentence
Tacos are my favorite food!

In Tune

Linking verbs

After students sing a few rounds of this grammar-related tune, they'll have no trouble naming examples of linking verbs!

Kacie Farmer, South Central Elementary, Elizabeth, IN

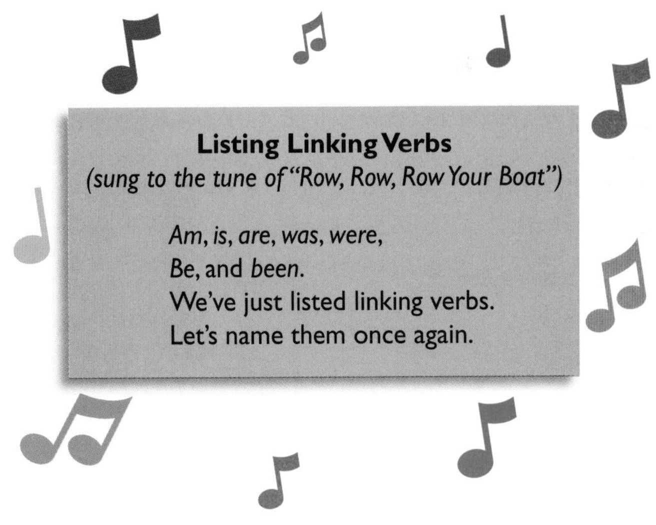

Listing Linking Verbs
(sung to the tune of "Row, Row, Row Your Boat")

Am, is, are, was, were,
Be, and *been.*
We've just listed linking verbs.
Let's name them once again.

Writing Tips & Tools

Direct the Troops

Distinguishing types of sentences

With help from a party-supply store purchase, students are sure to remember the difference between a statement and a command. In advance, obtain a plastic army helmet. To begin the activity, share a series of statements about your helmet and the upcoming activity, such as "I will put on this helmet," "When I wear the helmet, I am the general," and "I will give you commands, and I want you to follow them." Put the helmet on; then use a powerful voice to give a series of commands, such as "Stand up," "Clap your hands," and "Stop." Guide students to compare the sentences you shared aloud and identify which were statements and which were commands.

CLAP YOUR HANDS.

Linda Hill, Robert Wilson Elementary, Corpus Christi, TX

In the Cards

Varying sentence lengths

This partner activity challenges students to stay on topic while varying the lengths of their story's sentences. To prepare, remove the face cards from a deck of cards. Assign a topic or a prompt; then lead the duo to take the top card off the deck, write a sentence with the matching number of words, and then set the card aside. Partners take turns drawing a card and working together to write a sentence of the matching length. **To vary the activity's materials,** cover the faces of a die with masking tape and renumber the faces from three to eight. Direct the students to roll the die to determine the number of words to include in each sentence.

Keiran, Avery
I'm Bertie. I am a bird. I
start each day by singing. I
sing loudly. The other animals
seem to like it. Next, I eat.
Worms are my favorite food.

Patti Hoke, Florence Roche Elementary, Groton, MA

In Tune With Parts of Speech

Identifying coordinating conjunctions

Meet the needs of your auditory learners with this easy-to-remember song. After teaching students that a conjunction is a word that links sentences, phrases, or words, display a copy of the song on the top of page 71. Guide students to understand that the first letter of each conjunction in the song spells the word *fanboys*. Then lead students in singing a few rounds.

Amanda Reiser, Oak Park Elementary, Ocean Springs, MS

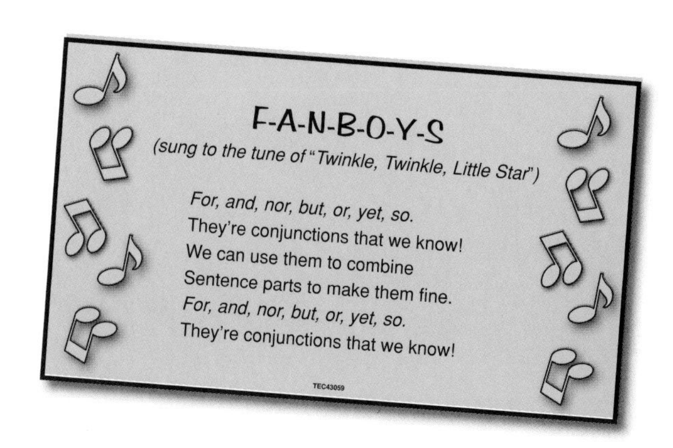
F-A-N-B-O-Y-S
(sung to the tune of "Twinkle, Twinkle, Little Star")
For, and, nor, but, or, yet, so.
They're conjunctions that we know!
We can use them to combine
Sentence parts to make them fine.
For, and, nor, but, or, yet, so.
They're conjunctions that we know!
TEC43059

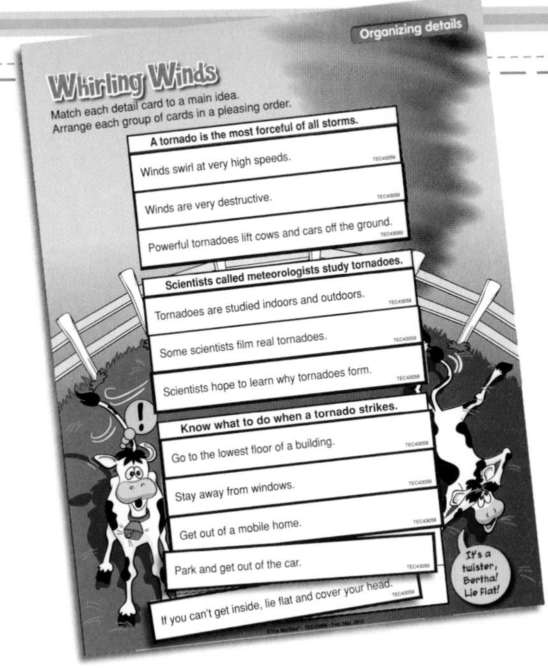
Organizing details
Whirling Winds
Match each detail card to a main idea.
Arrange each group of cards in a pleasing order.
A tornado is the most forceful of all storms.
Winds swirl at very high speeds.
Winds are very destructive.
Powerful tornadoes lift cows and cars off the ground.
Scientists called meteorologists study tornadoes.
Tornadoes are studied indoors and outdoors.
Some scientists film real tornadoes.
Scientists hope to learn why tornadoes form.
Know what to do when a tornado strikes.
Go to the lowest floor of a building.
Stay away from windows.
Get out of a mobile home.
Park and get out of the car.
If you can't get inside, lie flat and cover your head.
It's a twister, Bertha! Lie Flat!

Get Wind of This!

Organizing details

Want students to write up a storm? Then use this activity! To set up, make a copy of the bottom of page 71 on tagboard; then cut apart the detail cards and place them in a resealable plastic bag. Set out the cards with a copy of the sorting mat from page 72. To complete the activity, a student sorts each card under its matching topic sentence. When he is satisfied with the order of the sentences placed under each main idea, he uses the sentences to write a three-paragraph informative text on tornadoes. **For a shorter option**, direct the student to write only one of the three paragraphs.

Perfect Practice

Spelling

Mix up your review time with these fun activities!

Write the Right One: Write a current spelling word or a word students commonly misspell on the board three times, spelling it incorrectly two times. Each student writes the correct spelling on a portable dry-erase board and then holds it up for review.

No-Touch Tag: Ask a student to spell a word. If she spells it correctly, direct her to choose a different word and repeat, verbally "tagging" another child to spell the word.

Did You Hear That? Choose a child to spell a word from the list aloud. Direct the other students to write the letters as the child spells. The child selects a classmate to pronounce the word he spelled and, if she does so correctly, she spells the next word.

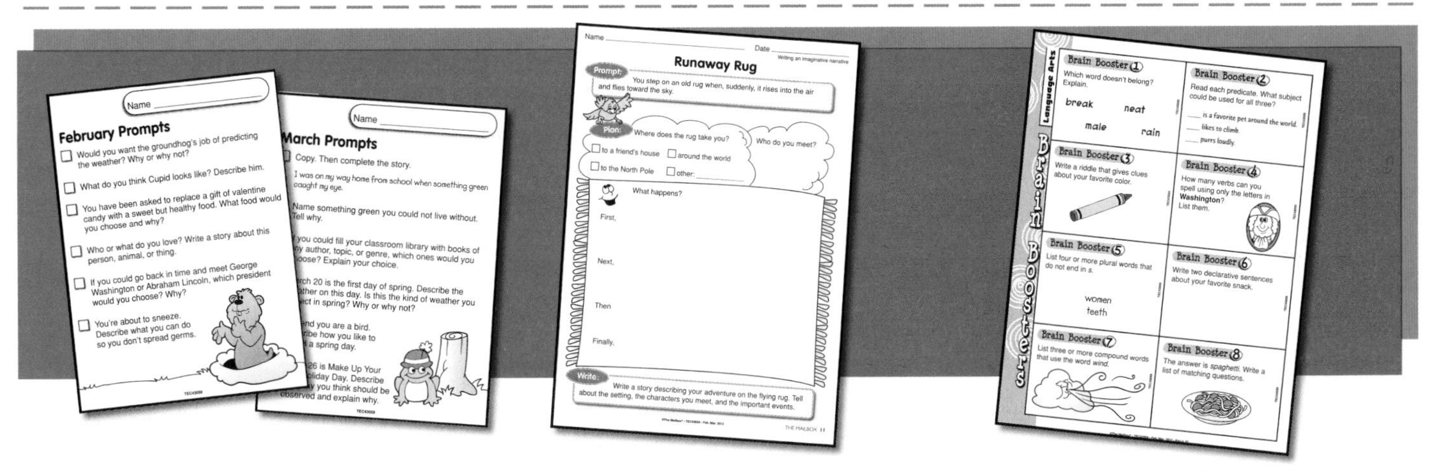
February Prompts
March Prompts
Runaway Rug
Brain Boosters

Encourage your youngsters to fall in love with writing! See the **prompts** on page 83.

Guide students' imaginations with the **graphic organizer** on page 89.

Do your early finishers need a challenge? Check out the **Brain Boosters** on page 55.

Writing Tips & Tools

What a View!

Writing poetry

This nature-inspired idea brings the outdoors in. Have each child fold a sheet of colored construction paper in half, cut out a rectangle, and unfold the paper to create a window shape. Give each student a clipboard and writing paper; then take students outside with their supplies. Instruct each child to hold up his window and focus on one of the sights around him, such as a flower, a cloud, or ants in the grass. Next, have him write words and phrases that come to mind as he looks through his window. Return to the classroom and have each child use his list to write a poem about his window view. **To extend the activity,** direct the child to add a small illustration and staple the window atop his poem.

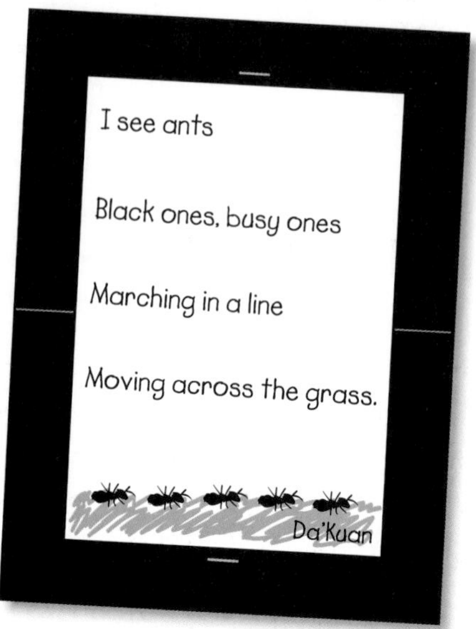
I see ants
Black ones, busy ones
Marching in a line
Moving across the grass.
Da'Kuan

Dawn Rainbowstar, The Colorado Springs School, Colorado Springs, CO

Wacky Words

Using more precise words

Encourage students to demonstrate an enriched vocabulary with this silly center. Post a list of words with unusual spellings or pronunciations; then review each word's meaning. Place a dictionary and a supply of paper near the display. Challenge students who visit the center to write sentences using three or more posted words. If needed, encourage them to use the dictionary to make sure each word is used correctly.

Isobel Livingstone, Rahway, NJ

doozy	putter
flimflam	rumpus
fusty	scoot
gizmo	vim
hoopla	yammer

Three for Me

Adding inflectional endings *-ed, -ing*

It may look like a game, but this activity requires students to listen, read, and make words. To begin, display one or both lists from page 73. Direct each student to draw a tic-tac-toe grid on a sheet of paper and write a different base word at the top of each section. Then read a word from the list. If a child has it on her paper, she rewrites the word in its space and adds *-ed* or *-ing*. If she doesn't have the word, she writes it with an inflectional ending under her grid. Continue reading words until a student has rewritten three words in a row horizontally, diagonally, or vertically and says, "That's three for me!" If desired, award the class three minutes of extra recess if the words are spelled correctly. **To make the activity more challenging,** cover the list's heading before displaying it.

bug	rain	help
skip	twirl	bob
hunt hunted	kiss kissed	hug hugged

laughed
tagged

Jennifer L. Kohnke, St. Charles, IL

Come Into Bloom

Using a graphic organizer

Give students a chance to reflect on how much they've learned and blossomed this year. Direct each child to draw a flower with four or more petals, like the one shown. Have him write a topic sentence in the middle and a detail on each petal. Next, instruct the student to use the graphic organizer to write a paragraph or more. If desired, have him lightly color his organizer. Post the organizers and the paragraphs on a display titled "We've Blossomed, and So Will You!" Keep the display posted into the next school year.

Valerie Wood Smith, Robeson Elementary Center, Morgantown, PA

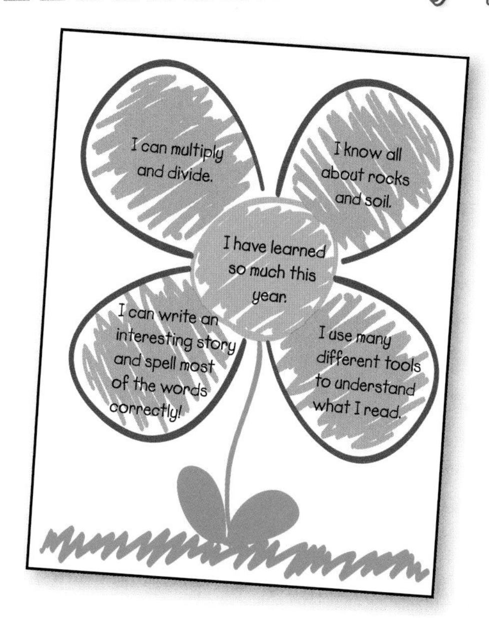
I can multiply and divide.
I know all about rocks and soil.
I have learned so much this year.
I can write an interesting story and spell most of the words correctly!
I use many different tools to understand what I read.

Have a Ball

Writing a narrative

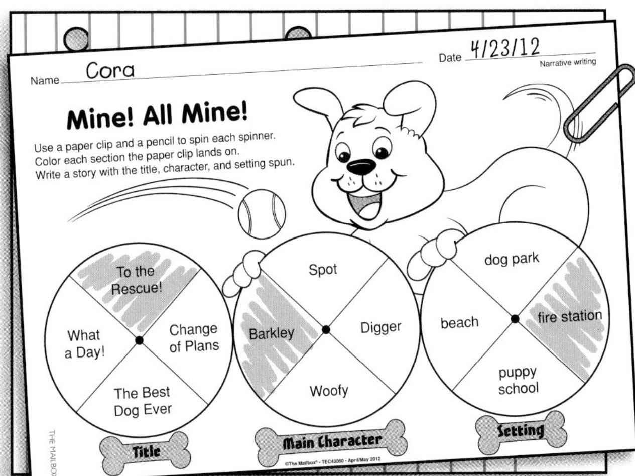
Name Cora
Date 4/23/12
Narrative writing
Mine! All Mine!
Use a paper clip and a pencil to spin each spinner.
Color each section the paper clip lands on.
Write a story with the title, character, and setting spun.
To the Rescue!
What a Day!
Change of Plans
The Best Dog Ever
Title
Spot
Barkley
Digger
Woofy
Main Character
dog park
beach
fire station
puppy school
Setting

Put a spin on narrative writing with this fun writing mat. Give each child a copy of page 74 and a paper clip. Direct the child to follow the directions on the page to write a story. Remind her to include a beginning, middle, and end with plenty of details. When the story is complete, instruct the child to paper-clip the mat to her final draft.

Points for Practice

Spelling review

Remind students that spelling is a valuable skill with this weekly review activity. To start, say a spelling word and instruct each child to write it on his paper. Next, roll a die and announce the number rolled; then spell the word aloud. If the student spelled the word correctly, he writes the number next to the word. If he spelled the word incorrectly, he writes a zero. Continue with each word on the list. After all the words are read, checked, and scored, direct each child to find his grand total. Award the student or students with the most points a small prize, such as a bonus point on the next test.

adapted from an idea by Kristen Peterson, Tea Elementary, Tea, SD

Liang

1. nickel +5
2. castle +2
3. mentel +0
4. puzzle +3
5. freckel +0
6. equal +6
7. coral +1
8. level +1
9. candle +2
10. shovel +5

25

Writing Tips & Tools

Quick Correction
Editing

Harness students' year-end energy with this review game. Write two similar sentences on the board, including the same type of grammatical errors in each. Put students into two teams and have each team stand in a line. Invite one player from each team to go to the board and, on your signal, have him make one correction to his team's sentence. When he has done so, he passes the dry-erase marker to the next player on his team. Students continue in this manner until each team feels all the necessary edits are made. The team members sit down to signal they are done. The first team that correctly edits its sentence earns a point. Continue play with new sentences as time allows.

"Can we go to Best Burger for dinner?" Kyle asked.
"I prefer to eat at Tiny's Tacos," Kara said.

Lois Werner, Martin Luther Lutheran School, Oshkosh, WY

The Right Route
Writing directions

Here's an idea that benefits your current students as well as next year's class. To start, have each child choose a different school destination, such as the gym, cafeteria, media center, restroom, playground, or office. Direct her to write directions that explain how to get from your classroom to the destination. Next, take students to each destination and have them look for important landmarks or details that would make their instructions clearer. Instruct students to rewrite their informational texts, adding these details; then bind the completed directions into a class book for next year's students to review and use as a resource.

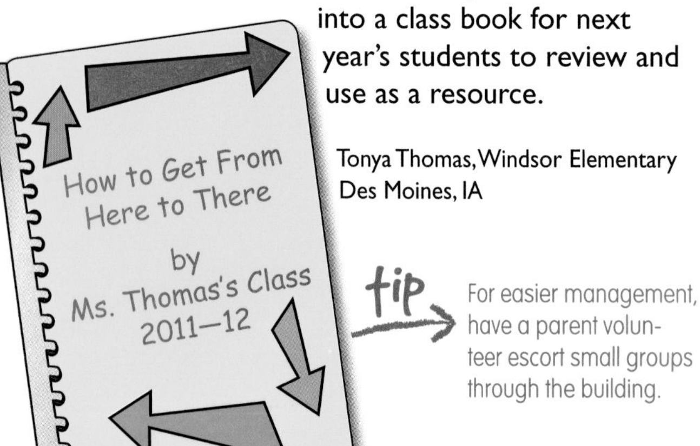

How to Get From Here to There
by
Ms. Thomas's Class
2011–12

Tonya Thomas, Windsor Elementary
Des Moines, IA

tip For easier management, have a parent volunteer escort small groups through the building.

Everything in Its Place
Writing reports

Repurposed file folders and envelopes make simple research organizers. In advance, determine how many subtopics you want each child to address in his report and list them on the board. Then, to make an organizer, have each child cut envelopes in half until he has one half for each subtopic. The student labels each envelope half with a different subtopic and then glues the halves to the inside of a file folder. Instruct the child to write facts related to each topic on separate index cards and place the index cards in the matching envelope. When the student is ready to write his report, he refers to his index cards and stores his drafts inside the folder.

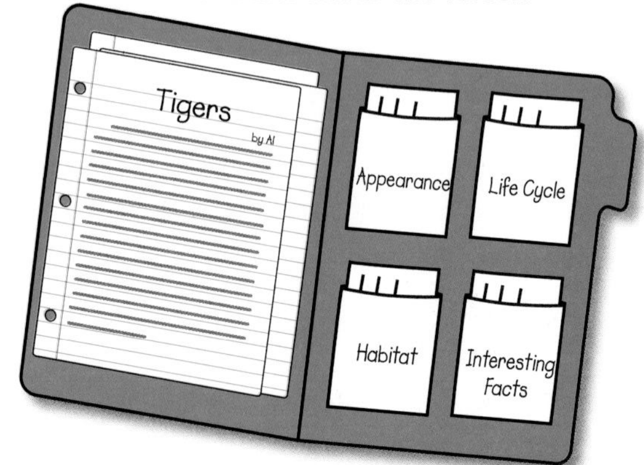

Tigers
by Al
Appearance
Life Cycle
Habitat
Interesting Facts

Get great **practice sheets** and more on pages 80–100.

Name ______________________ Date ______________

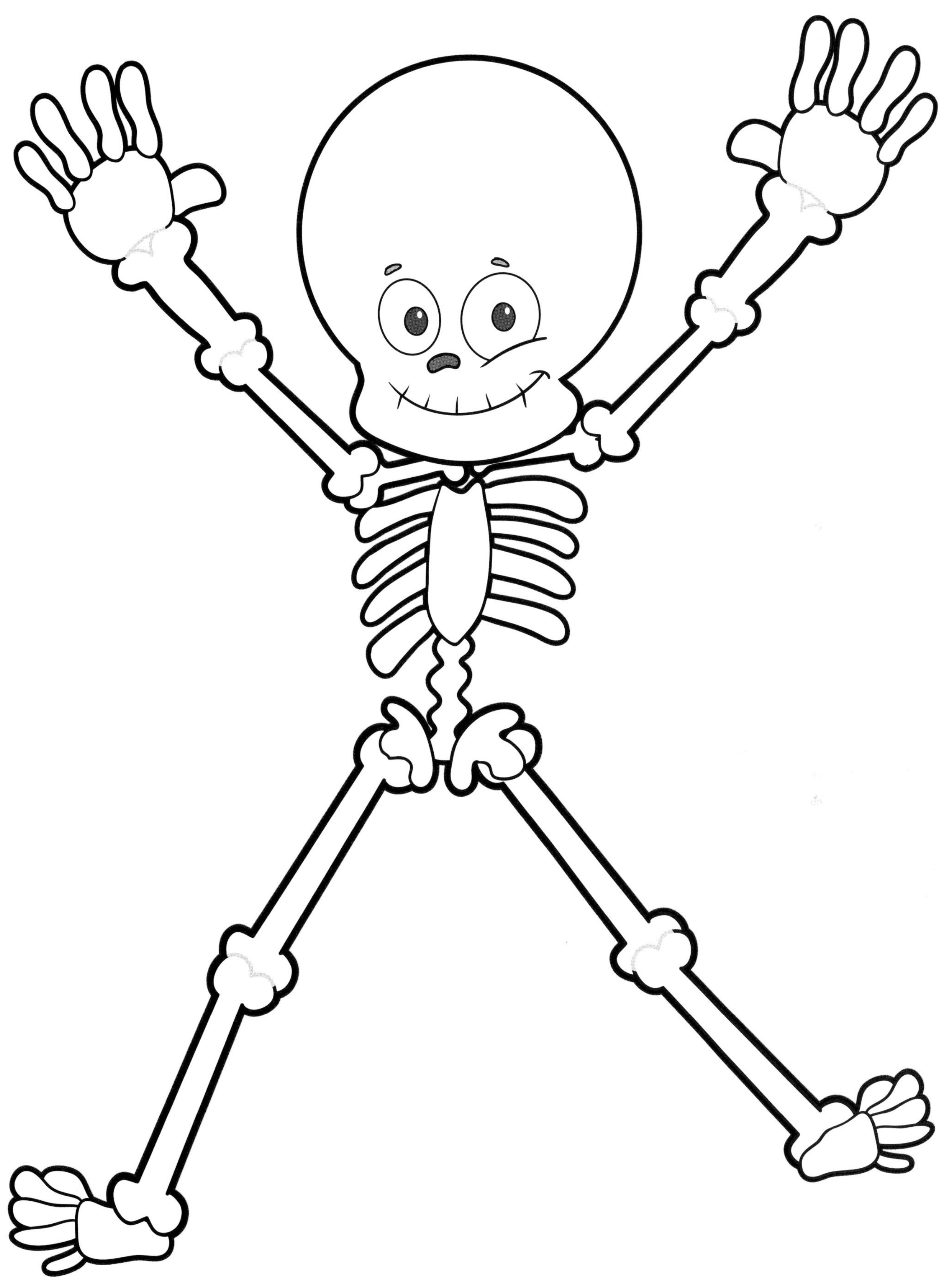

Note to the teacher: Use with "Boning Up" on page 58.

Around Town

Write a paragraph about your community.
Read the word bank. Choose a topic.

Paragraph Place
Topic Sentence
Detail Sentences
Closing Sentence
Topics
Places to Go
My Favorite Spot
A Town Celebration
NEVERL8
Word Bank
city
park
store
school
church
library
parade
downtown
festival
building
hospital
restaurant
fire station
movie theater

How to use Copy the activity card and put it in a plastic page protector for durability. Then set out the card and writing paper.

Name ______________________ Date ______________________

Revising

Tools for Writing

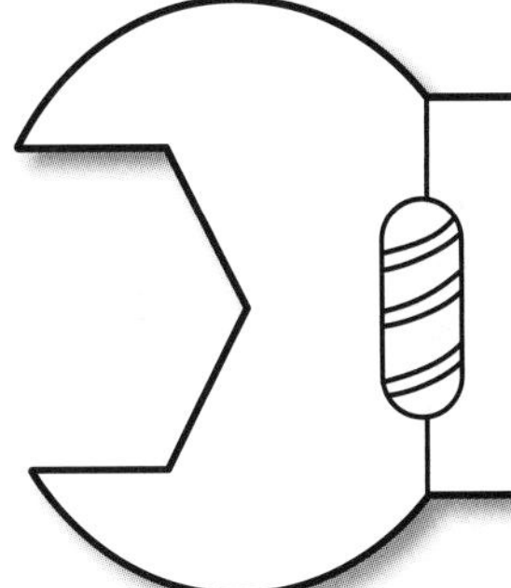

Arrange sentences in an order that makes sense.

Cross out sentences that do not belong.

Combine short, related sentences.

Circle words that can be replaced with more exact ones. Then change them.

Note to the teacher: Use with "Help at Hand" on page 60.

Taco Shell Pattern

Use with "Taco Time!" on page 61.

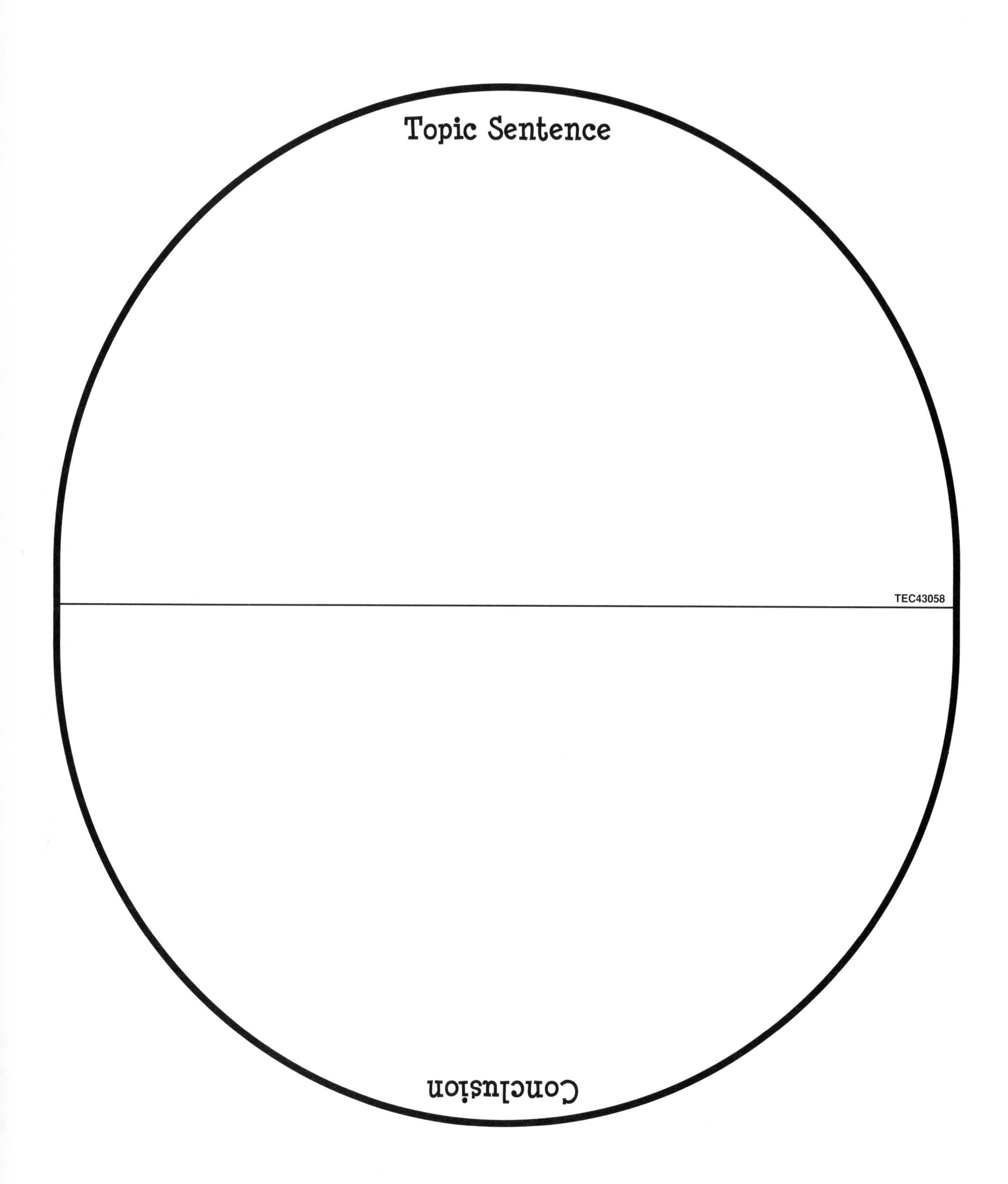
Topic Sentence
TEC43058
Conclusion

Song Card

Use with "In Tune With Parts of Speech" on page 62.

F-A-N-B-O-Y-S

(sung to the tune of "Twinkle, Twinkle, Little Star")

For, and, nor, but, or, yet, so.
They're conjunctions that we know!
We can use them to combine
Sentence parts to make them fine.
For, and, nor, but, or, yet, so.
They're conjunctions that we know!

TEC43059

Detail Cards

Use with "Get Wind of This!" on page 63 and the sorting sheet on page 72.

If you can't get inside, lie flat and cover your head. TEC43059

Winds are very destructive. TEC43059

Winds swirl at very high speeds. TEC43059

Tornadoes are studied indoors and outdoors. TEC43059

Park and get out of the car. TEC43059

Some scientists film real tornadoes. TEC43059

Go to the lowest floor of a building. TEC43059

Stay away from windows. TEC43059

Scientists hope to learn why tornadoes form. TEC43059

Powerful tornadoes lift cows and cars off the ground. TEC43059

Get out of a mobile home. TEC43059

Whirling Winds

Match each detail card to a main idea.
Arrange each group of cards in a pleasing order.

A tornado is the most forceful of all storms.

Scientists called meteorologists study tornadoes.

Know what to do when a tornado strikes.

!

It's a twister, Bertha! Lie flat!

Note to the teacher: Use with "Get Wind of This!" on page 63 and the detail cards on page 71.

Base Words Lists

Use with "Three for Me" on page 64.

Double the Ending Consonant

blot
bob
bug
dip
hop
hug
knit
nod
pat
plan
rap
rob
skip
tag
trap

TEC43060

Do Not Double the Ending Consonant

dream
help
hunt
jump
kiss
laugh
mind
pass
rain
reach
sew
ski
talk
twirl
walk

TEC43060

Name________________________ Date____________

Narrative writing

Mine! All Mine!

Use a paper clip and a pencil to spin each spinner.
Color each section the paper clip lands on.
Write a story with the title, character, and setting spun.

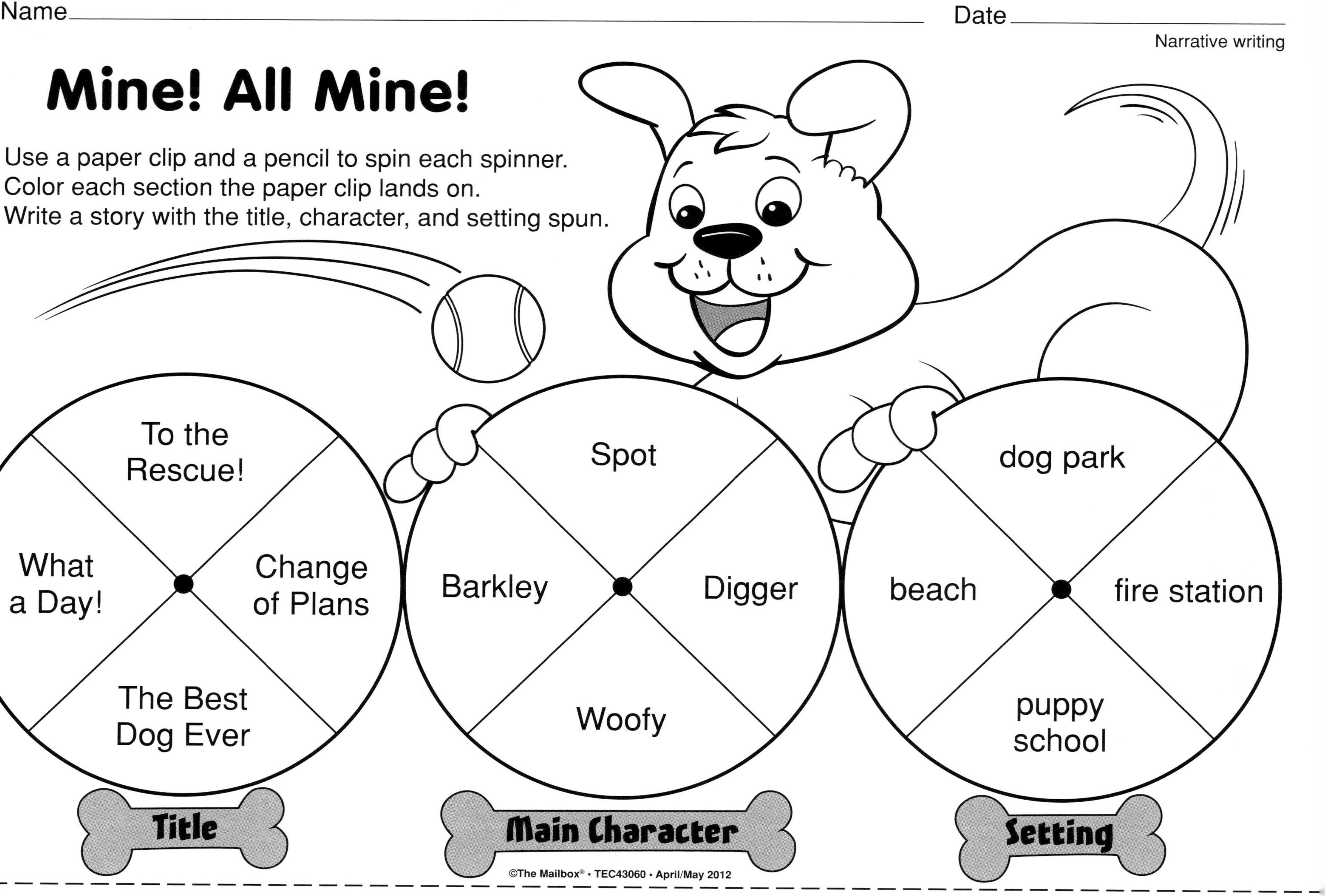
To the Rescue!
Change of Plans
The Best Dog Ever
What a Day!
Title
Spot
Digger
Woofy
Barkley
Main Character
dog park
fire station
puppy school
beach
Setting

Note to the teacher: Use with "Have a Ball" on page 65.

Going on Safari!

Independent Writing Activities

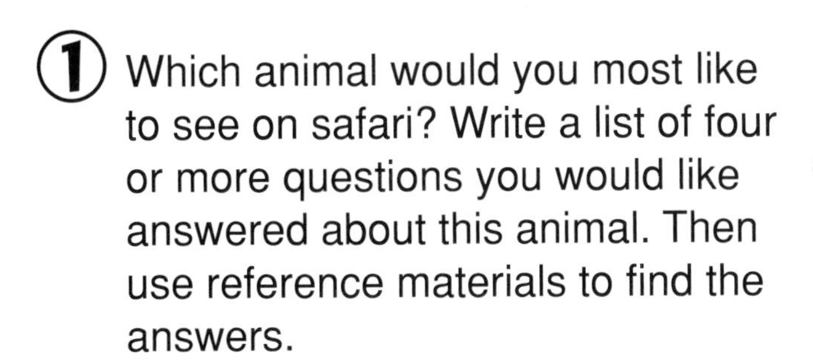

1. Which animal would you most like to see on safari? Write a list of four or more questions you would like answered about this animal. Then use reference materials to find the answers.

2. Make a list of animals you would not expect to see on safari. Write a paragraph telling why you wouldn't see them.

3. Pretend you are on safari. Write a poem about what you see and hear.

4. Write a letter inviting a friend to go on safari with you. Tell your buddy what you will do on your trip to convince him or her to join you.

Choose a prompt. Write the number and your response.

5. Pretend you are an animal that lives in Africa. You take a safari through part of the US. Write a story about your adventure.

Center Activity Card Copy this activity card and put it in a plastic page protector. Then place the activity card and paper at a center.

Build Writing Skills!

4
Ideas That Are Just
"Write" for the Job

1 Center of Attention
Nouns

With help from this silly clown, students show off their understanding of nouns! Enlarge the clown pattern on page 78, cut it out, and post it in an easy-to-access location. Next, have each child write on a piece of paper an example for each noun category listed on the clown. After reviewing students' responses, direct each student to write his examples on the corresponding sections of the clown. Keep the clown posted for students to use as a reference. **As an alternative,** give each child his own copy of the pattern on page 78 and have him list examples on it.

Amy Winner, Northwestern Primary, Darlington, PA

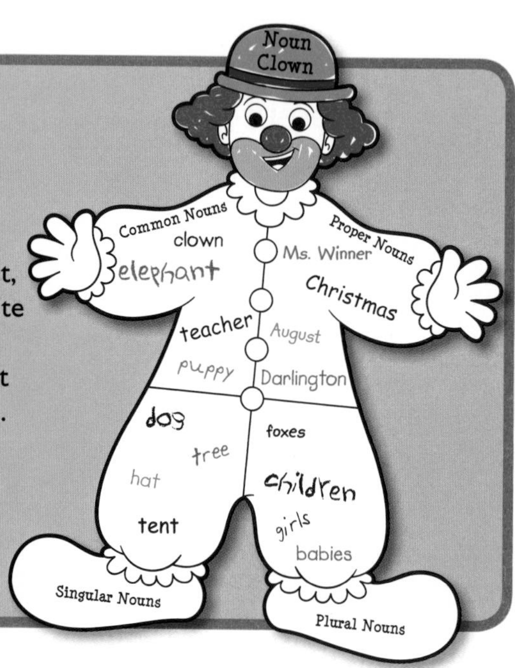
Noun Clown
Common Nouns
clown
elephant
Proper Nouns
Ms. Winner
Christmas
teacher
August
puppy
Darlington
dog
foxes
tree
hat
children
tent
girls
babies
Singular Nouns
Plural Nouns

Avery
zebra

declarative
My stripes are black and white.

interrogative
Will I find enough grass to eat today?

exclamatory
Lions scare me!

imperative
Don't leave the protection of the herd.

2 Guess Who
Types of sentences

Turn sentence-writing practice into a fun-filled guessing game! Post a list of nouns (like the one shown) and instruct each child to write one on her paper. Then direct her to write four sentences (declarative, interrogative, exclamatory, and imperative) from the noun's point of view. Provide time for the student to read her sentences aloud and encourage her classmates to guess the noun she chose.

Carolyn Burant, St. John Vianney School, Brookfield, WI

alarm clock	pencil
bear	pizza
cell phone	racecar
computer	stuffed animal
dog	tornado
football	whiteboard
helicopter	zebra

3 Manipulative End Marks
Ending punctuation

Use this hands-on activity to reinforce end marks. In advance, gather ring cereal, pretzel sticks, and string licorice. To begin, a student writes a statement, an exclamation, and a question on a large sheet of construction paper. Then the child glues a cereal ring to his paper in place of the period. He glues a pretzel stick and a cereal ring for the exclamation point; then he molds a licorice piece into the shape of a question mark and glues it above another cereal ring.

Kelly Garman, Lake Elementary, Millbury, OH

Eating cereal is a good way to start the day
Corn Clusters are the very best
Will you please help me pour the milk
Terrence

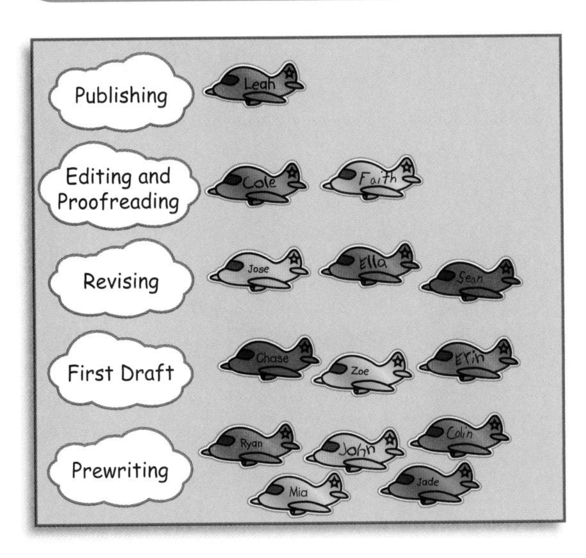
Publishing
Leah
Editing and Proofreading
Cole
Faith
Revising
Jose
Ella
Sean
First Draft
Chase
Zoe
Erin
Prewriting
Ryan
John
Colin
Mia
Jade

4 Flying High
Writing process

Take students on a trip through the writing process with this easy-to-prepare idea. To start, cover a wall or flat surface at student height with blue paper. Next, label each of five cloud cutouts with a stage of the writing process and attach them to the blue paper as shown. Then have each child personalize and cut out a copy of a plane pattern from below. If desired, laminate the planes for durability; then use Sticky Tac adhesive to place each plane next to the prewriting cloud. As a student soars through each stage of the writing process, direct him to move his plane next to the corresponding cloud.

Brooke Beverly, Dudley Elementary, Dudley, MA

Plane Patterns
Use with "Flying High" above.

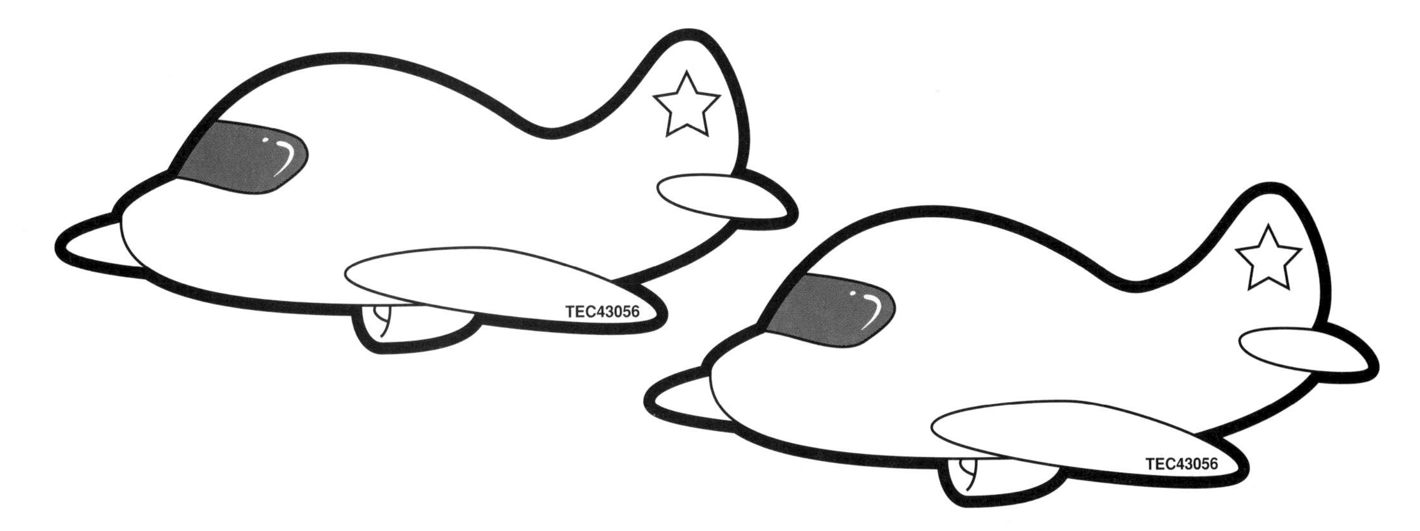
TEC43056
TEC43056

Clown Pattern

Use with "Center of Attention" on page 76.

Noun
Clown
Common Nouns
Proper Nouns
Singular Nouns
Plural Nouns
TEC43056

Time to Shine!

Four Stellar Ideas for Celebrating Your Student Authors!

1

Every budding author dreams of being published someday, so why not make the dream a reality and have each student publish his own anthology? Give each child two sheets of construction paper. On one sheet, have him design a cover that showcases his writing collection. On the other sheet, have him draw a self-portrait and write an "About the Author" paragraph. Laminate the pages; then guide the student to staple his favorite writing pieces between the two papers. Have him hole-punch the top left-hand corner of the book and insert a metal ring. Finally, invite the child to hang his anthology on a classroom display for other students to read and enjoy.

Jake's
Anthology

Meet the Author
About the Author

2

Put the spotlight on one student's writing each week. Display a child's favorite writing pieces on a bulletin board titled "Meet the Author." Include a photo of the student and an "About the Author" summary. Place sticky notes and pencils near the display. Throughout the week, have students visit the display and read the writing samples. Encourage each child to write a positive remark on a sticky note and post it on the display.

In addition to monthly birthdays and national holiday festivities, add another celebration to the calendar. Celebrate your writers! Send out invitations to guests, such as families, faculty members, or another class. Ask parent volunteers to donate beverages and breakfast bars or doughnuts. Before the get-together, have each student type her favorite writing sample. Then assemble the samples into a class literary magazine and make copies of it for your guests. On the day of the celebration, designate a special chair where each author sits and reads her selected piece aloud. After the readings, make the authors available for an autograph session with the invited guests.

Author

4

A classroom website is a great way to share your young authors' work. Each month, post a sample of each child's writing. With just the click of a mouse, family members from near and far can see his latest writing compositions!

tip For privacy purposes, assign each child a number and post his writing using the number rather than his name.

Name ____________________

August Prompts

- ☐ What is one thing you would like to learn this year? Why?
- ☐ Describe one thing about you that is true. Describe one thing about you that you wish was true.
- ☐ Copy and complete.
  I think ____ grade will be better than ____. Here's why.
- ☐ How do you feel when someone does not follow the rules? Explain.
- ☐ Would you rather buy one book at the store or borrow three from the library? Explain.
- ☐ Write a story titled "The Best Saturday Ever!"
- ☐ Tell about a fun summer memory.

TEC43056

Name ____________________

September Prompts

- ☐ It is your lucky day. Describe all the lucky things that happen to you!
- ☐ In what ways is your classroom like your home? How is it different?
- ☐ If you could spend all day in one room of your school, where would you choose? Why?
- ☐ Autumn starts on September 23. What is your favorite thing about autumn? Give two or more reasons.
- ☐ Copy. Explain.
  There are many things I can do to stay safe when I pack and carry my backpack.
- ☐ Ancestor Appreciation Day is September 27. What do you know about your ancestors? What would you like to know?

TEC43056

How to use Have each child staple a copy of this page in his writing journal. Or cut copies in half and distribute only one month's prompts at a time to students. When a student uses a prompt, he checks its box.

Name ____________________

October Prompts

- [ ] Pretend you are a judge at a jack-o'-lantern contest. Describe the winning pumpkin.
- [ ] Uh-oh. A fire has started on your stove! What do you do? Why?
- [ ] What does it mean to have a positive attitude? Include examples.
- [ ] Are fall sports better than spring sports? Explain why or why not.
- [ ] Copy the sentences. Then complete the story.

  It was a quiet, fall night. A full moon filled the sky.
- [ ] Tell about a time when you went somewhere new. Add details that explain what you saw and how you felt.

TEC43057

Name ____________________

November Prompts

- [ ] What are three good ways to stay warm when it is chilly outside?
- [ ] Why is it important for citizens to vote? Give two or more reasons to support your idea.
- [ ] If you were in charge of planning your family's Thanksgiving meal, what would you serve? Describe each food.
- [ ] You're playing outside a friend's house when a turkey trots up to you. What happens next?
- [ ] Pretend you are sailing on the *Mayflower*. Write a letter to a family member. Tell about your trip.
- [ ] What are you most thankful for this year? Why?

TEC43057

How to use Have each child staple a copy of this page in his writing journal. Or cut copies in half and distribute only one month's prompts at a time to students. When a student uses a prompt, he checks its box.

Name ______________________

December Prompts

- ☐ Pretend you are walking down the street when a neighbor's holiday lawn decoration comes to life. Tell what happens next.
- ☐ Which winter holiday would you like to know more about? Why?
- ☐ Copy. Then complete and explain.

  If I could give my family any gift, I would give…
- ☐ Think about the last day of school before winter break begins. Describe how you feel.
- ☐ If you could, would you like to hibernate during the winter? Why or why not?
- ☐ Describe how you have changed during the last year.

TEC43058

Name ______________________

January Prompts

- ☐ Copy. Explain.

  I plan to make 2012 the best year yet. Here's how!
- ☐ Pretend you have a chat with Old Man Winter. What do you say to him? How does he reply?
- ☐ Would you like to live in an igloo? Why or why not?
- ☐ To be "snowed under" means to be overworked or very busy. Write about a time you were snowed under at school.
- ☐ Would you rather be hot and need to cool down or be cold and need to warm up? Explain.
- ☐ How to Make a Snow Angel

TEC43058

How to use: Have each child staple a copy of this page in his writing journal. Or cut copies in half and distribute only one month's prompts at a time to students. When a student uses a prompt, he checks its box.

Name ____________________

February Prompts

- ☐ Would you want the groundhog's job of predicting the weather? Why or why not?
- ☐ What do you think Cupid looks like? Describe him.
- ☐ You have been asked to replace a gift of valentine candy with a sweet but healthy food. What food would you choose and why?
- ☐ Who or what do you love? Write a story about this person, animal, or thing.
- ☐ If you could go back in time and meet George Washington or Abraham Lincoln, which president would you choose? Why?
- ☐ You're about to sneeze. Describe what you can do so you don't spread germs.

TEC43059

Name ____________________

March Prompts

- ☐ Copy. Then complete the story.

  I was on my way home from school when something green caught my eye.
- ☐ Name something green you could not live without. Tell why.
- ☐ If you could fill your classroom library with books of any author, topic, or genre, which ones would you choose? Explain your choice.
- ☐ March 20 is the first day of spring. Describe the weather on this day. Is this the kind of weather you expect in spring? Why or why not?
- ☐ Pretend you are a bird. Describe how you like to spend a spring day.
- ☐ March 26 is Make Up Your Own Holiday Day. Describe a holiday you think should be observed and explain why.

TEC43059

How to use: Have each child staple a copy of this page in his writing journal. Or cut copies in half and distribute only one month's prompts at a time to students. When a student uses a prompt, he checks its box.

Name ____________________

April Prompts

- ☐ Write a story in which opening an umbrella inside brings a character good luck instead of bad luck.
- ☐ Imagine you are a raindrop. You plan to race another raindrop down a window. Describe what happens.
- ☐ What does it mean to *spring into action*? Write about a time you had to spring into action or a time you saw someone else spring into action.
- ☐ How are chocolate and jelly beans alike? How are they different?
- ☐ Copy a topic sentence. Complete the paragraph.

  April has the best weather!
  April has the worst weather!
- ☐ The Twelve Busy Bunnies

TEC43060

Name ____________________

May Prompts

- ☐ Pretend you are a flower named Bud. Explain why you like or dislike living in a flowerpot.
- ☐ Copy and complete the sentence starter. Describe what you would like to do as that animal.

  If I *could* be *any animal*, I *would choose* to be
- ☐ If you were a judge in a Mom of the Year contest, what three traits would you look for in the winning mom?
- ☐ Would you rather have a four-day school week or have each school day shortened by one hour? Explain.
- ☐ The Day the Bugs Moved Indoors
- ☐ Describe how to play flashlight tag. (If you don't know, make up your own rules!)

TEC43060

How to Use Have each child staple a copy of this page in his writing journal. Or cut copies in half and distribute only one month's prompts at a time to students. When a student uses a prompt, he checks its box.

Name ____________________

June Prompts

- ☐ Write a story about a time when you were so hot you thought you might melt.
- ☐ What does "learn by heart" mean? Describe something you learned by heart this year.
- ☐ Pretend you will spend your summer vacation in a jungle. What do you expect to see? What will you do?
- ☐ What should be done with school supplies that have survived the school year? Write a letter to your teacher to describe your ideas.
- ☐ Should kids have a later bedtime during summer? Why or why not?
- ☐ What do school buses do during the summer? Write a make-believe story to explain.

TEC43061

Name ____________________

July Prompts

- ☐ The Best Way to Spend a Summer Day
- ☐ What does freedom mean to you?
- ☐ Pretend you just saw the world's biggest firewo[rks] show. Describe it.
- ☐ Write directions telling how to make a mud pie.
- ☐ You're famous! Write a story telling how you became famous and what life is like for you now.
- ☐ Would you like to compete in a bicycle race? Why or why not?
- ☐ Describe an activity that is best done on a sunny day.

TEC43061

How to Use
Have each child staple a copy of this page in his writing journal. Or cut copies in half and distribute only one month's prompts at a time to students. When a student uses a prompt, he checks its box.

Name ____________________ Date ____________________

Writing with a beginning, middle, and end

Storytime!

Prompt: Check one.

- [ ] The Mystery in the Kitchen
- [ ] The Night I Met the Tooth Fairy
- [ ] I needed to clean my room, and fast!
- [ ] Did you hear what my new pet, Dino, did?

Plan:

Beginning Who is the main character?	When and where does the story take place?	What is the problem?
Middle What is one way the main character tries to solve the problem?	What is another way?	What is another way?
Ending How is the problem solved?	How does the main character feel?	How does the story end?

Write: Use your plan to write a story. Include all the important events from the beginning of the story to the end.

Name ____________________ Date ____________

Writing directions

Get Cooking!

Prompt: You have a new babysitter who wants to get things just right. Help her learn how to make one of these foods exactly the way you like it. Check one.

- ☐ My Favorite Cereal
- ☐ My Favorite Sandwich
- ☐ The Best Afterschool Snack
- ☐ The Perfect Taco

Plan: What items does she need to gather?

What steps should she follow?

How does she know that she has made it correctly?

Write: Write directions for your new babysitter. Tell her how to make the food you chose. Use specific details so she knows exactly what to do.

Name ______________________ Date ______________

Writing a friendly letter

Wish You Were Here!

Prompt: Your family takes a surprise trip to a faraway island. This island is so out-of-the-way that phones and email don't work. You just can't wait to tell a friend about this amazing place, so you write a letter.

Plan:

Who will you write to?	Where are you writing from?
What have you seen?	What fun things have you done?

Write: Write a letter to a friend. Write the date and a greeting. Then, in the body of your letter, tell about your surprise trip. End your letter with a closing and your signature.

Name ______________________ Date ______________________

Writing an imaginative narrative

Runaway Rug

Prompt: You step on an old rug when, suddenly, it rises into the air and flies toward the sky.

Plan: Where does the rug take you?

- ☐ to a friend's house
- ☐ around the world
- ☐ to the North Pole
- ☐ other: ______________

Who do you meet?

What happens?

First,

Next,

Then

Finally,

Write: Write a story describing your adventure on the flying rug. Tell about the setting, the characters you meet, and the important events.

Name ____________________ Date __________

Persuasive writing

The Best Pet to Get

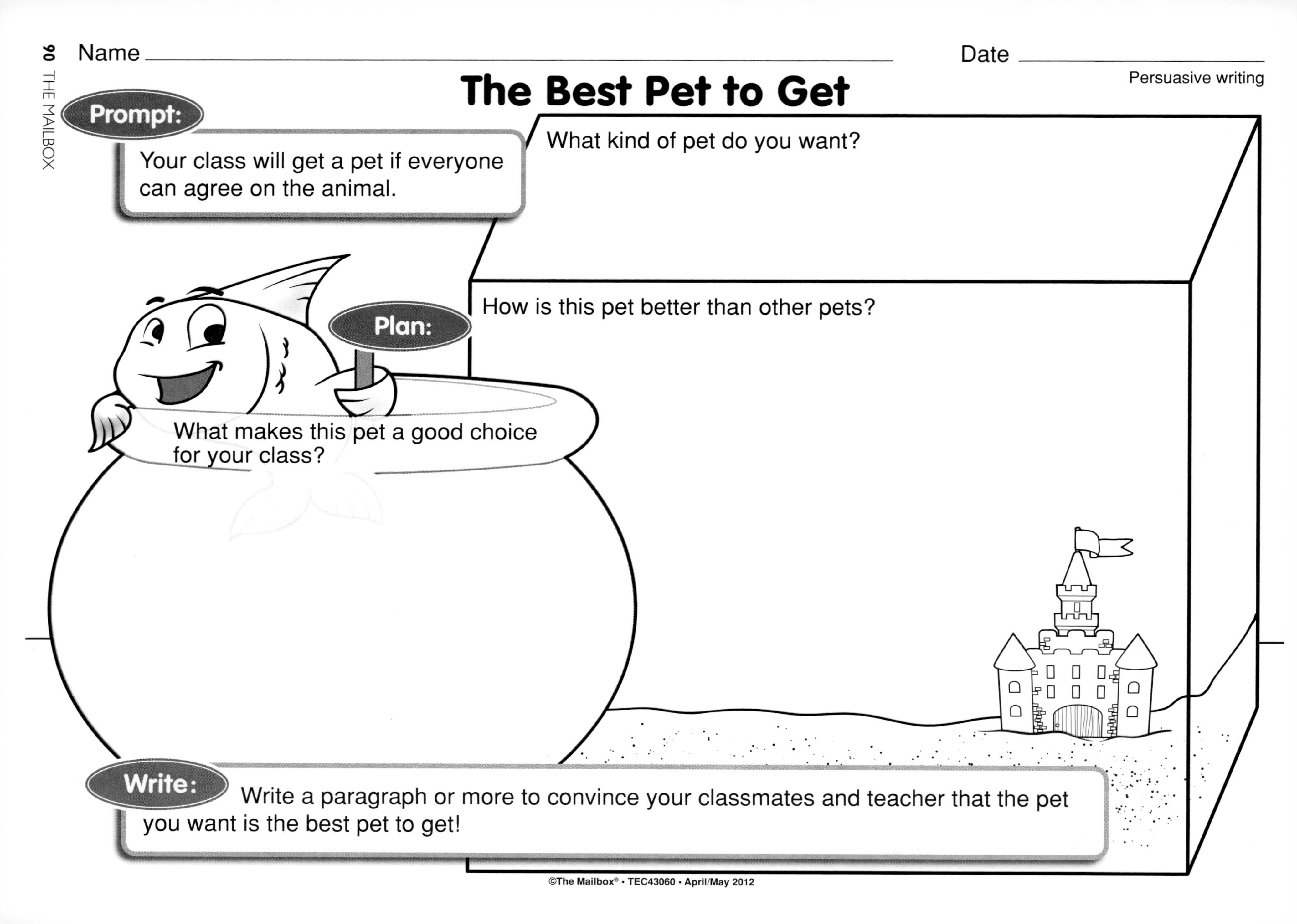

Prompt: Your class will get a pet if everyone can agree on the animal.

Plan:

What kind of pet do you want?

How is this pet better than other pets?

What makes this pet a good choice for your class?

Write: Write a paragraph or more to convince your classmates and teacher that the pet you want is the best pet to get!

Name ________________________ Date ____________

Personal narrative: lesson learned

No Time to Spare

12
3
9
6

Prompt:

Think about a time when you had an important project or chore to do, but you waited until the last minute to complete it.

Plan:

Describe the project or chore.	Why did you have to complete it at the last minute?
	What are some problems you had trying to finish the task?

What did you learn?

Write:

Write about doing your project or chore at the last minute. Use details to describe any problems you had and explain what you will do differently the next time you have an important project or chore to do.

Name ______________________________ Date ______________

Subjects and predicates

All Together Now!

Read.
If the phrase could be used as a subject of a sentence, write *S*.
If the phrase could be used as a predicate in a sentence, write *P*.

A *subject* names someone or something. A *predicate* tells what the subject is or does.

◯ The best band in town

◯ is my friend Baldie

◯ perform every Saturday morning

◯ is the lead singer

◯ pounds his drums

◯ The guitar player

◯ They

◯ Bertie

◯ Their shows

◯ Bertie's brother Blaze

◯ is called The Early Birds

◯ are always sold out

For each *S* above, find the matching *P* phrase.
Write each complete sentence.

1. ______________________________

2. ______________________________

3. ______________________________

4. ______________________________

5. ______________________________

6. ______________________________

Bonus: Write your own sentence about The Early Birds. Underline the subject. Circle the predicate.

Name ____________________ Date ____________________

Monsters at the Movies

Write the end mark for each sentence.
Color the ticket by the code.

1. Which movie do you want to see ☐
2. There are so many choices ☐
3. Have you seen Those Strange People From Earth ☐
4. What a scary choice ☐
5. The Monster Mummy Show looks funny ☐
6. Should we get our tickets now ☐
7. Let's go ☐
8. Wow, those tickets sure cost an arm and a leg ☐
9. Hand me your money ☐
10. Would you like popcorn ☐
11. Look at all that candy ☐
12. I think I'll be too scared to eat ☐
13. Find a seat quickly ☐
14. The movie is about to start ☐
15. Is it just me, or is it really dark in here ☐

Now Showing

Color Code
declarative = blue
interrogative = red
exclamatory = yellow
imperative = green

Bonus: Think of your favorite movie. Write a declarative, interrogative, exclamatory, and imperative sentence about the movie.

Name ______________________ Date ______________________

Subject-verb agreement

Pet Doctors

Circle the word that best completes each sentence.
Then write the circled word in the puzzle.

Down

1. Dr. Purr and Dr. Barker (is/are) veterinarians.
2. Every day they (treat/treats) many patients.
3. Dr. Purr (give/gives) medicine to a puppy with a fever.
4. So many pets (need/needs) a good doctor.
6. Dr. Barker (help/helps) a kitten with a sore paw.
9. Dr. Purr greets a snake as it (slither/slithers) into the office.
10. Next, a turtle with shell trouble (crawl/crawls) in.
11. Everyone (know/knows) these doctors are the best!
12. This animal clinic (is/are) one busy place!

Across

5. Dr. Purr and Dr. Barker (work/works) in an animal clinic.
7. The doctors (care/cares) for all kinds of pets.
8. Right now, Dr. Barker is (mend/mending) a bird's broken wing.
10. Dr. Purr (check/checks) a rabbit's ears.
13. Then a hamster in a ball (roll/rolls) through the doorway.

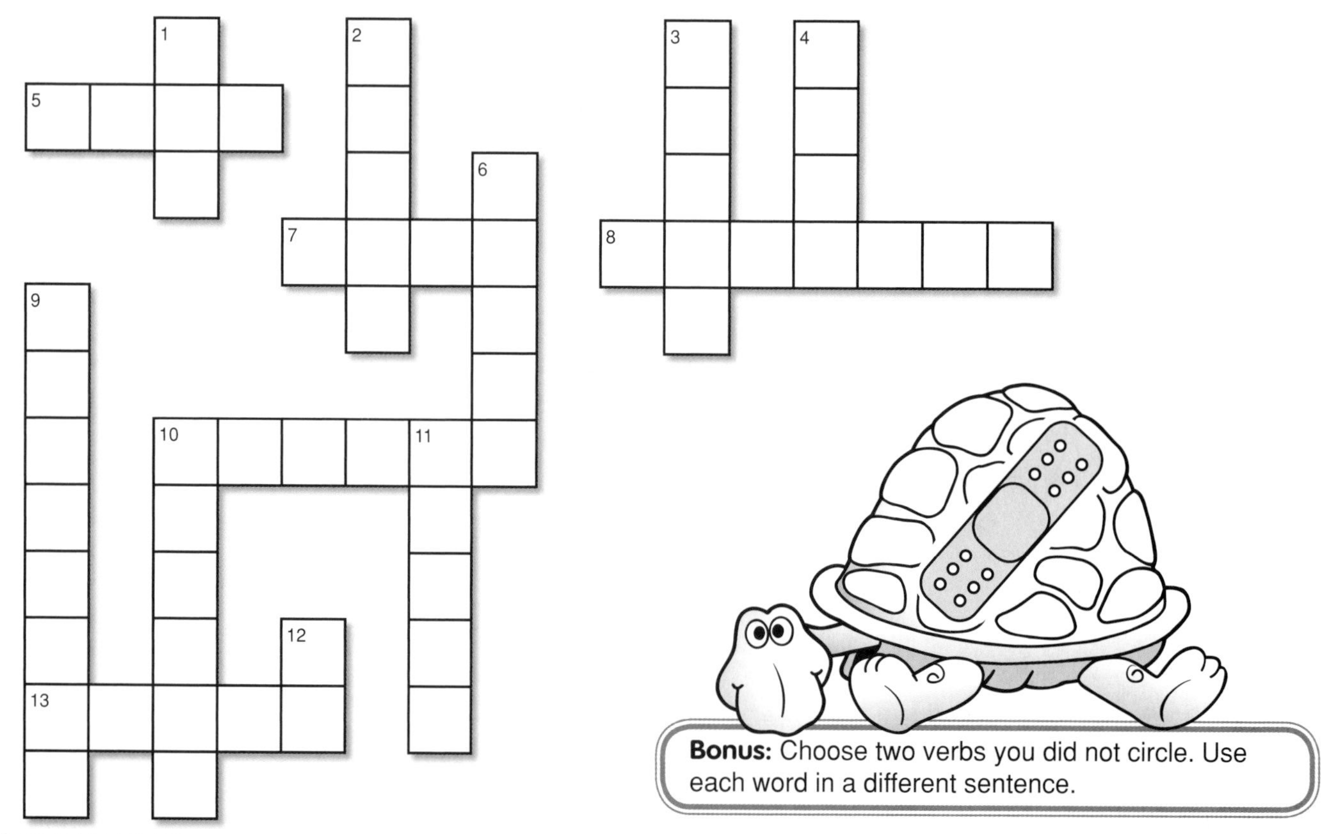
1
2
3
4
5
6
7
8
9
10
11
12
13

Bonus: Choose two verbs you did not circle. Use each word in a different sentence.

Sentence Search

What You Need

magazines or newspapers   highlighter   scissors   glue   paper

What You Do

Choose a skill. Write the number on your paper. Follow the directions.

1 Quotations

Find two sentences that name the speaker at the beginning of the quotation.
Find two sentences that name the speaker at the end of the quotation.
Find two sentences that name the speaker in the middle of the quotation.
Highlight the speaker and the verb.
Cut out the sentences. Glue.

2 Simple Sentences

Find four simple sentences.
Cut them out. Glue.
Write five simple sentences of your own.

Hint: A simple sentence has one complete subject and one complete predicate.

3 Compound Sentences

Find three compound sentences.
Cut them out. Glue.
Write three compound sentences of your own.

Hint: A compound sentence is made up of two or more simple sentences. They are joined by a comma and a conjunction (like *and*, *or*, and *but*).

4 Complex Sentences

Find two complex sentences.
Cut them out. Glue.
Write two complex sentences of your own.

Hint: *Complex sentence*—Because my grandpa lives far away, I don't see him very often.

Not a complex sentence—My grandpa lives far away.

5 Coordinating Conjunctions

Find a sentence for each conjunction.
Highlight the conjunctions.
Cut out the sentences.
Glue.
Then choose three conjunctions and write a different sentence with each.

and
but
or
yet
for
nor
so

6 Subordinating Conjunctions

Find a sentence for each conjunction.
Highlight the conjunctions.
Cut out the sentences.
Glue.
Use a reference book to list four other subordinating conjunctions.

although
because
since
though
whereas
while

Center Activity Card Put this activity card in a plastic page protector. Then place the activity card with magazines or newspapers, a highlighter, scissors, glue, and paper at a center.

Name ____________________ Date ____________________

Editing for capitalization, rules

Hard Rock

Underline the words that need capital letters.

1. the Rolling Rocks are going on tour!
2. The band will perform all over the united states.
3. The tour starts in april and ends in October.
4. Jerry jamz is the Rolling Rocks' lead singer.
5. The bass player is manny Mellow.
6. You will find billy D. Bang on the drums.

7. next weekend, the band will have its first concert.
8. Tickets are on sale now for friday night's show.
9. tickets can be purchased online.
10. You can also buy tickets at 54 main street.
11. Their first concert is in new york!
12. do you think that show will sell out?
13. The band leaves for a second show on saturday.
14. Then it will perform in boston before flying to Los Angeles.
15. the Rolling Rocks will rock your town soon!

Use the capitalization code to color each circle.

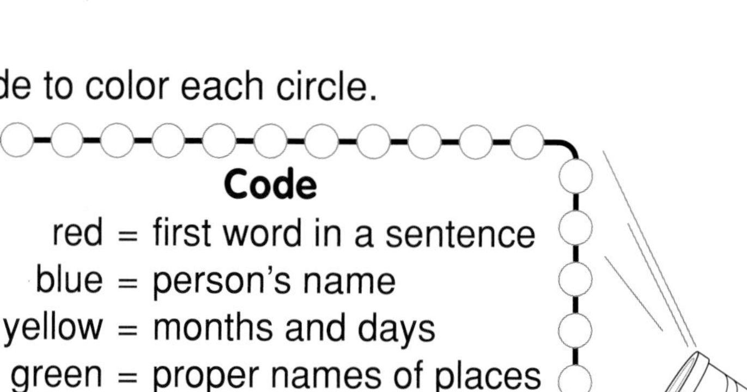

Code

red = first word in a sentence
blue = person's name
yellow = months and days
green = proper names of places

Bonus: Pretend you will see the Rolling Rocks in concert. Write a sentence telling who you will go with, when you will go, or where you will see them play. Circle each word with a capital letter.

Name ____________________ Date ____________

Ending punctuation

Kitty in the City

Write **.**, **?**, or **!** at the end of each sentence.

1. Where can I take you, pal
2. I would like to go to Tree House Tower
3. Are you in town for vacation or business
4. I'm here to see the sights
5. If you're hungry, I'd suggest stopping at Mouse's Deli first
6. Is the food there really that good
7. Absolutely
8. Thanks for the advice
9. No problem
10. After these two stops, I think I will see a show
11. What did you have in mind
12. Cats, of course
13. You have a busy day ahead
14. Yes, I do
15. Step on it

Bonus: Write three more sentences that the cat and cab driver might say. End one with a period, one with a question mark, and one with an exclamation point.

Name ______________________ Date ____________

Alphabetical order to the second and third letters

Test Your Strength

Write each group of words in alphabetical order.

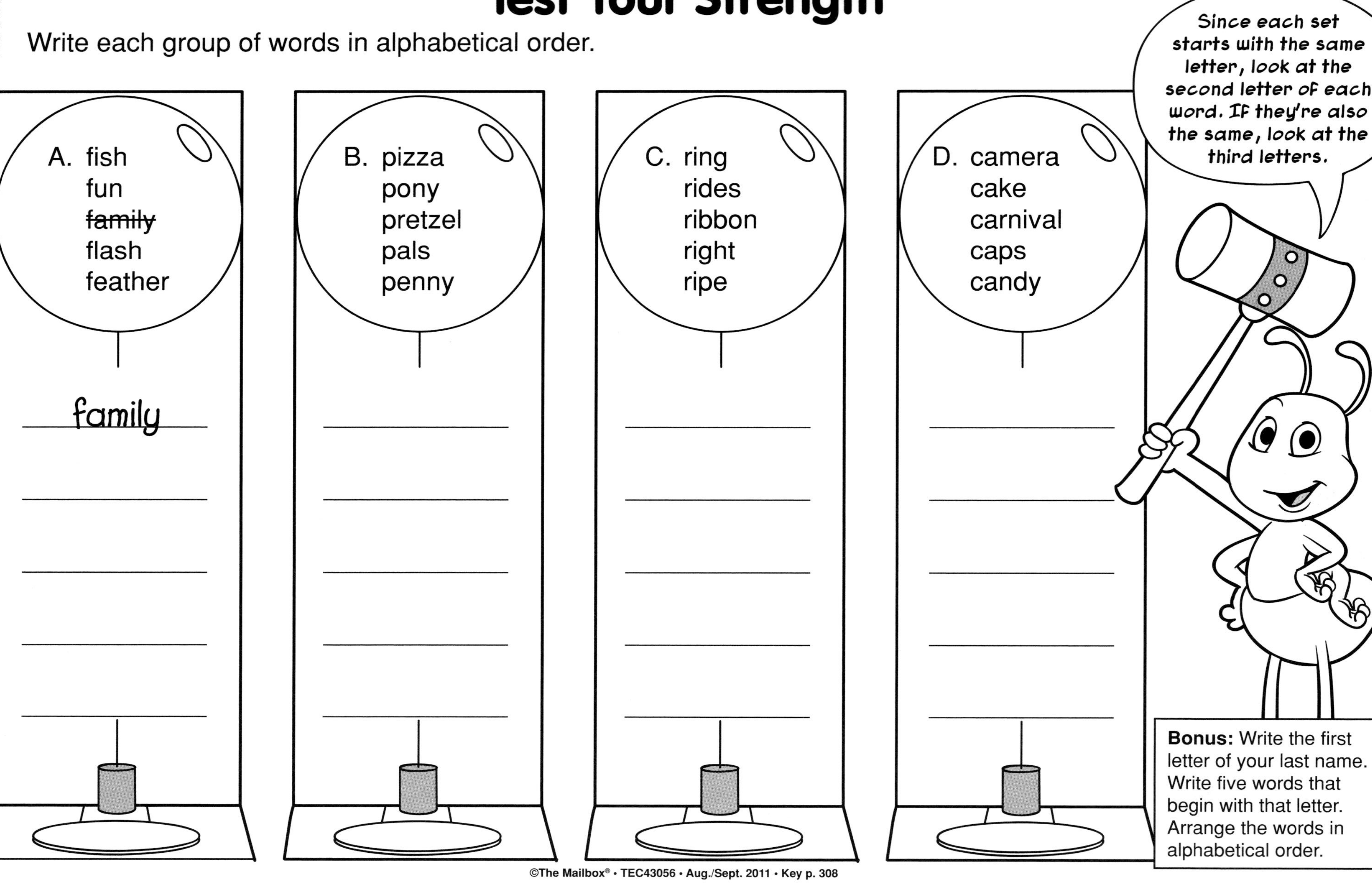
A. fish
fun
~~family~~
flash
feather
family
B. pizza
pony
pretzel
pals
penny
C. ring
rides
ribbon
right
ripe
D. camera
cake
carnival
caps
candy
Since each set starts with the same letter, look at the second letter of each word. If they're also the same, look at the third letters.

Bonus: Write the first letter of your last name. Write five words that begin with that letter. Arrange the words in alphabetical order.

Name ______________________ Date ______________

Moving Day

To complete each sentence, add *ed* or *ing* to the word.
Write the new word on the line.
Circle the word in the word search.

1. We are ______________ (move) to a new city.
2. We are ______________ (take) everything with us.
3. That means our pets are ______________ (come) too.
4. Yesterday, the movers ______________ (arrive) to pack the boxes.
5. I made sure they ______________ (tape) up the boxes well.
6. They ______________ (place) all the furniture on the truck.
7. Then the movers ______________ (stop) to take a break.
8. Meanwhile, many friends came by and ______________ (hug) us.
9. We aren't ______________ (leave) until the morning.
10. Mom ______________ (scrub) the house after the movers left.
11. Our pets will be ______________ (ride) in the car with us.
12. We will be ______________ (drive) a long way to our new house.

Bonus: Write the rule for adding *ed* or *ing* to a word that ends in silent *e*.

l	h	b	i	n	u	t	y	n	f
e	a	o	n	u	j	a	l	o	r
a	w	k	g	k	e	p	u	m	i
v	s	t	o	p	p	e	d	o	d
i	h	u	g	g	e	d	a	v	i
n	c	b	w	t	m	i	g	i	n
g	p	l	a	c	e	d	t	n	g
n	d	c	f	r	g	s	m	g	r
i	t	p	s	h	r	a	n	s	h
d	a	p	l	i	t	i	l	c	p
z	k	m	u	b	m	l	v	g	z
a	i	r	e	o	f	r	d	e	k
v	n	s	c	r	u	b	b	e	d
r	g	e	d	r	i	v	i	n	g

THIS END UP

Name ______________________ Date ______________

Plural nouns

Packing for Grandma's House

Write each word in a rectangle on the basket with the matching rule.
Then write the plural form of each noun.

Hint: One row on each basket will be empty.

wolf	lunch	flower	dish	scarf	berry
lady	cape	loaf	glass	story	basket

A. For most nouns, add **s**.

B. For nouns ending with *s*, *x*, *ch*, *sh*, or *ss*, add **es**.

C. For nouns ending with a consonant and *y*, change the **y** to **i** and add **es**.

D. For most nouns ending with *f*, change the **f** to **v** and add **es**.

Bonus: For each blank space, write a noun that matches the rule. Then write the plural form.

MATH

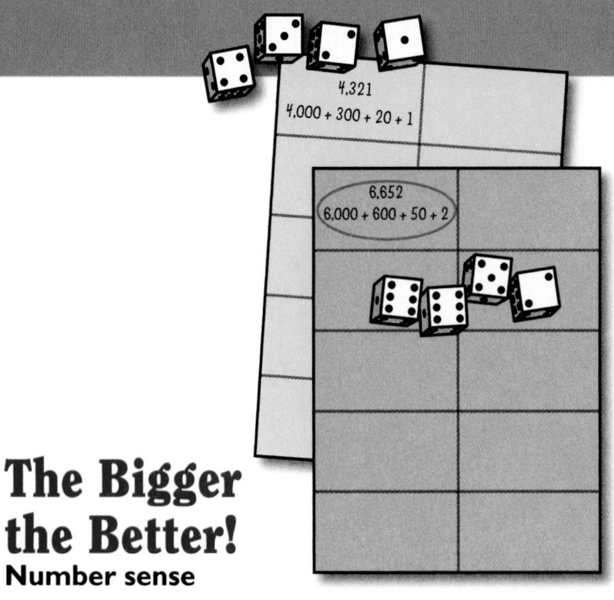
4,321
4,000 + 300 + 20 + 1
6,652
6,000 + 600 + 50 + 2

The Bigger the Better!
Number sense

To prepare for this partner game, instruct each child to divide a sheet of paper into ten equal sections. Give each partner a die for each digit he will practice (two dice for two-digit numbers, three dice for three-digit numbers, and so on). To play, each student rolls his dice and arranges them to create the largest number possible. Next, the student writes the number in standard form and expanded form in the first section of his chart. Each child reads his number aloud to his partner and the player with the larger number circles it. The first player to circle five numbers wins. **As an alternative,** direct students to create the smallest possible numbers instead.

Michelle Bayless, Zushi, Japan

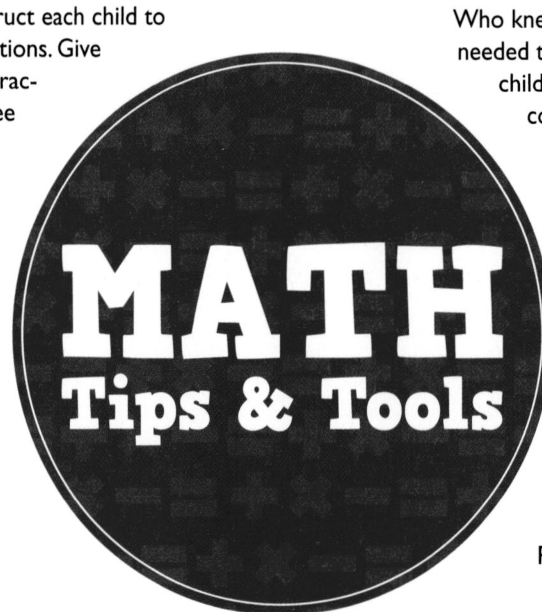
MATH
Tips & Tools

COLORFUL
CRAYONS
24 CRAYONS
Antwaan

Item	Number in My Desk	Even or Odd
crayons	24	even
pencils	3	odd
notebooks	2	even
textbooks	4	even
glue sticks	3	odd
bookmark	1	odd

Desk Discoveries
Odd and even numbers

Who knew that a desk contains everything needed to explore number sense? Direct each child to label a sheet of paper with the column headings shown. Next, have him list items found in his desk in the "Item" column. Then have the student count the corresponding items in his desk, write their respective numbers on the chart, and then determine whether each number is even or odd. Provide time for each child to share one item, its number, and its designation as even or odd.

Beth Pallotta
Eden Christian Academy
Pittsburgh, PA

Number Cruncher
Basic addition facts

For a fun twist on computation practice, introduce this origami fortune-teller! To begin, give each child a copy of the pattern on page 113; then have her cut out the large square and write her name in the middle. Next, announce a number range, such as 10 to 18. Direct the student to write on each empty triangle an addition problem whose sum equals a number in the range. If desired, have her create an answer key. Help the child fold her fortune-teller; then provide time for students to use their manipulatives to practice addition with a partner.

Dawn Hardy, David A. Perdue Primary, Warner Robins, GA

182 128
>
>

These are my running shoes. I wear them while I run for 45 minutes every day. What time of day do you think I wear them?

Ms. Palomba uses a toothbrush for two minutes twice a day. She brushes her teeth at 7:30 AM (morning) and 9:30 PM (evening).
Ms. Palomba uses a dog's leash for 30 minutes each day. She takes her dog for a walk at 4:30 PM (afternoon).
Ms. Palomba uses her running shoes for 45 minutes each day. She runs at 6:00 AM (morning).

Two Ways to Go

Comparing numbers

Point your mathematicians in the right direction with this tip and tool!

- **Comparing numbers tool:** Have each student draw a less than symbol on a 4¾" x 5" paper square. Direct the child to place the paper inside a clear CD case. Write two numbers on the board and have each student prop the case on her desk to show the matching symbol. Stand at the back of the class and take a quick glance to check students' understanding.
- **Comparing numbers tip:** When students are ready to write number comparisons, share this easy tip. Tell students to draw two dots next to the bigger number and one dot next to the smaller number. Guide students to connect the dots to reveal the correct symbol.

$$98 < 908$$

Colleen Dabney, Williamsburg, VA, and
Linda Morel, Amite Elementary, Amite, LA

Personal Routine

Time

Introduce facts about yourself while building knowledge of time with students. Each day for several days, bring in a personal item from home and share it with the class. Tell students what it is, how you use it, and for how long you use it. Then have students guess the time or times of day you use the item. After confirming the time, list it and the item on a chart as a reference. **As an extension**, invite a different child each day to share an item from home in a similar manner.

Melissa Palomba, St. Louis School, Louisville, OH

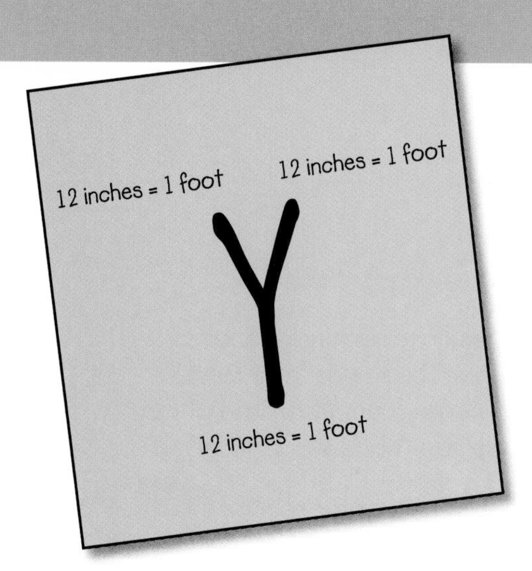
12 inches = 1 foot
12 inches = 1 foot
Y
12 inches = 1 foot

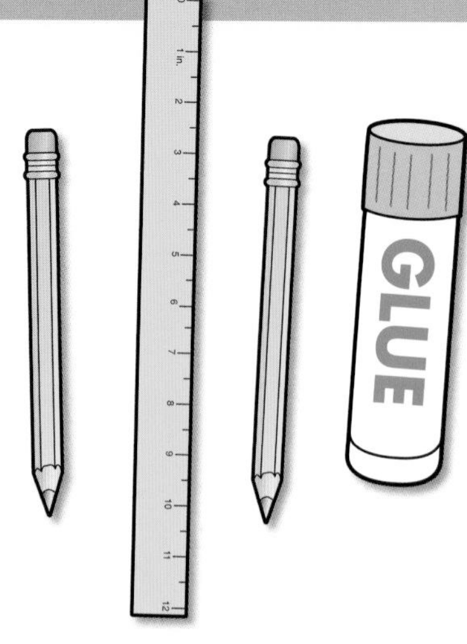
GLUE

Easy to See

Customary linear measurements

Simple and to-the-point, this visual aid helps students remember the number of inches and feet in a yard. A child draws a large Y (yard) on a piece of paper. Then he labels the end of each extension as shown. The student tapes the paper to his desk as a reminder or staples it into his math journal. Either way, it will be easy for students to see that one yard equals three feet or 36 inches.

Debra Gray, Pleasant Hill Elementary
Olive Branch, MS

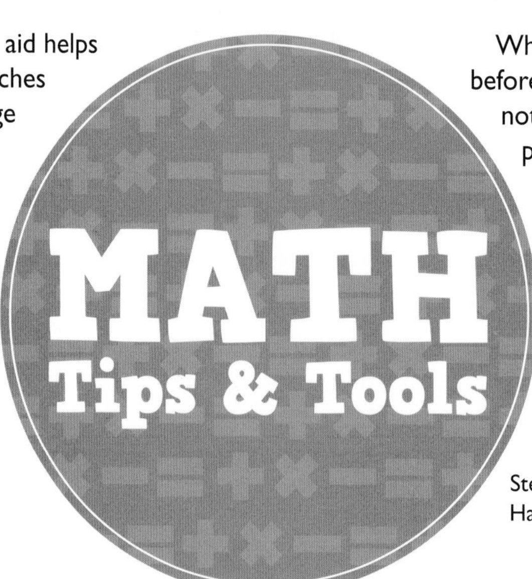
MATH
Tips & Tools

Make Every Minute Count!

Modeling and extending patterns

When you have a few minutes to spare before wrapping up your math time, why not give students a chance to practice pattern skills? Simply post a letter pattern on the board and challenge students to use whatever manipulatives they have at their desks to model and extend the pattern. Provide time for each student to share her pattern with a neighbor; then invite one or two students to share with the class.

Stephanie Brachtenbach
Harmony Elementary, Overland Park, KS

Cashing In

Comparing money amounts

With this easy idea, students spend a few minutes each day thinking about money! Once a week, give each small group a different set of manipulative coins to count. Have one student from each group draw his group's coins on the board and write the total. Throughout the week, refer to the money amounts when directing students to transition. For example, ask the group with the largest money amount to line up for lunch first or direct the groups with amounts less than 75 cents to report to the carpet area.

Beth Pallotta, Eden Christian Academy, Pittsburgh, PA

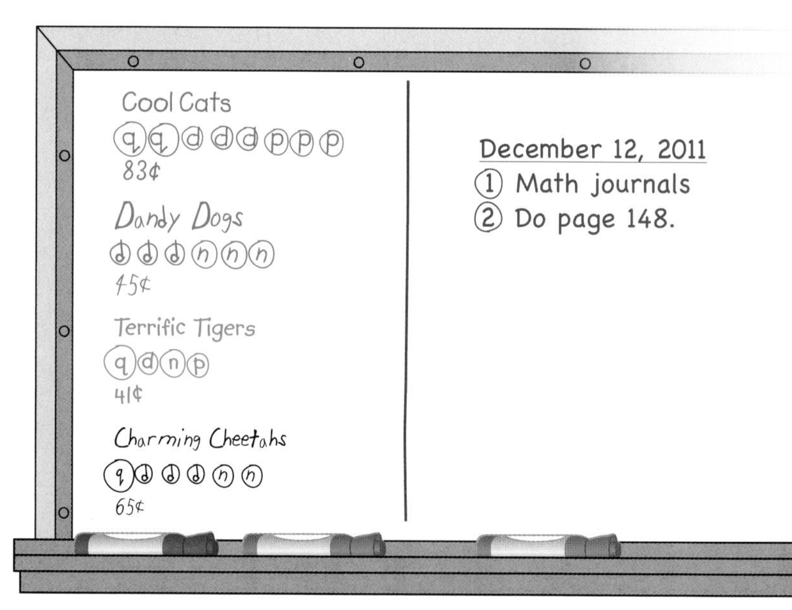
Cool Cats
q q d d d p p p
83¢
Dandy Dogs
d d d n n n
45¢
Terrific Tigers
q d n p
41¢
Charming Cheetahs
q d d d n n
65¢
December 12, 2011
① Math journals
② Do page 148.

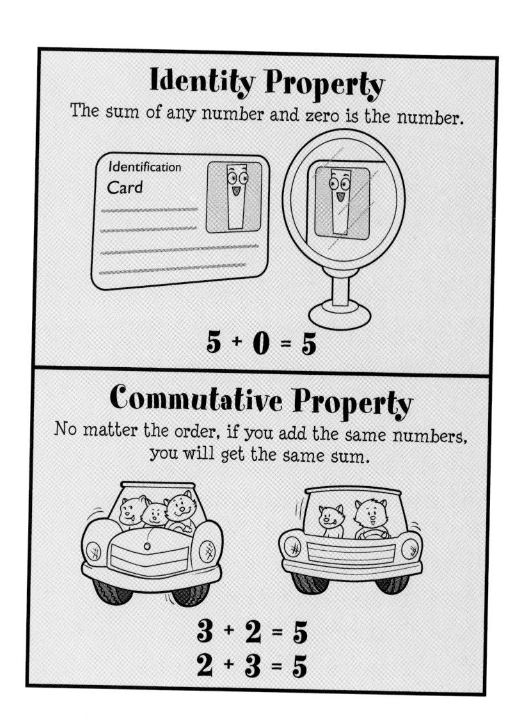
Identity Property
The sum of any number and zero is the number.
Identification Card
5 + 0 = 5
Commutative Property
No matter the order, if you add the same numbers, you will get the same sum.
3 + 2 = 5
2 + 3 = 5

Drive It Home

Recognizing properties of addition

Use these analogies to bring students to a better understanding of addition rules. Post an enlarged copy of page 114 and refer to it as you describe each property. For the **identity property**, hold up a mirror and an identification card, such as a driver's license. Tell students the mirror represents zero; then place the card in front of it. Lead students to understand that the image in the mirror is the same card, just as adding any number to zero will give you the same number. For the **commutative property**, have students imagine cars full of people traveling on a road. Explain that even though the cars move (commute) and switch positions with one another on the road, the number of people in each car and on the road doesn't change.

Bethany Hamilton, Running Brook Elementary, Columbia, MD

Head to Head

Reviewing basic facts

To prepare for this fun game, make a class set of pockets by cutting one-inch strips off the ends of discarded envelopes. Have each student write her name on a pocket and glue it to the middle of a sentence strip. Help the child wrap the strip around her head to make a headband and staple the ends together. While still wearing the headbands, divide students into two teams and select one player from each team to join you. To play, put a numbered playing card in each pocket and then call out the sum or product of the numbers on the cards. Each player looks at his opponent and subtracts or divides to guess the number on his own card. Award a point to the first player to correctly name her number; then remove the cards and choose two new students to play. The team with more points at the end of the game wins. **As an alternative**, invite three students to play the game during free time. Instruct the third child to be the dealer—distributing the cards, naming the sums or products, and awarding points.

Jeannie Pavlik, Pittsville Elementary, Pittsville, WI

6
Kenneth

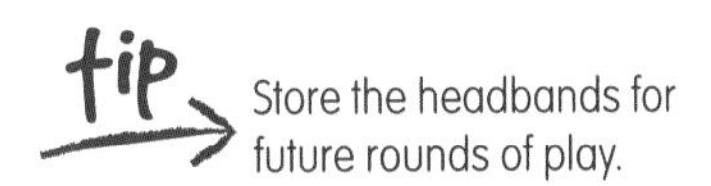
tip
Store the headbands for future rounds of play.

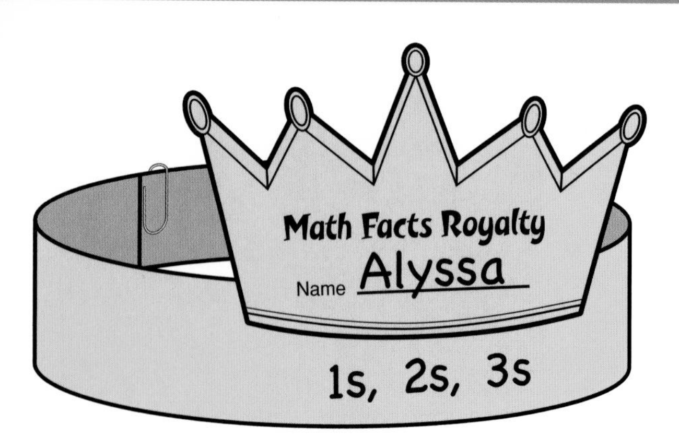
Math Facts Royalty
Name Alyssa
1s, 2s, 3s

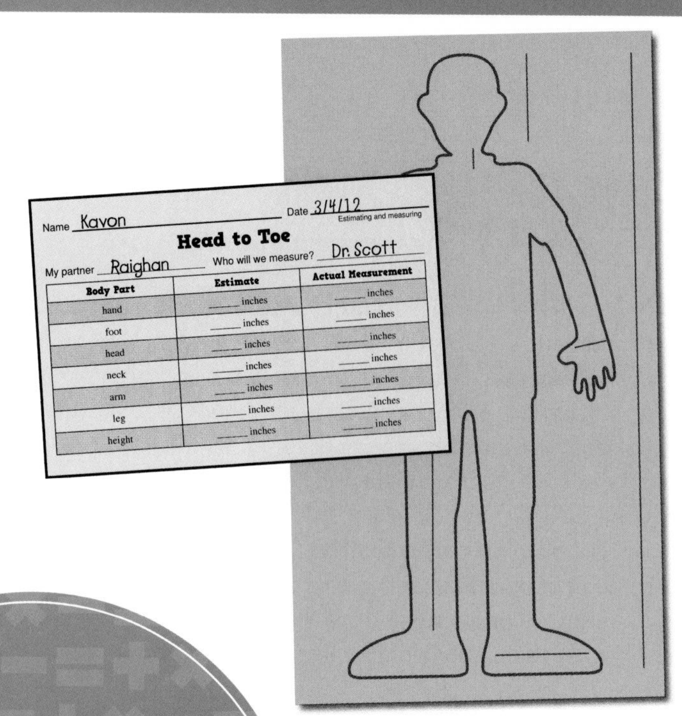

Name Kavon Date 3/4/12

Estimating and measuring

Head to Toe

My partner Raighan Who will we measure? Dr. Scott

Body Part	Estimate	Actual Measurement
hand	____ inches	____ inches
foot	____ inches	____ inches
head	____ inches	____ inches
neck	____ inches	____ inches
arm	____ inches	____ inches
leg	____ inches	____ inches
height	____ inches	____ inches

MATH Tips & Tools

Crowning Achievement
Addition and multiplication facts

A majestic incentive like this one will surely motivate students to master their facts! For each child, label a copy of the crown pattern from page 115 with her name and glue the pattern to a long paper strip. When the student masters her first set of facts, write its number on the paper strip and use paper clips to attach the ends together to form a headband. Invite the child to wear the crown for the day. At the end of the day, remove the paper clips to store the crown flat until the child masters another set of facts. If desired, recognize the first child in the class to successfully master each set of facts by also providing her with a simple cape to wear for the day.

adapted from an idea by Tonya Janicke
India Hook Elementary, Rock Hill, SC

Head to Toe
Estimate and measure length

Help students make real-life connections to measurement with this partner center. In advance, invite your principal or another staff member to lay on a large piece of bulletin board paper while you make a tracing of her body. Cut out the tracing; then write on it the staff member's name. Also draw a measurement line for each body part listed on page 115. Place the tracing at a center with rulers and student copies of page 115. Each student records his estimates on his paper; then he works with his partner to determine the actual measurements.

Beth Pallotta, Eden Christian Academy, Pittsburgh, PA

Tape the tracing to the floor or across a tabletop to keep the paper from curling.

Column by Column
Two-digit addition and subtraction

Use this catchy chant to steer students to work from right to left.

Laura Johnson, South Decatur Elementary, Greensburg, IN

Ones first and
Then the tens—
Follow this order;
Then use it again.

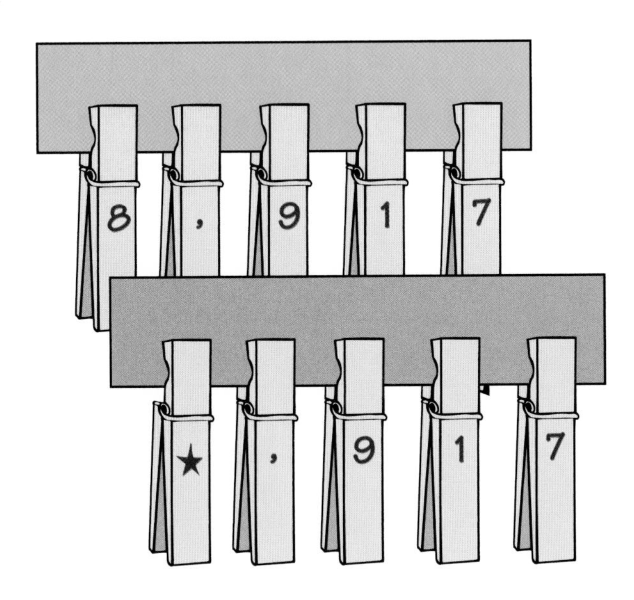
8
,
9
1
7
★
,
9
1
7

Clip It If You Can
Place value

The number of student teams is up to you, but the result is the same—a better understanding of numbers for everyone! For each team, cut a tagboard rectangle and label nine clothespins with a different digit from 0 to 9 (one digit will not be used); another clothespin with a star; and, if practicing numbers with more than three digits, one with a comma. To play, announce a number with different digits and have one player from each team show it by clipping the clothespins to the rectangle. If there's a digit that the team does not have, the student clips the star in its place. For each team, award one point for each correctly displayed digit but no points for the star. Continue as time allows. The team with the most points wins. **To make the game easier**, label the tagboard rectangle with place-value columns.

Marie E. Cecchini, West Dundee, IL

7
9
10
3
4
6
Miguel
Improper Fraction
Mixed Number
7/3
2 1/3

Mix and Match
Improper fractions and mixed numbers

Give students a chance to increase their understanding of fractions with this easy-to-prepare activity. To make the spinners, fold a sheet of paper in half, unfold it, and divide each half into four equal sections. Label each section as shown. On another sheet of paper, draw a T chart and label each column as shown. A student uses a pencil and paper clip to spin each spinner. He uses the numbers spun to write an improper fraction in the left column; then he rewrites the fraction as a mixed number in the right column. The child continues nine more times.

Stephanie Brachtenbach, Harmony Elementary, Overland Park, KS

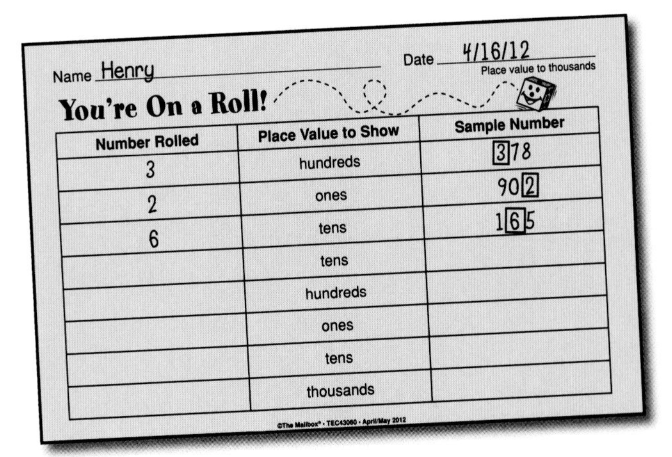

Name Henry Date 4/16/12

Place value to thousands

You're On a Roll!

Number Rolled	Place Value to Show	Sample Number
3	hundreds	[3]78
2	ones	90[2]
6	tens	1[6]5
	tens	
	hundreds	
	ones	
	tens	
	thousands	

©The Mailbox® • TEC43060 • April/May 2012

MATH Tips & Tools

On a Roll
Place value

Fun and flexible, this activity easily adapts for whole-group instruction, for small-group review, and even as a center! Give each child a copy of a recording sheet from page 116 and a die. Instruct the student to roll the die and write on his recording sheet the number he rolled. Next, have him write a multidigit number that uses the number he rolled to represent the named place value. Then he draws a box around the corresponding digit. The student repeats the steps to complete the page.

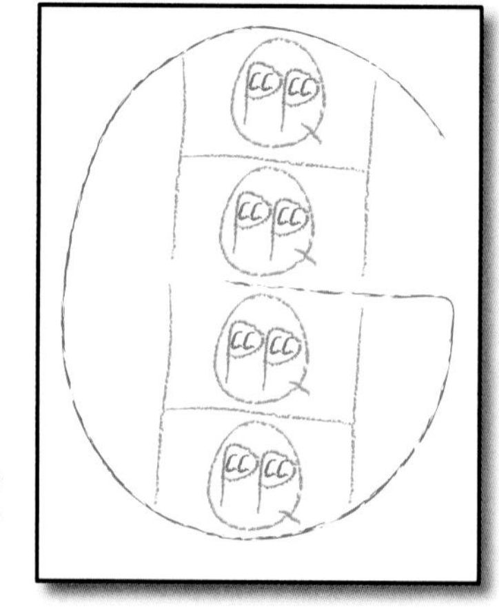

"G" Whiz!
Liquid capacity

Students will soak up measurement conversions with this graphic organizer. To start, instruct each child to draw a large *G* (gallon) on a sheet of paper. Next, have her draw within the *G* two large *H*s (half gallons) and, within each *H*, direct her to draw two *Q*s (quarts). Within each *Q* have the child draw two *P*s (pints) and, within each *P*, instruct her to draw two *C*s (cups). If desired, have the child make a key on her paper that indicates the meaning of each letter. Lead students to understand that different combinations of half gallons, quarts, pints, and cups can be made from this organizer. Encourage each child to use her graphic organizer when she completes capacity activities, and she'll be a gallon whiz in no time!

Michele Giarrusso, Lafayette Elementary, Wayne, NJ

Hardware Store Helpers
Line plots

Looking for a hands-on way to construct line plots? Use tile spacers! After posing a survey question and gathering results, label a large sheet of paper with the numbered responses. Then invite students to use these inexpensive manipulatives with your document camera, turning each spacer to look like an *X*. **As an alternative**, put out the spacers for students to use individually at a center.

Colleen Dabney, Williamsburg, VA

tip
Label a transparency sheet and complete the activity using an overhead instead.

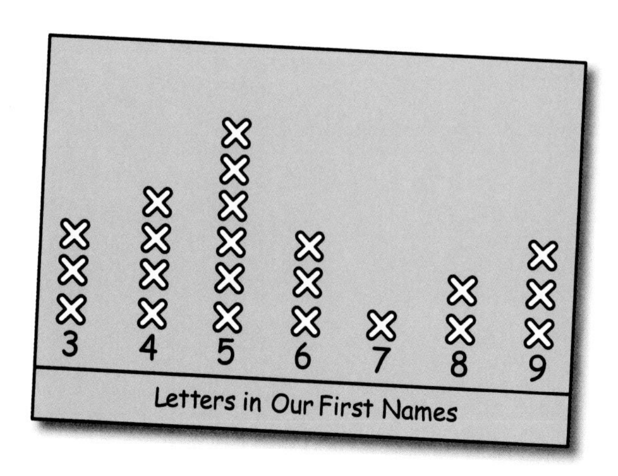
3
4
5
6
7
8
9
Letters in Our First Names

The Array Song
(sung to the tune of "Frère Jacques")

Rows and columns,
Rows and columns
Make an array,
Make an array.
Count each object
In each row.
Add them up.
Add them up.

Rows and columns,
Rows and columns
Make an array,
Make an array.
Count each row.
Count each column.
Multiply.
Multiply.

A Strategic Song
Arrays

Want to sing about a multiplication strategy? Here's your song!

Jackie Batkins, Seven Pines Elementary, Sandston, VA

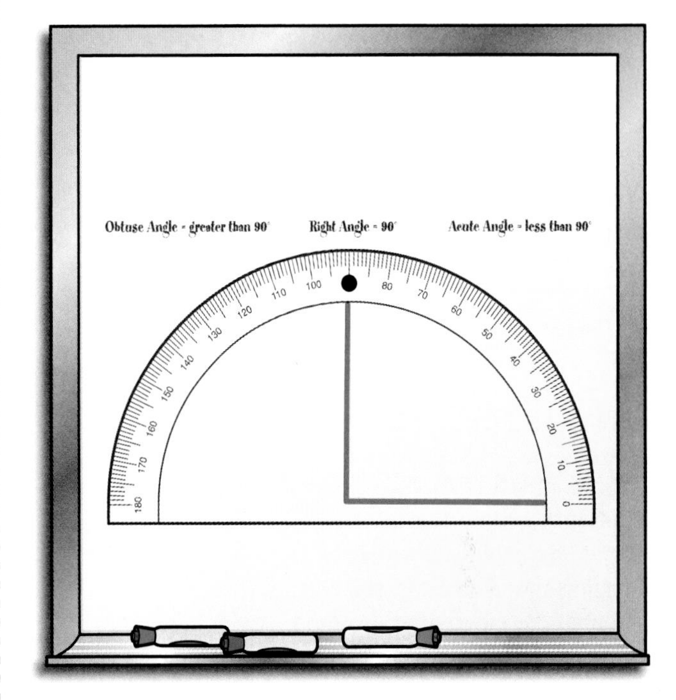
Obtuse Angle = greater than 90°
Right Angle = 90°
Acute Angle = less than 90°

Big, Little, and In Between
Right, acute, and obtuse angles

To show students how to use a protractor and help them size angles, project a copy of page 117 so it is easy to see. Use thin manipulatives, such as chenille stems or coffee stirrers, to model different angles. For each angle, name its measurement; then have students identify each as right, acute, or obtuse. After you've modeled examples of each kind of angle, have students refer to the measurements already marked as you announce new angle measurements. Guide them to use their arms to indicate about where each angle would fall on the protractor.

Wendy Scharich, Philander Lee Elementary, Canby, OR

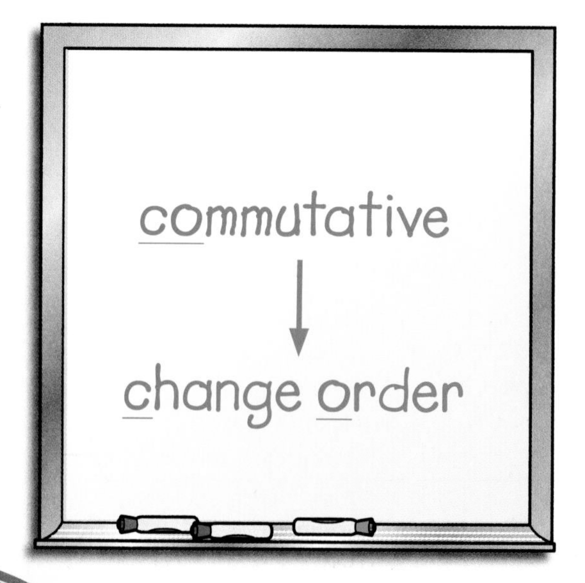
commutative
change order

MATH Tips & Tools

Like Climbing a Tree
Ordered pairs

Reference a fun outdoor activity to help students visualize plotting and finding coordinates. To start, ask students to close their eyes and imagine walking in a straight line to a tall tree. When they get to the tree, tell them to stop. Then instruct the students to imagine climbing straight up the tree. Direct students to open their eyes; then explain that using ordered pairs is similar to what they just envisioned. First, they move across the *x*-axis, like walking to the tree. Then they move up the *y*-axis, just like climbing the tree.

Nicole Pasceri, Errick Road Elementary, Tonawanda, NY

Short and Sweet
Commutative property

Help students remember the order property with this quick tip. Write the word *commutative* on the board. After explaining that with this property, the order of the numbers can change but the answer will be the same, underline the letters *co*. Tell students to think of the *c* as short for *change* and the *o* as short for *order*, because with the commutative property, only the addends or factors change order.

Kim Anthony, Richmond, VA

Steps to Understanding
Perimeter

Turn a walk around school into a learning opportunity—no materials required! Lead students to a large location, such as the blacktop or the cafeteria. While moving in a single-file line, instruct students to count their steps as they move around the outside edges of the space. Explain that the distance around a shape is its perimeter, and ask what they found the perimeter of the space to be. Choose a new location and repeat the process.

Michelle Hughes, Goleta, CA

Turn to pages 123–142 for **games and practice sheets.**

Disguise Your Dozen

Fact review, critical thinking

Whether you put this out as a center or a free-time activity, this game gets students thinking! Copy the gameboard on page 118 and put it in a plastic page protector. Set out the board with a supply of paper, 24 paper clips, a calculator, and two dice. To play, each child chooses a side of the gameboard. Player 1 rolls the dice and uses the numbers rolled to make a math fact with an answer shown on the mat. Player 2 checks the answer on the calculator and, if he's correct, Player 1 places a paper clip on the matching space; then he writes the fact on his paper. Player 2 takes a turn in the same manner, and play continues until one player covers all his numbers.

Rhonda Vogt, Seffner Christian Academy, Seffner, FL

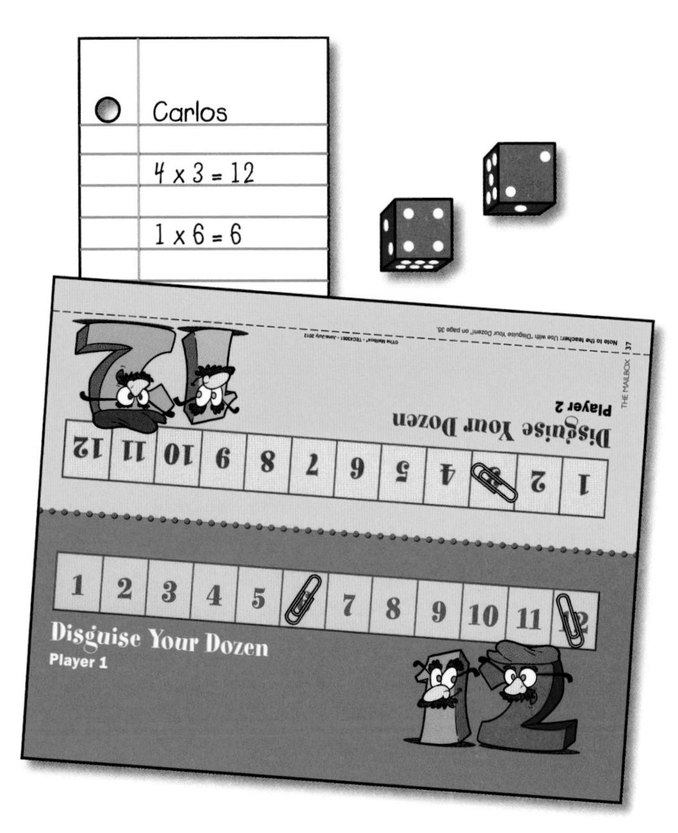
Carlos
4 x 3 = 12
1 x 6 = 6
Disguise Your Dozen
Player 2
1 2 3 4 5 6 7 8 9 10 11 12
1 2 3 4 5 7 8 9 10 11
Disguise Your Dozen
Player 1

Kendall, Katrina

coins = $1.75
ice pops = $2.99
We need $1.24 more.

coins = $0.88
lemon = $0.25
We would get back $0.63.

Shop 'til They Drop

Solving word problems involving money

To start this partner activity, have each duo divide a sheet of paper into four sections. Give each pair of students a random amount of manipulative coins and have them write the total on the first section of their paper. Next, display an item from a grocery store circular and instruct each twosome to record the name and price of the item. Have the students determine how much more money they'd need to buy the item or how much change they'd receive if they bought it, and record that amount in the same section. Direct each pair to leave the coins at their workspace and take their paper to a new workspace. After each pair records the total for their new set of coins, display a new item and have students repeat the activity. Repeat the process two more times.

Colleen Dabney, Williamsburg, VA

Luis
Steps to Problem Solving
1. Read the problem carefully. Underline the question. Circle key words and numbers.
2. Choose a strategy to try. Predict what the answer might be.
3. Solve the problem.
4. Look back at the problem. Does your answer make sense?
5. Check your work and label your answer.

G
L L Tia
A. 908, 918, 981
B. 515, 516, 517
C. 792, 797, 806

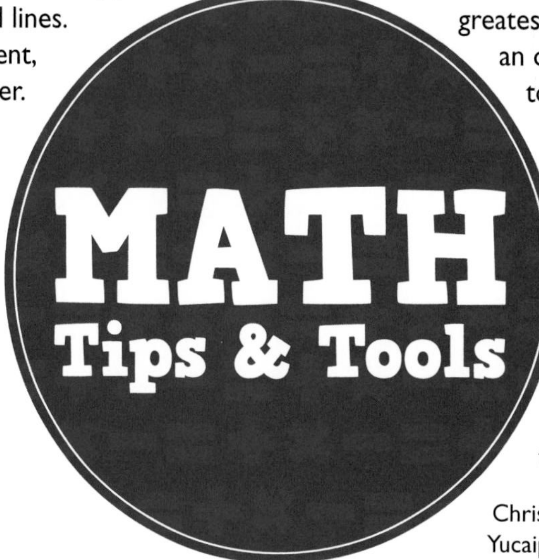
MATH
Tips & Tools

Right on Track
Solving word problems

These tents help students clear problem-solving hurdles! To make one, a child personalizes a copy of page 119 and then cuts along the bold lines. Next, he folds the cutout to make a tent, as shown, and glues or tapes it together. He places the tent on his desk so the "Steps to Problem Solving" panel is facing him. The child refers to each side of the tent as needed to successfully complete a problem-solving task or assignment.

adapted from an idea by Carolyn Burant, St. John Vianney School, Brookfield, WI

Mount Numbers
Ordering numbers

Use this simple drawing to help students write numbers from least to greatest or from greatest to least. Before students begin an ordering activity, direct each child to draw a simple mountain shape at the top of her paper. At each base, have her write the letter *L* (least). Then have her label the peak with *G* (greatest). Show students that, like the height of the mountain, numbers get bigger as they move from least to greatest (up the mountain) but smaller as they move from greatest to least (down the mountain).

Christine McLaughlin, Yucaipa Elementary, Yucaipa, CA

"Tic-Tac-Time"
Using an analog clock, determining elapsed time

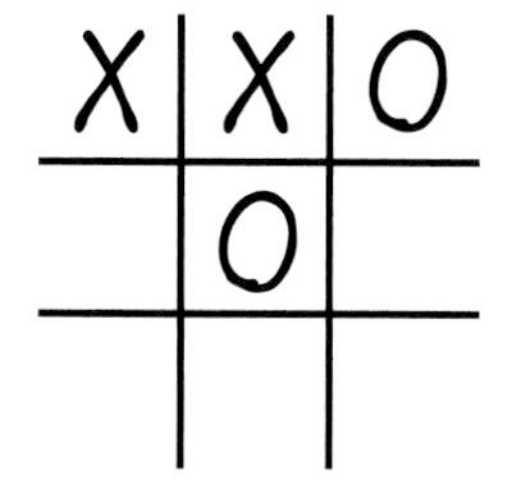
X X O
O

To prepare for this class game, copy the clock pattern on page 120. Draw a tic-tac-toe grid on the board and divide students into two teams. Before playing one of the versions below, remind students that, when naming a time, they start with the short hour hand (colored green for *go*) and end with the long minute hand (colored red for *stop*).

To practice identifying time, move the hands to a desired time and have a player name the time shown or announce a time for the student to show on the clock. A correct response earns the player an X or O for her team. The first team to place three marks on the grid horizontally, vertically, or diagonally wins.

To practice determining elapsed time, move the hands to a desired time. Announce a period of time earlier or later and have the student name or show the new time.

Michelle Bayless, Zushi, Japan, and Debbie Brun, Rumford, RI

12
1
2
3
4
5
6
7
8
9
10
11
hour
minute

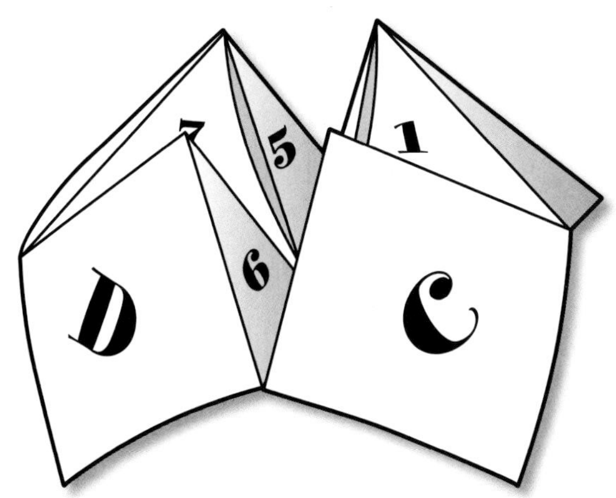
7
5
1
6
D
C

Fortune-Teller Pattern

Use with "Number Cruncher" on page 102.

Cut out the large square and flip the paper writing-side down. Fold each corner toward the center. Flip the folded paper over again. Then fold each corner toward the center. Fold the square in half so the letters are on the outside. Place your thumbs and index fingers under the flaps and squeeze them together.

A 5 3 B

7 1

8 2

D 6 4 C

TEC43056

Identity Property

The sum of any number and zero is the number.

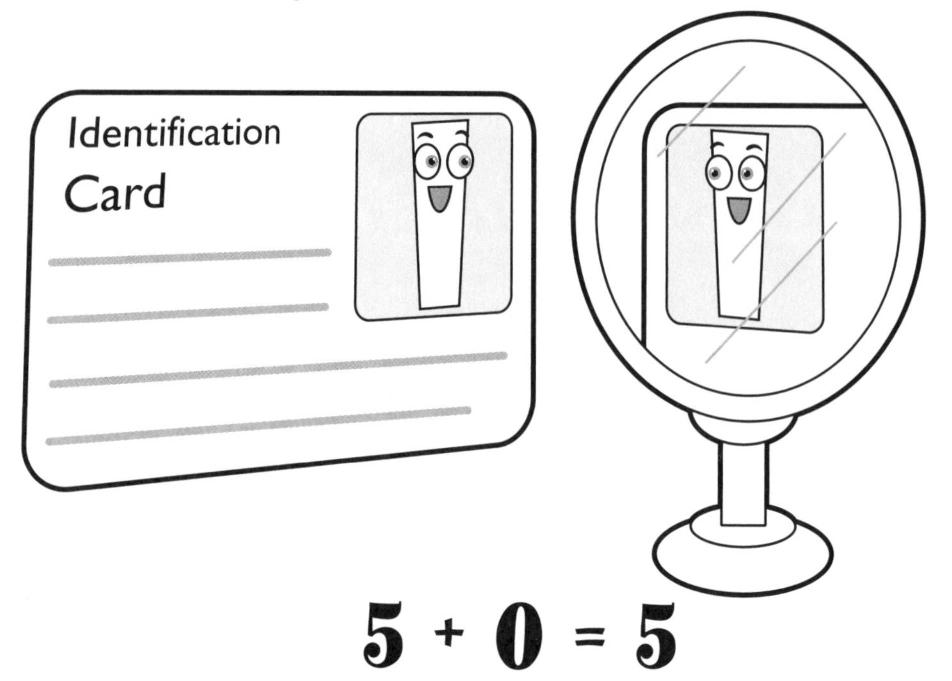
Identification
Card

5 + 0 = 5

Commutative Property

No matter the order, if you add the same numbers, you will get the same sum.

3 + 2 = 5

2 + 3 = 5

 Note to the teacher: Use with "Drive It Home" on page 105.

Crown Pattern

Use with "Crowning Achievement" on page 106.

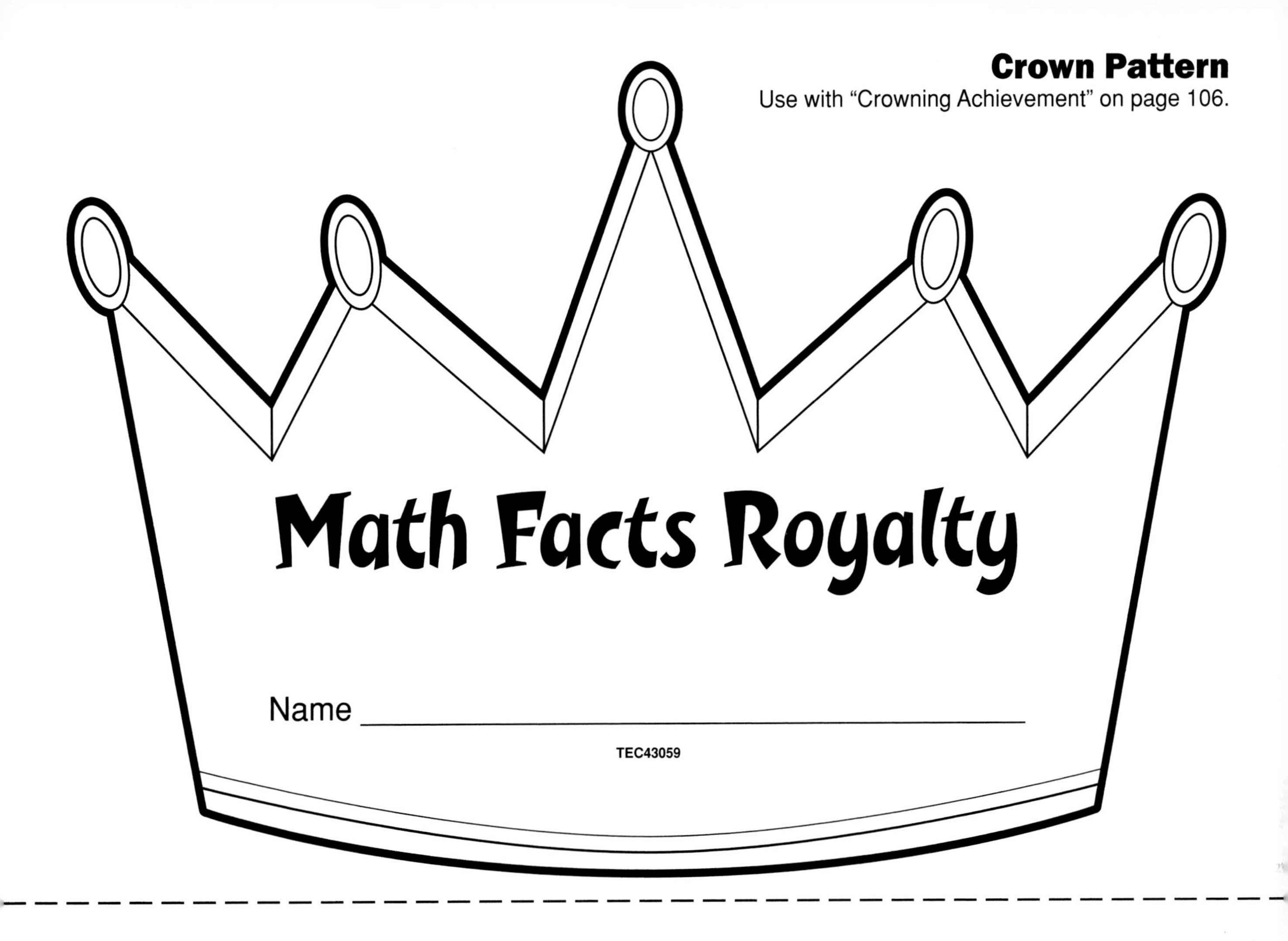

Math Facts Royalty
Name ______________________________
TEC43059

Name ______________________________ Date ______________

Estimating and measuring

Head to Toe

My partner ______________ Who will we measure? ______________

Body Part	Estimate	Actual Measurement
hand	_______ inches	_______ inches
foot	_______ inches	_______ inches
head	_______ inches	_______ inches
neck	_______ inches	_______ inches
arm	_______ inches	_______ inches
leg	_______ inches	_______ inches
height	_______ inches	_______ inches

Note to the teacher: Use with "Head to Toe" on page 106.

Name ______________________ Date ______________

Place value to thousands

You're On a Roll!

Number Rolled	Place Value to Show	Sample Number
	hundreds	
	ones	
	tens	
	tens	
	hundreds	
	ones	
	tens	
	thousands	

Name ______________________ Date ______________

Place value to ten thousands

You're On a Roll!

Number Rolled	Place Value to Show	Sample Number
	thousands	
	ones	
	hundreds	
	thousands	
	hundreds	
	tens	
	ten thousands	
	ten thousands	

 Note to the teacher: Use with "On a Roll" on page 108.

Obtuse Angle = greater than 90° **Right Angle = 90°** **Acute Angle = less than 90°**

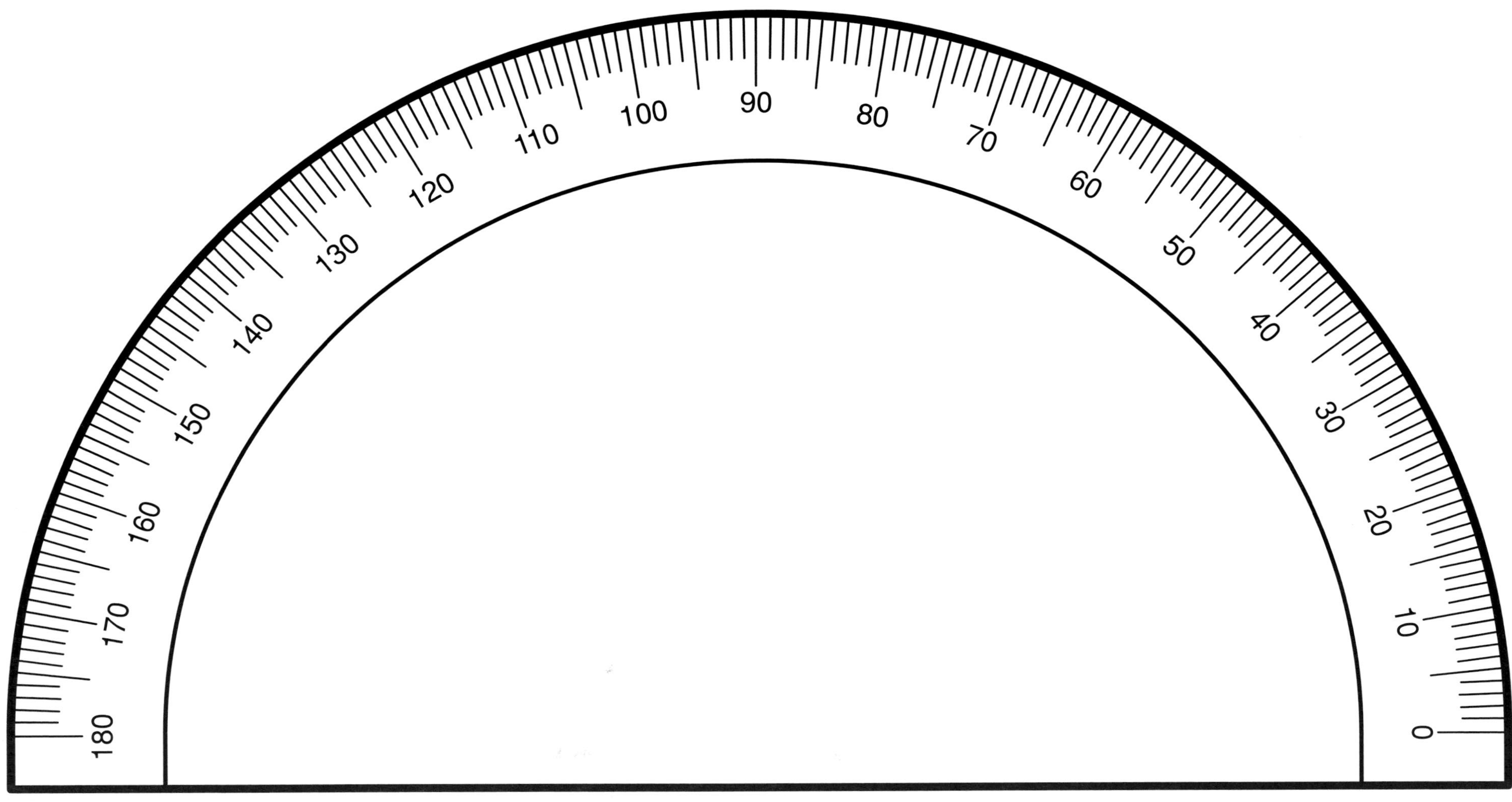
0
10
20
30
40
50
60
70
80
90
100
110
120
130
140
150
160
170
180

Note to the teacher: Use with "Big, Little, and In Between" on page 109.

Disguise Your Dozen

Player 1

1	2	3	4	5	6	7	8	9	10	11	12

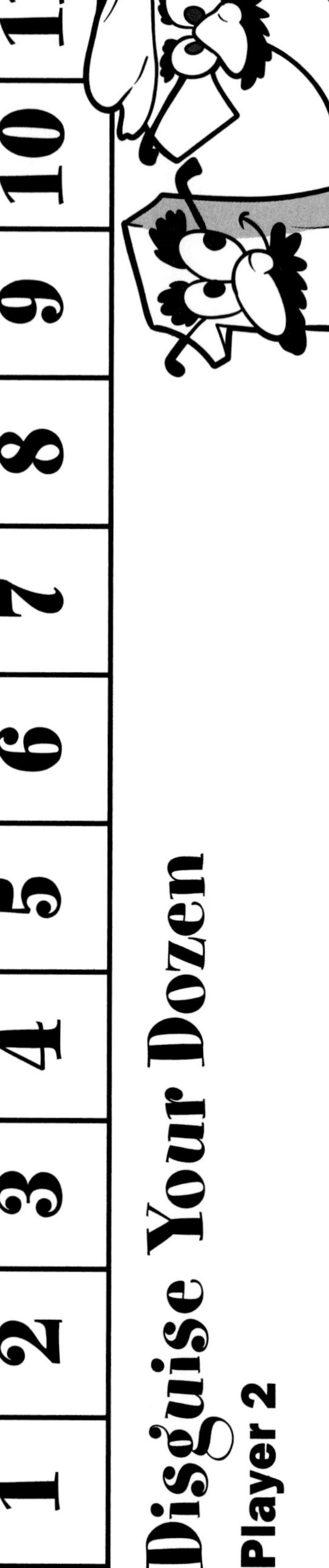

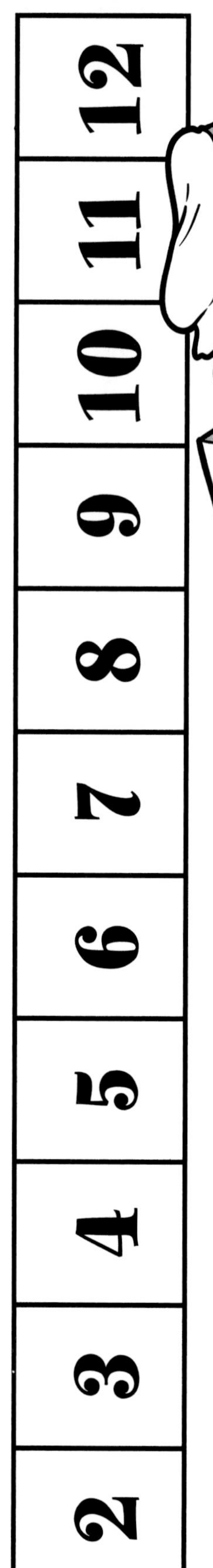

Disguise Your Dozen

Player 2

1	2	3	4	5	6	7	8	9	10	11	12

Note to the teacher: Use with "Disguise Your Dozen" on page 111.

Steps to Problem Solving

1. Read the problem carefully. Underline the question. Circle key words and numbers.
2. Choose a strategy to try. Predict what the answer might be.
3. Solve the problem.
4. Look back at the problem. Does your answer make sense?
5. Check your work and label your answer.

Strategies

Draw a picture.
Work backward.
Use or make a table or graph.
Act it out.
Look for a pattern.
Make a list.
Make a model.
Guess; then check.
Write a number sentence.
Solve a simpler problem.

Key Words

Add	Multiply	Subtract	Divide
in all	times	how many more	in each
altogether	twice	difference	split
total	at this rate	left	shared equally
both		change	
combined		remains	
		fewer, heavier, longer, shorter, faster, slower, farther (comparing words)	

Note to the teacher: Use with "Right on Track" on page 112. If students won't be multiplying or dividing during the year, cover those columns in the Key Words section before copying.

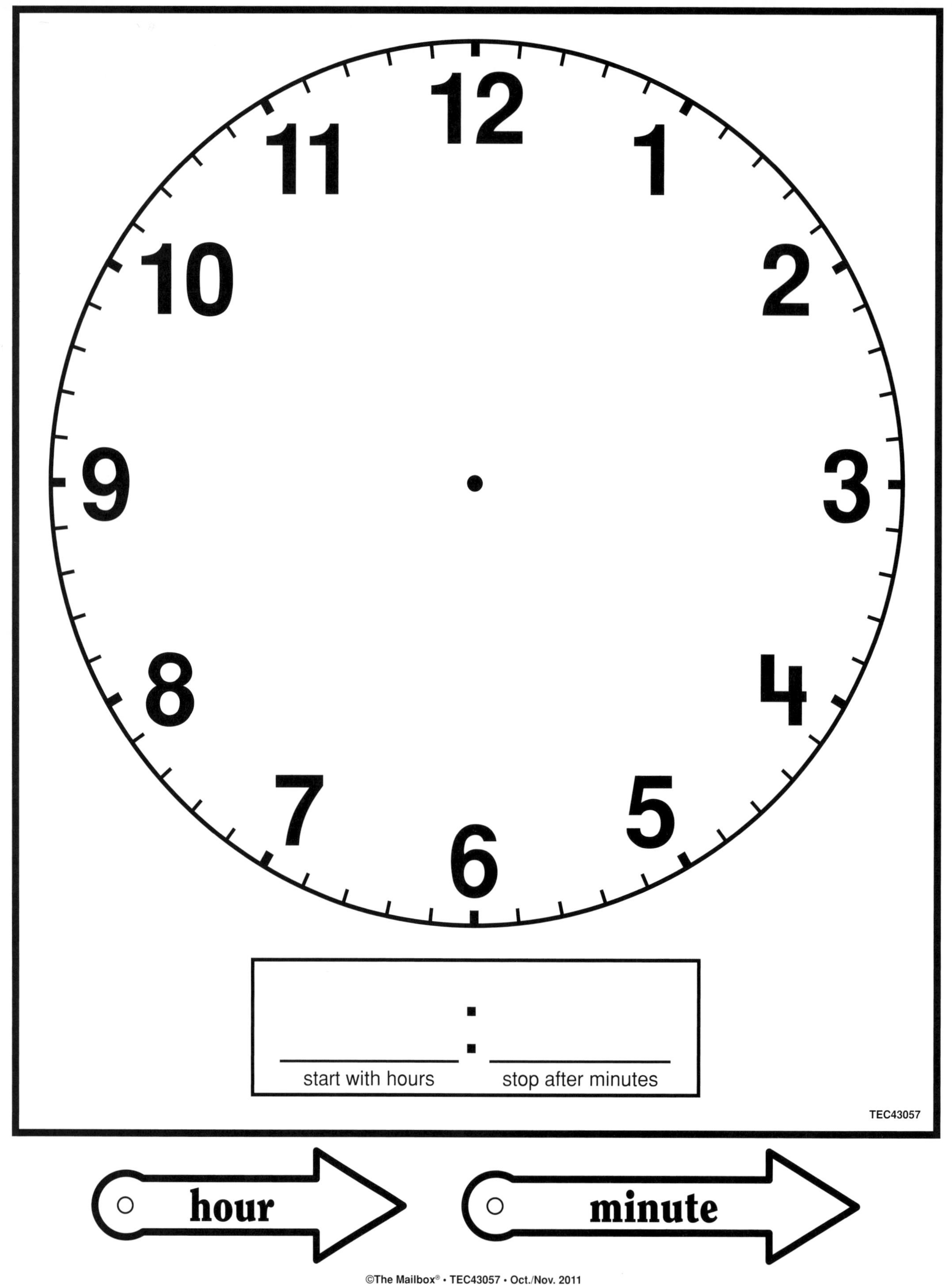
12
1
2
3
4
5
6
7
8
9
10
11
:
start with hours
stop after minutes
TEC43057
hour
minute

Note to the teacher: Use with "'Tic-Tac-Time'" on page 112 and "On the Clock" on page 121. Copy this page, then color the hour hand green and the minute hand red. Laminate it for durability. Cut out the hands and use a brad to secure them to the clock. Before using the manipulative, remind students to name a time by starting with the green hour hand (go) and ending with the red minute hand (stop).

A-One, A-Two, A-One, Two, Three, Four!

Simple Songs for Reinforcing Math Skills

On the Clock

Short and sweet, this little number reminds students about the **hands on a clock**. If desired, assemble the manipulative clock on page 120 to demonstrate.

Suzanne Clark, Middle Creek Elementary, Apex, NC

(sung to the tune of "Are you Sleeping?")

Clocks have two hands.
Clocks have two hands—
Short and long,
Short and long.
Short hand points to hours.
Long hand points to minutes.
Short and long,
Short and long.

What Is the Property?

Help students differentiate between the **commutative and identity properties** with this catchy tune.

Stephanie Brachtenbach, Harmony Elementary, Overland Park, KS

(sung to the tune of "Did You Ever See a Lassie?")

Oh, the order doesn't matter.
The order, the order,
The order doesn't matter.
That's the commutative property.
For two plus five is seven,
And five plus two is seven.
The order doesn't matter.
That's the commutative property!

And any number plus zero
Is the number, the number.
Any number plus zero,
That's the identity property!
For five plus zero is five,
And three plus zero is three.
Any number plus zero,
That's the identity property!

Keep or Lift?

After a few rounds of this song, students are sure to remember **whether to change the digit being rounded**.

Lisa Hutchinson, Horn Lake Elementary, Horn Lake, MS

(sung to the tune of "This Old Man")

Zero, one, two, three, four,
Boy, these numbers are a bore!
Keep that [ten]
Just the same.
Rounding, rounding is the game!

Five, six, seven, eight, and nine,
Man, these numbers sure look fine!
Raise that [ten]
Up by one.
Rounding, rounding sure is fun!

Multiply Understanding With These Hands-On Helpers!

"Array" for Cookies!

Bake up some fun and understanding with this edible idea. Give each child a sheet of gray construction paper (baking sheet) and some cookie-flavored cereal. Next, instruct each student baker to arrange 12 cereal pieces on her baking sheet so each row has the same number of pieces. Invite students to share how they arranged their cookies; then lead students to understand that 12 can be shown several different ways. Explain that an array is an arrangement of items in rows and columns. Also tell students that a multiplication problem can be re-created as an array. Continue the activity with a different number of cookies; then provide time for students to snack on the cereal. **For another edible option**, have students break a Hershey's milk chocolate bar along the seams and use its pieces to form arrays.

Nicholas Sveum, Edgerton, WI, and Jamie Galindo, East Primary School, Kermit, TX

tip

For added fun, use a sheet of aluminum foil instead of gray paper.

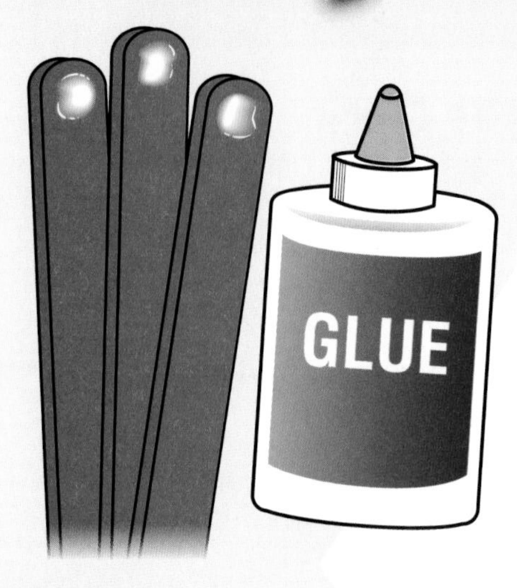
GLUE

Dot Demo

You can count on these sticks to help students connect multiplication and repeated addition! Give each child nine craft sticks and a bottle of glue. Direct him to put one bead of glue at the top of each stick. When the glue is dry, pose a problem, such as 3 x 1. Explain that "times" means the same as "sets of" and that the answer can be found by adding together three sets of one. Then instruct students to set out three sticks and find the answer. Encourage students to touch the dots as needed. Repeat with other ones facts. When students are comfortable with the ones, direct each child to add another dot of glue to each stick. Repeat with the twos facts; then continue the process until students have nine beads of glue on each stick. **As an alternative**, have students add a small pom-pom to each glue dot or provide puff paint instead of glue.

adapted from an idea by Susan Marsh, White Township Consolidated School, Belvidere, NJ

Cool Stuff!

To sort out the answers to multiplication problems, have students use plastic ice cube trays! Label each tray space with a different number from 0 to 12. Place the trays and a supply of beans in an accessible location. When a child needs help determining a product, he fills spaces with beans to match the problem. For example, to solve 6 x 4, the child fills each space from one to six with four beans. Then he counts the total number of beans used.

Stacy Goodwin, Parklane Academy, McComb, MS

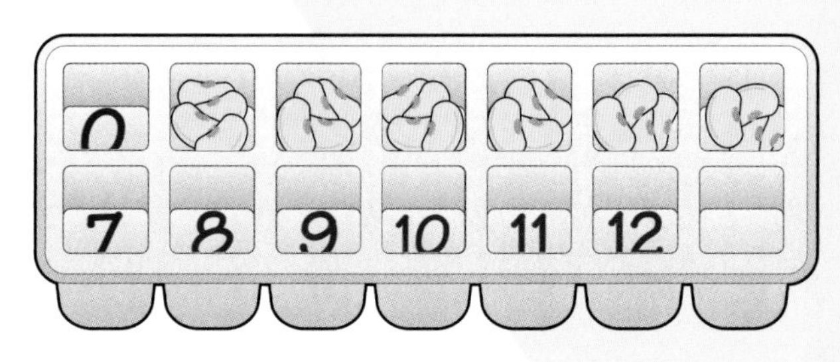
0
7
8
9
10
11
12

Mind Builders

Mind Builder 1

Write a number to complete each fact family set.
Then write the facts for each set.

A. 3, 5, ?
B. 7, 4, ?

___ + ___ = ___ ___ − ___ = ___

___ + ___ = ___ ___ − ___ = ___

TEC43056

Mind Builder 2

Would you rather have two hundred fifty or two hundred five of your favorite things? Explain.

TEC43056

Mind Builder 3

Draw two different examples of this repeating pattern.

AABCAABCAABC

TEC43056

Mind Builder 4

Look at the table.
Draw all the different one-scoop ice cream cone possibilities.

Flavors	Cones
chip, chocolate, vanilla	sugar, cake

TEC43056

Mind Builder 5

Copy. Complete the chart.

Standard Form	Expanded Form
29	
	600 + 30 + 5
1,697	
	8,000 + 90 + 1
	4,000 + 500 + 3

TEC43056

Mind Builder 6

Do you spend more time in your classroom before lunch or after lunch? Explain how you know.

MILK

TEC43056

Mind Builder 7

Copy and complete each sentence.

A. I count __ small triangles.
B. I count __ large triangles.
C. I count __ small squares.
D. I count __ large squares.
E. I count __ rectangles.

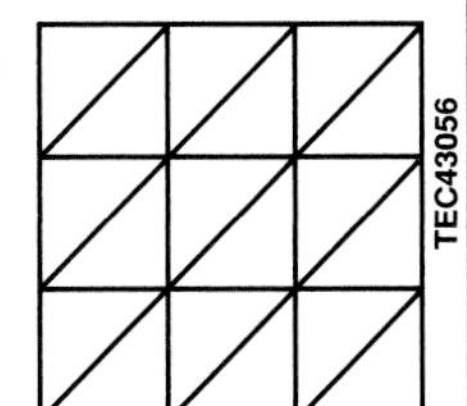

TEC43056

Mind Builder 8

You have $3.00.
Write a shopping list that has two or more items.
Solve to find your change.

$0.75	$0.35	$1.25	$2.45

TEC43056

How to use Give each student a copy of this page (or one card at a time) to work on during free time. Have the student solve the problems on a separate sheet of paper.

Math

Mind Builders

Mind Builder 1

Copy and complete each pattern.

A. 9, 12, 15, ____, ____
Write the rule.

B. 5, 10, 15, ____, ____
Write the rule.

TEC43057

Mind Builder 2

What time do you wake up on a school day? ____:____ Write the time in a different way.

What time do you eat lunch? ____:____
Write the time in a different way.

What time do you go to bed? ____:____
Write the time in a different way.

TEC43057

Mind Builder 3

Write the value of each underlined digit.

392	574	876
188	269	680
401	321	138

List the numbers shown in order from greatest to least.

TEC43057

Mind Builder 4

Estimate the number of pencils in your classroom. Explain how you reached this estimate.

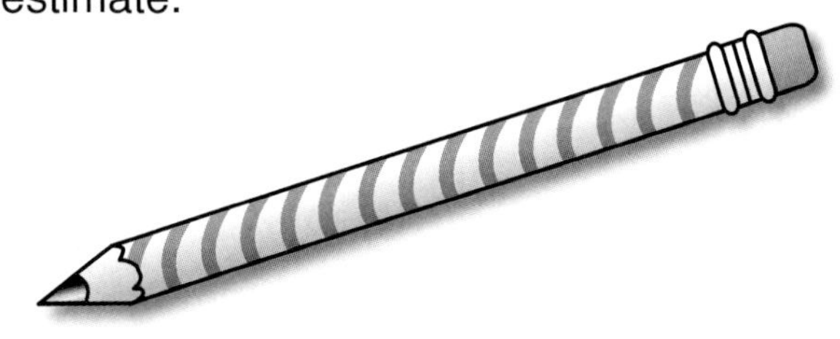

TEC43057

Mind Builder 5

Write a two-digit number.

- Write a number that is ten more than the number.
- Write a number that is ten less than the number.
- Name two numbers that can be added together to total the number.

TEC43057

Mind Builder 6

Name four different shapes that each have three or more corners. Draw each shape.

TEC43057

Mind Builder 7

The class makes a tally chart to show favorite pets. Use the information to make a bar graph.

dog	𝍸 II	gerbil	III
cat	𝍸	fish	IIII

TEC43057

Mind Builder 8

2 x 3 = 6
rows
columns
product

Draw two more arrays. Write the number sentence for each array.

TEC43057

How to use Give each student a copy of this page (or one card at a time) to work on during free time. Have the child solve the problems on his own paper.

Mind Builder 1

Copy the chart. Find four more ways to make 23¢.

Quarters	Dimes	Nickels	Pennies
0	2	0	3

TEC43058

Mind Builder 2

Copy each number pair. Write < or > between each pair.

A. 33 17
B. 48 22
C. 63 71
D. 44 59
E. 27 68
F. 35 53
G. 48 44
H. 10 39

TEC43058

Mind Builder 3

Write the fact families.

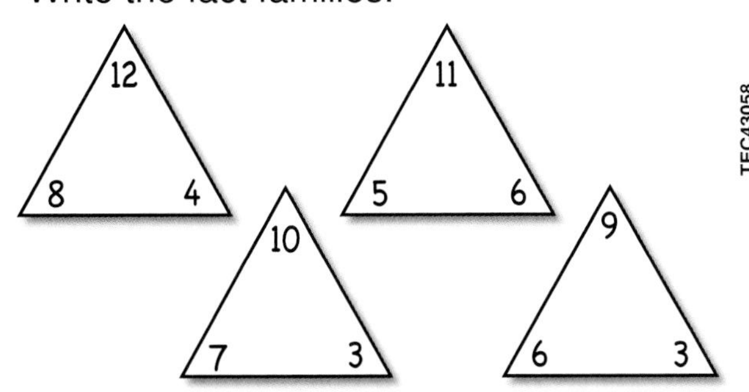
12
8
4
11
5
6
10
7
3
9
6
3

TEC43058

Mind Builder 4

Choose three different digits from 1 to 9. Use the digits to make as many three-digit numbers as you can. Explain your method.

TEC43058

Mind Builder 5

A. Draw a rectangle with a perimeter of 12 cm.

B. Draw a square with a perimeter of 16 cm.

TEC43058

Mind Builder 6

Write and answer three questions about the graphs.

Circus Tickets Sold
Number of tickets sold
150
125
100
75
50
25
Thursday
Friday
Saturday
Sunday
Days of the week

TEC43058

Mind Builder 7

A. Your family is eating a pizza. If the pizza is shared equally, what fraction will you get? Draw the pizza.

B. If a friend joins you for dinner, what fraction of the pizza will you get? Draw the pizza.

TEC43058

Mind Builder 8

Patrick, Sarah, and Charlie each have a different pet. Patrick does not have a cat. Sarah has a fish. Which pet does each child have? Explain how you found each answer.

cat

dog

fish

TEC43058

How to use: Give each student a copy of this page (or one card at a time) to work on during free time. Have the child solve the problems on his own paper.

Math

Mind Builders

Mind Builder 1

Study the part of the hundred chart shown. Write the missing numbers.

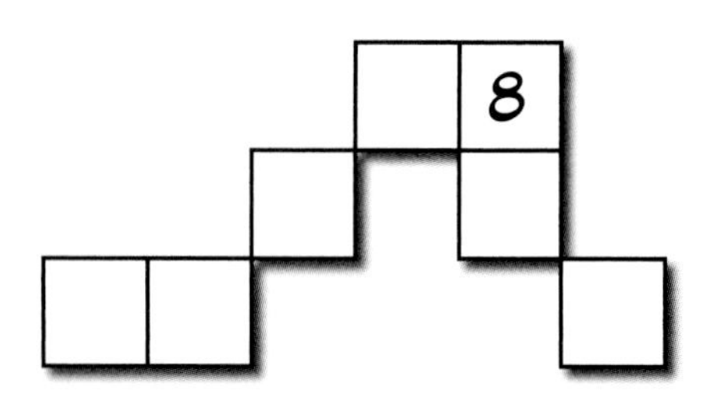

8

TEC43059

Mind Builder 2

Write and answer four questions about the calendar.

February 2012						
Sun.	Mon.	Tues.	Wed.	Thurs.	Fri.	Sat.
			1	2	3	4
5	6	7	8	9	10	11
12	13	14	15	16	17	18
19	20	21	22	23	24	25
26	27	28	29			

TEC43059

Mind Builder 3

Write five or more comparisons.

For each comparison, use a number from a square and a number from a circle.

Use >, <, or =. 140 > 104

140

256

197

308 380 104

TEC43059

Mind Builder 4

The hens in the coop laid 4 eggs on Monday, 8 eggs on Tuesday, and 12 eggs on Wednesday. If the pattern continues, on what day will the hens lay 2 dozen eggs? Tell how you know.

TEC43059

Mind Builder 5

3 x 15 = 45

Explain how using this fact will give you the answer for 45 ÷ 15.

TEC43059

Mind Builder 6

Estimate each sum. Then solve each problem.

A. 28 + 51 is about ________.
   28 + 51 = ________

B. 104 + 89 is about ________.
   104 + 89 = ________

C. 67 - 48 is about ________.
   67 - 48 = ________

TEC43059

Mind Builder 7

A mistake was made in each problem. Describe each mistake and tell how to correct it.

A.
```
  $88.90
+  29.07
--------
 $107.97
```

B.
```
   6
 x 3
 ---
   9
```

TEC43059

Mind Builder 8

Describe the pattern on the graph. Predict how long it will take to eat 10 pies.

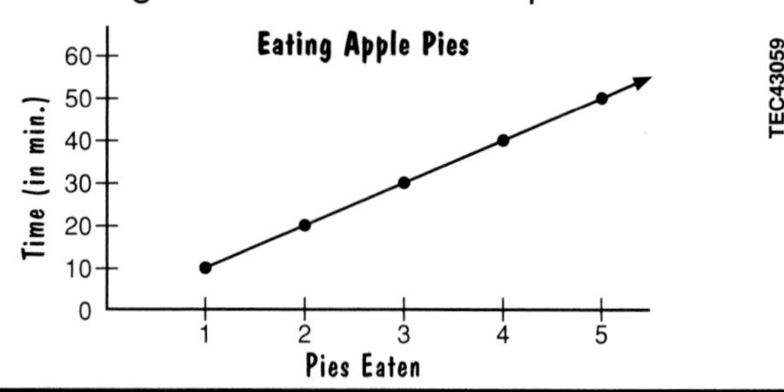

Eating Apple Pies
Time (in min.)
0
10
20
30
40
50
60
1
2
3
4
5
Pies Eaten

TEC43059

How to use: Give each student a copy of this page (or one card at a time) to work on during free time.

Math

Mind Builders

Mind Builder 1

Name something that can be done in each amount of time.

A. 15 seconds
B. 20 minutes
C. 8 hours

TEC43060

Mind Builder 2

Allie skip-counted by threes until she reached 30.

A. Did she say 18?
B. Did she say 23?
C. Did she say 27?

TEC43060

Mind Builder 3

Write two statements about the Venn diagram.

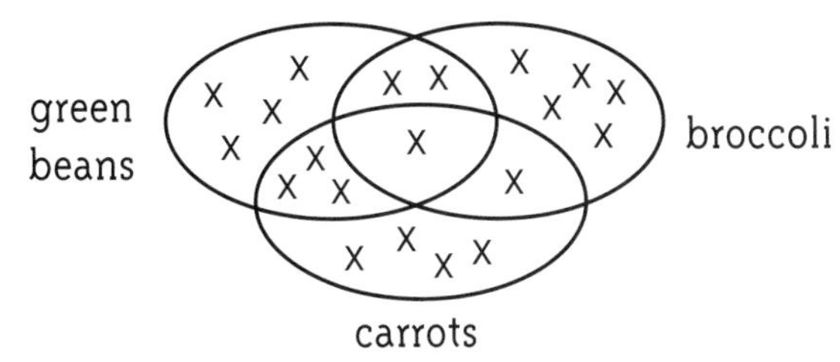

Foods Students Like
green beans
broccoli
carrots

TEC43060

Mind Builder 4

Solve this riddle.

How can you make seven even?

TEC43060

Mind Builder 5

You have one $5 bill, two $1 bills, eight quarters, and two dimes. A movie ticket costs $7.50.

A. Do you have enough money for a ticket?
B. Can you buy a bag of popcorn for $1.50 too?

TEC43060

Mind Builder 6

Copy and complete the chart.

	round to the nearest 10	round to the nearest 100
58		
143		
216		

TEC43060

Mind Builder 7

If you had to jump over a puddle, would you rather jump over one that was 30 inches wide or one that was one yard wide? Explain.

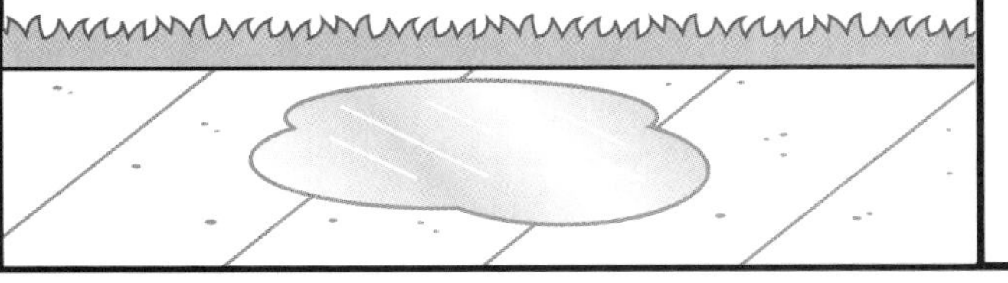

TEC43060

Mind Builder 8

5

A. Write a division problem with this as the quotient.
B. Write a division problem with this as the divisor.
C. Write a division problem with this as the dividend.

TEC43060

How to Use Give each student a copy of this page (or one card at a time) to work on during free time.

Math

Mind Builders

Mind Builder 1

Find the value of each missing number. Explain the steps you took for each.

A. [ice cream cone] + 9 = 16

B. 25 – [sun] = 17

TEC43061

Mind Builder 2

Use the numbers to write and solve two different addition problems.

Then write and solve two different subtraction problems.

141 89 23 17

TEC43061

Mind Builder 3

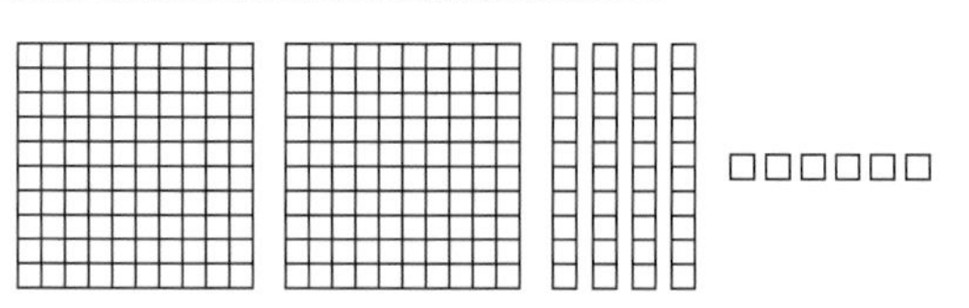

A. What is the number shown?

B. What number is 10 more? What number is 10 less?

C. What number is 100 more? What number is 100 less?

TEC43061

Mind Builder 4

Write and answer three questions about the data table.

Second-Grade Lunches	
Sandwiches	Number Eaten
peanut butter	14
ham	7
grilled cheese	28
turkey	32

TEC43061

Mind Builder 5

Uh-oh! Only three buttons work. Which three can you press to make a problem with the answer shown? (Hint: One button may be pressed more than once.)

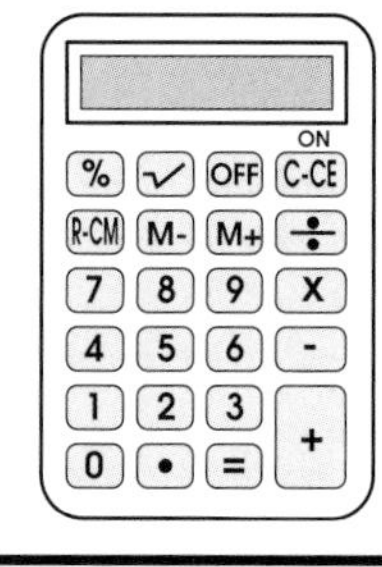
ON
% OFF C-CE
R-CM M- M+ ÷
7 8 9 X
4 5 6 -
1 2 3 +
0 • =

36

TEC43061

Mind Builder 6

A. Write a three-digit number where all the digits are different.

B. Write the number rounded to the nearest 10.

C. Write the number rounded to the nearest 100.

Repeat these steps with three different numbers.

TEC43061

Mind Builder 7

A. 

B. 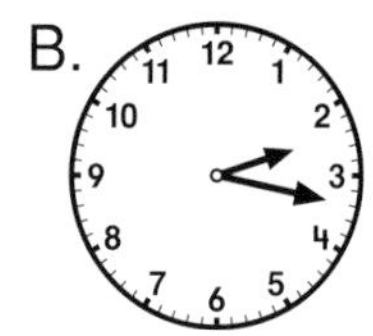

C. 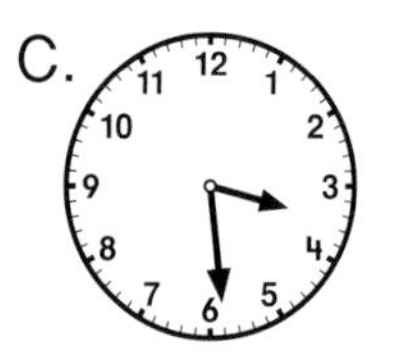

Write the time for each clock.

Describe the pattern.

TEC43061

Mind Builder 8

Use the plates of cookies to write three problems.

Write an addition problem.

Write a multiplication problem.

Write a division problem.

TEC43061

How to Use Give each student a copy of this page (or one card at a time) to work on during free time.

Name ______________________ Date ______________

Place value to thousands

A Mountain of Meatballs

Circle the value of the underlined digit.
Write the letter on the meatball with the matching value.

549	4 tens **M**	4 ones **N**	4 hundreds **O**
73	3 hundreds **K**	3 ones **L**	3 tens **M**
3,592	5 ones **Y**	5 thousands **Z**	5 hundreds **A**
8,601	8 hundreds **L**	8 tens **M**	8 thousands **N**
6,395	9 hundreds **N**	9 tens **O**	9 thousands **P**
102	1 ten **A**	1 thousand **B**	1 hundred **C**
427	7 ones **E**	7 hundreds **F**	7 tens **G**
9,570	9 tens **G**	9 hundreds **H**	9 thousands **I**
2,441	4 thousands **J**	4 hundreds **K**	4 tens **L**
706	7 hundreds **R**	7 tens **S**	7 ones **T**
1,059	1 thousand **U**	1 hundred **V**	1 ten **W**
4,928	2 hundreds **B**	2 ones **C**	2 tens **D**

40
700
3
9,000
7
20
90
400
500
1,000
100
8,000

What do you call fake spaghetti?

To find out, write each letter from above on its matching numbered line or lines.

"____ ____ ____ ____-____ ____ ____ ____ ____"
40 90 100 400 500 700 90 8,000 9,000

Name ______________________ Date ______________

Comparing and ordering numbers

A Packed Parking Lot

Write < or > between each pair of numbers.
Complete each task.

A. 24 ____ 15 63 ____ 84

Write the numbers from **least** to **greatest.**

______, ______, ______, ______

B. 88 ____ 79 70 ____ 69

Write the numbers from **greatest** to **least.**

______, ______, ______, ______

C. 81 ____ 62 25 ____ 52

Write the numbers from **least** to **greatest.**

______, ______, ______, ______

D. 54 ____ 52 46 ____ 53

Write the numbers from **greatest** to **least.**

______, ______, ______, ______

E. 121 ____ 143 152 ____ 135

Write the numbers from **least** to **greatest.**

______, ______, ______, ______

F. 260 ____ 268 321 ____ 123

Write the numbers from **greatest** to **least.**

______, ______, ______, ______

G. 119 ____ 125 132 ____ 126

Write the numbers from **least** to **greatest.**

______, ______, ______, ______

H. 307 ____ 319 311 ____ 314

Write the numbers from **greatest** to **least.**

______, ______, ______, ______

Name ______________________ Date ______________

Addition and subtraction without regrouping

Tracker Takes the Case!

Find the footprints that match each letter.
Use the numbers to write an addition and a subtraction problem.
Solve.

A	B	C	D
36 + 12 = 48; 36 − 12 = 24	+ ___ − ___	+ ___ − ___	+ ___ − ___
E	**F**	**G**	**H**
+ ___ − ___	+ ___ − ___	+ ___ − ___	+ ___ − ___
I	**J**		
+ ___ − ___	+ ___ − ___		

74 47 56 63 53 45 35 36 82 13

10 12 31 64 31 21 32 24 43 12

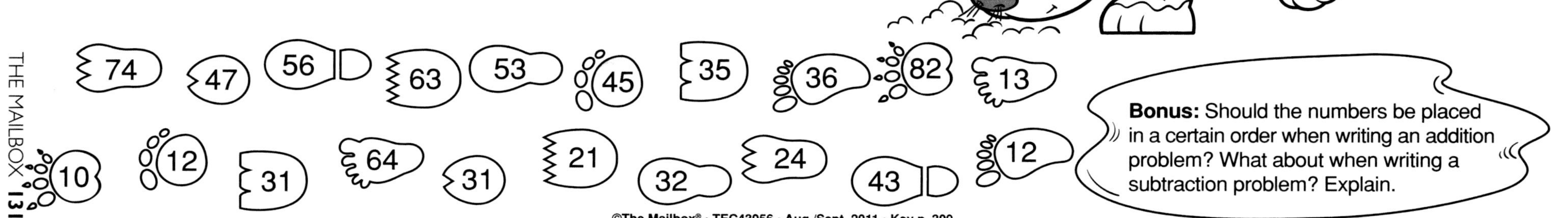

Bonus: Should the numbers be placed in a certain order when writing an addition problem? What about when writing a subtraction problem? Explain.

Name ______________________ Date ______________

Estimating sums and differences

"Essssstimating"

Fill in the circle next to the best estimate.

1. 13 + 16 ○ 20 ○ 40 ○ 30	2. 21 + 68 ○ 80 ○ 90 ○ 70	3. 56 + 22 ○ 80 ○ 70 ○ 60
4. 33 + 21 ○ 30 ○ 60 ○ 50	5. 12 + 55 ○ 80 ○ 70 ○ 60	6. 37 + 32 ○ 70 ○ 60 ○ 80
7. 43 − 22 ○ 20 ○ 10 ○ 30	8. 19 − 12 ○ 10 ○ 20 ○ 30	9. 67 − 31 ○ 20 ○ 40 ○ 50
10. 75 − 31 ○ 50 ○ 30 ○ 40	11. 88 − 26 ○ 80 ○ 70 ○ 60	12. 57 − 22 ○ 20 ○ 30 ○ 40

Solve each problem.
Color the rock by the code.

Color Code

My estimate was reasonable. = yellow

My estimate was not reasonable. = brown

Bonus: Write steps to explain how you found the estimate for problem 1.

Name ______________________ Date ______________

Time to five minutes

Feeding Time

Write each time.
Find the pattern for each row.
Use the pattern to draw and write the last time.

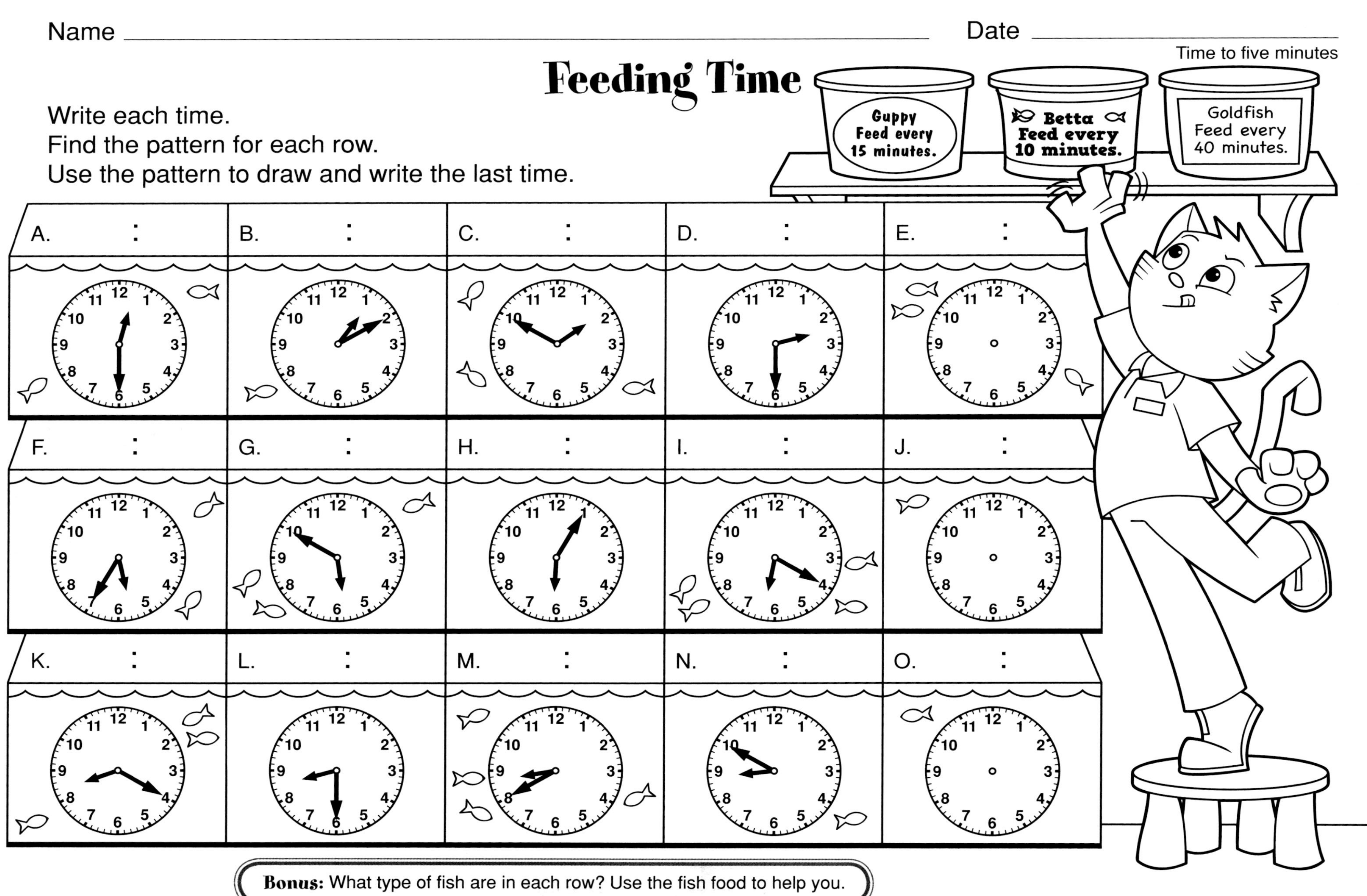
Guppy
Feed every
15 minutes.
Betta
Feed every
10 minutes.
Goldfish
Feed every
40 minutes.
A. :
B. :
C. :
D. :
E. :
F. :
G. :
H. :
I. :
J. :
K. :
L. :
M. :
N. :
O. :

Bonus: What type of fish are in each row? Use the fish food to help you.

Name ______________________ Date ______________

Telling time to the minute

Up, Up, and Away

Write the time shown on each clock.
Color the balloon with the matching time.
Hint: Not all the balloons will be used.

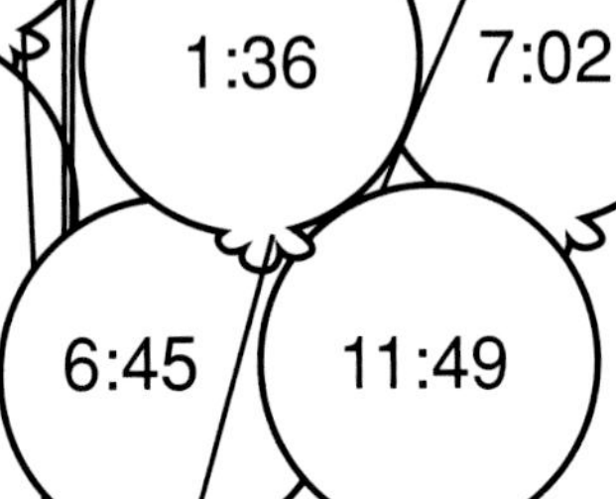

12:09
6:37
8:41
5:11
4:55
9:52
3:23
10:29
1:36
7:02
2:15
6:45
11:49

A.

B.
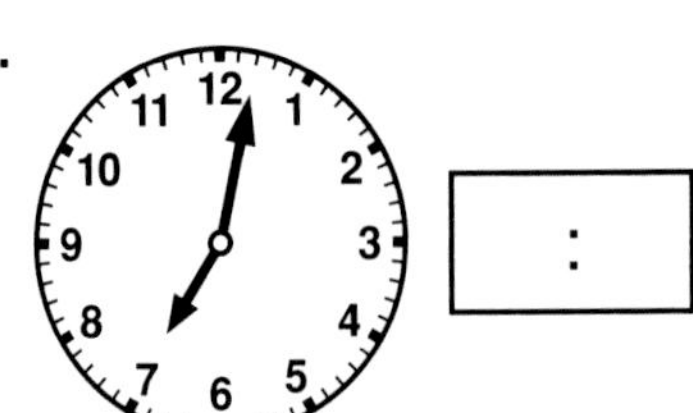

C.
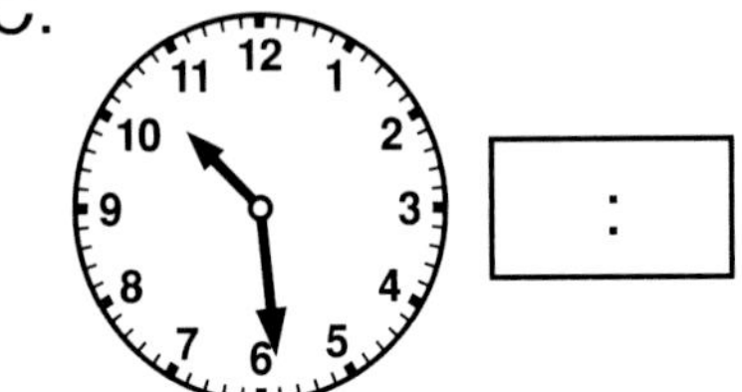

D.
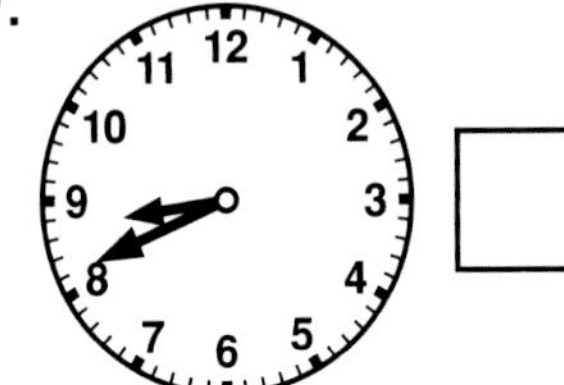

E.
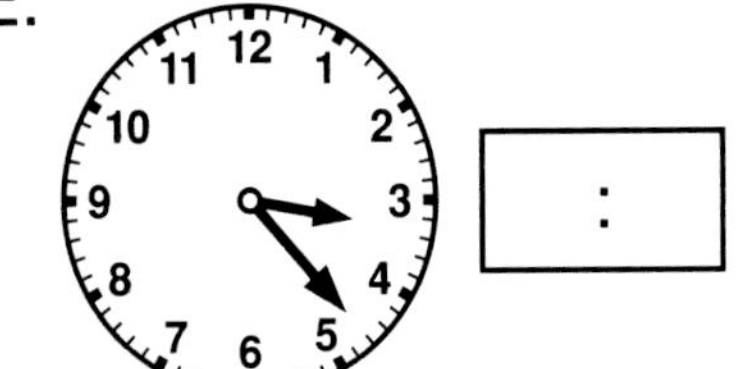

F.
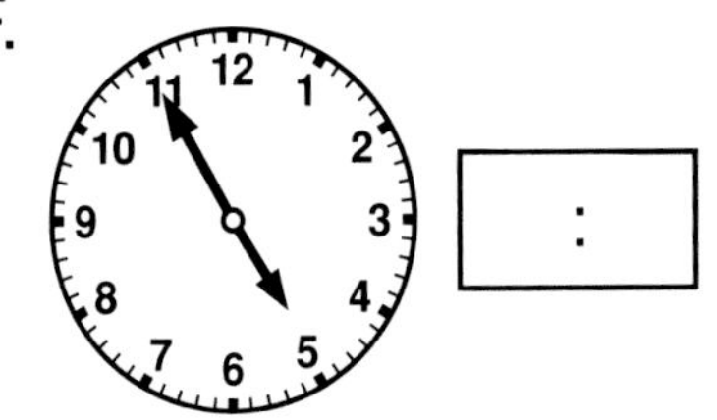

G.

H.
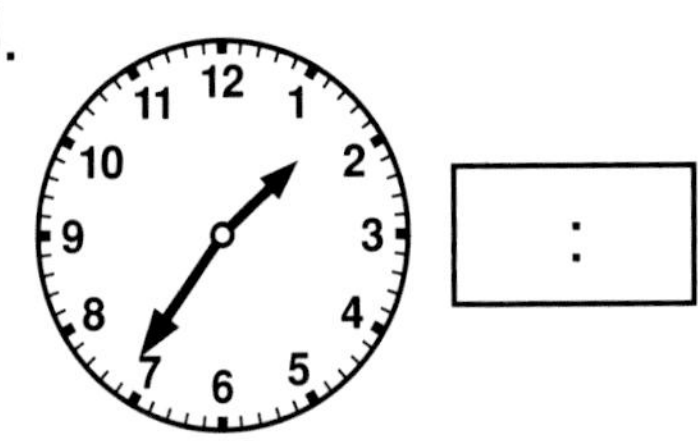

I.
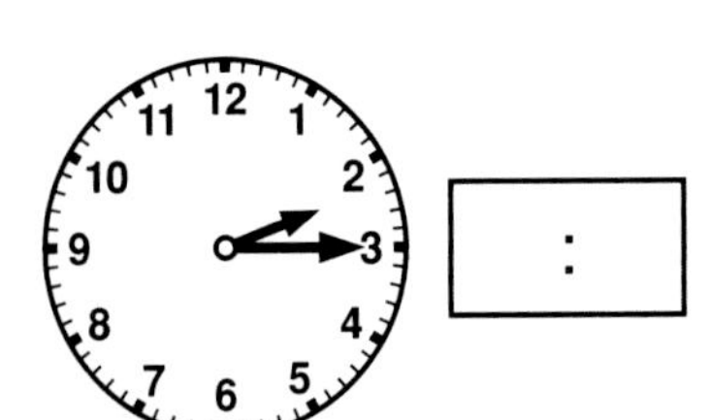

J.
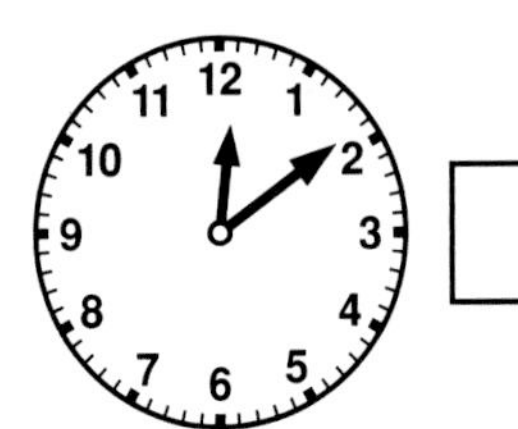

K.
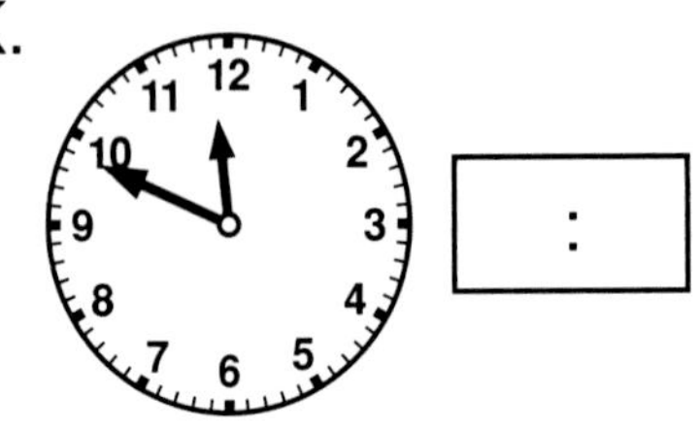

L.
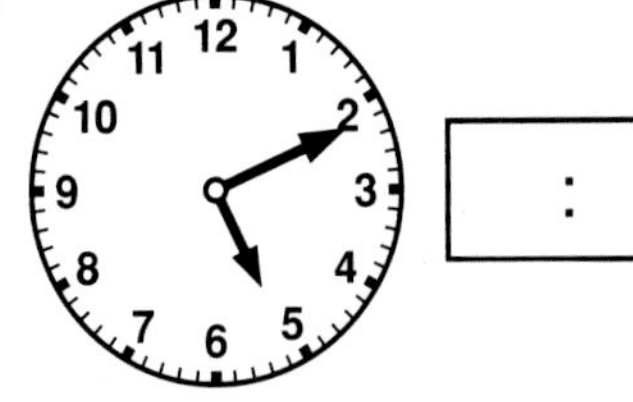

Bonus: Draw a clock to match the time on the uncolored balloon.

Name ______________________ Date ______________

Time

What's the Scoop?

Pick a prompt.
Write your response.

1. Stan the Ice Cream Man starts work when the long hand on the clock points to 12 and the short hand points to 11. What time does he start? How do you know?

2. Stan takes breaks at 1:15, 3:40, and 5:55. Use words and drawings to show each time two different ways.

3. Stan sells ice cream during the day. His shift ends at 7:00. Is that AM or PM? Explain why you think so.

Name ______________________ Date ______________

Measurement

Gone Fishing!

Pick a prompt.
Write your response.

1. You measure a worm for bait. Do you use a ruler or a yardstick? Tell why.

2. There are 8 fish. Each fish is 2 inches long. If these fish swim in a straight line, will the line be longer than 1 foot? Explain how you know.

3. Fish A is 4 feet long. Fish B is 38 inches long. Which is longer? Explain.

Math prompts: Project a set of prompts for all students to see. Direct each child to choose a prompt, copy its number onto his paper, and then write his response. If desired, have each child respond to all three prompts.

Name ______________________ Date ______________

Measurement, money

Numbers to Noodle On

Read and respond.

There are about 100,000 hairs on the average person's head. Each hair grows a little over 12 centimeters every year.

A. Name two items that are about 12 centimeters long. ______________

____

B. About how much does one hair grow each month? ______________

Your digestive system is a group of tubes and organs that help you turn food into fuel. If you could stretch it out, your digestive system would be nearly 30 feet long!

C. About how many yards long is your digestive system? (Hint: there are three feet in one yard.)

____

D. How tall are you? (If you're not sure, have a friend help you measure.) ______________

Write an equation to compare your height to the length of the digestive system. Use < or >.

______________ ○ ______________

A dollar bill weighs 1 gram. Its average lifespan is 42 months. There are 294 different ways to make change for a dollar.

E. About how many years will a dollar bill last? ______________

F. Name two or more items that weigh as much as a dollar bill.

____

____

G. On another sheet of paper, write or draw several different ways you might make change for a dollar.

Zorba was a record-setting dog. This Old English Mastiff weighed 343 pounds. He was 8 feet 3 inches long from nose to tail.

H. Think about how much you weigh. About how many of you would it take to equal this dog's weight?

____

I. Think about how tall you are. About how many of you would it take to equal this dog's length?

____

J. If you named the dog's length in inches only, how long would it be? (Hint: there are 12 inches in one foot.)

____

Name ______________________ Date ______________

Word problems: dollars and coins

Munching at the Movies

Read.
Solve.
Color the popcorn piece with the matching answer.

$3.50 $6.80 $4.70 $3.49

$3.20
$2.25
$4.67
$3.25

1. A movie ticket costs 6 dollars, 2 quarters, and 3 dimes. How much does each ticket cost?

2. Lemonade costs 1 dollar and 3 quarters. Frozen lemonade costs 50 cents more. How much is frozen lemonade?

3. Cal brought 3 dollars, 2 dimes, and 5 pennies to buy snacks. He lost his pennies. How much money does Cal have to spend?

4. Kyle has 3 dollars, 2 dimes, and 1 nickel. He needs 25 cents more to buy popcorn. How much does popcorn cost?

5. Nachos cost 4 dollars, 3 dimes, 1 nickel, and 2 pennies. Extra cheese costs 30 cents more. How much are nachos with extra cheese?

6. Carly brought 2 dollars, 4 quarters, and 5 nickels for candy. How much money does she have in all?

7. Katie has 3 dollars, 2 quarters, 1 nickel, and 4 pennies. If she buys pizza, she will have ten cents left. How much does pizza cost?

8. Kevin bought two pretzels. Each pretzel costs 2 dollars, 3 dimes, and 1 nickel. How much did he spend in all?

Bonus:
Carly decided to buy a bag of licorice. The licorice costs 1 dollar, 1 dime, and 3 pennies. How much money does she have left? (Hint: Use your answer from problem 6 to find this answer.)

Name ______________________ Date ______________

Comparing fractions

Baking Banana Bread

Color each loaf to show the fraction.
Write <, >, or = in each ○.

A.

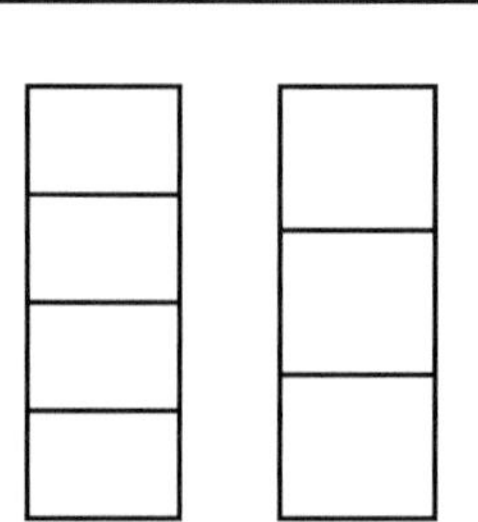

$\frac{2}{3}$ ○ $\frac{1}{2}$

B.

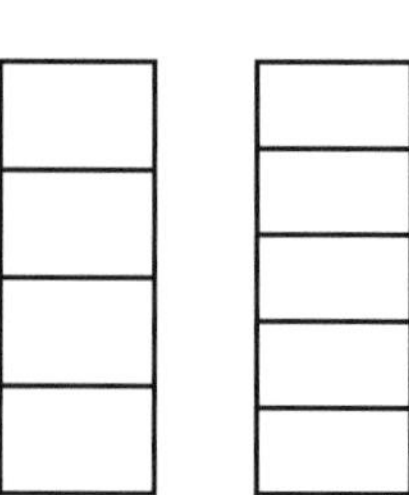

$\frac{1}{4}$ ○ $\frac{1}{3}$

C.

$\frac{2}{4}$ ○ $\frac{3}{5}$

D.

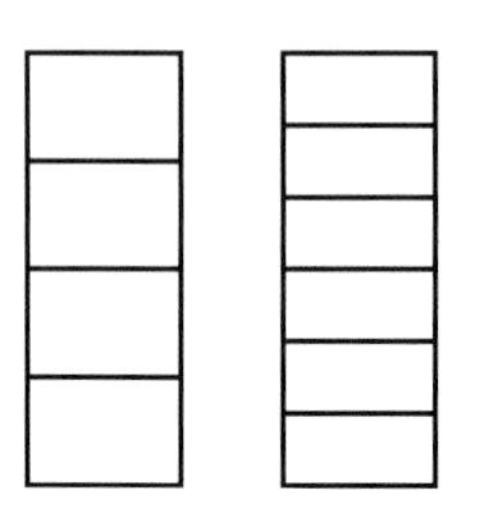

$\frac{3}{4}$ ○ $\frac{2}{6}$

E.

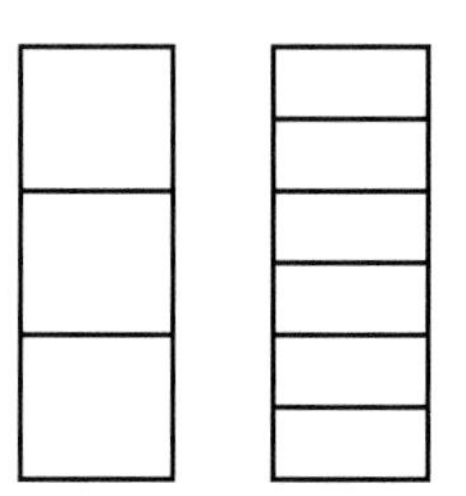

$\frac{2}{3}$ ○ $\frac{4}{6}$

F.

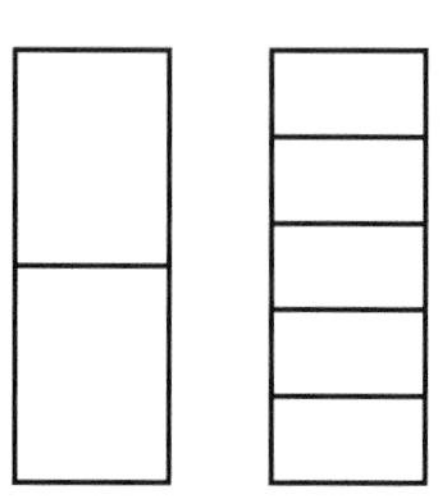

$\frac{1}{2}$ ○ $\frac{3}{5}$

G.

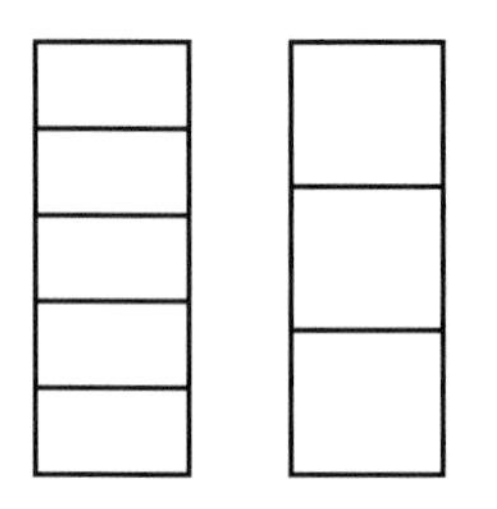

$\frac{2}{5}$ ○ $\frac{2}{3}$

H.

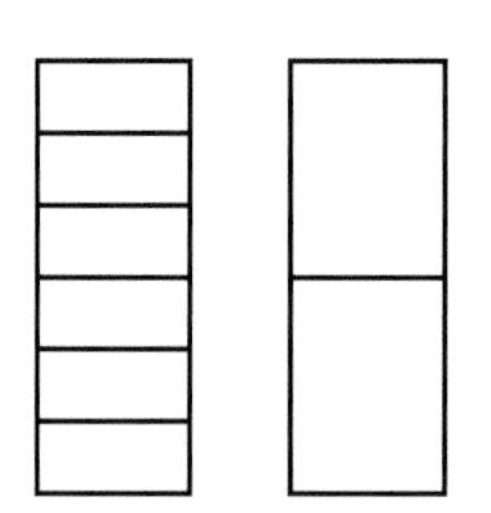

$\frac{2}{6}$ ○ $\frac{1}{2}$

I.

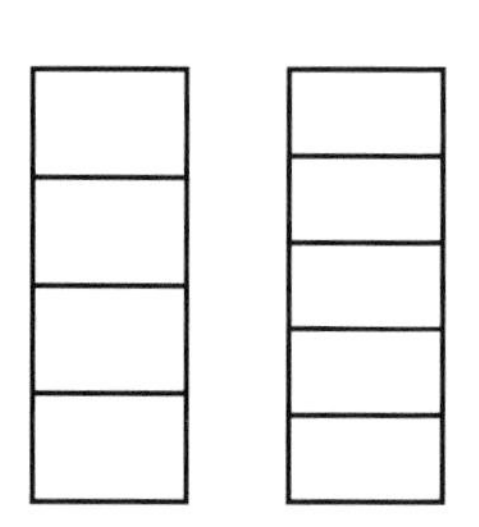

$\frac{1}{4}$ ○ $\frac{1}{5}$

J.

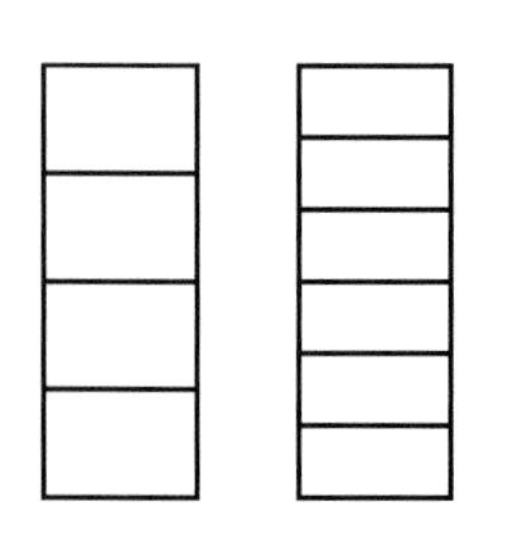

$\frac{3}{4}$ ○ $\frac{5}{6}$

K.

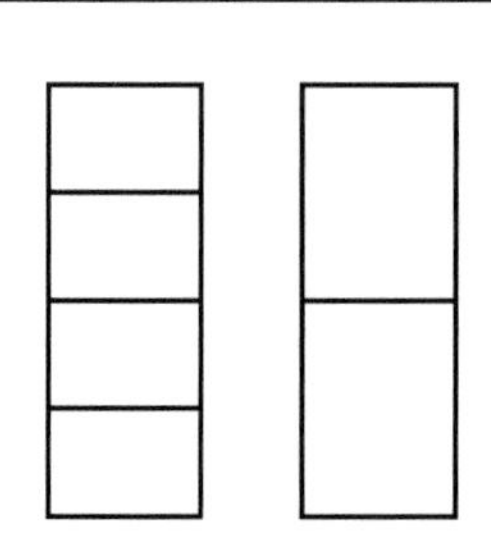

$\frac{2}{4}$ ○ $\frac{1}{2}$

L.

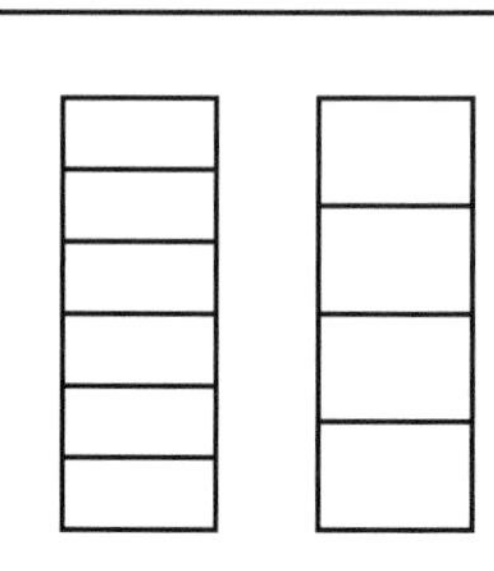

$\frac{3}{6}$ ○ $\frac{1}{4}$

Bonus: Would you rather have $\frac{2}{3}$ of a loaf of banana bread or $\frac{2}{6}$ of a loaf? Explain.

Name ____________________ Date ____________

Fractions on a number line, equivalent fractions

He's Got the Beat

Write each fraction on the matching number line. Then color the music note.

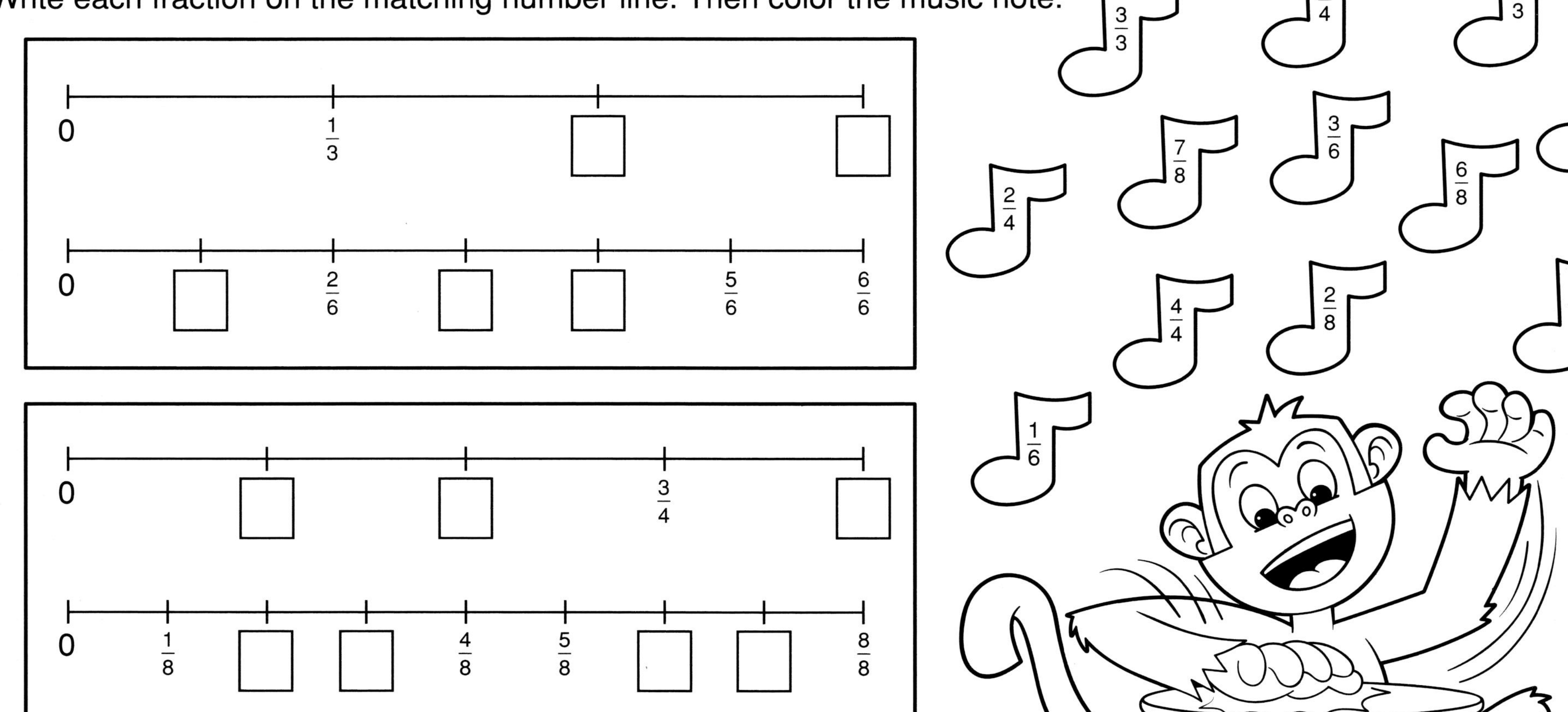
0
1/3
0
2/6
5/6
6/6
0
3/4
0
1/8
4/8
5/8
8/8
3/3
1/4
2/3
3/8
2/4
7/8
3/6
6/8
4/4
2/8
4/6
1/6
Bonus: Look at the number lines. Which fraction is equal to 2/8? Explain how you know.

Draw a blue box around each fraction from above equal to $\frac{1}{2}$.

Draw a yellow box around each fraction from above equal to $\frac{3}{4}$.

Draw a red box around each fraction from above equal to 1.

Name ______________________________ Date ______________

Identifying polygons

A Splashy Movie

Color each polygon.

1. D

2. 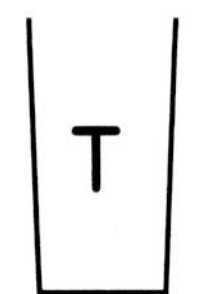
T

3. 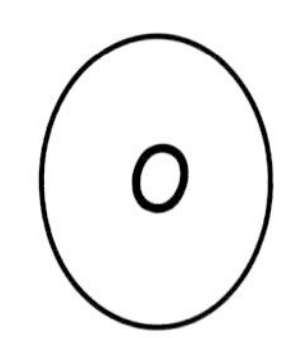
O

4. 
E

5. 
W

6. 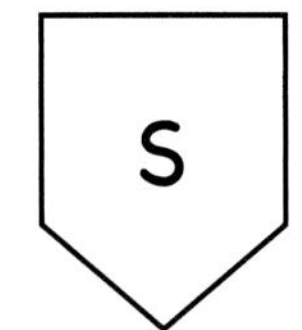
S

7. 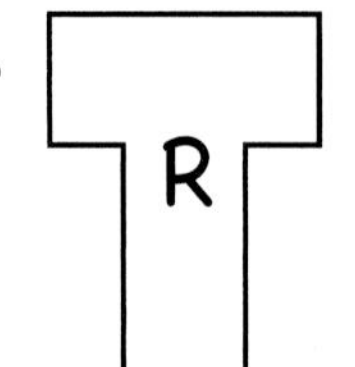
R

8. 

J

9. 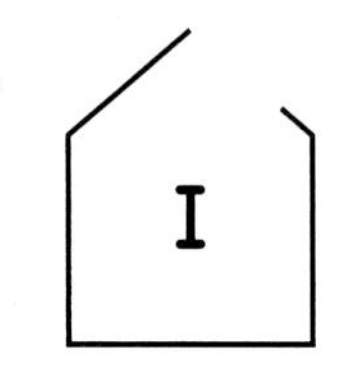
I

10. 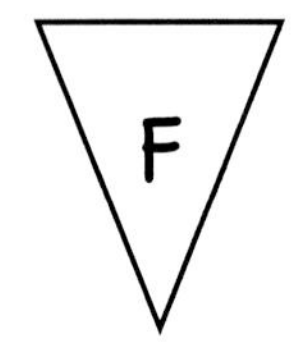
F

11. 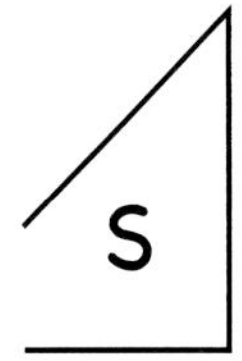
S

12. 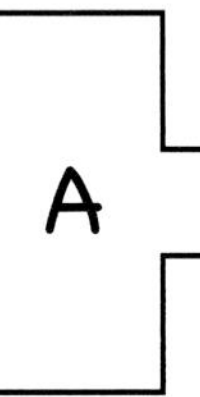
A

13. 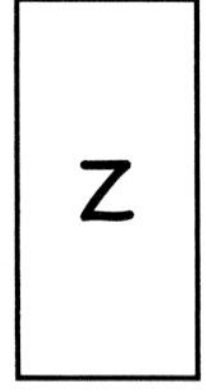
Z

14. 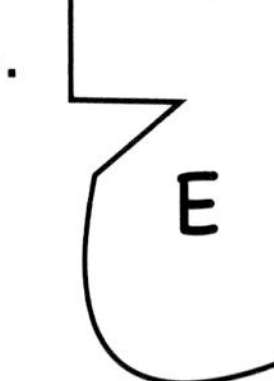
E

15. 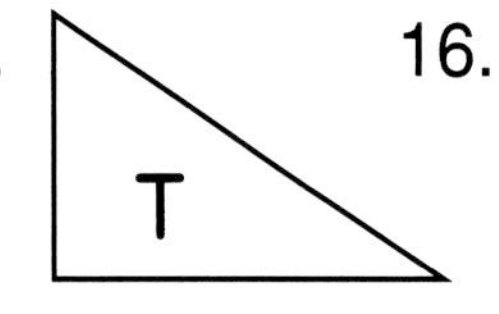
T

16. W

17. 
J

18. 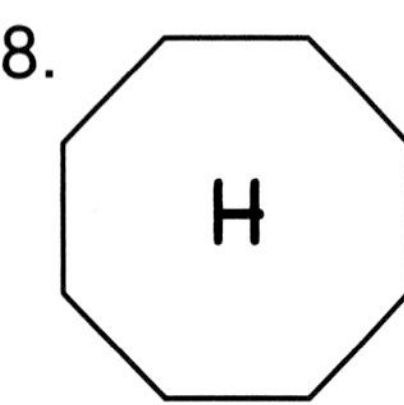
H

19. 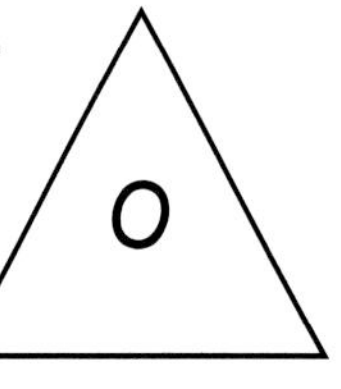
O

20. 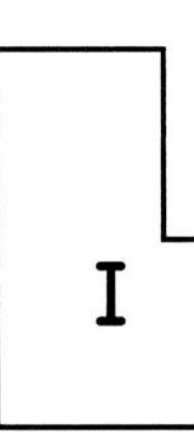
I

A **polygon** is a closed figure. Each of a polygon's sides is a line segment.

Exit

What's a shark's favorite movie?

To solve the riddle, write each colored polygon's letter on its matching numbered line or lines.

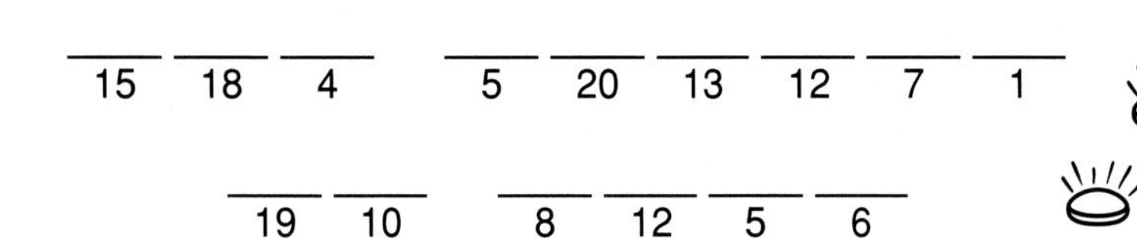

15 18 4 5 20 13 12 7 1
19 10 8 12 5 6

Bonus: Circle the number beside each quadrilateral.

Name ____________________ Date ____________

Probability

Which Color Will Be Revealed?

Color two balls red.
Color four balls yellow.
Color one ball blue.
Color two balls green.

Freddy hides these balls under cups. Decide if each sentence is *true* or *false*.
Write each answer.

1. It is **certain** that Freddy will reveal a red ball. ____________
2. It is **unlikely** that Freddy will reveal a blue ball. ____________
3. It is **likely** that Freddy will reveal a yellow ball. ____________
4. It is **impossible** that Freddy will reveal a green ball. ____________
5. It is **unlikely** that Freddy will reveal a red ball. ____________
6. It is **certain** that Freddy will reveal a yellow ball. ____________
7. It is **likely** that Freddy will reveal a blue ball. ____________
8. It is **unlikely** that Freddy will reveal a green ball. ____________
9. It is **likely** that Freddy will reveal a red ball. ____________
10. It is **impossible** that Freddy will reveal a pink ball. ____________
11. It is **certain** that Freddy will reveal a round ball. ____________
12. It is **impossible** that Freddy will reveal a blue ball. ____________

Bonus: Draw a cup of five balls to match this statement: It is certain that a red ball will be picked.

Name ______________________ Date ______________

Multiplication: two-digit by one-digit

Merry Mr. Frog

Multiply.

(A) 20 x 6	(B) 40 x 4	(D) 10 x 9	(E) 60 x 6	(G) 70 x 5
(H) 30 x 8	(I) 50 x 4	(M) 80 x 4	(N) 20 x 7	(R) 90 x 2
(T) 50 x 3	(U) 30 x 7	(V) 40 x 2	(Y) 60 x 5	

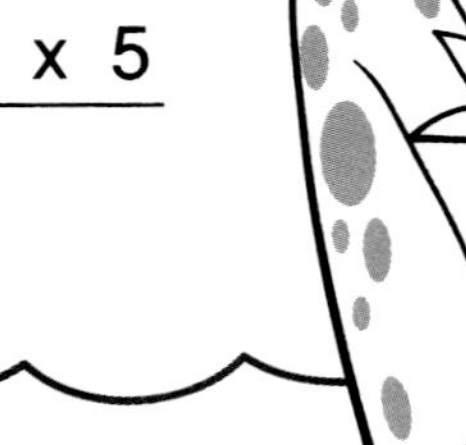

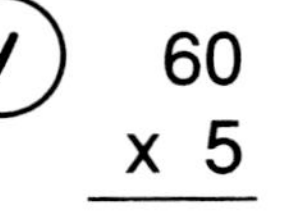

Why is Mr. Frog so happy?

To solve the riddle, write each letter on its matching numbered line or lines.

__ __   __ __ __   __ __ __ __ __ __ __ __ __ __
240 360   120 150 360   360 80 360 180 300 150 240 200 140 350

__ __ __ __   __ __ __ __ __ __   __ __ __ .
150 240 120 150   160 210 350 350 360 90   240 200 320

Bonus: Why do all the answers on this page have a zero in the ones place?

SCIENCE

simply
science

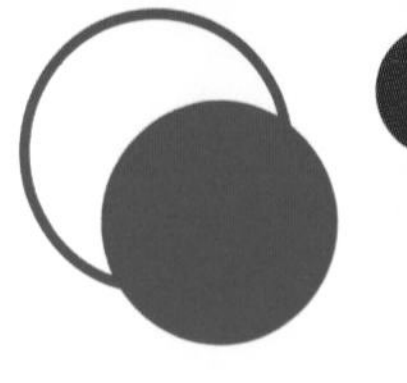
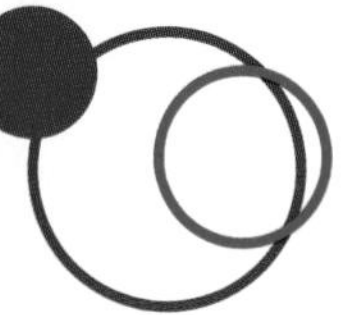

Observation skills

More Than Meets the Eye

In advance, snap a few pictures around a common campus location (such as the playground) and print them out. Then divide students into small groups; give each group a photo and two different colored markers. Using one color marker, have the students describe and record all the things they see in the photo. Next, take students to the location and direct each group to take their paper and other marker to the specific area from their photo. Direct students to record observations of what they feel, smell, hear, and measure there. (Encourage nonstandard measurements.) After returning to the room, lead students to understand that observing is more than meets the eye: it requires different senses and tools of measure. **To extend the activity**, head outside at a different time of day or during a different season. Have students compare their outdoor observations.

Elizabeth Searls Almy, Greensboro, NC

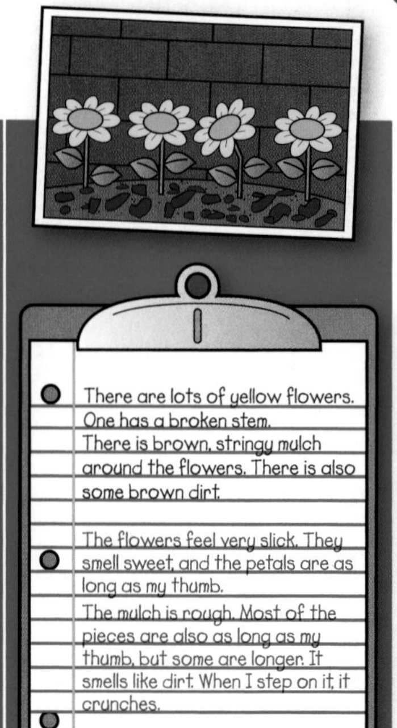
There are lots of yellow flowers. One has a broken stem.
There is brown, stringy mulch around the flowers. There is also some brown dirt.
The flowers feel very slick. They smell sweet, and the petals are as long as my thumb.
The mulch is rough. Most of the pieces are also as long as my thumb, but some are longer. It smells like dirt. When I step on it, it crunches.

Science journals

Under the Microscope

Train your young scientists to record data and communicate ideas with this simple routine. To start, model for students how to complete an entry in their science journals. After the first science activity and journal entry, choose one or two exceptional samples. Label the pages as shown and then display the journals in a specifically designated location. Before starting science instruction, share the journals and discuss why they are featured. Repeat the activity throughout the year with different students' journals and no doubt your scientists will wow you with their work!

Pam Temerowski, Green Acres Elementary, Warren, MI

Featured Science Journal
Sept. 12, 2011
Today we practiced
observation skills. We used
apple slices.
Great diagram!

Wind direction

Go With the Flow

Here's a hands-on demonstration that flows nicely with your weather unit! To prepare, obtain a hair dryer with an extension cord. Tape several crepe paper streamers to the end of a yardstick. Then cut apart a copy of the direction signs on page 150. After sharing with students that wind is named from its starting direction, give each of eight students a different sign. Direct the students to sit in a circle as though they are a large compass. Invite another student to stand in the middle of the circle with the yardstick. Use the hair dryer to move the streamers and ask students to name the wind direction. **As an alternative,** name a wind direction and have a student direct the air to model that movement. Elizabeth Searls Almy

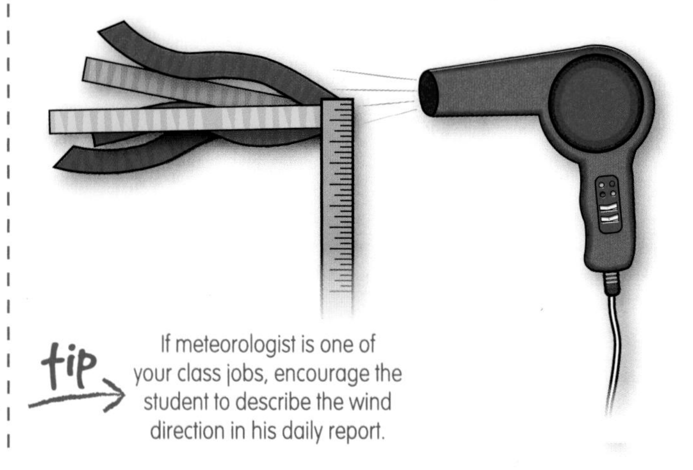

tip If meteorologist is one of your class jobs, encourage the student to describe the wind direction in his daily report.

simply
science

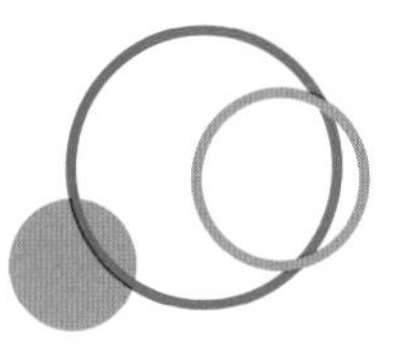
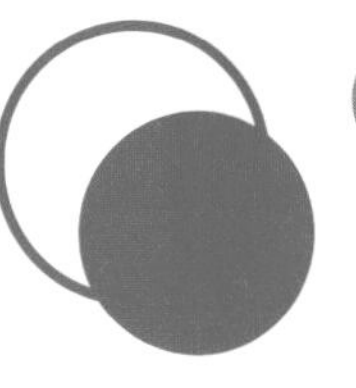
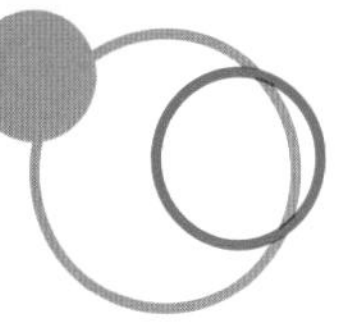
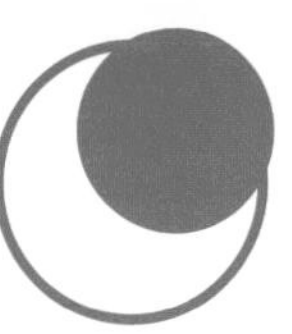

Properties of water

Molecules on the Move

Does temperature affect how fast water molecules move? This low-prep demonstration uncovers the answer. Begin by asking students to predict if the temperature of water will affect how fast its molecules move and have them write their responses in their science journals. Next, fill a clear glass jar with very cold water, another jar with an equal amount of room temperature water, and a third jar with a matching amount of very hot water. Instruct students to pay careful attention as you place a drop of food coloring in each jar because the water with the fastest moving molecules (the hot water) will be the one in which the color spreads fastest. Finally, have each student write in his journal an explanation of the demonstration and its results.

Elizabeth Searls Almy
Greensboro, NC

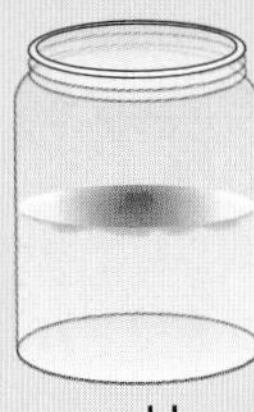
cold

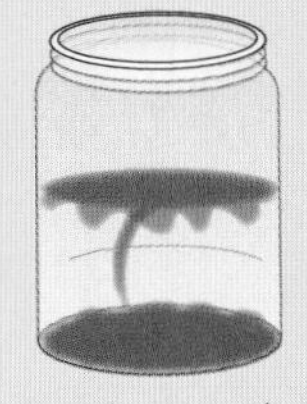
room temperature

hot

Animal diets

O Is for Omnivore

Lend a hand to help students remember which kinds of animals eat what kinds of food. Lead students in reciting the definitions shown. As students say the first line, have them raise their left hands. Then direct students to raise their right hands as they say the second line. When they recite the third line, instruct students to link their hands to form an *O* above their heads.

Suzan Quesenberry, Donahoe Elementary, Sandston, VA

Herbivores eat plants.
Carnivores eat meat.
Omnivores eat both plants and meat.

What is plasma?
More to Explore Science Questions

Scientific thinking

Extra Answers

Encourage your curious scientists to ask questions that go beyond the scope of your lessons with this simple routine. Decorate a box like the one shown. At the end of a science activity, provide time for each student who has an additional question to jot it down on a paper strip and place it in the box. Designate a regular time to review the questions and provide answers. For more challenging questions, use this time to demonstrate how to find the answers through the use of reference materials. Not only will students get the answers they're looking for, they'll also see how to answer questions on their own!

Angela Arndt, Sicklerville, NJ

simply
science

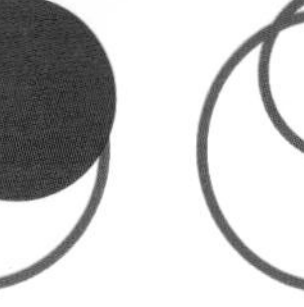

Moon phases

Calendar Connection

In advance, copy the moon phase cards on page 151 and cut them out. Select a student to serve as the night sky watcher each week and have him identify which moon phase he sees. Then direct him to use resources, such as a daily newspaper or a website, to confirm it. Have the child post the corresponding card on a labeled classroom calendar. Encourage the rest of the class to identify patterns in the moon's changes.

Audrey Hurst, Mallard Creek Elementary, Charlotte, NC

What's Up This Month?

December

				1		3
4	5	6	7	8	9	
11	12	13	14	15	16	17
	19	20	21	22	23	24
25	26	27	28	29	30	31

Weather, temperature

Fun for All!

To prepare, enlarge the thermometer pattern on page 151. Color-code the temperature ranges as shown to indicate cold temperatures, warm temperatures, and hot temperatures; then post the thermometer. As a class, brainstorm activities students could do outside for each temperature range. Then give each child three sheets of paper and direct her to draw and write her own activity for each range. When she's finished, have her color the background to correspond to colors on the thermometer. Bind the completed pages in three separate books.

Jennifer Mross, Kiel Elementary, Kinnelon, NJ

I could go snowboard when it is cold outside.
Madison
hot
warm
cold

Push	Pull
opening the art room door	opening the paper drawer
hitting the tetherball	Ms. S. moving the milk cart

Forces of motion

On the Move

Students will be amazed at how much motion occurs at school! At the beginning of the day, have each child label a chart in her science journal like the one shown. Tell students to keep the journal handy all day long. Throughout the day, leave a few minutes early for special classes, lunch, and recess. When you arrive at your destination, instruct each child to record any movement she observes in the matching column. If a student has free time while in the classroom, encourage her to do the same. At the end of the day, provide time for students to share a few of their observations aloud.

Elizabeth Searls Almy, Greensboro, NC

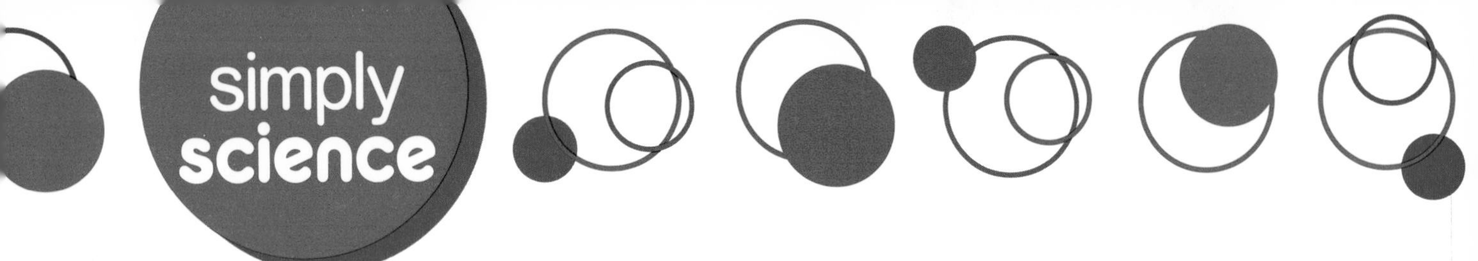
simply
science

Force and motion

Number Push

Make a variation of shuffleboard part of your science instruction! Here's how. Use masking tape to make a triangular shuffleboard court like the one shown. Direct a student to place a penny at the base of the triangle and have him use a pencil to push the penny (applying force) onto the first numbered space. Select a different child to repeat the process with another penny, this time aiming for the second numbered space. Continue in this manner until a penny has been aimed at each section, leading students in a discussion of how the amount of force applied results in the pennies moving different distances and how the amount of force should change as the distance increases. If desired, keep the court set up and invite student pairs to visit it as a center or free-time activity.

Cynthia Wicks, Eastwood Elementary, Roseburg, OR

5
3
4
1¢
1
2
Start
1¢

Fossils

A Not-So-Big Dig

To lead students to a greater appreciation for paleontologists' work, give each student a chocolate chip cupcake, a paper towel, and two toothpicks. Challenge each child to carefully extract the chocolate chips (fossils) from the cupcake (earth) without damaging the chips. Give students a short period of time to work independently on this task. Then have them stop and share with a small group of classmates what worked well for them. After sharing ideas, give students time to apply what they learned from their classmates. Not only will your youngsters have a better understanding of the time and patience paleontologists put into their work, but they'll also practice how scientists share ideas.

Jeannie Pavlik, Pittsville Elementary, Pittsville, WI

States of matter

Working the Room

Not only does this activity reinforce properties of solids and liquids, but it's also a great way to get out students' wiggles! Tell students they will be acting like water molecules; then define the space you wish for them to move in. Play an upbeat, tropical tune and direct students to move around the space, acting as the molecules in a liquid do. Then change the music to a classical song. Tell students that the water has frozen and that they should demonstrate how the molecules in ice (a solid) move by coming together as one unit. After students connect the music to the two different states, switch back and forth between the songs to see if they can demonstrate each state of matter without direction.

Elizabeth Searls Almy, Greensboro, NC

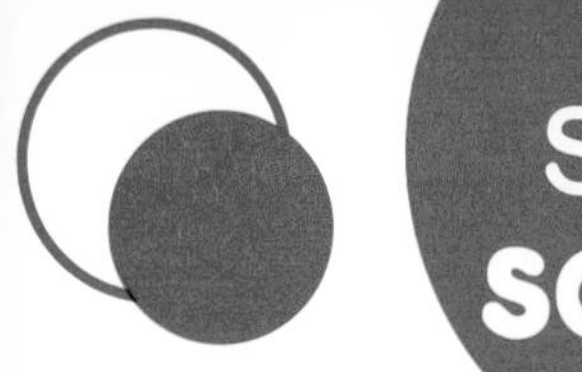
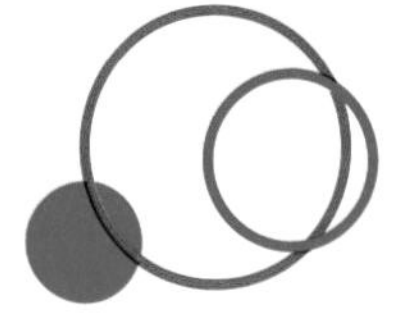

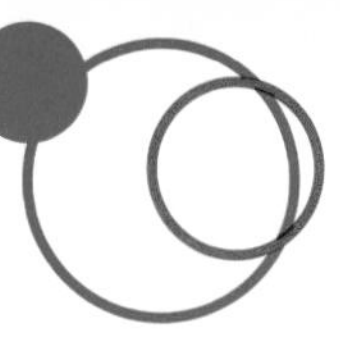
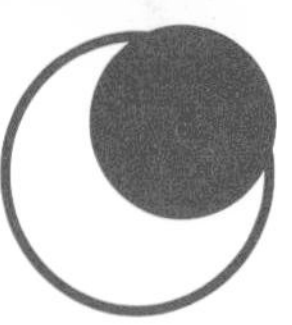

Earth's resources

Three Cheers for Earth!

Add some extra flair to your classroom with these instructional pennants. First, have students name ways they can take care of the earth's water, air, and land as you write the ideas on the board. Next, provide each child with a large triangle cut from recycled paper (pennant). Direct the student to write on his pennant an idea from the board and illustrate it. When all the pennants are complete, punch two holes in each one as shown, feed a length of yarn through the holes, and hang the pennants for all to see.

Elizabeth Searls Almy, Greensboro, NC

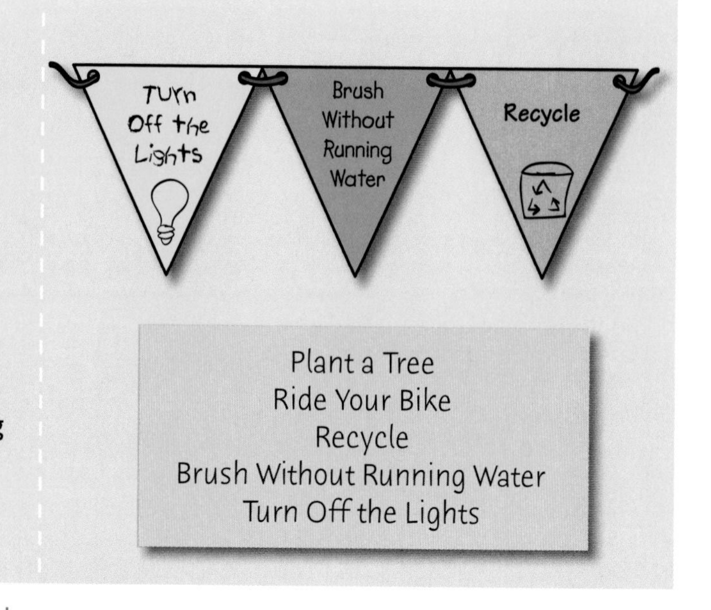
Turn Off the Lights
Brush Without Running Water
Recycle
Plant a Tree
Ride Your Bike
Recycle
Brush Without Running Water
Turn Off the Lights

Life cycles

In Full Bloom

Here are two ways your budding botanists can learn how flowering plants grow!

For a kinesthetic approach, have students act out the stages of a flowering plant's life cycle as you name each step.

seed: sit on the floor (soil) in a tight ball
sprout: start to rise up while still crouching
plant with buds: stand with arms up and hands in fists (buds)
bloom: open hands (petals)
seed dispersal: bend to the side as if the wind is blowing

For a visual approach, a student divides a paper plate into five parts. In each section, the child draws a different picture of the flowering plant's life cycle. Next, he cuts five paper flower petals and writes a description of each stage on a different petal. He glues each petal next to its illustration.

Cynthia Wicks
Eastwood Elementary
Roseburg, OR

Weather

Morning Meeting Meteorologist

Start each day with a peek at the weather, courtesy of one of your student reporters. Assign a day for each child to act as your class meteorologist and give her a copy of page 152. Have her use weather forecasts from television, newspapers, or the Internet to complete her report ahead of her assigned day. When it's her turn, have her read the report aloud to the class. **For a fun twist**, project a map of your state or region on your interactive whiteboard for the child to stand in front of during her report.

Christy Kirby
Montgomery Elementary
Cincinnati, OH

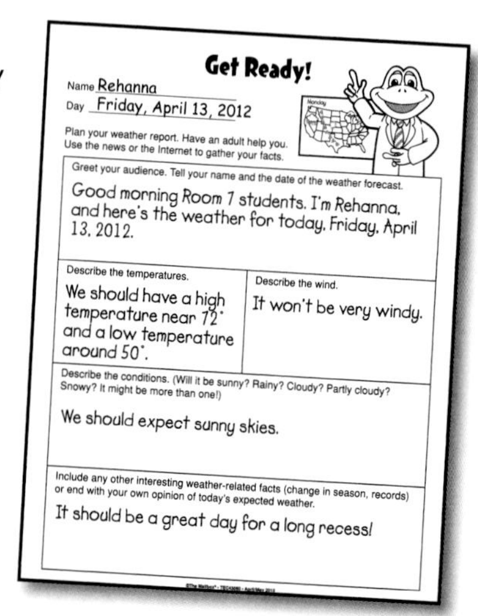

Get Ready!

Name Rehanna
Day Friday, April 13, 2012

Plan your weather report. Have an adult help you. Use the news or the Internet to gather your facts.

Greet your audience. Tell your name and the date of the weather forecast.
Good morning Room 7 students. I'm Rehanna, and here's the weather for today, Friday, April 13, 2012.

Describe the temperatures.
We should have a high temperature near 72° and a low temperature around 50°.

Describe the wind.
It won't be very windy.

Describe the conditions. (Will it be sunny? Rainy? Cloudy? Partly cloudy? Snowy? It might be more than one!)
We should expect sunny skies.

Include any other interesting weather-related facts (change in season, records) or end with your own opinion of today's expected weather.
It should be a great day for a long recess!

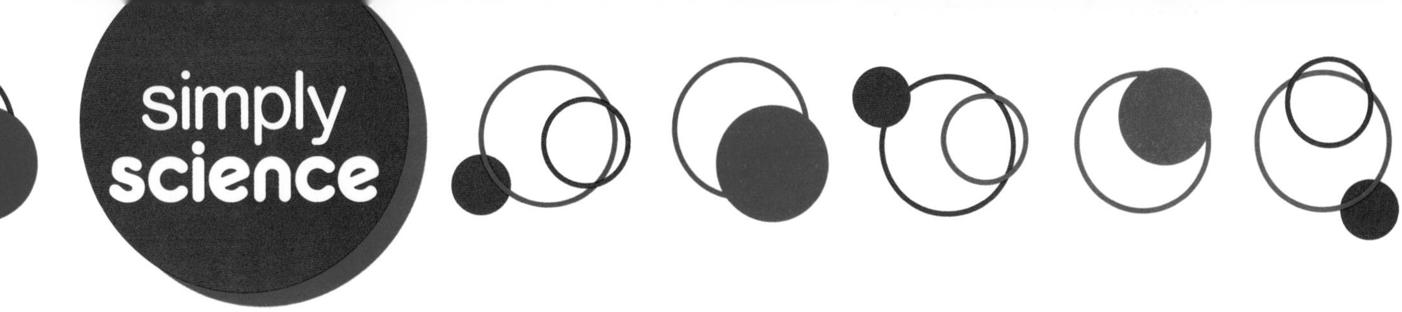
simply
science

Habitats

Homebodies

To prepare this game of knowledge and skill, place five similar-size cardboard boxes side by side in an open space. Label each box with a different habitat students have studied. Divide the class into two teams and give each team a lightweight ball. To play, call out an animal name and have the first player from each team try to roll, kick, or toss the ball into the box with the matching habitat without tipping it over. Award one point to each team that gets its ball into the matching box. Continue playing as time allows, and declare the team with more points the winner. **As an alternative,** write the animal names on index cards and have students place each card in the matching box.

Elizabeth Searls Almy, Greensboro, NC

Caribou.
tundra

Sun, light

Around Town

Build understanding of shadows with this fun center. Put out building blocks or LEGO blocks. Invite students to make buildings for a miniature community that includes their school, homes, and stores. After the community is built, direct individual students to take turns using a flashlight to simulate the sun rising in the east and setting in the west, while the rest of the class records observations about the shadows cast across their community.

Elizabeth Searls Almy

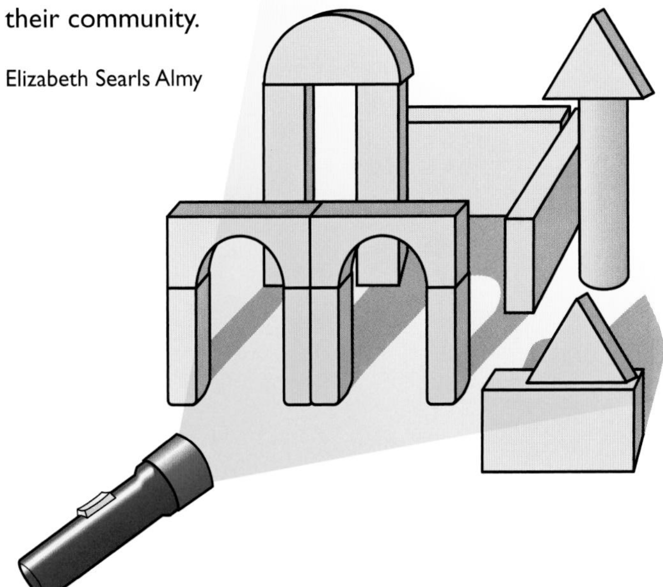

Food chains

Linked In

This activity for two challenges students' memories and their knowledge of how living things interact. First, the student pair cuts out the cards from a copy of page 153, shuffles the cards, and places them facedown on the workspace. Each child takes a turn flipping over two cards. If the cards show animals in the same food chain or a matching animal and habitat, she takes the cards. If not, she turns the cards back over. The activity ends when one child completes a food chain of six cards.

Elizabeth Searls Almy

Grassland
grass
grasshopper
mouse
snake
hawk

Direction Signs

Use with “Go With the Flow” on page 144.

TEC43056 **Northeast** Northeasterly	TEC43056 **Northwest** Northwesterly	TEC43056 **Southeast** Southeasterly	TEC43056 **Southwest** Southwesterly
TEC43056 **North** Northerly	TEC43056 **South** Southerly	TEC43056 **East** Easterly	TEC43056 **West** Westerly

Moon Phases Cards

Use with "Calendar Connection" on page 146.

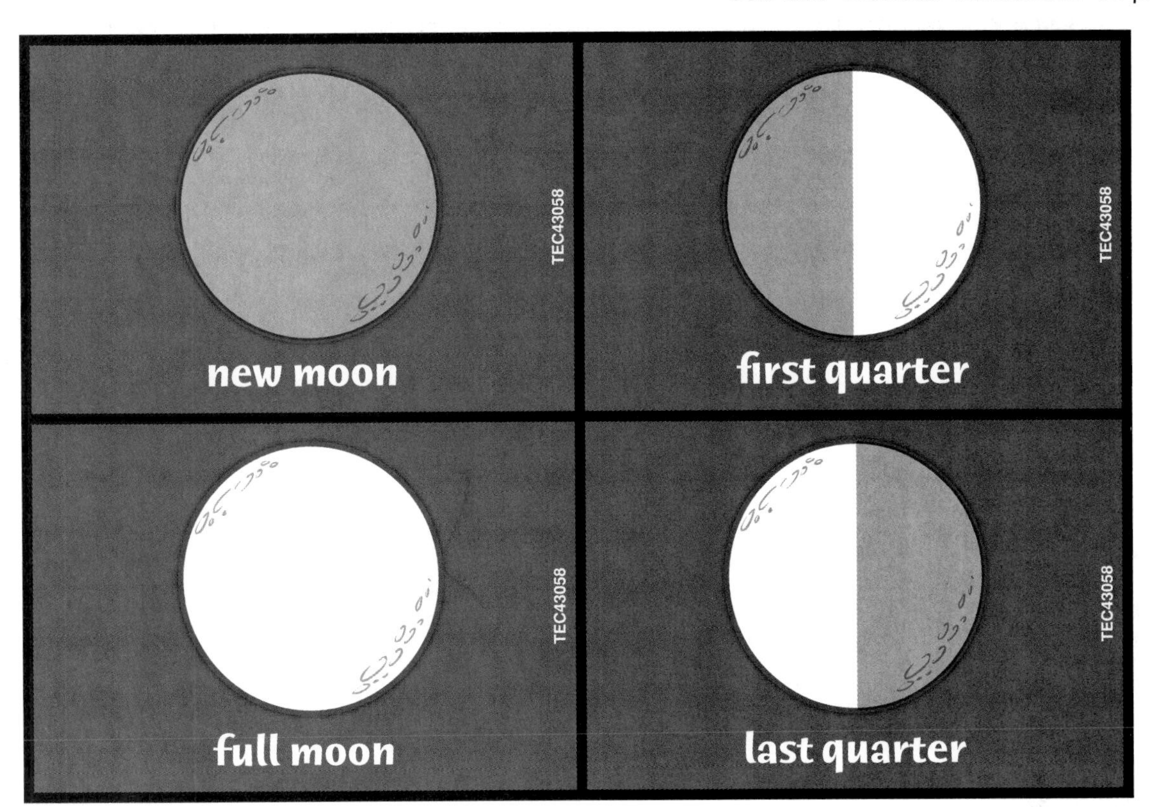
new moon
TEC43058
first quarter
TEC43058
full moon
TEC43058
last quarter
TEC43058

Thermometer Pattern

Use with "Fun for All!" on page 146.

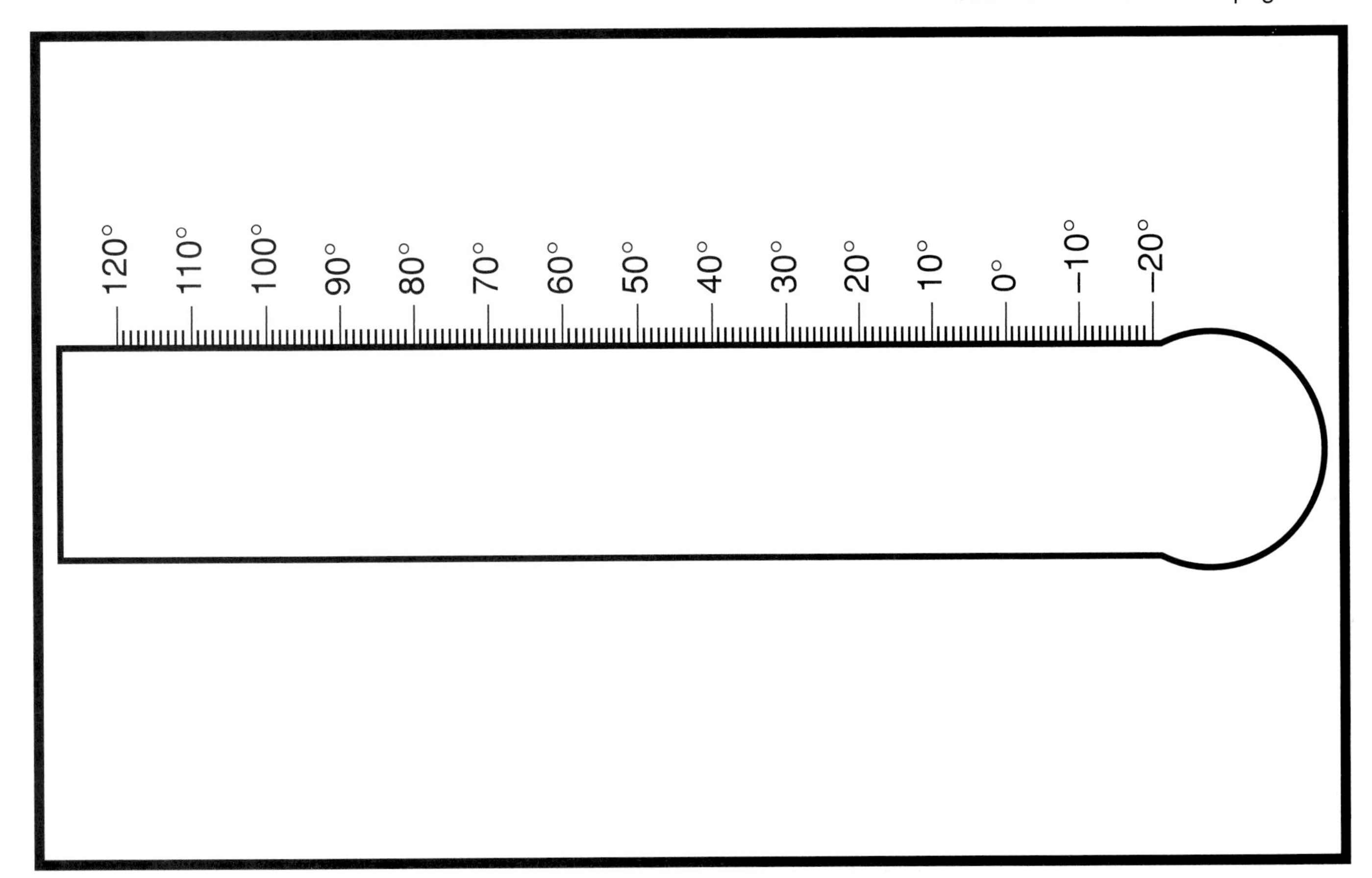
120°
110°
100°
90°
80°
70°
60°
50°
40°
30°
20°
10°
0°
–10°
–20°

Get Ready!

Name____________________________

Day ____________________________

Plan your weather report. Have an adult help you. Use the news or the Internet to gather your facts.

Monday

Greet your audience. Tell your name and the date of the weather forecast.	
Describe the temperatures.	Describe the wind.
Describe the conditions. (Will it be sunny? Rainy? Cloudy? Partly cloudy? Snowy? It might be more than one!)	
Include any other interesting weather-related facts (change in season, records) or end with your own opinion of today's expected weather.	

Note to the teacher: Use with "Morning Meeting Meteorologist" on page 148.

Food Chain Cards

Use with "Linked In" on page 149.

hawk TEC43061	eagle TEC43061	shark TEC43061
snake TEC43061	raccoon TEC43061	seal TEC43061
mouse TEC43061	fish TEC43061	big fish TEC43061
grasshopper TEC43061	water beetle TEC43061	small fish TEC43061
grass TEC43061	algae TEC43061	plankton TEC43061
Grassland TEC43061	Pond TEC43061	Ocean TEC43061

Name ____________________ Date ____________

Reading a diagram

On the Hunt

Use the diagram to answer the questions.

1. What color eyes does a great horned owl have? ____________ Draw a star next to the part that tells you so. Then color the eyes.

2. What's another word for feathers that cover a bird's body? ______________ Color this area brown but leave the white throat patch uncolored.

3. Which body part helps the owl hear? ____________
   How? ______________________________
   ____

4. What are **ear tufts** made of? ____________
   What is their purpose? ______________________
   ____

5. What's another word for **talons**? ____________
   How do they help the owl? ____________
   ____

6. For what does the owl use its **hooked beak**? ________
   ____

Bonus: Name something in your classroom that is about as long as the great horned owl's wingspan.

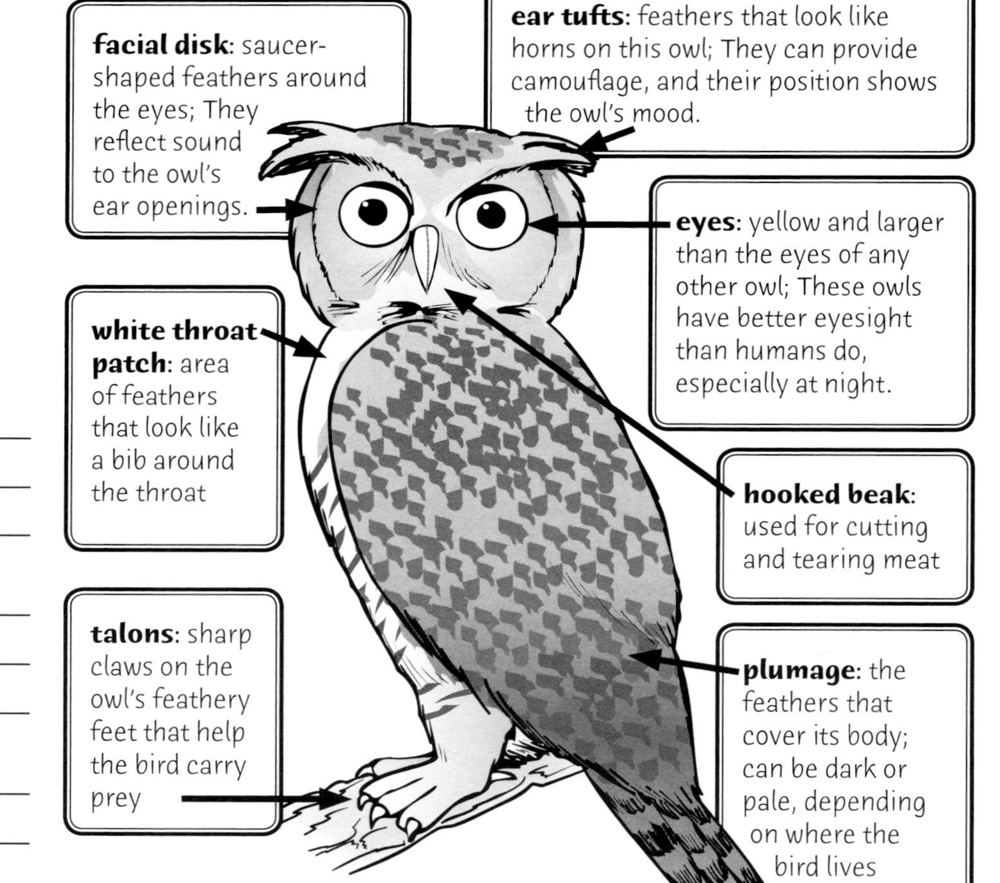
facial disk: saucer-shaped feathers around the eyes; They reflect sound to the owl's ear openings.
ear tufts: feathers that look like horns on this owl; They can provide camouflage, and their position shows the owl's mood.
eyes: yellow and larger than the eyes of any other owl; These owls have better eyesight than humans do, especially at night.
white throat patch: area of feathers that look like a bib around the throat
hooked beak: used for cutting and tearing meat
talons: sharp claws on the owl's feathery feet that help the bird carry prey
plumage: the feathers that cover its body; can be dark or pale, depending on where the bird lives

The Great Horned Owl

The most common owl in North America, this bird can grow up to 25 inches tall. Its **wingspan**, or length from the tip of one outstretched wing to the tip of the other, can be as wide as 57 inches.

Social Studies

Exploring Social Studies

A Good Citizen...

Hand in Hand

Citizenship

To highlight the qualities of good citizens, draw a student-size outline on a piece of bulletin board paper. Post the outline near your class rules. Direct each student to write on a sticky note what being a good citizen means to him. Provide time for each child to share his meaning aloud; then have him post the sticky note on the outline. Keep the outline displayed as a reminder that good citizens and good classmates go hand in hand. **As an alternative**, choose a student as citizen of the week. Have each child explain on a sticky note what makes the student a good citizen. At the end of the week, place each sticky note on an index card and bind the index cards into a book for the child to keep.

Tara Durning, Mother Teresa Academy, Clifton Park, NY

Practical "Place-map"

World geography

This dual-purpose activity provides practice with map skills and keeps desktops clean! To begin, give each child a pattern page of continents. Have her color the continents and cut them out. Next, direct the child to glue the cutouts to a large sheet of blue construction paper and label it as shown. If desired, have each student place a small sticker on the map to represent her location. Laminate the maps and encourage students to use them during snacktime or send them home to use during meals.

Cindy Enher, Bet Yaakov Ateret Torah, Brooklyn, NY

Me Box

Personal histories

Get to know your students with this special project. To start, a child covers a shoebox and its lid with colorful paper. Next, he labels each face of the box with a different favorite and then adds matching pictures. After that, the child writes his first name on the lid; then he glues to the lid a self-portrait or a copy of a personal photo. The student flips the lid over and writes his full name and where he was born. He creates a personal timeline that starts with his birthday and names important life events up to this year. Set aside time for each child to share his box.

Connor
My favorite color is yellow!
My favorite food is pizza!

Lori Knight, Adamston Elementary, Clarksburg, WV

Exploring Social Studies

Vote Here!

Civic responsibility

Turn two discarded boxes into the perfect polling place for your classroom! To make a voting booth, cut the flaps off a large box. Cover the box with blue paper or a blue paper tablecloth. Add decorations such as white paper stars. To make a ballot box, simply place an empty tissue box inside the large box. Whenever your students have a topic to vote on, place a class supply of ballots next to the ballot box and send individual students over to vote.

Tara Durning, Mother Teresa Academy, Clifton Park, NY

A Mini Model

Native Americans, shelter

Shape students' understanding of the Plains Indians' former dwelling, the tepee. First, explain to students that this portable tent was made of buffalo skin that was stretched over poles. Next, guide each child to glue together two overlapping craft sticks (poles) as shown. The student uses markers to add decorative details to half of an eight-inch tortilla (buffalo skin). Then he overlaps the ends to make a cone shape and secures the shape with liquid glue. When the glue is dry, the child stands the poles and places the buffalo skin over them, as shown.

adapted from an idea by Pat Biancardi, Homan Elementary, Schererville, IN

Branching Out

Family histories

Plant seeds of understanding with this personalized graphic organizer. To start, discuss with students the meaning of family and acknowledge that every family is different. Next, send home small apple patterns with each child. Have her write on the apples the names of family members and how they're related to her, enlisting her parents' help as needed. To create the graphic organizer, the child draws a tree on a large sheet of paper, labels the trunk as shown, and colors it. Then she cuts out her apple patterns and arranges them by generation on her paper. She glues the apples to her paper and then draws leaves and branches to complete her tree.

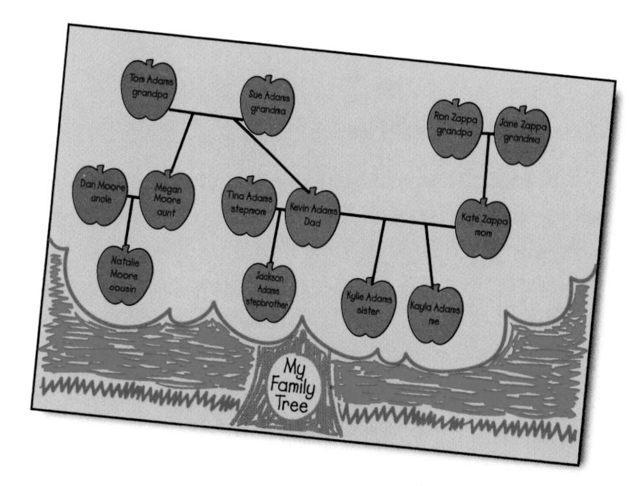
Tom Adams grandpa
Sue Adams grandma
Ron Zappa grandpa
Jane Zappa grandma
Dan Moore uncle
Megan Moore aunt
Tina Adams stepmom
Kevin Adams Dad
Kate Zappa mom
Natalie Moore cousin
Jackson Adams stepbrother
Kylie Adams sister
Kayla Adams me
My Family Tree

Monica Sabec, Dunrankin Drive Public School, Mississauga, Ontario, Canada

Exploring Social Studies

Mock Meeting
Local government

To start this demonstration, have students brainstorm the pros and cons of a local issue, such as building a new skate park or holding a citywide celebration. Then choose five students to serve as a city council and one student to serve as mayor. Provide time for each child to briefly share his views on the issue and then have the council take a vote. Choose a different group of six students to repeat the process. Discuss similarities and differences between the two councils and the factors that may have led to each decision. As time allows, organize different scenarios, such as an all-girl or all-boy council, letting only the mayor vote, or having a council member abstain from voting.

Cynthia Wicks, Eastwood Elementary, Roseburg, OR

Why do leaders need to communicate well?
Why is honesty important for a leader?
Was Dr. King confident? Give examples to explain why or why not.
How important is compassion to being a good leader? Give examples.
How did Alexander the Great persevere?

That Special Something
Traits of leaders

Share biographies of strong leaders, such as Martin Luther King Jr., Harriet Tubman, or Alexander the Great. Then have students generate a class list describing the traits of a good leader. Use the traits to write a different question on each of five sheets of chart paper and post the charts around the room. Guide small groups of youngsters to rotate from chart to chart, reading and responding to each question. When students have returned to their starting charts, call on one group at a time to share the answers aloud; then use the responses to further discuss the qualities of great leaders.

Stephanie Brachtenbach, Harmony Elementary, Overland Park, KS

A Well-Known Destination
Community features

Students show what they know about their own community by making visitors' guides. Instruct each child to list on separate sheets of paper information about his community, such as things to do, places of historic significance, local celebrations, and a restaurant guide. Direct him to add colorful details to each page and include related drawings and captions for each list. Then have him staple the pages together and place his visitors' guide in your class library. **As an alternative**, have students use the format to describe other communities studied.

Dawn Gomez, Sunset Hills Elementary, Tarpon Springs, FL

Tarpon Springs
Visitors' Guide

Exploring Social Studies

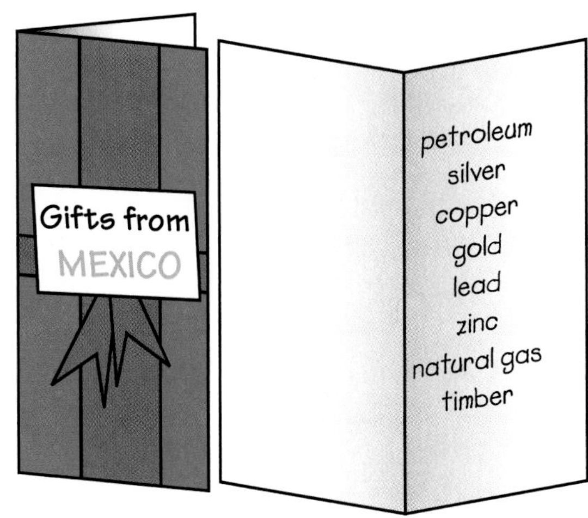
Gifts from
MEXICO
petroleum
silver
copper
gold
lead
zinc
natural gas
timber

For each community you study, fold a large sheet of construction paper in half. Decorate the outside to look like a wrapped gift box and write a title similar to the one shown. Explain to students that natural resources are like precious gifts that each community can share with its citizens and with citizens of other communities. Then open the paper and direct students to name the community's natural resources as you write them on the paper. If desired, list next to each resource examples of products that could be made from it. Post each list to compare two or more communities' natural resources.

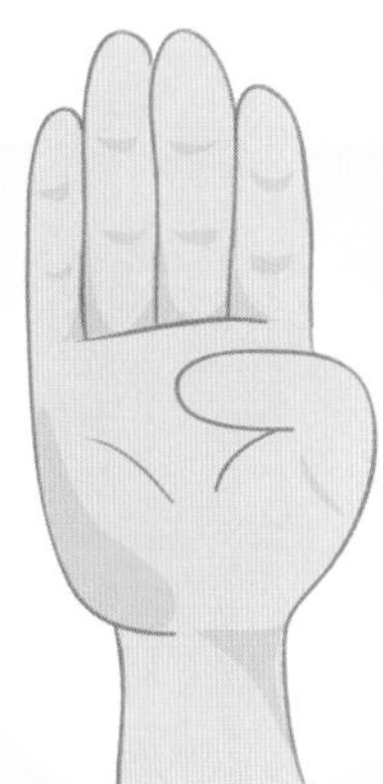

B for Barter

Economics

Take students on a trip back in time with a picture book. Before reading aloud *A New Coat for Anna*, by Harriet Ziefert, explain that bartering is a way of getting goods by trade instead of using money. Instruct each student to signal examples of bartering in the story by signing the letter *b* in American Sign Language. Wrap up the activity by providing time for each child to share with a partner his definition of *bartering* along with one example from the story.

Chelsea Forbus LaVere, Chesapeake, VA

tip → Also use the story to compare and contrast how people lived after World War II to how people live now.

Location Round-Up

Maps and globes

Students discover there's a world of difference between maps and globes with this hands-on activity. To begin, give each child a copy of a labeled world map. Direct him to color two countries he thinks are on opposite sides of the globe. Next, have him draw a line to signal the shortest distance between the two countries. Invite the child to check his prediction on a globe. Use students' results to lead a discussion about maps and globes and how it can be difficult to visualize distances on a map compared to a globe, especially when the shortest distance may involve crossing the poles.

Stephanie Brachtenbach, Harmony Elementary, Olathe, KS

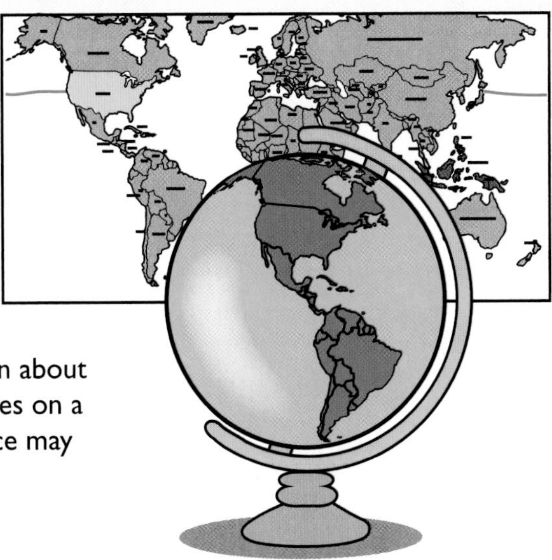

Exploring Social Studies

Past and Present
Changes over time

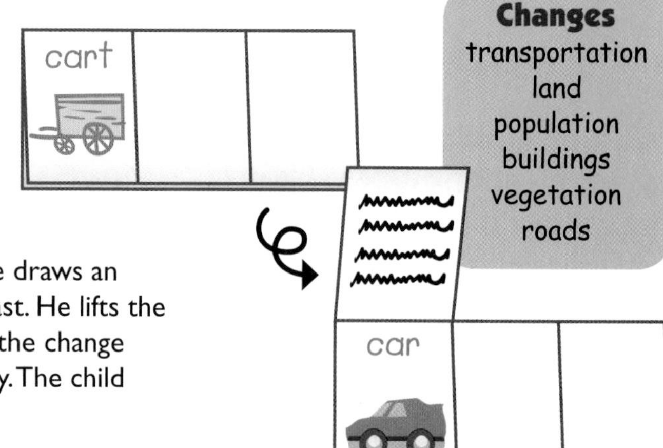

cart
car
Changes
transportation
land
population
buildings
vegetation
roads

To begin, make a list of changes that have occurred in your community, such as the one shown. Discuss the items and changes with students. Next, have each student fold a sheet of paper in half lengthwise and then cut the top layer into three equal sections. On the first front flap, he draws an example of what one item from the list looked like in the past. He lifts the flap and writes on the underside a brief explanation of why the change occurred. Then he draws a picture of what it looks like today. The child repeats with different examples on the other two flaps.

Cynthia Wicks, Eastwood Elementary, Roseburg, OR

April 16, 2012
date

Pay to the order of scarcity
word

The meaning of this word is wants are greater than resources can provide

An example of this word in the real world is There was a scarcity of hula hoops in PE class. Not everyone was able to have one, and many students had to wait while others used them.

Cara
signature

Check This Out!
Economic vocabulary

This simple activity pays dividends to you and your students! Post a list of economic terms being studied. Make a supply of check cutouts (pattern below) and place them near the list. When a student sees an example of one of the words, direct her to complete a check and post it near the list. Review each check and, if desired, invite each student who posted one to cash it in for a small prize.

Jennifer Winkler, Georgetown, TX

Check Pattern
Use with "Check This Out!" above.

____
date

Pay to the order of ______________________________
word

The meaning of this word is ______________________________

____

An example of this word in the real world is ____________________

____

____
signature

Exploring Social Studies

Time-Saving Treats

Specialization and division of labor

Students' hard work and planning result in a tasty treat the whole class will enjoy. To start, post a list of materials such as those shown and provide each small group with a copy of page 162. Challenge each group to plan how to assemble a packaged snack for each child in the quickest manner possible. Assign each group one day the following week to assemble its snacks, and use a timer to determine the amount of time each group takes to complete its plan. Keep track of each group's time and, at the end of week, discuss which method was the quickest and most efficient.

Stephanie Brachtenbach, Harmony Elementary, Overland Park, KS

- bite-size snack foods such as small cookies, cereal, crackers, or raisins
- foil or plastic wrap
- resealable plastic bags
- plastic gloves

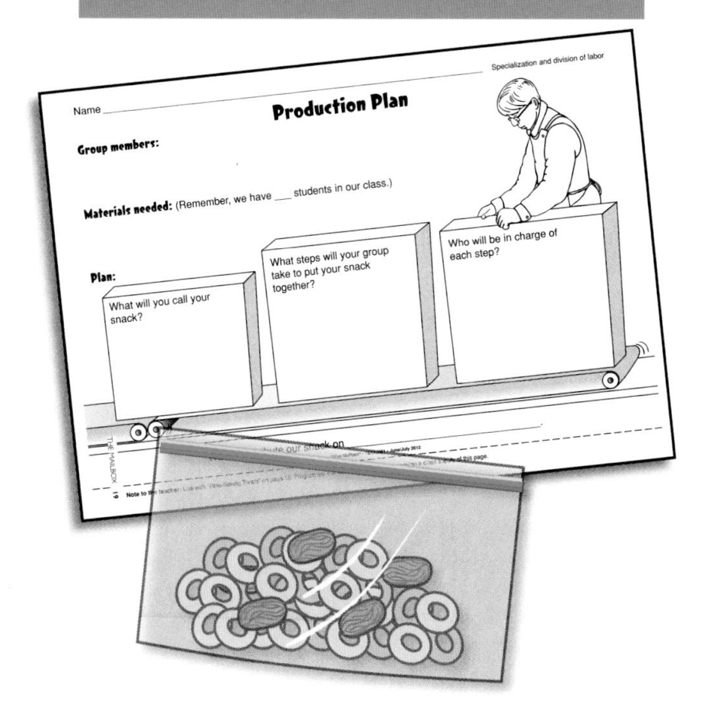

Specialization and division of labor

Name

Production Plan

Group members:

Materials needed: (Remember, we have ___ students in our class.)

Plan:

What will you call your snack?

What steps will your group take to put your snack together?

Who will be in charge of each step?

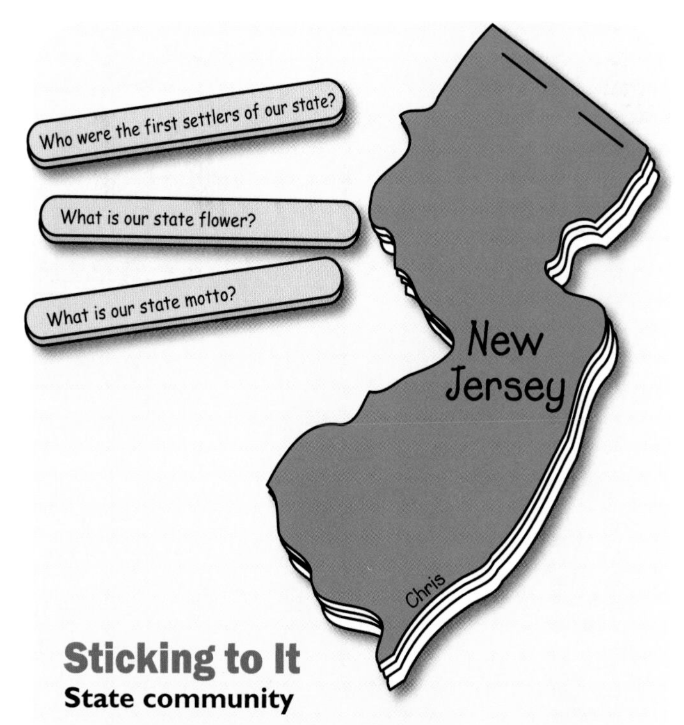
Who were the first settlers of our state?
What is our state flower?
What is our state motto?
New Jersey
Chris

Sticking to It

State community

Perfect for the end of the year, this activity motivates students to research and record state-specific facts. First, program questions like the ones shown on a supply of crafts sticks and place the sticks in a jar. Next, create several tagboard templates of your state outline. Have each child trace a template onto lined paper to make a booklet page for each question in the jar; then have him cut out the pages. Also have the child trace the template onto construction paper, cut out the tracing (cover), and label the cover with the name of the state. Each day, choose a question and provide time for students to research the answer. Instruct each child to write his response in a complete sentence on a booklet page. When all the questions have been answered, help students staple their booklet pages together. If desired, reward students for their efforts with an ice-pop party.

Kathryn Davenport, Partin Elementary, Oviedo, FL, and Patricia Swiatek, Cedar Hill Elementary, Towaco, NJ

Name________________________

Production Plan

Group members:

Materials needed: (Remember, we have ___ students in our class.)

Plan:

What will you call your snack?

What steps will your group take to put your snack together?

Who will be in charge of each step?

We will distribute our snack on ________________________.

Note to the teacher: Use with "Time-Saving Treats" on page 161. Program the number of students before copying a class supply of this page.

Name ______________________ Date ______________________

Historical figure: Christopher Columbus

Ready to Explore?

Use reference materials to find the answers.

1. When and where was Columbus born?

2. What plan did Columbus have in the 1480s?

3. Which country gave money to Columbus to pay for his planned trip?

4. What were the names of his three ships?

5. About how many men were part of his crew?

6. In what year did he start his trip?

7. Which ocean did he cross after he left Spain?

8. When did he first see land?

9. What name is used today for the place Columbus landed?

10. In what month is Columbus Day?

Check the references you used.

☐ atlas ☐ encyclopedia

☐ book ☐ Internet

Bonus: What is the date of Columbus Day this year?

How to use For a research center, whole-class lesson, or computer lab activity, copy a class supply of this page. Give student pairs access to reference materials such as biographies, atlases, and online encyclopedias to answer the questions.

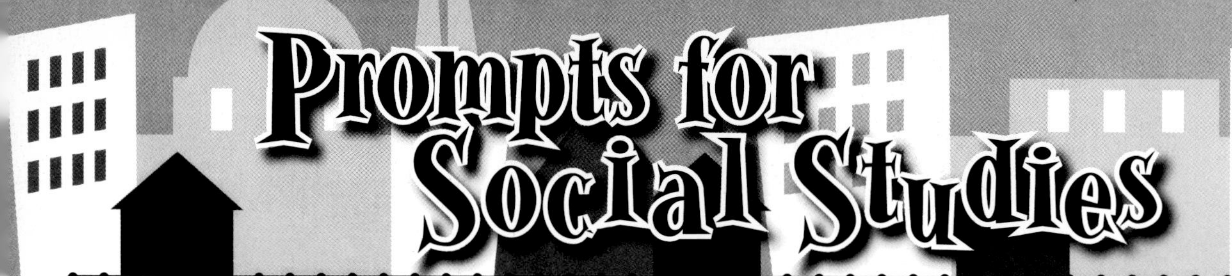

Prompts for Social Studies

Rules and Laws

What is the most important rule to have in your classroom? Explain.

What is the most important law to have in your community? Explain.

Families

Write a meaning for *family*. Then tell how you can be a responsible member of your own family.

Maps and Globes

If you wanted to find the route from your school to your house, would you use a map or a globe?
Why is one a better choice than the other?

Roles of Leaders

Name an activity you do that requires a leader.
What does the leader do to make sure the activity runs smoothly?

Technology

List two ways technology is used in your community. Tell what your community would be like without technology.

How to use: Have each child staple a copy of this page in his writing journal. Or cut copies in sections and distribute only one prompt at a time to students.

Prompts for Social Studies

Geography

What are the benefits of living near mountains? What are the challenges?

Holidays and Cultural Celebrations

Why do people celebrate holidays and special occasions? Give two or three reasons and include examples.

Communities

If it were up to you, would you live in a rural community, a suburban community, or an urban community? Explain.

Time and Change

What changes have you seen in your community lately? What do you think caused these changes? How do you think these changes will affect your community in the future?

GRAND OPENING!

Economic Resources

Economic resources are things of value that allow a business or community to provide goods and services. How do adults at your school serve as economic resources?

How to use: Have each child staple a copy of this page in his writing journal. Or cut copies in sections and distribute only one prompt at a time to students.

Prompts for Social Studies

Economy

Income is money earned from providing goods or services. Why do you think some jobs have higher incomes than other jobs?

20
UNITED STATES
THE
OF AMERICA
20
E
TWENTY
20
TWENTY DOLLARS
20

Community Resources

Most communities get revenue (money) through taxes. What do you think your community should spend its revenue on?

Interdependence of People

List some jobs in your school. How do the people who do these jobs depend on each other? What happens if someone does not do his or her job?

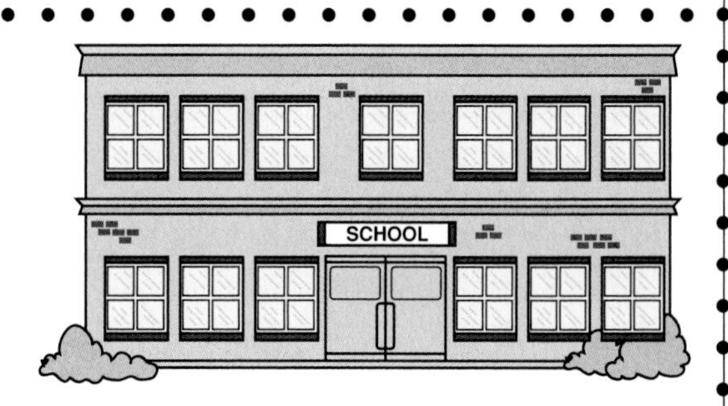
SCHOOL

Community Leaders

Can a community have too many leaders? Why or why not?

Historic Figures

Many people we think of as important historic figures overcame problems during their lives. Do you think we would consider these people to be important if they did not have those experiences? Explain.

Jackie
Robinson

How to Use Have each child staple a copy of this page in her writing journal. Or cut copies into sections and distribute only one prompt at a time to students.

Learning Centers

Learning Centers

Moveable Parts

Practicing spelling words

Materials:
craft sticks programmed with letters or letter pairs
spelling list

A student silently reads the first word on the list to himself. He gathers the letter sticks that make the word, arranges them on his desktop, and then says each letter to himself. He returns the sticks to the group and repeats the steps for each remaining word on the list. **As an alternative**, trace over each letter with puffy paint and allow drying time before setting out the sticks. A student traces the letters with his finger after forming each word.

Karen Slattery
Dunrankin Drive Public School
Mississauga, Ontario, Canada

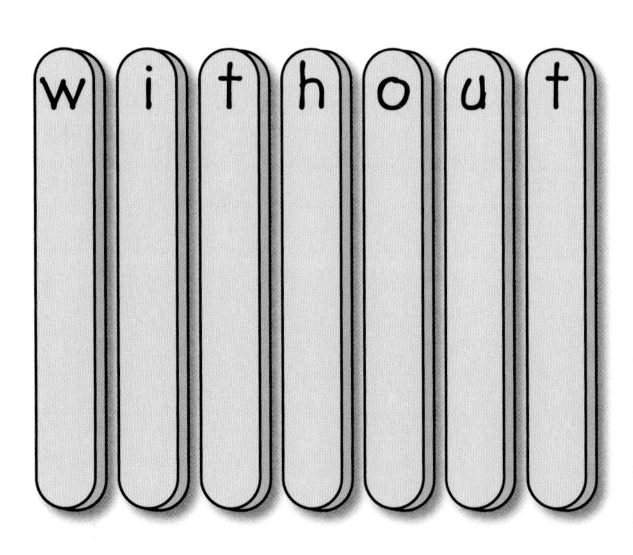
w
i
t
h
o
u
t

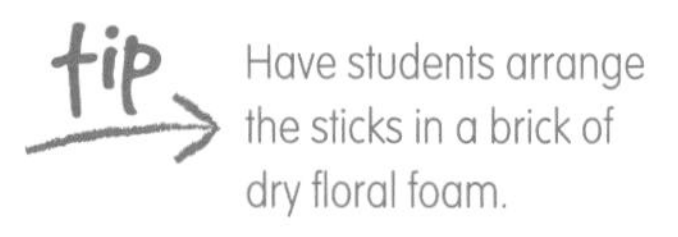
tip
Have students arrange the sticks in a brick of dry floral foam.

Past and Present

Identifying and using antonyms

Materials:
highlighter
paper

A child draws a T chart on her paper and labels each column as shown. In the left column, she writes a phrase that describes summer. In the right column, she writes a related phrase that uses an antonym for a word in the left column. The child highlights the antonym pair and repeats the steps as time allows.

Carolyn Burant
St. John Vianney School
Brookfield, WI

Cassie

Summer	School
stay up late	wake up early
warm weather	cool weather
eat outside	eat inside
empty backpack	full backpack
short pants	long pants

Bull's-Eye!
Addition

Materials:
magnetic dartboard and darts
masking tape
paper

Hang the dartboard on a wall. At a reasonable distance away, mark a line on the floor with tape. A student stands behind the throwing line and tosses each dart at the board. On his paper, he records the numbers the darts land on and then finds the sum. The child repeats the steps as time allows.

Piper Porter
Mountain Way Elementary
Granite Falls, WA

20
1
13
6
10
15
2
17
3
19
7
16
8
11
9
5

An Indoor Grill
Modeling patterns

Materials:
cutout copies of the food cards on page 180
flat-tipped wooden skewer or dowel
paper

A child chooses two or more types of food cutouts. She places the cutouts atop the skewer to form a repeating pattern. Then she draws the pattern on her paper and labels it. **As an alternative**, write a variety of patterns on index cards. Place the cards at the center. A child selects a card and writes the pattern on her paper. She uses the materials to model the pattern and then draws the pattern on her paper.

Tara Durning
Mother Teresa Academy
Clifton Park, NY

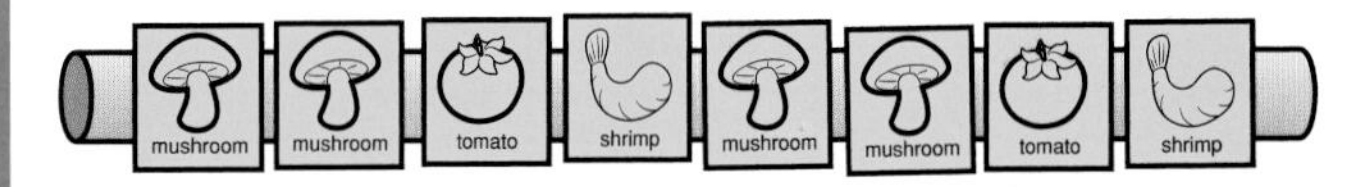
mushroom
mushroom
tomato
shrimp
mushroom
mushroom
tomato
shrimp

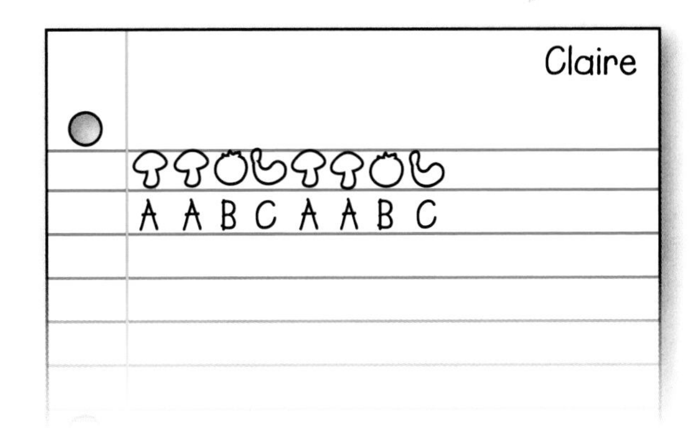
Claire
A A B C A A B C

Learning Centers

Race to Write!
Classifying words

Materials:
student copies of page 181
timer

In advance, make a copy of the recording sheet from page 181 and label the top row with a time period and letters. Label the left column with categories like the ones shown. Then make student copies of the labeled sheet. A child sets the timer for the designated length of time. Then he tries to list a different word in each section before time expires. **To add more variety to the center**, put cards labeled with letters in one container and cards labeled with categories in another. The student pulls five letter cards and four category cards from each container and uses them to label his recording sheet.

Dee Dee Cooper, Monterey Elementary, Monterey, LA

Name Brandon Date 11/2/11

Category Challenge

Classifying words

Give me 20!

Time 3 min.	B	S	G	R	A
animal	bear	snake	goat	rat	ape
food	banana	soup	gravy	ravioli	apple
girl's name	Beth	Sarah	Gloria	Risha	Allison
city	Boston	San Diego	Galveston	Rockville	Atlanta

Real or Imposter?
Base words, suffixes

Materials:
2 bags, each labeled as shown
copy of the cards on page 182
dictionary
paper

To prepare, cut apart the cards and place them in the corresponding bags. To complete the activity, a student labels her paper as shown. She takes a card from each bag and places the cards together. If the word and suffix combine to make a real word, she writes it in the "Real" column and sets the cards aside. If the word and suffix don't create a real word, she writes the combination in the "Imposter" column and sets the cards aside. She continues until all the cards are used. Then she checks her answers in the dictionary.

Beth Pallotta, Eden Christian Academy, Pittsburgh, PA

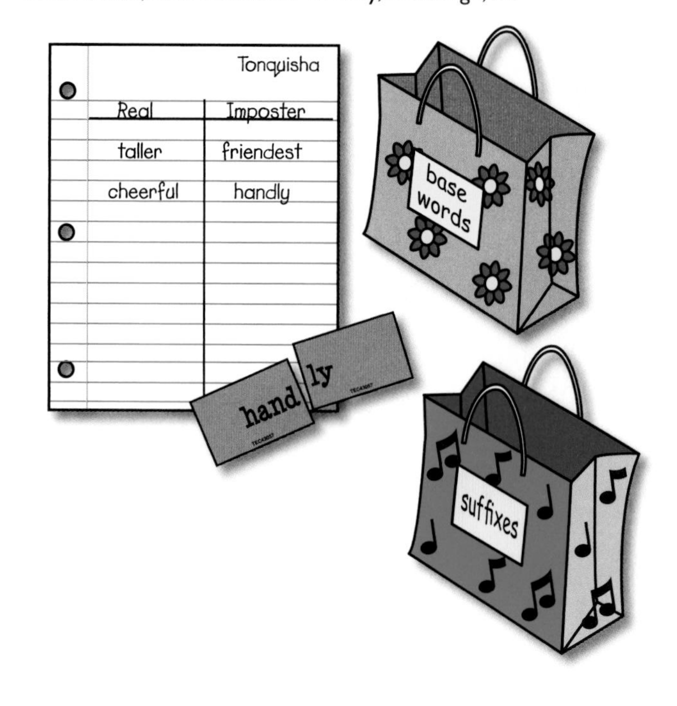
Tonquisha
Real
Imposter
taller
friendest
cheerful
handly
hand
ly
base words
suffixes

A Handful of Ways to Make...

Modeling money amounts

Materials:
manipulative coins
paper

To prepare, draw a hand outline on a sheet of paper and number each digit as shown. Write a desired money amount on the palm and place the handprint at a center with the other materials. A student numbers his paper and labels it with the money amount. On each digit, he lays coins that equal the amount. When he's confident with his groupings, he removes the manipulatives from one digit at a time and draws the matching coins and their values on his paper. **To make the center more challenging**, limit the number of coins students can use to make the target amount.

Beth Pallotta, Eden Christian Academy, Pittsburgh, PA

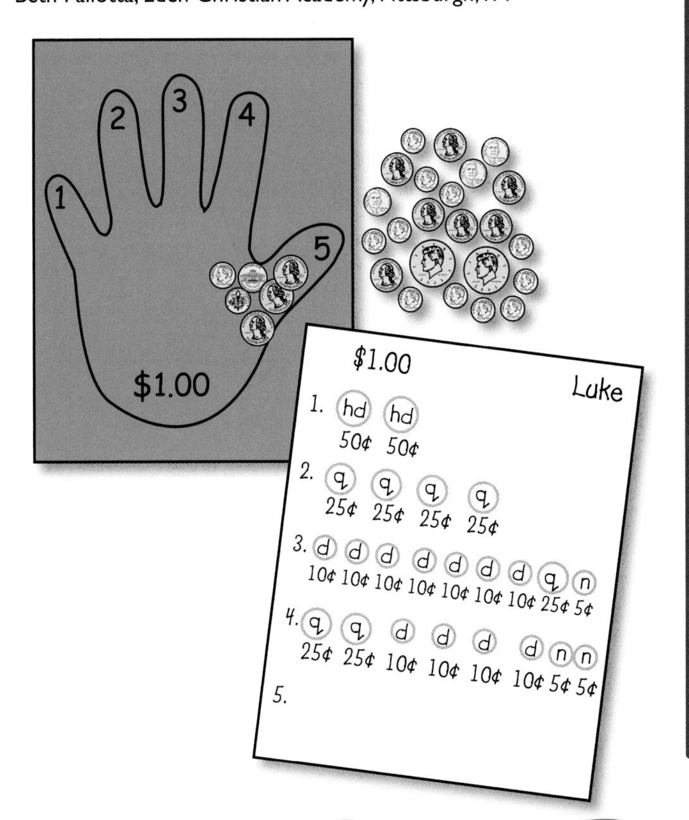
1
2
3
4
5
$1.00
$1.00
Luke
1. hd hd
50¢ 50¢
2. q q q q
25¢ 25¢ 25¢ 25¢
3. d d d d d d d q n
10¢ 10¢ 10¢ 10¢ 10¢ 10¢ 10¢ 25¢ 5¢
4. q q d d d d n n
25¢ 25¢ 10¢ 10¢ 10¢ 10¢ 5¢ 5¢
5.

Start With Today

Extending number patterns

Materials:
cards labeled with number patterns
paper

A child writes on her paper the number of days she's been in school or the number for the day's date (For example, for October third, she would write "3."). She takes a card and writes a matching number pattern that uses five more numbers. She copies the card below the pattern and then she chooses another card. The child continues in this manner as time allows, starting each pattern with the same number.

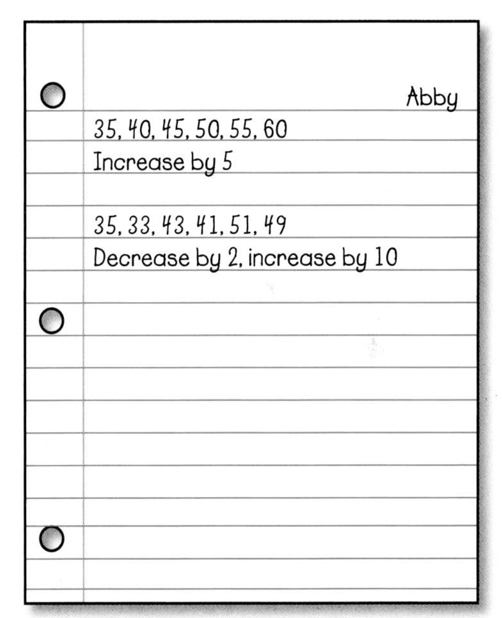
Abby
35, 40, 45, 50, 55, 60
Increase by 5
35, 33, 43, 41, 51, 49
Decrease by 2, increase by 10

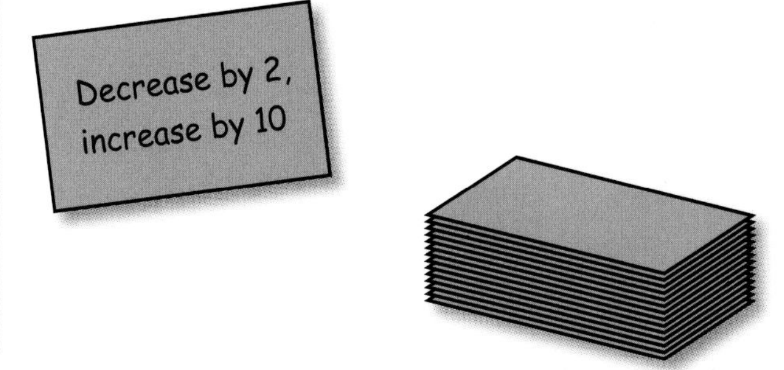
Decrease by 2,
increase by 10

Learning Centers

Trim the Tree
Main idea and details

Materials:
student copies of the ornament patterns on page 183
green paper
scissors
glue

After reading, a child cuts a tree shape from green paper and then labels it with the main idea. Next, he writes on each ornament a different detail that supports the main idea. The student cuts out the patterns and glues each cutout to the tree. **As an alternative**, use die-cut shapes and change them out each season. Try circles (flower's stigma) and petals for spring, pumpkins and seeds for fall, and snowmen with snowflakes as another option for winter.

Nicole Terrell, T. A. Hendricks Elementary, Shelbyville, IN

Two in One
Guide words

Materials:
dictionary
spelling list
paper

A student makes a T chart and labels each column as shown. She finds the first spelling word in the dictionary. Then she writes the word and its guide words on her paper. She continues with each of the remaining words.

Brooke Beverly, Dudley Elementary, Dudley, MA

Wandalynn

Word	Guide Words
quickly	queen post–quiet
beautiful	bearish–beautifulness
monthly	monteith–moonquake

Fishing for Sums

Two-digit addition with and without regrouping

Materials:
cutout copy of the fish cards on page 183
plastic container (tank)
paper

In advance, place the fish cards in a tank. A child labels his paper as shown and takes two fish cards from the tank. He stacks one card above the other and then mentally adds the ones column. If the sum is a two-digit number, he writes and solves the entire problem in the "Regroup" column. If the sum is a one-digit number, he writes and solves the entire problem in the "Do Not Regroup" column. The student returns the cards to the tank and repeats the process as time allows.

Beth Pallotta, Eden Christian Academy, Pittsburgh, PA

23
36
57
40

Colin

Regroup	Do Not Regroup
	23 + 36 59

Sweet Sets

Congruent shapes

Materials:
cutout copy of the candy cards on page 184

To prepare for this partner activity, place the candy cards at a center. The students shuffle the cards and place them facedown in rows. Each child takes a turn flipping over two cards. If the cards are congruent, she sets them aside. If not, she flips the cards over and the other student takes a turn. Students continue until all pairs are matched. **To extend the activity**, each child writes on a sheet of paper a definition for *congruent* and then draws two pieces of candy to illustrate the definition.

Carolyn Burant, St. John Vianney School, Brookfield, WI

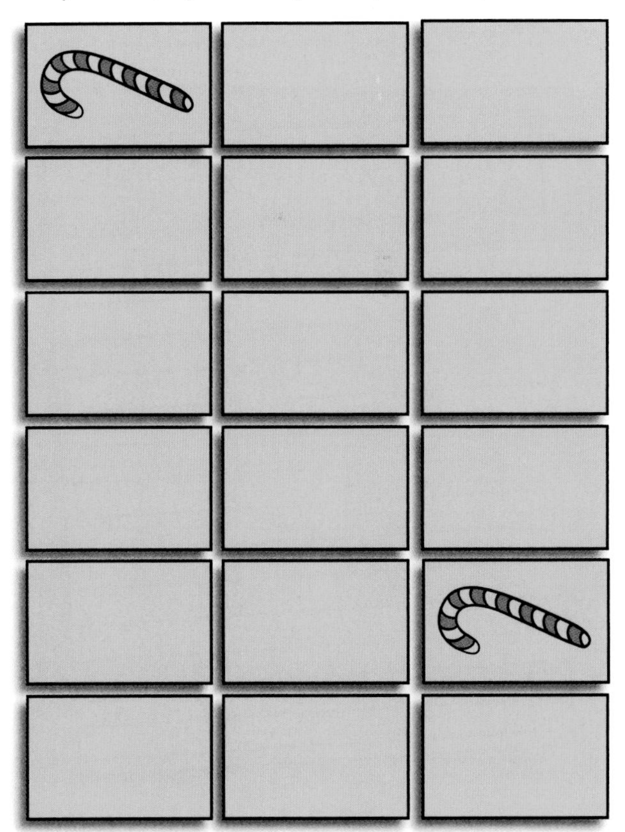

Learning Centers

Diagnose the Problem
Editing sentences

Materials:
copy of the bandage cards on page 185
an empty bandage box
paper

In advance, cut apart the cards and place them in the bandage box. To start the activity, a student removes the cards from the box. He selects a boldfaced sentence and identifies the error. Then he finds the card with the matching editing rule and places it on top of the sentence. The student continues to match each sentence with the correct editing rule. After all the cards are matched, he writes on his paper the letters of each pair and then writes the sentence correctly.

D.
Add a question mark at the end of the sentence.
H.
Do you eat oatmeal for breakfast
Chandler
D and H
Do you eat oatmeal for breakfast?

For the Love of Words
Syllabication

Materials:
paper heart with a heart cut out
a collection of news articles and reading passages
paper

A child folds her paper into fourths, unfolds it, and labels each section as shown. She places the heart atop a section of an article or a passage; then she identifies the number of syllables for each word inside the heart. The student writes each word under the appropriate heading on her paper. As time allows, she repeats the steps using a different section on the article or passage. **To vary the activity**, she labels her paper with designated spelling patterns, affixes, or parts of speech and records them instead.

Race Today!
BIG,
SA
JOE'S F
1 syllable
2 syllables
3 syllables
4 syllables
Avery

Split the Difference
Comparing fractions

Materials:
ten 3"-tall cardboard tubes
small rubber ball
masking tape
paper

To set up, use the masking tape to mark a bowling lane on a tabletop. Place the tubes at the end of the lane. To begin, a student gently rolls a ball toward the tubes. He writes two fractions: one to represent the tubes knocked down and one for the tubes still standing. Then the student writes ">," "<," or "=" between the two numbers to compare the fractions. He stands the tubes and repeats the steps as time allows. **As an alternative**, the student writes a subtraction sentence to show the fractional difference between the number of tubes standing and the number of tubes knocked down.

Stephanie Brachtenbach
Harmony Elementary
Overland Park, KS

Saleem
$\frac{2}{10} < \frac{8}{10}$

tip Choose a table placed against a wall to better control where the ball travels.

Kitties in the Corners
Multiplication

Materials:
cutout copy of the cards on page 186

For this partner activity, one student places the START card in the center of the workspace. Then each student selects nine cards and places them face up. To begin, Student 1 matches a corner of a card to a corner on the START card. Then Student 2 matches a corner of one of her cards to a corner of a card placed on the workspace. Anytime a student cannot match a card, her turn ends. If a student wants to place a card that touches more than one corner, all touching problems and products must match before she sets the card in place. The activity ends when all the cards have been correctly matched and all the kitties are positioned around the outside corners.

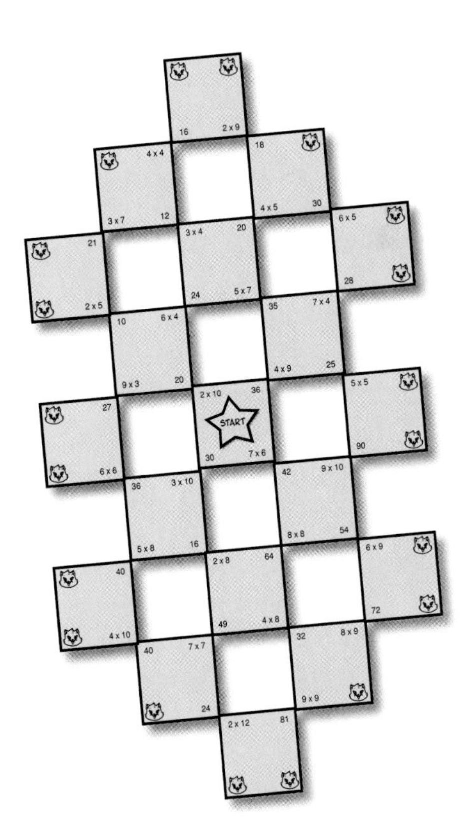

Learning Centers

Growing Entry Words
Using the dictionary

Materials:
5 flowerpot cutouts, patterns on page 187
copy of the entry word strips on page 187, cut apart
paper
glue

Label each flowerpot with a pair of guide words as shown. Put a thin line of glue along the bottom and side edges of each pot, leaving the top free of glue. Then glue each cutout on a sheet of paper (mat), making sure the open edge is at the top. Put out the mat and entry word strips. A student sorts the word strips into the matching flowerpots. If desired, have the student arrange the cards in alphabetical order and then copy each set of words onto a sheet of paper.

Barbara Duran
Rockwall, TX

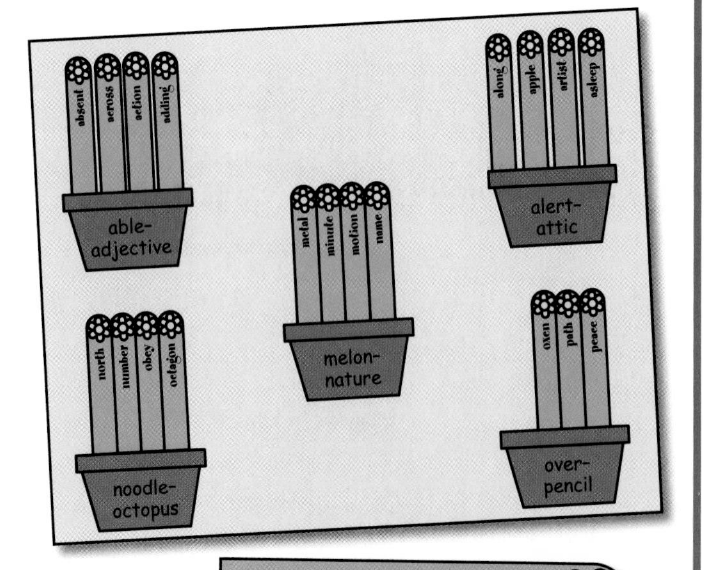
absent
across
action
adding
able-
adjective
along
apple
artist
asleep
alert-
attic
metal
minute
motion
name
melon-
nature
north
number
obey
octagon
noodle-
octopus
oxen
path
peace
over-
pencil
owner

Quick Thinking
Vocabulary, classifying

Materials:
index cards programmed with different categories and letters
timer
paper

A child places the index cards facedown and sets the timer for one minute. He selects a card and writes on his paper a word for each letter that matches the category. When time is up, the child stops writing, draws one tally mark for each letter of each word, and totals his score. If desired, the child prints his initials and his score on the back of the index card. When all students have completed the center, determine who had the highest score for each category.

Michelle Bayless
Croughton, England

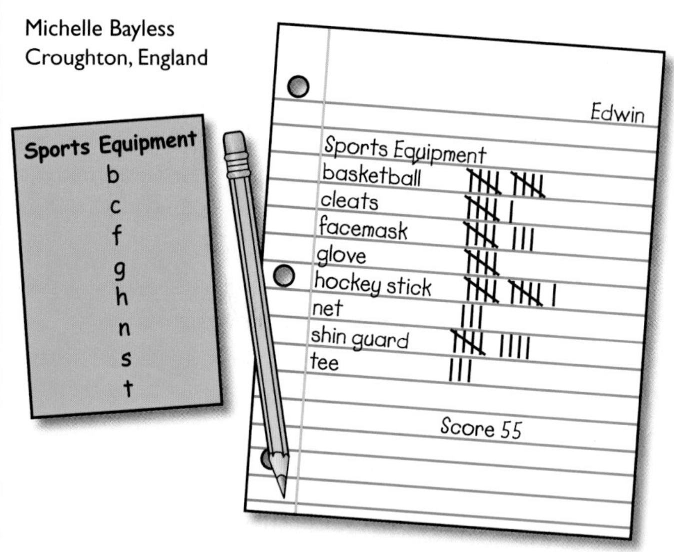
Sports Equipment
b
c
f
g
h
n
s
t
Edwin
Sports Equipment
basketball
cleats
facemask
glove
hockey stick
net
shin guard
tee
Score 55

Possible Categories

Furniture in a House	Animals With Fur
Things Found in a Closet	Winged Creatures
Things With Buttons	Items Found at School
Items in a Grocery Store	Things With Wheels
Plants We Eat	Sports Equipment

Savvy Savings
Adding and subtracting money

Materials:
5 grocery coupons or programmed copies of the coupon patterns on page 188
copy of the grocery receipt recording sheet on page 188
play money
calculator

To prepare, place the coupons in an envelope. Also program a copy of the grocery receipt with the names of the grocery items that match each coupon and a reasonable price for each item. Place student copies of the programmed grocery receipt, play money, the coupon envelope, and the calculator at a center.

A student selects a coupon and finds that grocery item on the receipt. He gathers the money needed to pay for the item. Then he deducts the coupon savings and writes the new price on the grocery receipt. The student continues with the other coupons. At the bottom of the receipt, he writes the total number of items sold. He uses the calculator to find the totals for the original prices and the sale prices; then he determines the difference between the original balance due and the sale price total.

Cheryl Sergi
Greene, NY

COUPON
Save $ 0 . 25
on any one
Bread
COUPON
Save $ 0 . 50
on any one
Super Crunch Cereal
COUPON
Save $ 0 . 75
on any one
Pudding Cups

Shopper: ________

B. Thrifty Mart

☐ Super Crunch Cereal $ 3 . 54
Sale price .... $ __ . __

☐ Pudding Cups $ 2 . 89
Sale price .... $ __ . __

☐ Farm Fresh Bread $ 2 . 15
Sale price .... $ __ . __

☐ Crackers $ 3 . 00
Sale price .... $ __ . __

☐ Cheese $ 3 . 99
Sale price .... $ __ . __

Total Number of Items Sold ____
Original Balance Due $ __ . __
Sale Price Total $ __ . __

Your Total Savings Today! $ __ . __
Thank You for Shopping!

Feeling Full
Capacity

Materials:
3 or 4 empty cardboard cartons of similar shapes but different sizes labeled as shown
2 or 3 lbs. of rice or dry beans in a large bowl
measuring cup
paper

A child creates a chart like the one shown. She estimates the number of cups of rice (or beans) it takes to fill each carton and records the values on the chart, arranging the order of the boxes from least to greatest capacity. Next, she uses a measuring cup to fill each box with rice. The student records the actual number of cups needed to fill the box; then she empties the contents back into the bowl.

Stephanie Brachtenbach
Harmony Elementary
Overland Park, KS

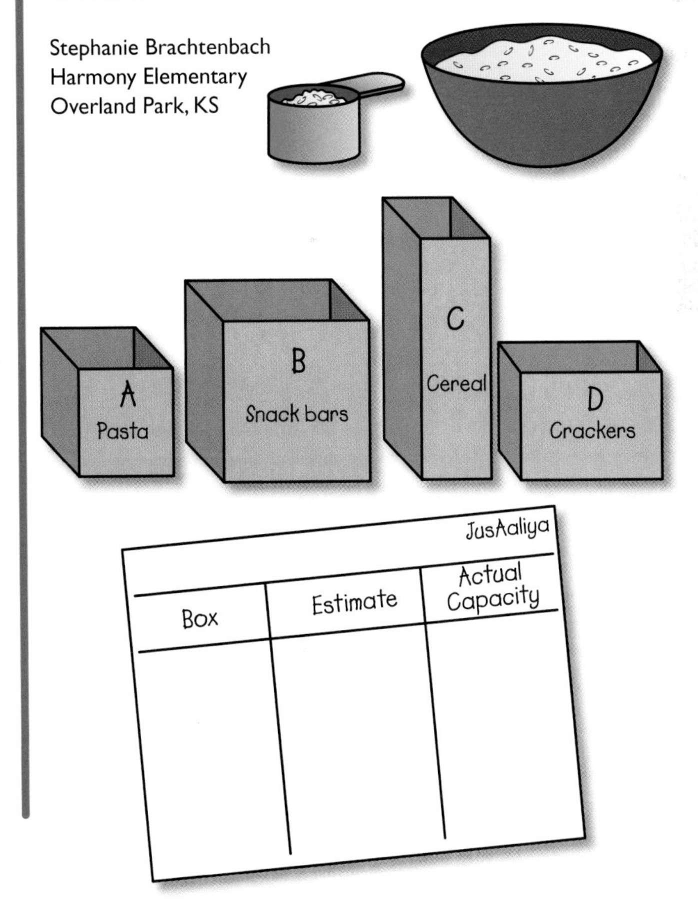
A
Pasta
B
Snack bars
C
Cereal
D
Crackers
JusAaliya
Box
Estimate
Actual Capacity

Learning Centers

Piecing It Together
Synonyms

Materials:
4 or 5 greeting cards

In advance, remove the front pictures from the greeting cards. Cut each picture into five puzzle pieces. Turn the pieces of each puzzle over and label each piece with a word that has the same meaning as the other four pieces, using a different word set for each picture. Scatter the puzzle pieces word-side up at a center. To complete the center, a student sorts the puzzle pieces into word groups with similar meanings. Then she turns each set over to check that all the puzzle pieces fit together.

Kathryn Davenport, Partin Elementary, Oviedo, FL

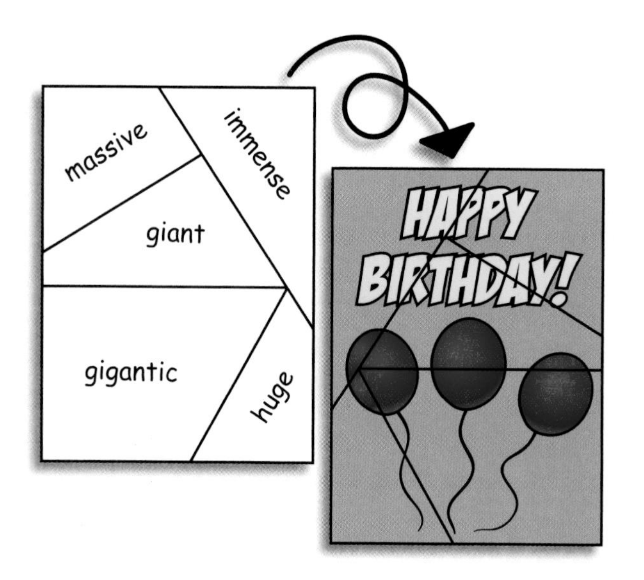
massive
immense
giant
gigantic
huge
HAPPY BIRTHDAY!

Summer Means...
Dictionary skills

Materials:
index card programmed as shown
dictionary
paper

A student divides his paper into a 3 x 3 grid. He thinks of a word that reminds him of summer and draws a picture of it in the center square. Then he refers to the index card and uses a dictionary to complete the remaining squares on his paper.

Entry Word	Pronunciation	Number of Syllables
Guide Words		Part(s) of Speech
Number of Meanings	Other Spellings of the Word	Name of Dictionary and Page Number

beach	(beech)	one syllable
battleship – bear		noun and verb
two meanings	beaches beached beaching	Children's Dictionary page 70

Zach

Terrific Toppings

Comparing fractions

Materials:
copy of the fraction cube on page 189, cut out and assembled
2 paper plates
16 red and yellow counters
paper

A child rolls the cube and reads the fraction. She arranges eight pepperoni on one plate (pizza) so the numerator is represented by red-side-up counters and the denominator is represented by yellow-side-up counters. The child rolls the cube again and uses the other plate to display the remaining counters. Next, she draws on her paper a picture of both pizzas and labels each with the matching fraction; then she draws a greater than, less than, or equal to symbol between the plates.

Denise Dayton, Gardner, MA

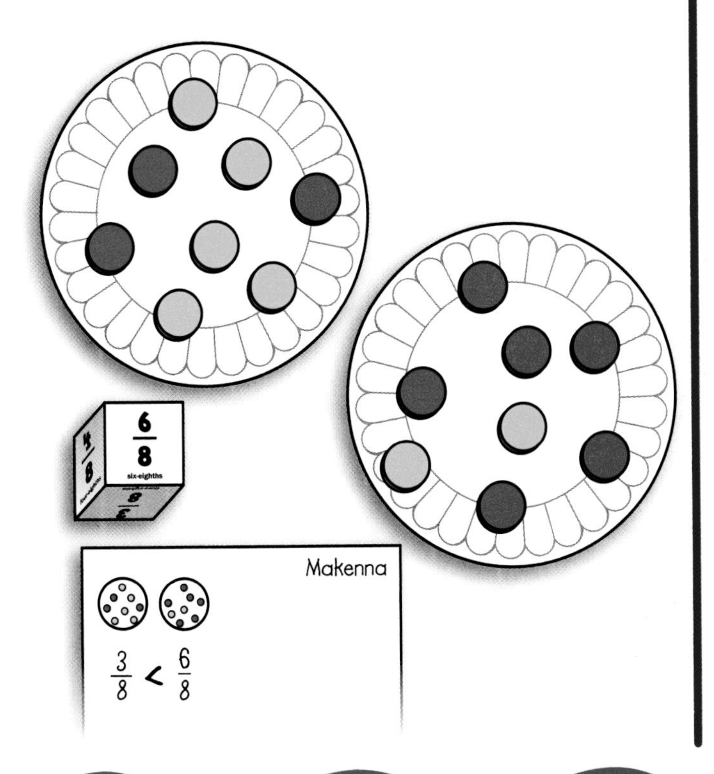

6/8
Makenna
3/8 < 6/8

That's "Sum" Product!

Multiplication as repeated addition

Materials:
student copies of the recording sheet on page 190
cutout copy of the picture cards on page 190

A student selects a card and reads the name of the group. He writes in the first column of his recording sheet the total number of groups. Then he counts and writes in the second column the number in each group. Using the numbers from the first two columns, the child writes a repeated addition sentence and its sum in the next two columns. He completes the last two columns in the row by writing the related multiplication sentence and its product. The student draws another picture card and repeats the process to complete the chart.

Denise Laudenslager, Palmer Elementary, Easton, PA

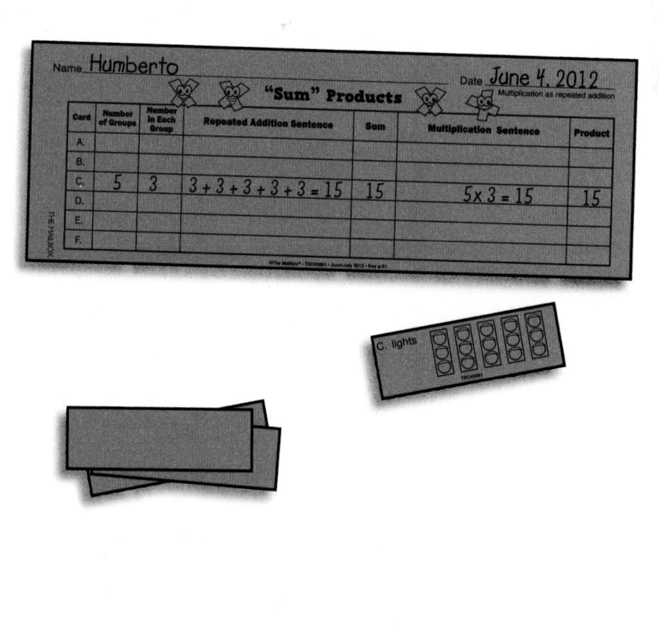

Name Humberto
Date June 4, 2012
"Sum" Products
Multiplication as repeated addition
Card | Number of Groups | Number in Each Group | Repeated Addition Sentence | Sum | Multiplication Sentence | Product
C. | 5 | 3 | 3 + 3 + 3 + 3 + 3 = 15 | 15 | 5 x 3 = 15 | 15
C. lights

Food Cards

Use with "An Indoor Grill" on page 169.

TEC43056 mushroom	TEC43056 mushroom	TEC43056 mushroom	TEC43056 mushroom	TEC43056 mushroom	TEC43056 mushroom
TEC43056 tomato	TEC43056 tomato	TEC43056 tomato	TEC43056 tomato	TEC43056 tomato	TEC43056 tomato
TEC43056 shrimp	TEC43056 shrimp	TEC43056 shrimp	TEC43056 shrimp	TEC43056 shrimp	TEC43056 shrimp
TEC43056 olive	TEC43056 olive	TEC43056 olive	TEC43056 olive	TEC43056 olive	TEC43056 olive
TEC43056 onion	TEC43056 onion	TEC43056 onion	TEC43056 onion	TEC43056 onion	TEC43056 onion
TEC43056 pepper	TEC43056 pepper	TEC43056 pepper	TEC43056 pepper	TEC43056 pepper	TEC43056 pepper
TEC43056 chicken	TEC43056 chicken	TEC43056 chicken	TEC43056 chicken	TEC43056 chicken	TEC43056 chicken

Name ______________________ Date ______________

Classifying words

Category Challenge

Give me 20!

Time					

Note to the teacher: Use with "Race to Write!" on page 170.

Base Word and Suffix Cards

Use with "Real or Imposter?" on page 170.

tall TEC43057	cheer TEC43057	loud TEC43057	most TEC43057
hard TEC43057	friend TEC43057	sweet TEC43057	thought TEC43057
help TEC43057	kind TEC43057	mean TEC43057	rich TEC43057
color TEC43057	dark TEC43057	smart TEC43057	tough TEC43057
bright TEC43057	cold TEC43057	hand TEC43057	warm TEC43057
er TEC43057	er TEC43057	er TEC43057	est TEC43057
est TEC43057	est TEC43057	ly TEC43057	ly TEC43057
ly TEC43057	ful TEC43057	ful TEC43057	ful TEC43057

Ornament Patterns

Use with "Trim the Tree" on page 172.

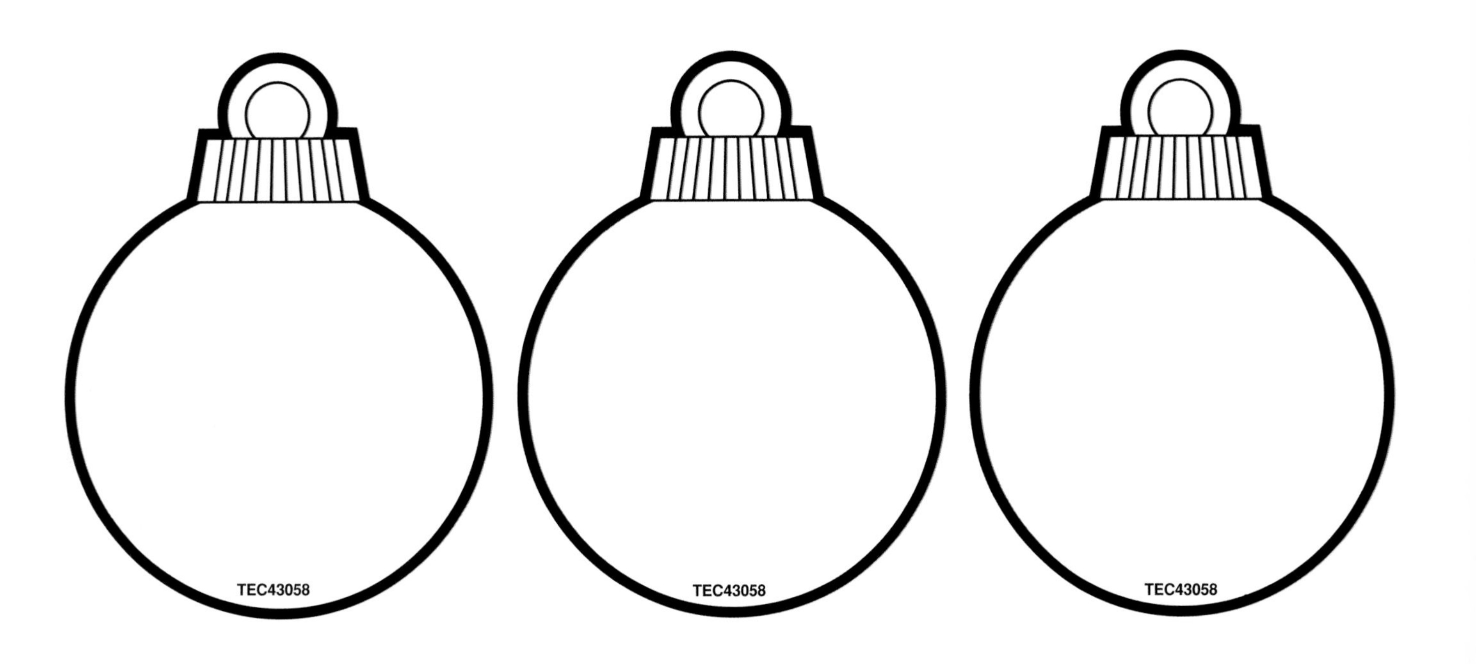
TEC43058
TEC43058
TEC43058

Fish Cards

Use with "Fishing for Sums" on page 173.

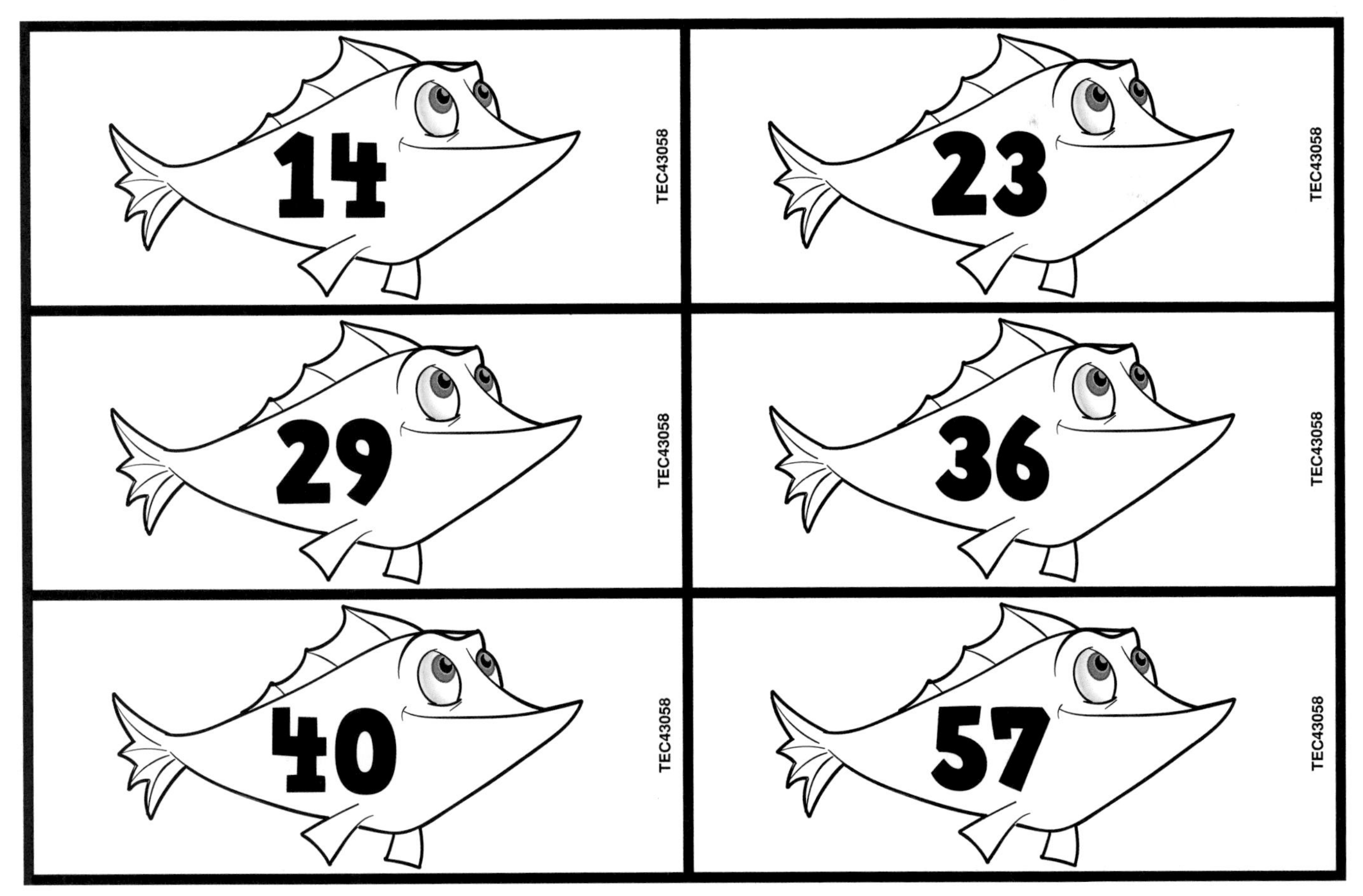
14
TEC43058
23
TEC43058
29
TEC43058
36
TEC43058
40
TEC43058
57
TEC43058

Candy Cards

Use with "Sweet Sets" on page 173.

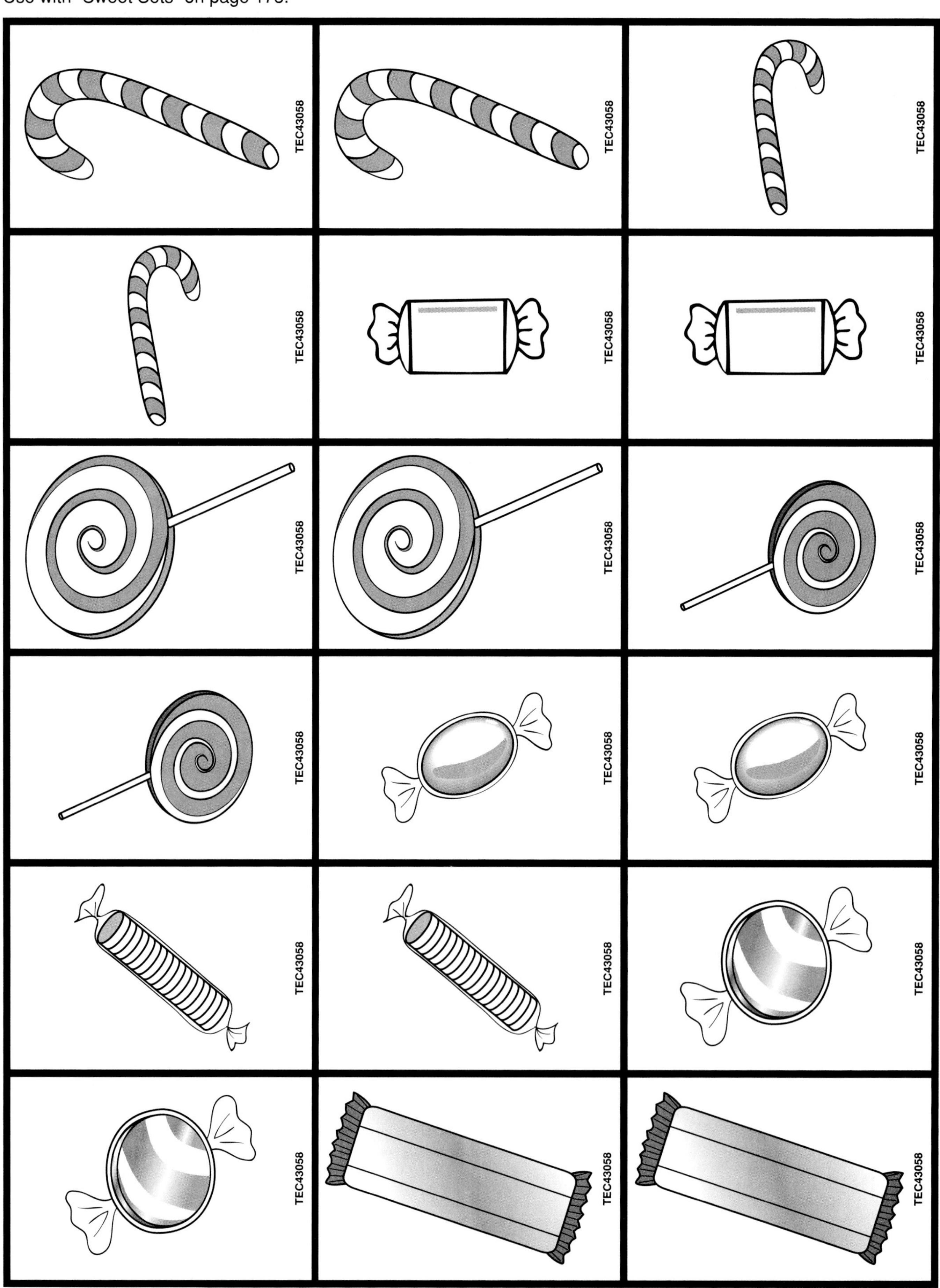
TEC43058
TEC43058
TEC43058
TEC43058
TEC43058
TEC43058
TEC43058
TEC43058
TEC43058
TEC43058
TEC43058
TEC43058
TEC43058
TEC43058
TEC43058
TEC43058
TEC43058
TEC43058

Bandage Cards

Use with "Diagnose the Problem" on page 174.

A. Capitalize the beginning of the sentence. TEC43059	H. **Do you eat oatmeal for breakfast** TEC43059
B. Add a period at the end of the sentence. TEC43059	I. **Ella didnt practice the piano on Monday.** TEC43059
C. Capitalize a person's name. TEC43059	J. **why do crickets chirp?** TEC43059
D. Add a question mark at the end of the sentence. TEC43059	K. **The puppies are small soft and very cuddly.** TEC43059
E. Add an apostrophe to the contraction. TEC43059	L. **On tuesday evenings, I go to karate practice.** TEC43059
F. Add commas to separate the words in a series. TEC43059	M. **Did george washington carver invent peanut butter?** TEC43059
G. Capitalize days of the week. TEC43059	N. **Robert has never been to the zoo** TEC43059

Cards

Use with "Kitties in the Corners" on page 175.

Card	Top left	Top right	Bottom left	Bottom right
START	2 x 10	36	30	7 x 6
	6 x 5		28	
	32	8 x 9	9 x 9	
	40	7 x 7		24
		21		2 x 5
	5 x 5		90	
	10	6 x 4	9 x 3	20
	36	3 x 10	5 x 8	16
		27		6 x 6
	6 x 9		72	
	3 x 4	20	24	5 x 7
	35	7 x 4	4 x 9	25
		40		4 x 10
		4 x 4	3 x 7	12
	42	9 x 10	8 x 8	54
	2 x 8	64	49	4 x 8
	2 x 12	81		
	18		4 x 5	30
			16	2 x 9

TEC43059

Flowerpot Patterns and Entry Word Strips

Use with "Growing Entry Words" on page 176.

TEC43060

TEC43060

action	path
north	oxen
motion	absent
adding	name
apple	peace
octagon	artist
along	obey
metal	minute
asleep	number
owner	across

TEC43060

Grocery Receipt Recording Sheet and Coupon Patterns

Use with "Savvy Savings" on page 177.

Shopper: ____________________

~ B. Thrifty Mart ~

☐ ____________________ $___.___

Sale price .... $___.___

☐ ____________________ $___.___

Sale price .... $___.___

☐ ____________________ $___.___

Sale price .... $___.___

☐ ____________________ $___.___

Sale price .... $___.___

☐ ____________________ $___.___

Sale price .... $___.___

Total Number of Items Sold ______

Original Balance Due $___.___

Sale Price Total $___.___

Your Total Savings Today! $___.___

Thank You for Shopping!

COUPON

Save $ ___.______

on any one

____

____

TEC43060

COUPON

Save $ ___.______

on any one

____

____

TEC43060

COUPON

Save $ ___.______

on any one

____

____

TEC43060

COUPON

Save $ ___.______

on any one

____

____

TEC43060

COUPON

Save $ ___.______

on any one

____

____

TEC43060

Cube Pattern

Use with "Terrific Toppings" on page 179.

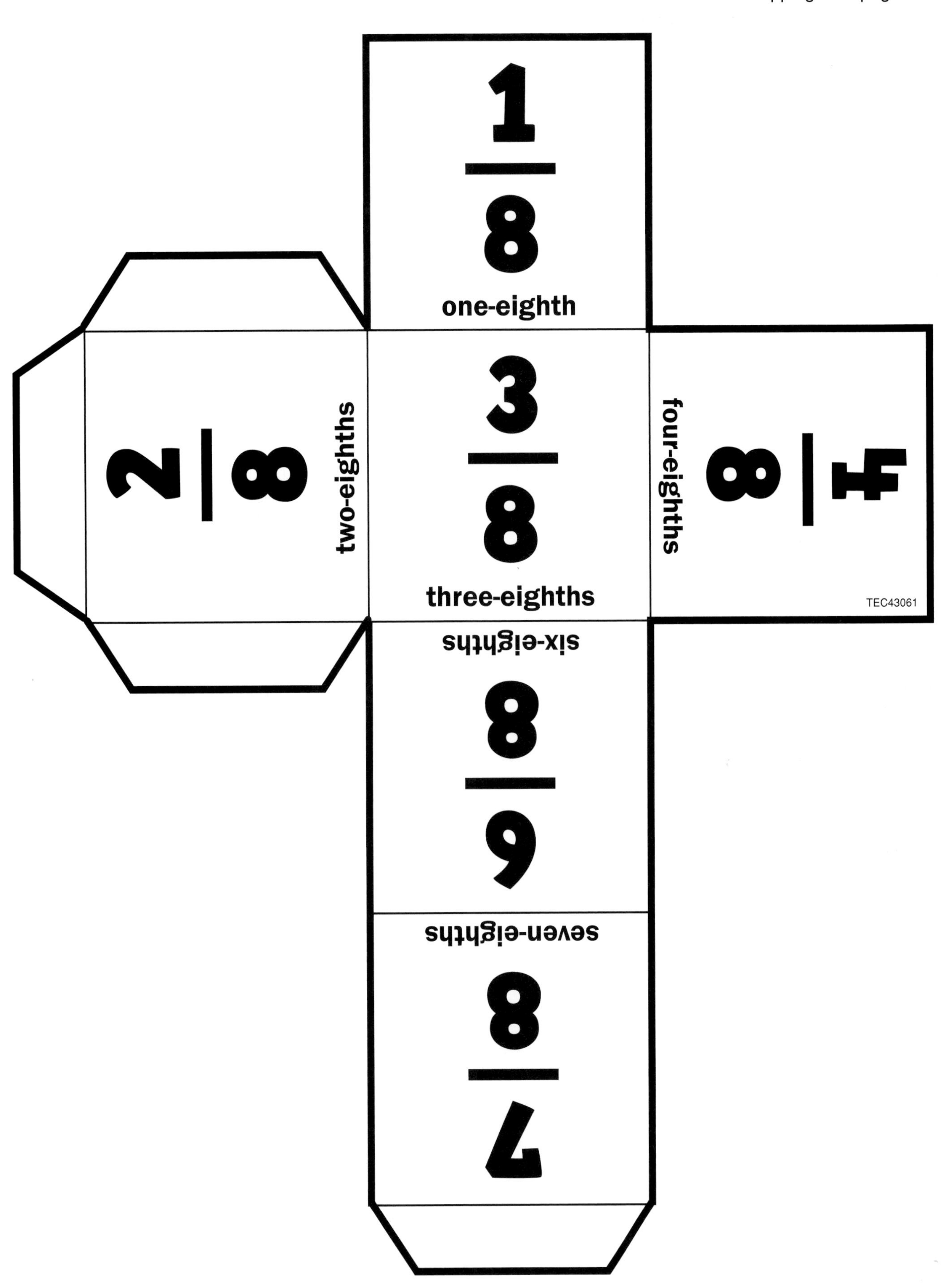

1/8
one-eighth
2/8
two-eighths
3/8
three-eighths
4/8
four-eighths
6/8
six-eighths
7/8
seven-eighths
TEC43061

Picture Cards

Use with "That's 'Sum' Product!" on page 179.

A. arms TEC43061	B. points TEC43061	C. lights TEC43061
D. wheels TEC43061	E. legs TEC43061	F. toes TEC43061

Name ____________________ Date ____________

Multiplication as repeated addition

"Sum" Products

Card	Number of Groups	Number in Each Group	Repeated Addition Sentence	Sum	Multiplication Sentence	Product
A.						
B.						
C.						
D.						
E.						
F.						

Note to the teacher: Use with "That's 'Sum' Product!" on page 179.

When Were They Made?

What You Need

student copies of page 192
box of pennies
scoop

What You Do

1. Take a scoopful of pennies.

2. Look at the year printed on each penny. Draw a tally mark in the matching column.

IN GOD WE TRUST
LIBERTY
1989

3. Write the total number of pennies.

4. Return the pennies to the box.

5. Repeat Steps 1–4 two more times.

Step-by-step center: Copy this activity card and put the activity card with the needed materials at a center.

Name ______________________________ Date ______________

Collecting data

IN GOD WE TRUST
LIBERTY
2010
UNITED STATES OF AMERICA
E PLURIBUS UNUM
ONE CENT
UNITED STATES OF AMERICA
ONE CENT
IN GOD WE TRUST
LIBERTY
1989
IN GOD WE TRUST
LIBERTY
2001

When Were They Made?

	Before 1980	From 1980 to 1989	From 1990 to 1999	From 2000 to 2009	After 2009
Trial 1					
Trial 2					
Trial 3					

Note to the teacher: Use with "When Were They Made?" on page 191.

Personalized Poultry

What You Need

construction paper: brown, red, orange
black ink pad
scissors
glue

What You Do

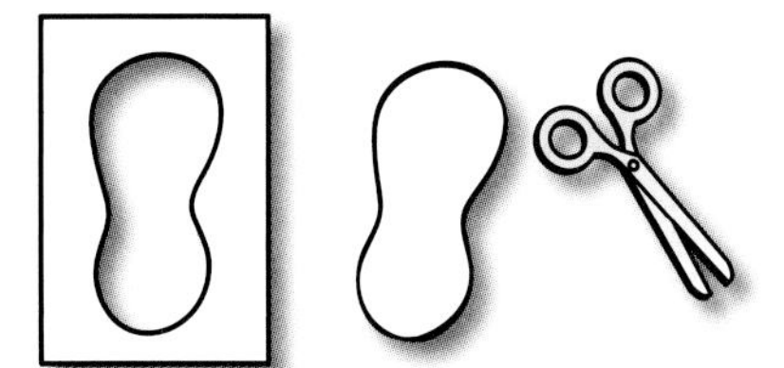

1. Trace your shoe. Cut out the tracing (body).

2. Fold two sheets of paper in half. Trace a hand on each paper. Cut out the tracings to make four sets of feathers.

GLUE

3. Fan out the feathers. Glue the body to the feathers.

4. Cut out an orange triangle. Cut out a red wattle. Glue them to the body.

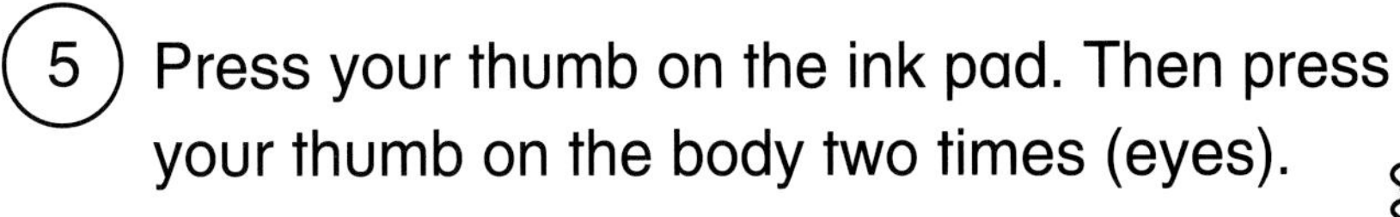

5. Press your thumb on the ink pad. Then press your thumb on the body two times (eyes).

6. Clean your thumb.

7. Turn your turkey over. Write your name and the date.

Step-by-step center: Copy this activity card and put the activity card with the needed materials at a center. If desired, put a container of baby wipes at the center to use for Step 6.

What's in a Name?

What You Need

beans
6 rubber bands
die
paper

What You Do

1. Draw 2 lines.

2. Write your first and last name. Count the letters. Set aside the same number of beans.

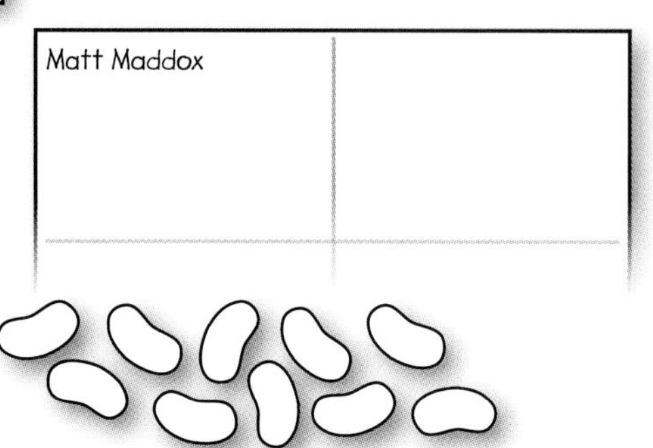
Matt Maddox

3. Roll the die. Put out the same number of rubber bands.

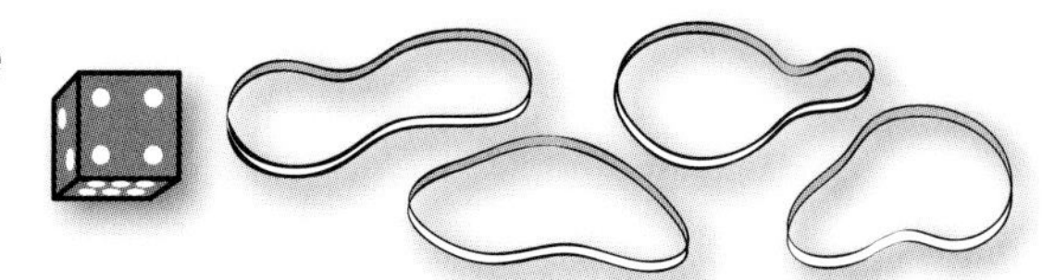

4. Equally divide the beans among the rubber bands. Draw a matching picture.

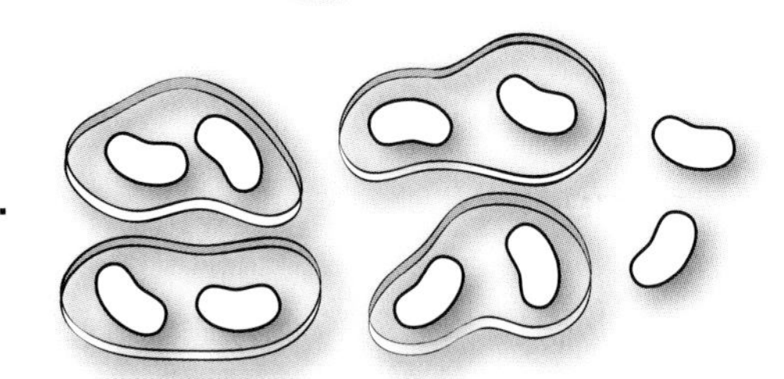

5. Copy and complete the sentence.

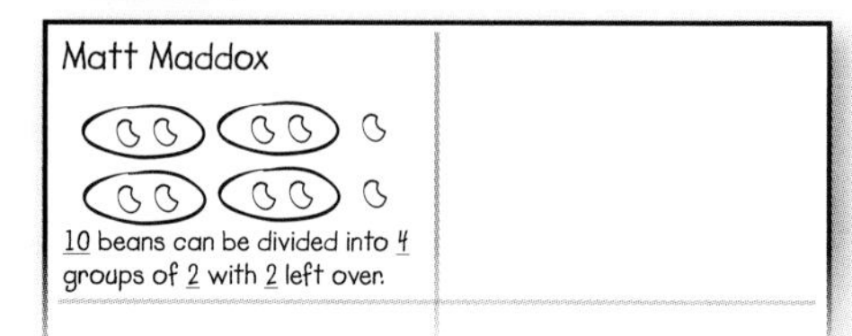
Matt Maddox
10 beans can be divided into 4 groups of 2 with 2 left over.

6. Repeat Steps 2–5 three more times. Use a different friend's name each time.

Step-by-step center: Copy this activity card and put the activity card with the needed materials at a center.

Love in Bloom

What You Need

muffin liner
green, white, and blue paper
ruler
scissors
glue

What You Do

1. Measure and cut a 1" x 6" green paper strip (stem).

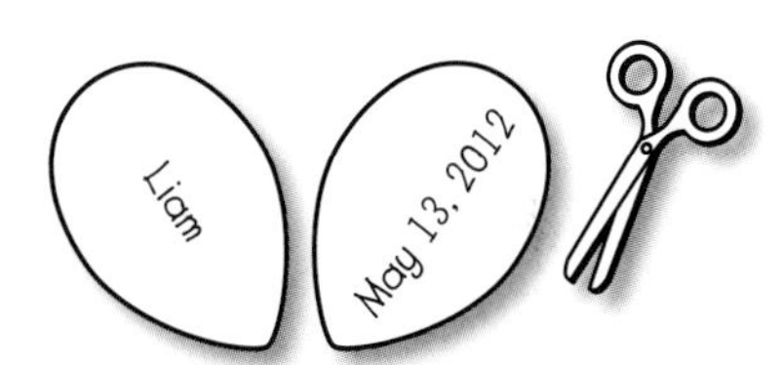
Liam
May 13, 2012

2. Cut 2 leaf shapes from green paper. Write your name on one and the date of Mother's Day on the other.

3. Glue the leaves and stem to the blue paper.

helpful

4. Cut 3 heart shapes (petals) from white paper. On each petal, write a different word or words to describe your mom or an important female loved one.

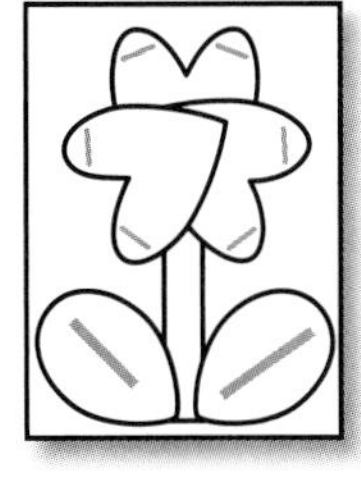

5. Glue the petals to the blue paper.

Mom

6. Label the muffin liner with the name of the woman you described in Step 4. Glue the liner to the petals.

Step-by-step center: Copy this activity card and put it with the needed materials at a center.

Break It Up!

What You Need

magazines or catalogs
scissors
glue
paper
marker

What You Do

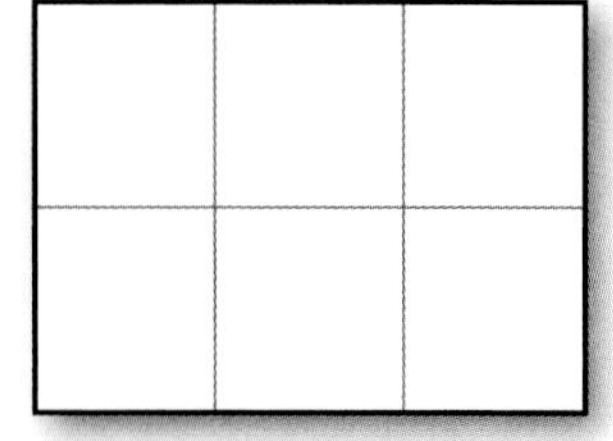

1. Draw 3 lines.

Toy Catalog

2. Find a picture of an object with a two-syllable name. Cut out the picture. Find and cut out 5 more pictures.

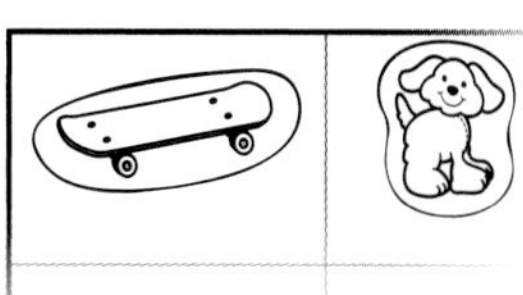

3. Glue 1 picture inside each box on your paper.

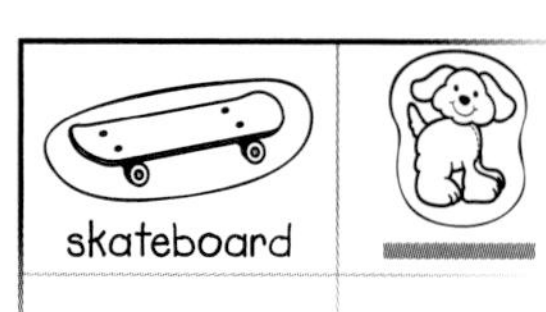
skateboard

4. Write the name of each object.

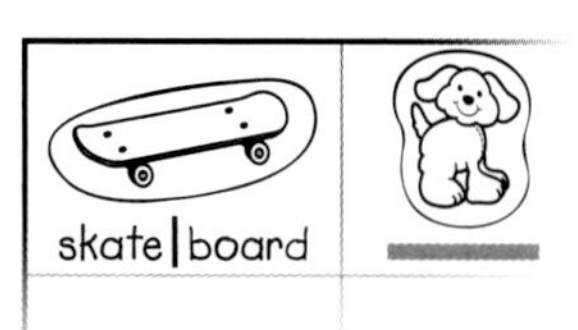
skate|board

5. Use the marker to draw a line between the syllables in each word.

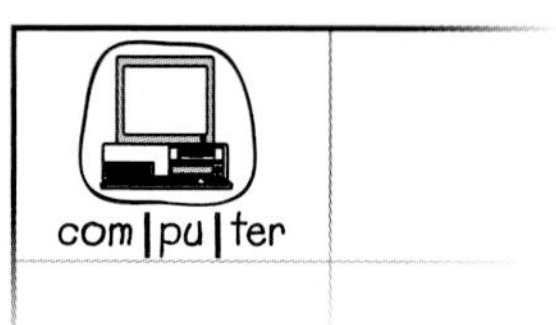
com|pu|ter

6. Turn your paper over. Repeat Steps 1–5. Find and cut out pictures with three-syllable names.

 Step-by-step center: Copy this activity card and put it and the needed materials at a center.

Celebrate the Season!

Celebrate the Season!

Motivating Messages
Problem solving

Walt Disney said, | "All our dreams | can come true, | if we have | the courage | to pursue them."

Start your school year with a cooperative group activity that is sure to inspire your students! To prepare, copy the message strips on page 199. Cut each strip to make word cards and give each student group a set of cards. Instruct students to arrange the cards to the quotation. After you've approved each group's arrangement, direct students to glue the cutouts to a construction paper strip and discuss what the quotation means. Provide time for each group to share its quotation and meaning; then post the messages around the room for year-round inspiration.

Mary Burgess, Howell Valley Elementary, West Plains, MO

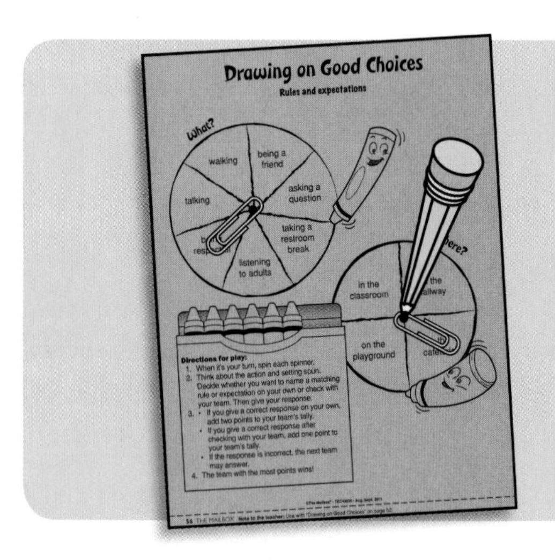
Drawing on Good Choices
Rules and expectations
What?
walking
being a friend
talking
asking a question
taking a restroom break
listening to adults
in the classroom
on the playground

Drawing on Good Choices
Rules and expectations

With this fun game, students show what they know about making good decisions in your classroom! After reviewing your rules and expectations, put students into teams. Project a copy of page 200 on the board and draw a tally chart to record team points. Show students how to use a pencil and paper clip to spin the spinners on an overhead projector or on the paper under a document projector. Play as directed and use any missed responses to guide a class review.

Wonderful Workers!
Commas in a series

For Labor Day, invite students to take a closer look at the people who help their school run smoothly! First, have each child choose a school employee and write three tools the employee uses when she works. Next, direct the student to write a sentence about the employee and the tools she uses, separating the tools with commas. Then have him trace each comma with a brightly colored crayon. Repeat the steps by having the student list three things the employee often wears and three things the employee does.

If desired, have each student publish his sentences by having him fold a sheet of paper in half. He writes the employee's name and job title on the front cover; then he writes a separate sentence on each page. He completes the project by illustrating each sentence and tracing each comma with a brightly colored crayon.

Mrs. Baker-cafeteria worker
spoon
pots
stove
Mrs. Baker uses a spoon, pots, and the stove.
apron
gloves
hairnet
She wears an apron, gloves, and a hairnet.

Cynthia Wicks, Eastwood Elementary, Roseburg, OR

Get more stuff on **pages 201-204**.

Use with "Motivating Messages" on page 198.

Confucius said, | "It does not | matter | how slowly you go | so long as | you do not | stop." TEC43056

John Wooden said, | "Do not let | what you cannot do | interfere | with what you can do." TEC43056

Walt Disney said, | "All our dreams | can come true, | if we have | the courage | to pursue them." TEC43056

Thomas Jefferson said, | "I find that | the harder I work, | the more luck | I seem to have." TEC43056

An Ethiopian proverb says, | "When spiderwebs | unite, they | can tie up | a lion." TEC43056

An unknown author said, | "No one is | perfect... That's | why pencils | have erasers." TEC43056

Drawing on Good Choices

Rules and expectations

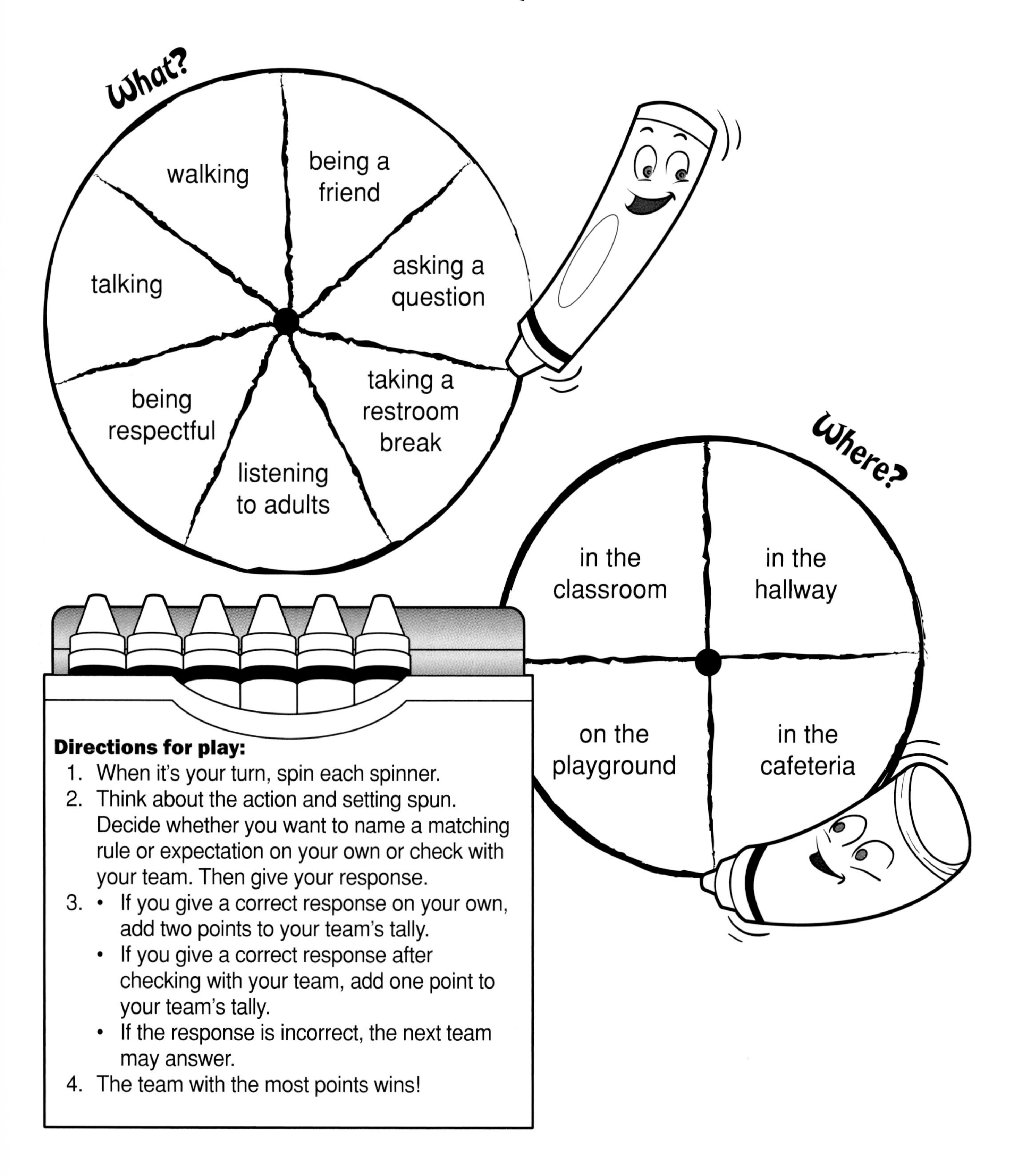
What?
walking
being a friend
asking a question
taking a restroom break
listening to adults
being respectful
talking
Where?
in the classroom
in the hallway
on the playground
in the cafeteria

Directions for play:

1. When it's your turn, spin each spinner.
2. Think about the action and setting spun. Decide whether you want to name a matching rule or expectation on your own or check with your team. Then give your response.
3.
   - If you give a correct response on your own, add two points to your team's tally.
   - If you give a correct response after checking with your team, add one point to your team's tally.
   - If the response is incorrect, the next team may answer.
4. The team with the most points wins!

Note to the teacher: Use with "Drawing on Good Choices" on page 198.

Name ______________________ Date ____________

Making text-to-self connections

Connecting With Classmates

Read.

1. Last year, Tabby's dad drove her to school. This year, Tabby will be a bus rider for the first time. She feels grown up!
2. Calvin got a new pet this summer. He can't wait to tell his classmates about it.
3. Kitty's mom took her shopping. Kitty is excited to show off her new school clothes, lunchbox, and backpack.
4. When Dusty gets to the lunchroom, he can't find his lunch money. He is upset.
5. Tom is nervous about who will be in his new class. He wonders who he will play with during recess.

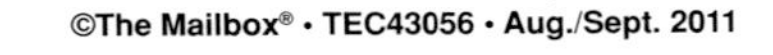

Choose two events.
Write each number in a box.
Explain how each event is like something that happened to you.

☐ ____________________________________

____

____

____

☐ ____________________________________

____

____

____

Bonus: Write the title of a book you have read or heard lately. Tell how one event from the story is like something that happened to you.

Name ______________________________ Date ________________

Number sense

So Many Apples!

Write the number.
Cross off the matching number.
(Hint: Some numbers will not be crossed off.)

15	82
23	85
38	99
45	127
53	146
59	162
67	215
69	268
74	283

A 5 tens, 3 ones = ________

B 9 tens, 9 ones = ________

C 2 tens, 3 ones = ________

D 1 hundred, 4 tens, 6 ones = ________

E 6 tens, 7 ones = ________

F 3 tens, 8 ones = ________

G 2 hundreds, 6 tens, 8 ones = ________

H 8 tens, 2 ones = ________

I 6 tens, 9 ones = ________

J 2 hundreds, 1 ten, 5 ones = ________

K 1 hundred, 6 tens, 2 ones = ________

L 8 tens, 5 ones = ________

M 1 ten, 5 ones = ________

N 4 tens, 5 ones = ________

O 1 hundred, 2 tens, 7 ones = ________

Bonus: List each number not crossed off. Write the hundreds, tens, and ones for each number.

How to use Copy and cut out the cards. Use them as center or free-time activities.

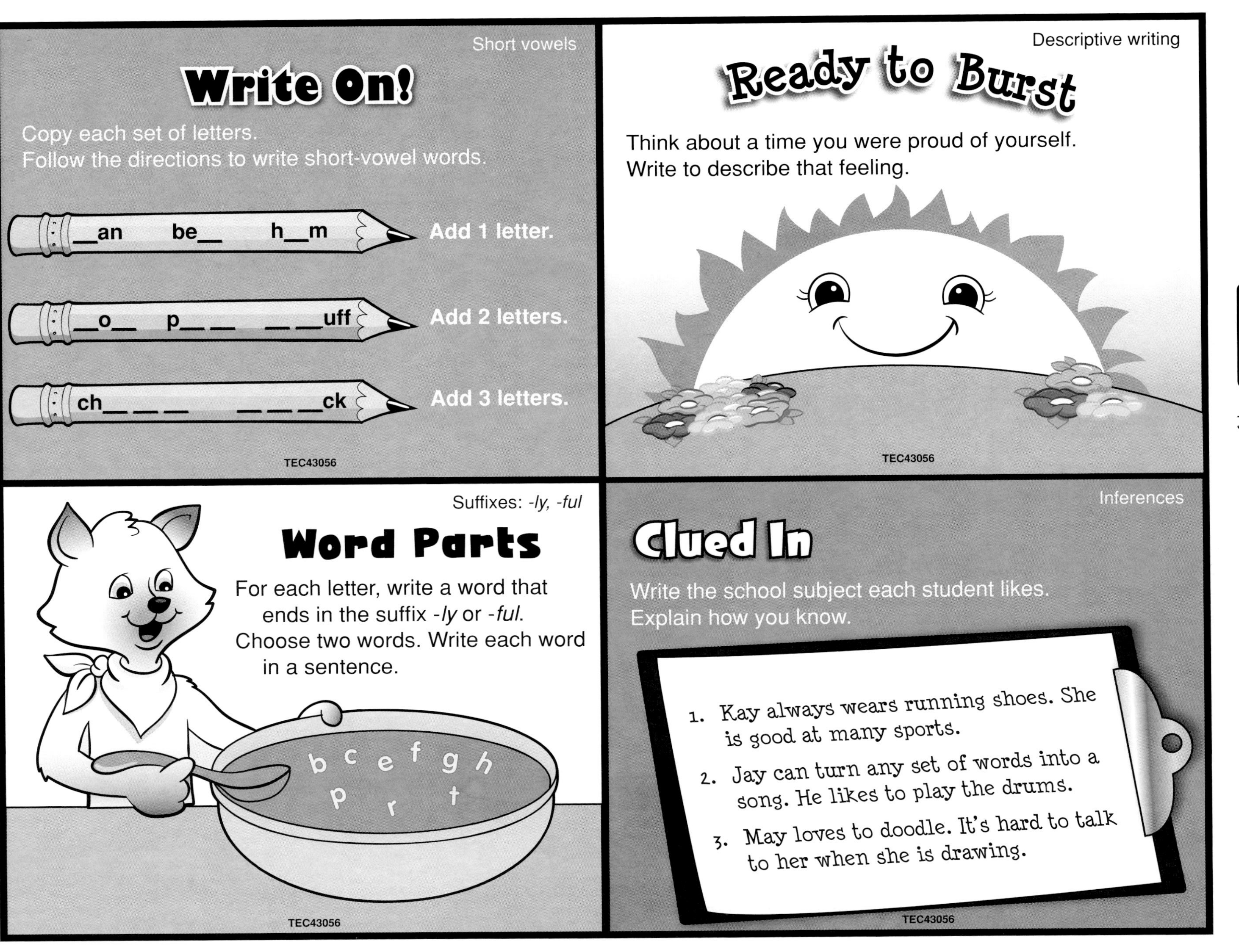
Short vowels
Write On!
Copy each set of letters.
Follow the directions to write short-vowel words.
__an be__ h__m
Add 1 letter.
__o__ p__ __ __ __uff
Add 2 letters.
ch__ __ __ __ __ __ck
Add 3 letters.
TEC43056
Descriptive writing
Ready to Burst
Think about a time you were proud of yourself.
Write to describe that feeling.
TEC43056
Suffixes: -ly, -ful
Word Parts
For each letter, write a word that ends in the suffix -ly or -ful.
Choose two words. Write each word in a sentence.
b c e f g h
p r t
TEC43056
Inferences
Clued In
Write the school subject each student likes.
Explain how you know.
1. Kay always wears running shoes. She is good at many sports.
2. Jay can turn any set of words into a song. He likes to play the drums.
3. May loves to doodle. It's hard to talk to her when she is drawing.
TEC43056

Math Activity Cards

How to use Copy and cut out the cards. Use them as center or free-time activities.

Basic facts
Fact Factories
Copy each problem.
Solve.
A. 8 + 8 =
B. 3 + 7 =
C. 10 - 8 =
D. 6 + 6 =
E. 18 - 9 =
F. 14 - 7 =
G. 10 - 7 =
H. 5 + 5 =
I. 8 - 4 =
J. 6 + 4 =
K. 9 + 9 =
L. 12 - 6 =
M. 8 + 2 =
N. 10 - 9 =
O. 7 + 3 =
TEC43056
Estimating and measuring length
Sizing Up the Room
Make a list of ten or more items.
Estimate each item's length.
Measure to check.
A paper clip is about one inch long.
TEC43056
Comparing numbers
Chomp, Chomp!
Write two numbers.
Leave a space between them.
Draw <, >, or = to make a true sentence.
Repeat nine or more times.
1,075
2,932
5,678
4,190
1,750
2,239
3,284
5,876
3,824
4,910
TEC43056
Using a schedule
Mom's Reminders
Read the schedule.
Write and answer four or more questions about it.
On School Days
7:00 Turn off alarm!
7:05 Eat breakfast.
7:20 Brush teeth and wash face.
7:25 Get dressed.
7:35 Get lunchbox and backpack. Go to bus stop.
7:45 Bus arrives. Don't be late!
TEC43056

Start Here!

Lead students into a fun-filled year with these fabulous first-day activities!

Name ____________

☐ Find the United States map. Which state is flagged on the map? ________

☐ Find the classroom library. How many books are in the biography tub? ______

☐ Find the teacher. What is her favorite third-grade subject? ________

Welcome Back!

Introduce students to their new classroom with this fun scavenger hunt! Prepare a list of items and locations for each child to find, including one that sends students to you. Below each item, write a question that, when answered, confirms that the student has found the location. What a great way for students to learn about their new surroundings! *Sheree Knight, Oregon City, OR*

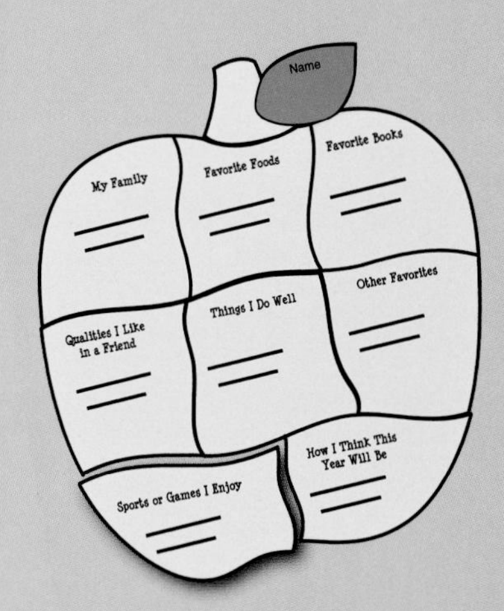

Name
My Family
Favorite Foods
Favorite Books
Other Favorites
Things I Do Well
Qualities I Like in a Friend
How I Think This Year Will Be
Sports or Games I Enjoy

Bring 'em Together!

Help students get to know one another with these appealing puzzles! Have each student complete a copy of page 206. Then have him cut apart the puzzle pieces. Divide the class into small groups and put the group members' pieces in the same bag. The group shakes the bag, empties it onto a common workspace, and works together to assemble each member's puzzle. As a follow-up activity, have each student glue his completed puzzle to a sheet of paper and post the puzzles on a display titled "Apples of My Eye." *Amy Barsanti, Pines Elementary, Plymouth, NC*

Summer Window

Revisit students' favorite summertime memories! After students complete the project, provide time for them to share their work. Then post the completed projects on a display titled "Take a Peek at Our Super Summers!"

Materials for each student:

3" x 5" index card
8½" x 11" sheet of white paper
8½" x 11" sheet of colored paper
scissors
crayons
glue

Steps:

1. Use the index card to trace four rectangles onto the colored paper.
2. Cut out the rectangles to make a window frame.
3. Glue the window frame to the white paper.
4. In each pane, draw or write about a different summer memory.
5. Write your name on the window frame.

Amy Barsanti

zzzzzz
1
Landon

tip: Use summer-themed scrapbook paper instead of colored paper. Then have the student write his name with a marker.

Getting acquainted

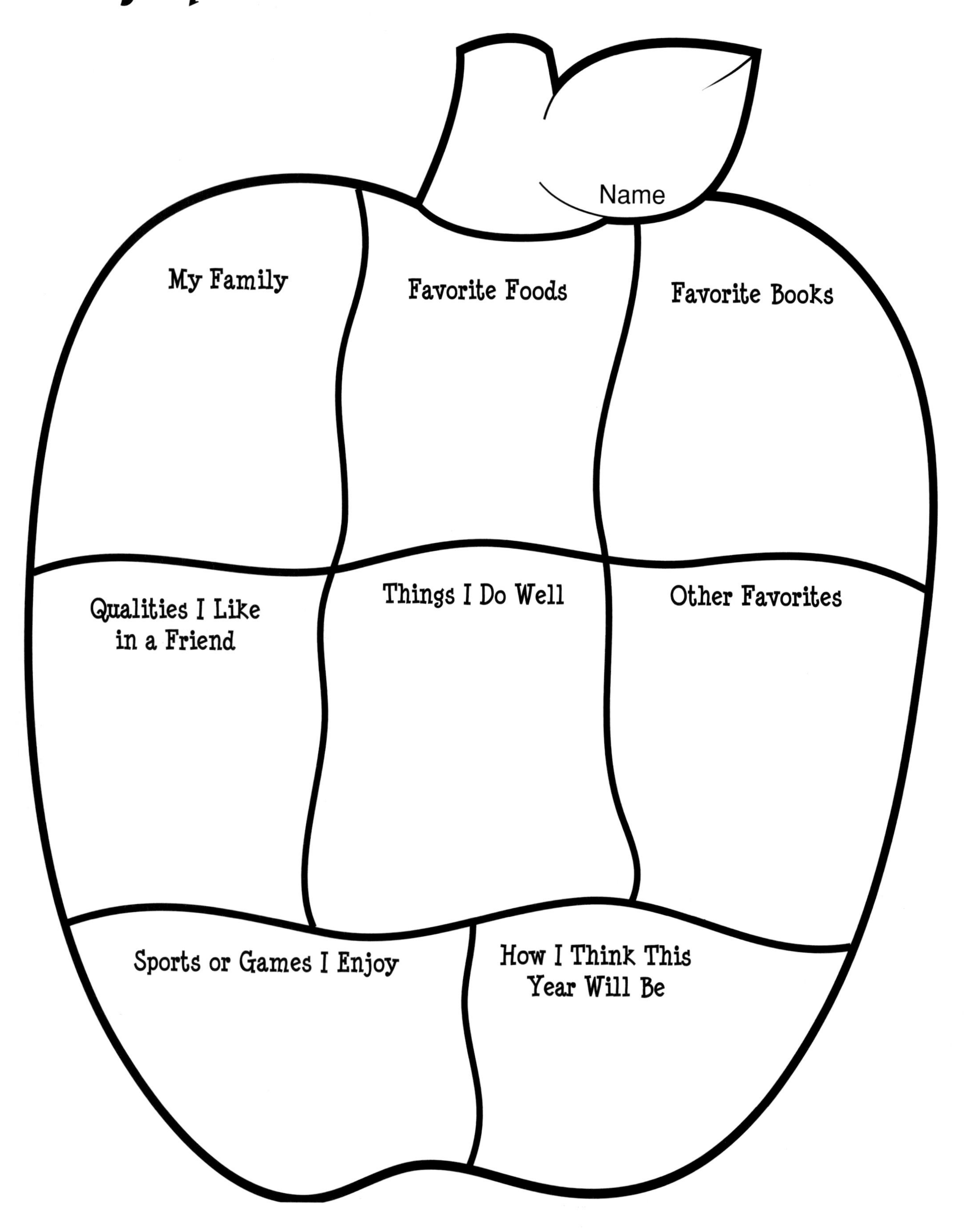
Name
My Family
Favorite Foods
Favorite Books
Qualities I Like in a Friend
Things I Do Well
Other Favorites
Sports or Games I Enjoy
How I Think This Year Will Be

Note to the teacher: Use with "Bring 'em Together!" on page 205.

"Whoooo's" Ready for Open House?
You Are!
School
Ms. Ammons

Welcome to Ms. Knust's Second Grade! 2011–12

Important Info

Save time and ensure consistent communication with this tip! Before school starts, create a computerized slide presentation that lists class rules, expectations, and schedules. Present the slide show to students on the first day of school and then use the presentation with parents at open house. Not only will you save time preparing for open house, but students and parents will hear (and see) the same information.

Unique Invitation

If your open house occurs after school starts, then the smiling student faces on these personalized invitations are sure to get parents' attention! In advance, print a supply of invitations on card stock. Next, plan a simple message about open house that has as many characters as you have students. Then give each child a letter, number, or punctuation card and arrange students to spell the message. Photograph the students and insert the image onto the bottom front half of the invitation. Fold the invitations and send them home in advance of the big day!

OPEN HOUSE
IS SEPT.
15, 2011!

tip If your school or district's photo policy keeps you from including every child in the photo, have each child design a letter for your message. Then display the letters on the board and photograph the letters.

Set up a simple bulletin board display to connect with parents! See "Snips of the Past" on page 272!

Treasure Hunt

To keep families moving while directing them to all the important places you want them to see, plan a treasure hunt. Give each family a preprinted treasure hunt checklist; when it's complete, have the student turn it in for a homework pass. Or have the student exchange the checklist for a raffle ticket and a chance to win a small prize such as a book!

Desk Display

Before open house, invite each student to choose five items to display on her desk. Also display student work on your classroom computers. Make these locations two stops on the treasure hunt.

Get Personal

Include a stop that displays personal effects—such as photos of you in the grade you're teaching, family photos, or personal favorites—to help students and their families get to know you better. Also include a stop that directs the child to talk to you. After families see these personal items, conversation will be a breeze!

Sign 'em Up!

Be sure to include one item on the treasure hunt checklist that directs parents to volunteer and conference sign-up forms. Another stop might encourage families to visit any newly updated areas of your school and to say hello to the principal.

Conferences

Terra Knust, Otwell Elementary, Otwell, IN; Andria Ammons, McNab Elementary, Pompano Beach, FL; Julie Lewis, J. O. Davis Elementary, Irving, TX; Pam Sanderson, Davis Drive Elementary, Apex, NC; Krista Rojas, Ocean View Elementary, Whittier, CA; Kelli Higgins, P. L. Bolin Elementary, East Peoria, IL; Robyn Johnson, Jefferson Elementary, Oregon, IL

Hip-Hip-Hooray!

September 17 is Constitution Day and Citizenship Day!

Stop and Go Situations

What better way to honor Constitution Day and Citizenship Day than by discussing the importance of rules? First, prepare a list of positive and negative school situations, like the ones shown. Next, give each child a copy of page 210 and direct her to color the scroll and feather on the positive-behavior section green (go) and the scroll and feather on the negative-behavior section red (stop). Instruct the student to cut out the pattern, fold it in half, and glue the sections back to back. Read each situation aloud and have the child flip her sign to identify the behavior. Discuss with students why some behaviors are those they should go ahead and do while others require stopping and choosing a better alternative.

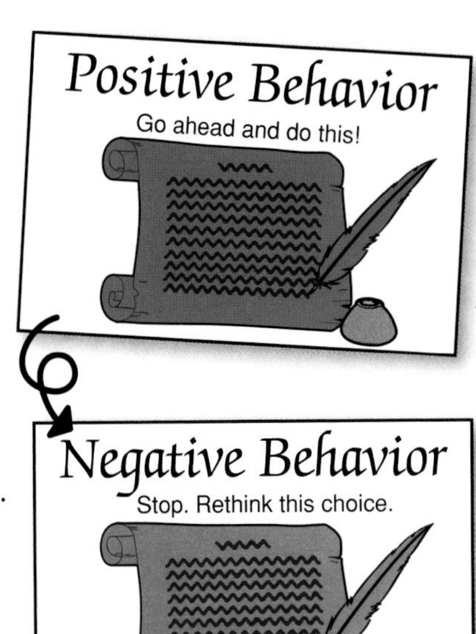
Positive Behavior
Go ahead and do this!
Negative Behavior
Stop. Rethink this choice.

Carolyn Burant, St. John Vianney School, Brookfield, WI

1. Our class walks quietly through the halls. *(positive)*
2. In the cafeteria, a classmate takes food off your tray and tells you not to tell anyone. *(negative)*
3. During recess, a classmate pushes you to the ground. *(negative)*
4. Students listen when the teacher speaks. *(positive)*

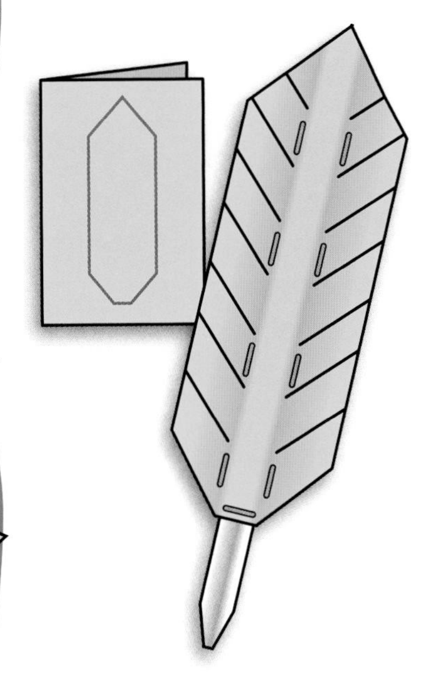

Old-Fashioned Fun

Recognize the signing of the Constitution with this quaint quill project. Have students use the quill to write Constitution-related words or spelling words in the air.

Materials for each student:

- tagboard feather template
- drinking straw
- sheet of construction paper
- scissors
- stapler
- tape

Steps:

1. Fold the construction paper in half.
2. Trace the feather onto the paper. Cut out the tracing, cutting through both paper halves.
3. Insert the straw between the cutouts (feather). Staple as shown.
4. Cut the end of the straw to form a point. Wrap the point with tape.
5. Cut one-inch angled strips along the outside edges of the feather.

Amy Barsanti, Pines Elementary, Plymouth, NC

Perfectly Timed Prompts

- What makes you a good citizen?
- Write a letter to a friend or family member. Explain why we celebrate Constitution Day and Citizenship Day.
- How would life be different if the US Constitution had never been written?

Constitution Card

Use with "Stop and Go Situations" on page 209.

Positive Behavior

Go ahead and do this!

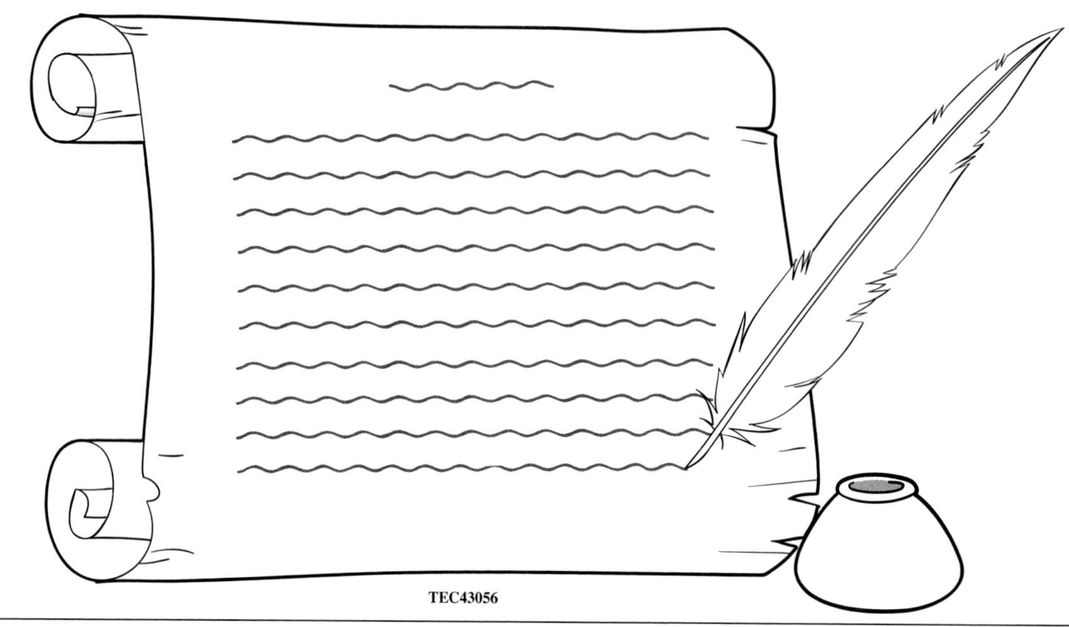

TEC43056

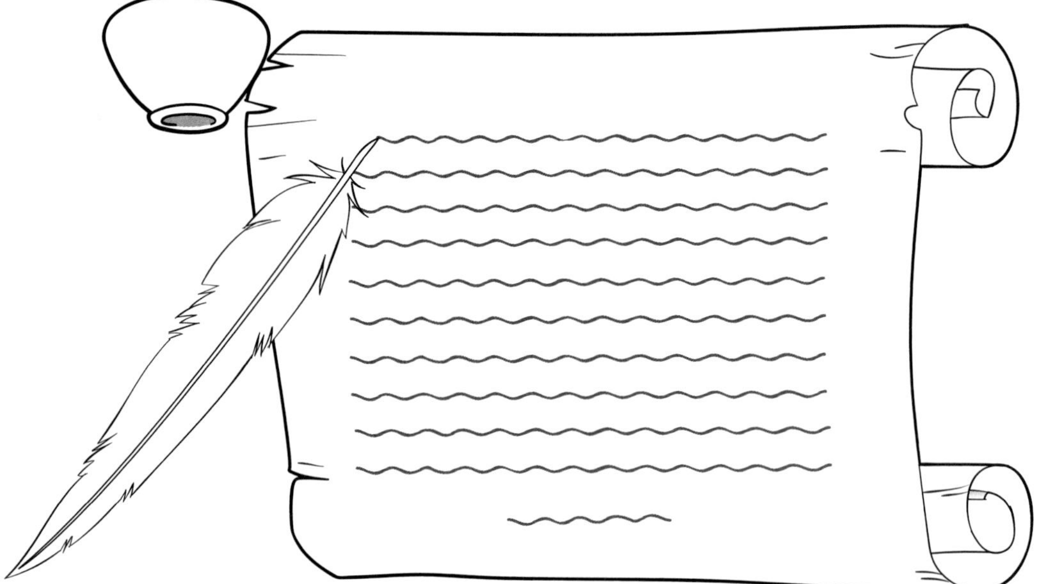

Stop. Rethink this choice.

Negative Behavior

Celebrate the Season!

Short and Sweet
Vocabulary

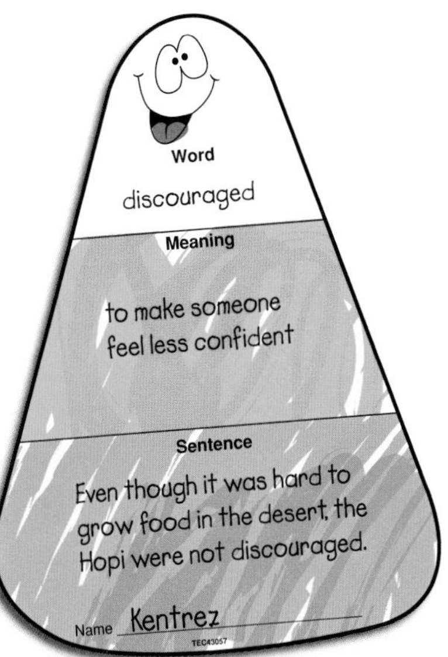
Word
discouraged
Meaning
to make someone feel less confident
Sentence
Even though it was hard to grow food in the desert, the Hopi were not discouraged.
Name Kentrez

This quick activity makes a sweet impression! First, give each child a copy of the candy corn pattern from page 212 and direct him to read an assigned selection. Direct the student to write on the pattern a new word from the reading. Have the child locate the word in a dictionary and write its meaning. Next, instruct him to write a sentence that uses the word and addresses the content of the reading. Finally, have the child color his pattern to resemble a candy corn. Post the completed projects with the title "New Vocabulary: What a Sweet Treat!"

Carolyn Burant, St. John Vianney School, Brookfield WI

Collecting Treats
Coordinate pairs

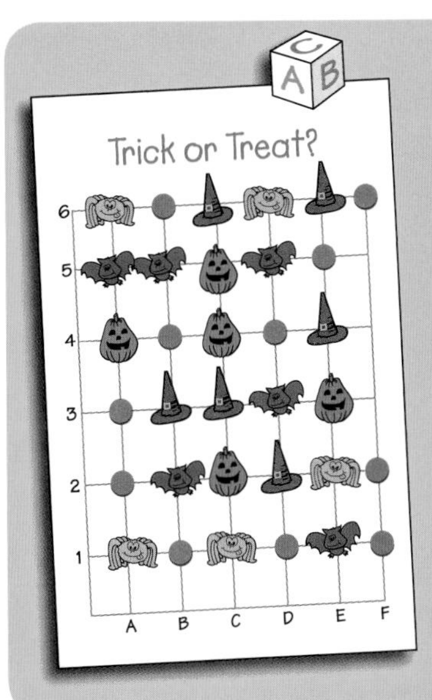
Trick or Treat?
6
5
4
3
2
1
A B C D E F

To set up this Halloween-themed math game, cover a die with masking tape and label each side with a different letter from *A* to *F*. Also make a coordinate grid like the one shown. Place the grid and the die at a center with 36 small items (such as pumpkin-shaped erasers or plastic spider rings), a bag of two-sided counters, and a traditional die. Before starting play, the two students put one treat on each coordinate (excluding those along the *x*-axis); then each player chooses one color on the counter. To begin, Player 1 rolls both dice and finds the matching coordinate. She takes the treat and replaces it with a counter of her color. Player 2 takes a turn in a similar manner. If a player rolls a coordinate that is already covered, her turn ends. The first player to cover three coordinates in a row horizontally, vertically, or diagonally wins; if neither partner does so, the partner with the most covered points at the end of play wins.

Kimberly Collatos, Portland, TN

Pilgrims at Work
Prepositions

'Tis the season for Thanksgiving fun! To begin, have students name prepositions and prepositional phrases as you write each one on the board. Next, have each child color and cut out a copy of the *Mayflower* and pilgrim patterns on page 212. Direct her to use her patterns to model as many of the prepositions from the list as she can. Then have the child glue her patterns to a sheet of paper and write a sentence about their placement using a preposition.

Carolyn Burant

Attach magnetic tape to the back of a set of patterns or set up your document camera. Invite different students to model each preposition for the class.

Prepositions
next to
near
far from
behind
in front of
above
below
under
over
on top of
The pilgrim is far from the Mayflower.

Candy Corn Pattern

Use with "Short and Sweet" on page 211.

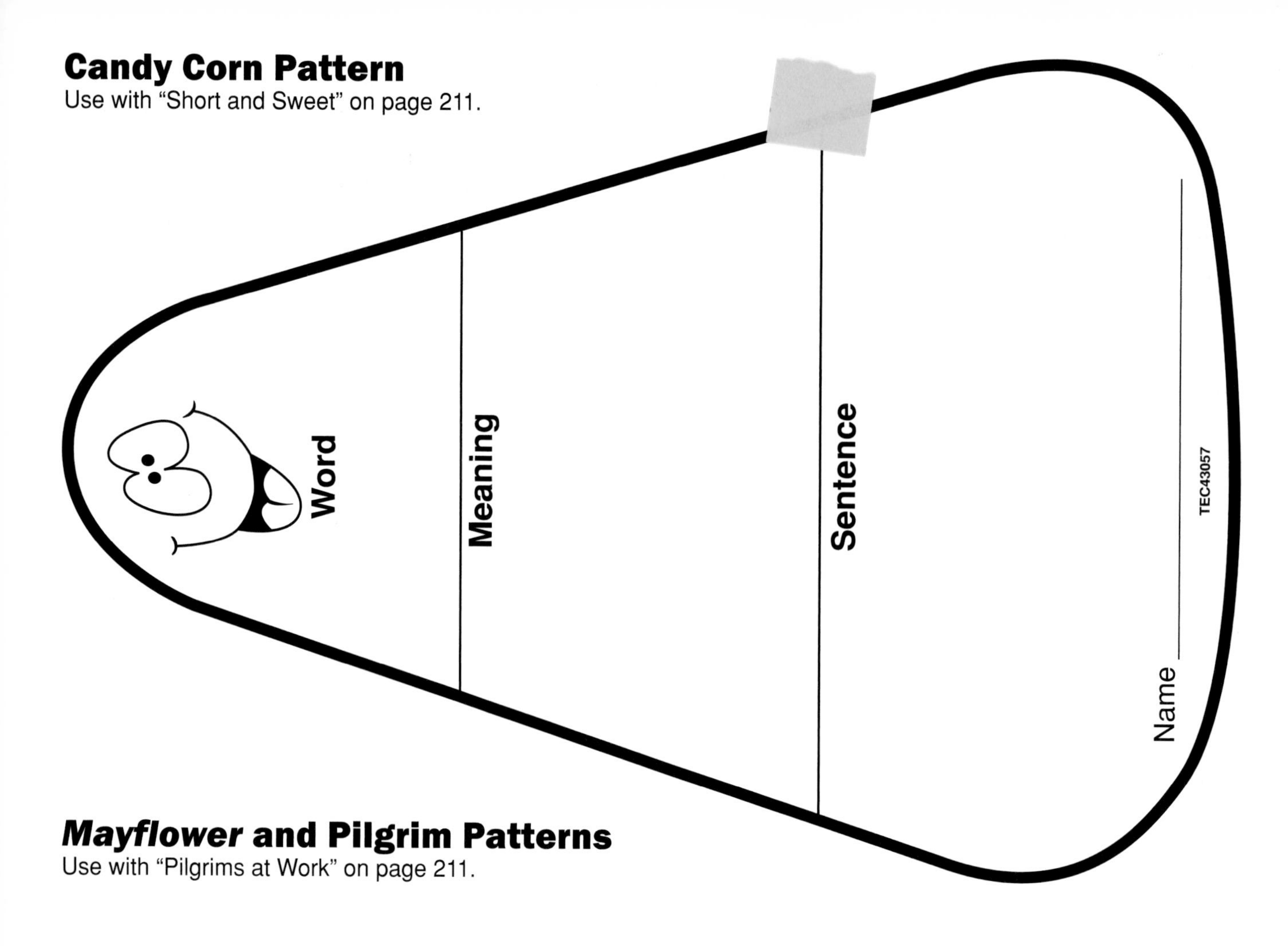
Word
Meaning
Sentence
Name
TEC43057

Mayflower and Pilgrim Patterns

Use with "Pilgrims at Work" on page 211.

TEC43057
TEC43057

Name ______________________________ Date ______________

Constructing and analyzing graphs

Patrolling the Pumpkin Patch

Complete the last column of the tally chart.
Then use the chart to complete the graph.

Things Seen at the Patch		
Object	**Tally Marks**	**Total**
pumpkins	卌 卌 II	
gourds	卌 I	
spiders	卌 III	
owls	III	
tractors	II	

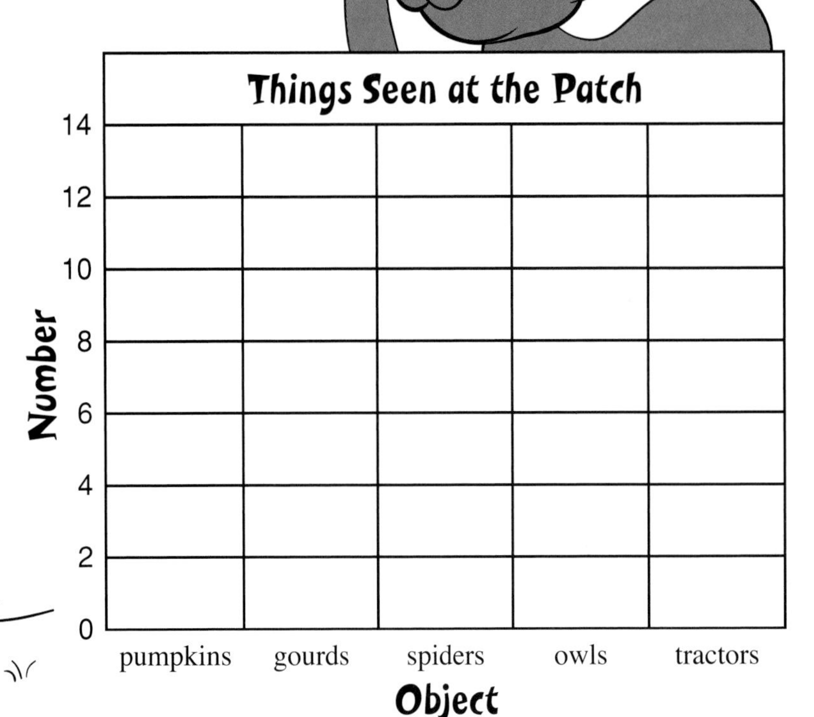

Things Seen at the Patch
14
12
10
8
6
4
2
0
Number
pumpkins
gourds
spiders
owls
tractors
Object

Answer the questions.

A. Which object was seen the most? ______________________

B. Which object was seen the least? ______________________

C. How many animals were spotted? ______________________

D. How many more spiders than owls were seen? ______________________

E. How many gourds and pumpkins were seen altogether? ______________________

Write the matching number sentence. ______________________

F. How many more pumpkins than gourds were seen? ______________________

Write this number as tally marks. ______________________

G. How many tractors were spotted? ______________________

H. How many total objects were seen at the pumpkin patch? ______________________

Bonus: Explain how you found the answer to question H.

Name ______________________ Date ______________

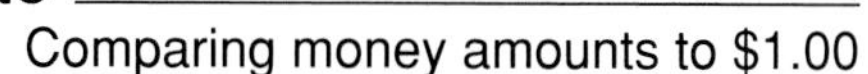

Comparing money amounts to $1.00

No Tricks, Only Treats!

Write each amount.

A. ______¢
B. ______¢
Sour Skulls
C. ______¢
D. ______¢
E. ______¢
RAISINS
F. ______¢
Goblin Gum
G. ______¢
Monster Choco Bar

Read and respond.

H. Circle the treat that costs more.  or 
RAISINS
Sour Skulls

I. Circle the treat that costs more. or

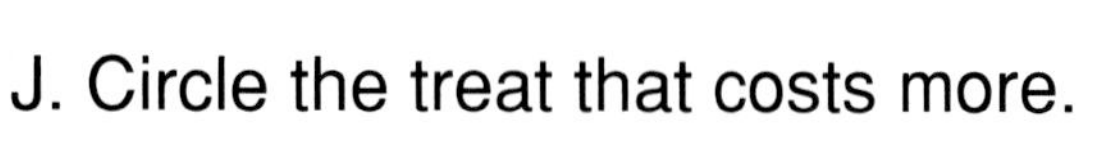

J. Circle the treat that costs more.  or

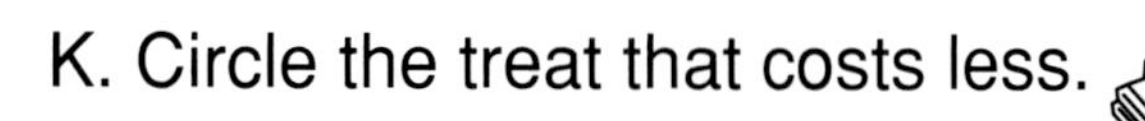

K. Circle the treat that costs less.  or
Goblin Gum

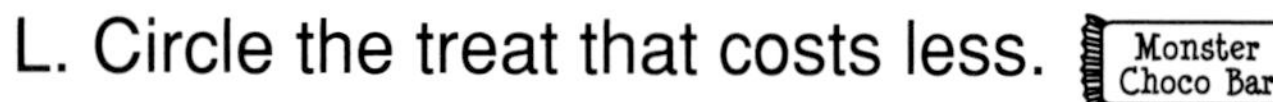

L. Circle the treat that costs less.  or
Monster Choco Bar

M. Color the treat that costs the most brown.

N. Color the treat that costs the least orange.

O. Color the two treats that cost the same green.

Bonus: Circle each cost greater than 50¢. Write these costs from least to greatest.

Name ______________________ Date ______________

Similarities and differences across nonfiction text

Happy Thanksgiving!

Read each fact sheet.

Thanksgiving Day in the United States

- The first Thanksgiving took place in 1621. The people of the Plymouth colony were grateful that they lived through their first year away from England. They also wanted to give thanks for their first harvest of crops.
- In 1863, President Lincoln made the last Thursday in November a day for all Americans to give thanks.
- In 1939, President Roosevelt changed the holiday to the fourth Thursday in November. This date became a federal holiday in 1941.
- In 2011, Thanksgiving Day will be on November 24. Many Americans will enjoy turkey, time with family, and parades on this day.

Thanksgiving Day in Canada

- The first Thanksgiving took place in 1578. An explorer in Canada wanted to give thanks after a long trip from England.
- For many years, this holiday was held on the last Monday in October.
- Since 1957, it has been held on the second Monday in October.
- In 2011, Thanksgiving Day will be on October 10. Many Canadians will eat turkey, spend time with family, and watch parades on this day.

Complete the Venn diagram.

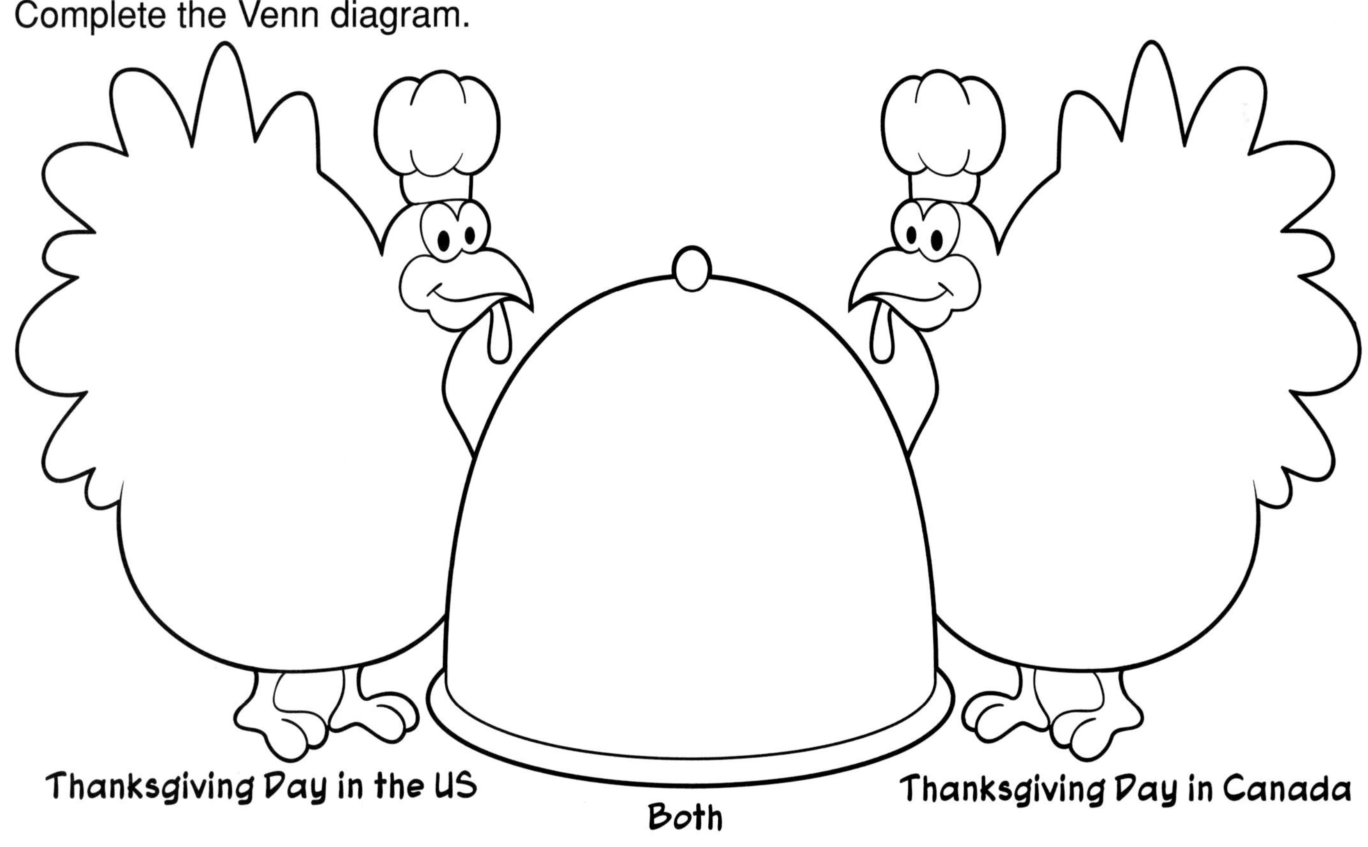
Thanksgiving Day in the US
Both
Thanksgiving Day in Canada

Language Arts Activity Cards

How to use Copy and cut out the cards. Use them as center or free-time activities.

Sounds of *c*
Serving Up Some Cs
List 8 or more words that start like *candy*.
List 8 or more words that start like *cider*.
Try to include one proper noun in each list.
TEC43057
Adding *-er*
More, More, More!
Rewrite each word by adding *er*.
Draw an orange circle around each real word.
fat
thin
round
beautiful
old
small
fancy
orange
big
long
careful
smooth
Change an ending y to i before adding er.
Some short-vowel words get an extra final consonant before adding er.
TEC43057
Sentences of different lengths
Awesome Autumn
Follow the directions to answer the question three times.
What do you like most about fall?
Write an answer with 3 or 4 words.
Write an answer with 5 or 6 words.
Write an answer with 7 or more words.
TEC43057
Friendly letter
Giving Thanks
Write a letter to someone special.
Tell what you are thankful for.
Greeting,
Date
Body
Closing,
Signature
TEC43057

How to use Copy and cut out the cards. Use them as center or free-time activities.

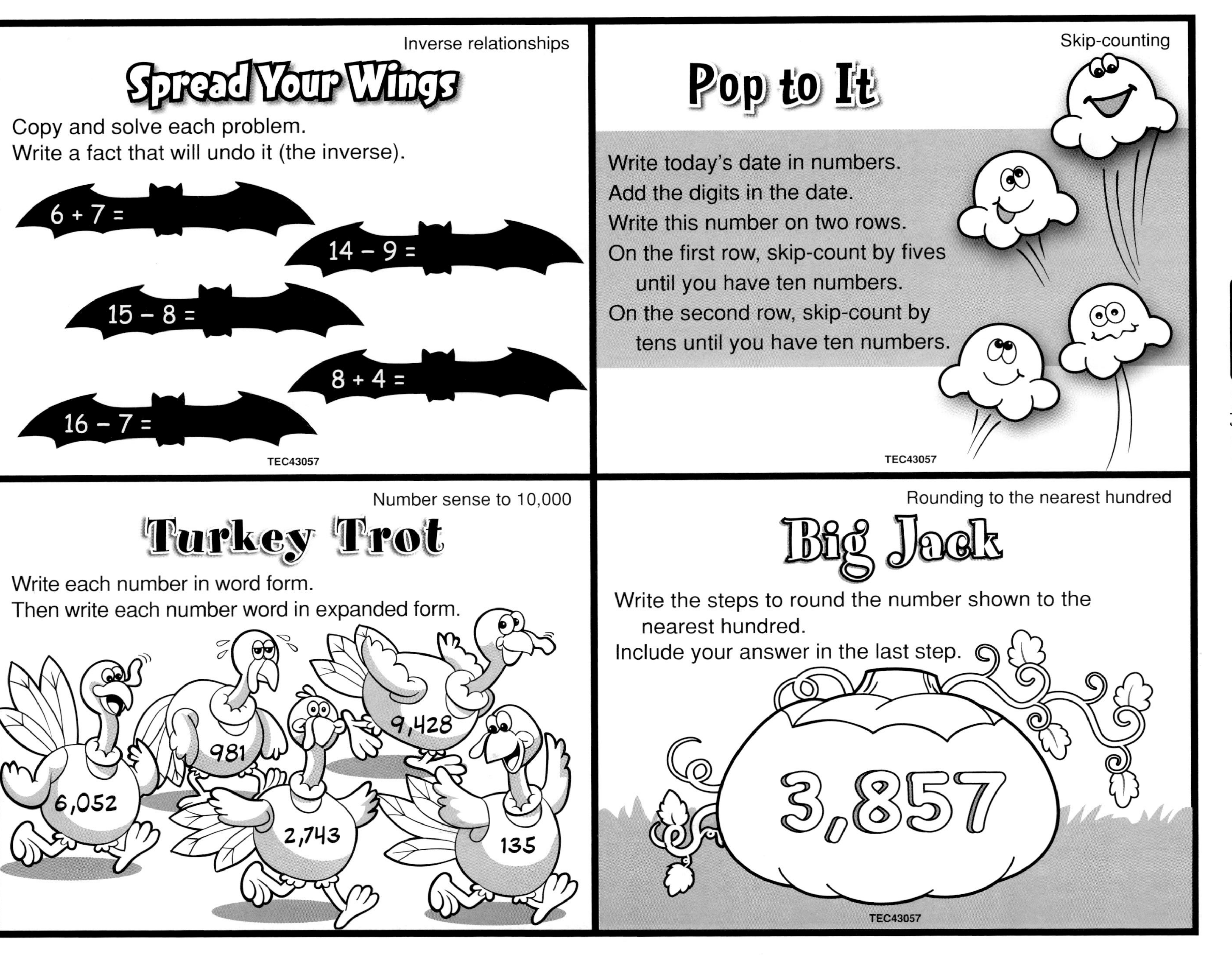

Inverse relationships

Spread Your Wings

Copy and solve each problem.
Write a fact that will undo it (the inverse).

6 + 7 =
14 – 9 =
15 – 8 =
8 + 4 =
16 – 7 =

TEC43057

Skip-counting

Pop to It

Write today's date in numbers.
Add the digits in the date.
Write this number on two rows.
On the first row, skip-count by fives until you have ten numbers.
On the second row, skip-count by tens until you have ten numbers.

TEC43057

Number sense to 10,000

Turkey Trot

Write each number in word form.
Then write each number word in expanded form.

9,428
981
6,052
2,743
135

Rounding to the nearest hundred

Big Jack

Write the steps to round the number shown to the nearest hundred.
Include your answer in the last step.

3,857

TEC43057

Pile On the Learning

Students will fall in love with these leaf-based activities!

Foliage From Far and Wide

Friendly letters

This activity will have students falling for letter–writing and will "leaf" them wanting to write more! First, request from each student's parents the name of a friend or family member who lives in a different community, preferably a different state. (Provide a name and address for students who are unable to supply one.) Next, have each child write a letter to the designated recipient and request samples of leaves from her community. When the response arrives, invite the child to read the letter aloud. Follow up the activity by having each child write a thank-you note. If desired, have him post the letter and its contents on a display that features a large US map.

Corine Mack, Chaparral Elementary, Gilbert, AZ

Sept. 19, 2011

Dear Anthony,

Thank you for your letter! It was so nice to hear from you. As you requested, I have sent several leaves from beautiful Massachusetts. They are from red maple and chestnut trees. I also included some photos of the trees in my town. I hope you enjoy them.

Your favorite relative,
Uncle Ben

tip

Use these leaves for the activities below or for research projects, science investigations, or math graphs.

Audrey

Item	Measurement (in leaves)
length of calendar	8 leaves
height of desk	
length of keyboard	
width of reading rug	
length of math book	

"Leaf" Room for Math

Nonstandard measurement

Turn fall leaves into math manipulatives! Direct each child to gather two or more leaves of the same shape and about the same size. Then list on the board classroom items you want students to measure. Demonstrate how students should hold their leaves (upright or on their sides) as you model how to measure one item. Instruct each student to copy the list, use her leaves to measure the objects, and record each nonstandard measurement. Discuss students' results and lead them to understand that since their leaves vary in size, so will the measurements. If desired, follow up the activity by having students use a ruler to measure each object and have them compare the nonstandard measurements to the standard measurements.

Cynthia Wicks, Eastwood Elementary, Roseburg, OR

Birds of a Feather

Arts and crafts

Fall leaves, paper plates (six-inch and eight-inch), plus a few basic craft supplies are all you need to put together these adorable bird crafts!

To make a turkey, a student colors a six-inch and an eight-inch plate brown. Next, he cuts from construction paper two yellow legs, two black eyes, one orange beak, and one red wattle. He glues the legs to the back of the eight-inch plate and glues the facial features to the six-inch plate. Then he glues the six-inch plate atop the eight-inch plate. Finally, the child tapes leaves (feathers) to the back of the eight-inch plate.

To make an owl, a child staples a six-inch plate (head) to an eight-inch plate (body). Next, she glues two brown leaves (ear tufts) to the back of the smaller plate. Then she glues brown leaves atop the plates. Finally, the child adds construction paper eyes and a beak.

Leaf Patterns

Use with the ideas on page 218.

4 Seasonal Centers You'll Fall For!

Nutty Words

Inflectional endings

Materials:

student copies of the booklet page from page 221
base word list like the one shown
construction paper
stapler

Base Words
bake
call
copy
dance
jump
laugh
play
shout
walk
work

laugh
laughs
laughed
laughing
My sister laughs at clowns.
I laughed at the joke.
We were laughing all day.

A student chooses a word from the list and writes it at the top of a booklet page. Then he rewrites the word on each line within the acorn, adding a different inflectional ending every time. On the lines under the acorn, the student writes one sentence for each new word. He repeats the steps with different base words and then staples the pages inside a folded sheet of construction paper.

Carolyn Burant, St. John Vianney School, Brookfield, WI

The "Eyes" Have It

Multiplying by two

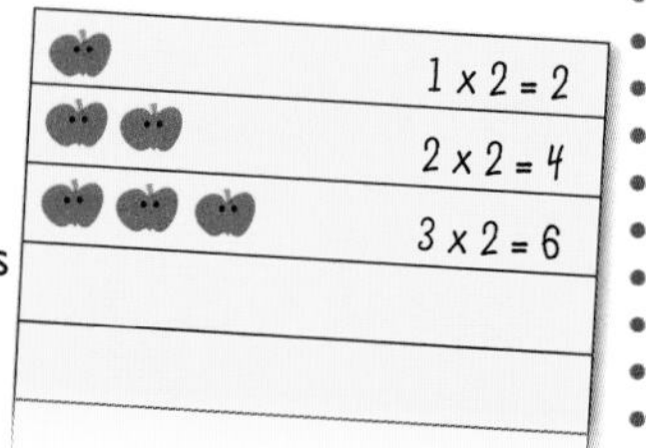
1 x 2 = 2
2 x 2 = 4
3 x 2 = 6

Materials:

orange and green colored pencils
fine-tipped black marker
paper

A child divides his paper into ten equal sections. He draws one pumpkin in the first section; then he uses the marker to add two simple eyes. The child writes a matching multiplication sentence in the same section. He repeats the steps in the next section, this time drawing two pumpkins. The student continues adding one pumpkin to each section until he has made ten pumpkins in the last section and has written the matching multiplication problem.

A Sweet Weigh-in

Estimating and measuring weight

Materials:

candy corn
balance scale
light objects
paper

Jaida

Item	Estimate	Weight
seashell	8 candy corns	11 candy corns

The child draws and labels a three-column chart as shown. She writes the name of one object in the first column. Next, she estimates its weight in candy corn and writes the estimate in the second column. The student checks her prediction by using the balance scale to find the object's weight; then she writes the weight in the third column. The child repeats the steps with each object.

Stuck on Words

Vocabulary

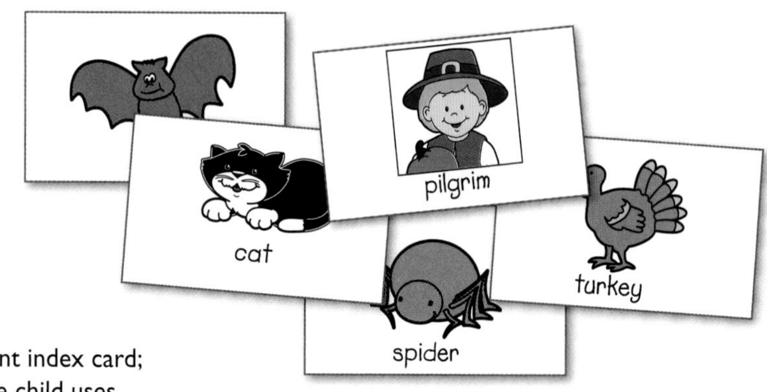
pilgrim
cat
turkey
spider

Materials:

copy of the task list on page 221
five or more seasonal stickers
five or more unlined index cards
marker

In advance, attach each sticker to a different index card; then label the card with a matching word. The child uses the word cards to complete each task on the list.

A Web of Word Tasks

1. List the words in ABC order.
2. Write five words. Next to each word, write four or more adjectives that describe the word.
3. Write four silly sentences. Use two or more words in each one.
4. Write a poem. Use five or more words in your poem.
5. Write three riddles. Use one or more words in each one.
6. Write a story. Use four or more words in your story.

Note to the teacher: Use the booklet page (top) with "Nutty Words" on page 220 and the task list (bottom) with "Stuck on Words" on page 220.

Celebrate the Season!

Chilly Chatter
Writing dialogue

"I love making snow angels!" Sammy cried.
"Me too," Sid said.
"Let's make some more over here," Sammy said.

Here's a fun winter activity students will talk about for days! To begin, read aloud *Snowmen at Night* by Caralyn Buehner. Periodically stop reading and lead students in a discussion of what the snowmen might be saying as they play. After reading, guide each child to write three or four sentences of dialogue that may have been spoken between the snowmen. Next, have the student copy his edited sentences onto sentence strips. To add a wintry touch, direct him to glue a pair of mini marshmallows (snowballs) atop each set of quotation marks. Provide time for each student to share his cool conversation with the class.

Kelly Garman, Lake Elementary, Millbury, OH

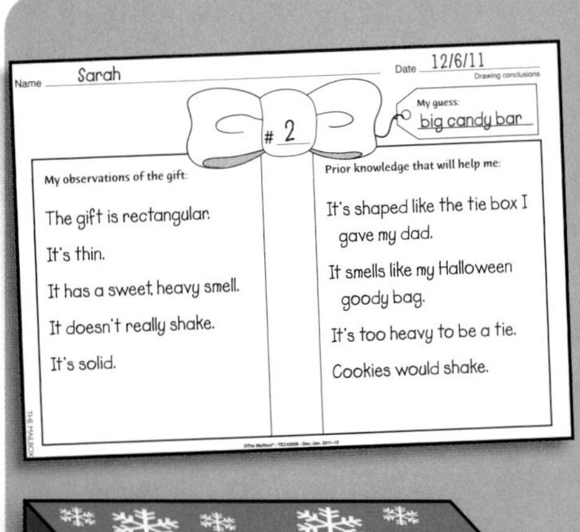
Name Sarah
Date 12/6/11
Drawing conclusions
2
My guess: big candy bar
My observations of the gift:
The gift is rectangular.
It's thin.
It has a sweet, heavy smell.
It doesn't really shake.
It's solid.
Prior knowledge that will help me:
It's shaped like the tie box I gave my dad.
It smells like my Halloween goody bag.
It's too heavy to be a tie.
Cookies would shake.
2

Unwrap a Guess
Drawing conclusions

Students combine clues and prior knowledge to uncover the mystery behind these gifts. To prepare, display several gift-wrapped packages that contain easy-to-guess items, such as a tennis racket, a fragrant box of chocolates, or a set of building blocks. Number each gift for easy identification. Give each child a copy of the chart on page 223; then direct her to choose one package and write its number on her paper. Guide the student to record her observations in the left column, inviting her to hold, shake, and smell the package. Then have her use her prior knowledge to complete the rest of the chart. Next, guide the student to combine her observations with her prior knowledge to draw a conclusion about the contents of the gift and write it on the gift tag. Set aside time for students to share their predictions; then unwrap the packages to reveal each gift. Lead students to understand that a similar process can be used to draw conclusions when they read.

Michelle Bayless, Zushi, Japan

Trim the Tree
Organizing a paragraph

Make the most of Christmastime excitement and inspire students to plan orderly paragraphs. To begin, invite students to name their favorite holiday traditions as you list their preferences on the board. Give each child a copy of page 224 and direct him to write his choice in the star. Then instruct him to complete the organizer. Wrap up the activity by having each student use his plan to write a paragraph.

Karen Almond, Royston Elementary, Royston, GA, and
Carolyn Burant, St. John Vianney School, Brookfield, WI

Name Terrell
Date 12/14/11
Graphic organizer
Topic: making cookies
Main idea: Making gingerbread cookies is fun.
Detail: using cookie cutters to cut out the shapes
Detail: decorating the baked cookies
Detail: making gingerbread people that look like people in my family
Conclusion: Making gingerbread cookies is one of my favorite holiday traditions.

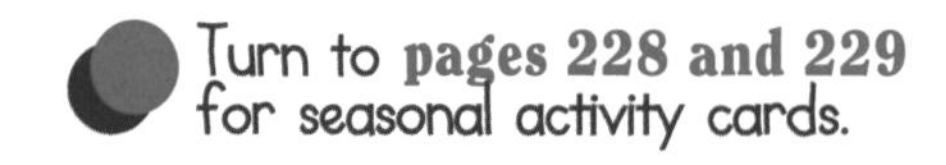
Turn to pages 228 and 229 for seasonal activity cards.

Name ______________________ Date ______________

Drawing conclusions

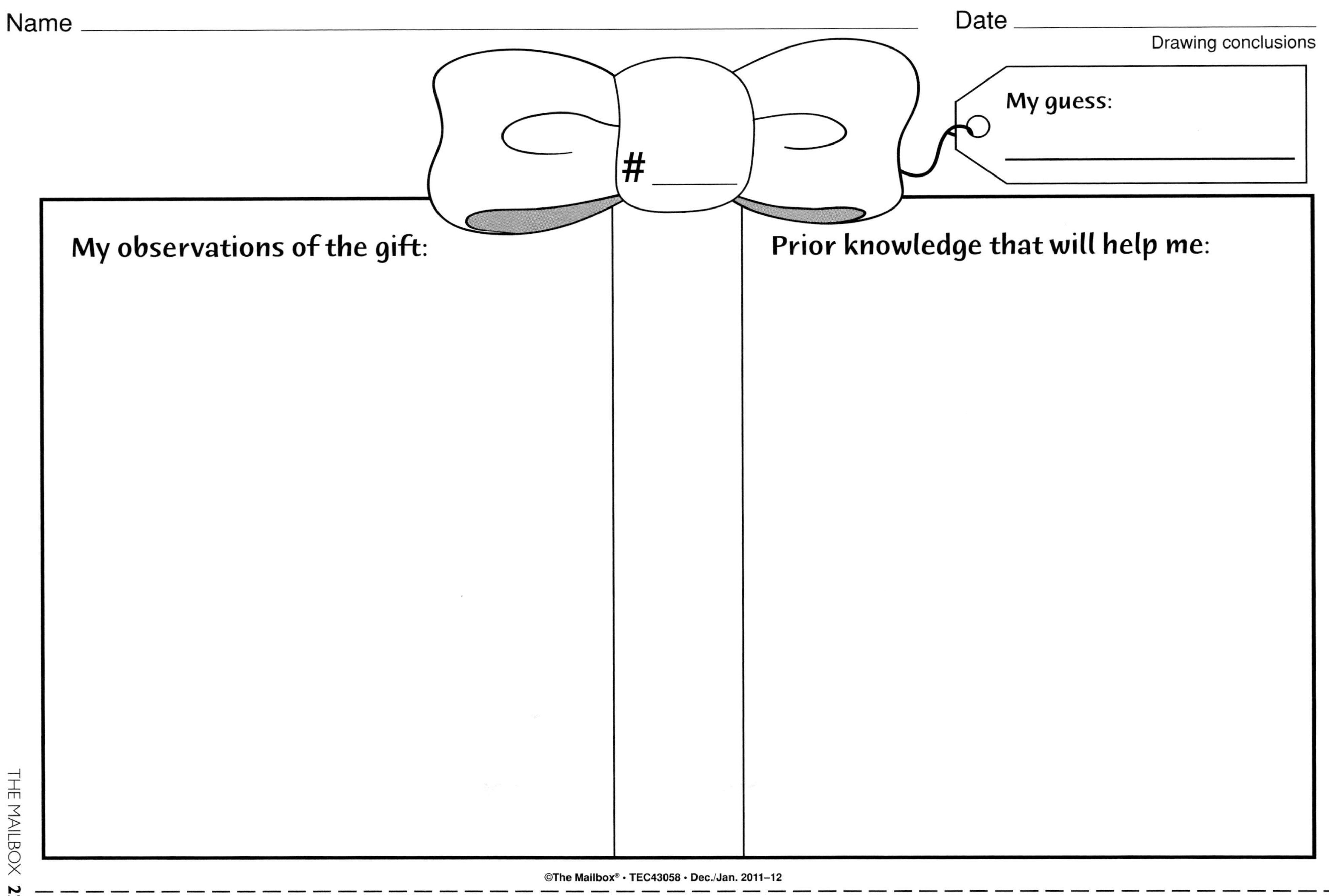
#____
My guess:
My observations of the gift:
Prior knowledge that will help me:

Note to the teacher: Use with "Unwrap a Guess" on page 222.

Name ______________________ Date ______________

Graphic organizer

Topic:
Main idea:
Detail:
Detail:
Detail:
Conclusion:

 Note to the teacher: Use with "Trim the Tree" on page 222.

Name ______________________ Date ______________

Verb tenses

Celebration Lights

If the underlined verb is used correctly, color the candle in front of the sentence.

1 We are celebrating the first night of Hanukkah.

2 Last year, we was at my cousin's house.

3 I has waited for this all year!

4 I am excited to open the gifts.

5 Grandma were going to come over tonight.

6 Now she is going to wait until tomorrow.

7 Dad has gone to get the matches.

8 Mom are lighting the menorah.

9 I was playing games with my sister.

10 The first candle is now lit.

11 We is going to spin the dreidel.

12 Dad have kept it in his desk drawer all year.

Write the number of each uncolored candle. Next to each number, write the correct verb for the matching sentence.

Bonus: For each helping verb you've written, write a different sentence.

Name ______________________ Date ______________

Elapsed time

Countdown to Christmas

Write the end time for each activity.
Color the candy that has the matching time.

Activity	Start Time	Elapsed Time	End Time
1. singing carols	6:20	1 hour	
2. shopping	12:25	1 hour, 20 minutes	
3. wrapping presents	3:00	25 minutes	
4. picking out a tree	10:30	20 minutes	
5. hanging ornaments	2:15	35 minutes	
6. visiting Santa	3:55	40 minutes	
7. hanging stockings	3:30	15 minutes	
8. addressing cards	9:10	1 hour, 5 minutes	
9. making a gingerbread house	8:25	30 minutes	
10. watching a parade	1:45	20 minutes	
11. eating dinner	5:45	30 minutes	
12. reading stories	8:15	15 minutes	
13. decorating the house	11:00	1 hour, 15 minutes	
14. looking at lights	7:30	45 minutes	
15. baking cookies	4:45	45 minutes	

10:15
3:25
6:15
5:30
8:15
7:20
3:45
2:05
10:50
8:55
12:15
1:45
4:35
8:30
2:50

Bonus: Last night's Christmas party began at 6:45. If it ended at 9:30, how long did it last? Explain how you found the answer.

Name ______________________ Date ______________

Capitalization, sequence

The Life of Martin Luther King Jr.

Circle each word that should be capitalized.
Use the color code.
Then number the sentences in order from the earliest to the latest date.

______ A. Martin marries coretta scott in 1953.

______ B. Martin Luther King Jr. dies on april 4, 1968, in memphis, Tennessee.

______ C. in 1964, King accepts the Nobel Peace Prize.

______ D. in 1948, martin becomes a minister.

______ E. Martin is born on january 15, 1929.

______ F. In 1954, Martin is a pastor in montgomery, alabama.

______ G. Martin gives his "I Have a Dream" speech on august 28, 1963.

______ H. Martin goes to Morehouse College in Atlanta, georgia, in 1944.

______ I. Dr. king organizes peaceful protests in 1965.

______ J. In 1955, King meets rosa parks and begins the bus boycotts.

Color Code

name = red
month = blue
city = green
state = orange
first word in the sentence = purple

Bonus: Write three or more sentences about Martin Luther King Jr. Use the code to circle each capital letter.

Language Arts Activity Cards

How to use Copy and cut out the cards. Use them as center or free-time activities.

Author's purpose
Celebrating Books
Copy the chart.
Write three or more story and book titles for each purpose.
Use book titles from your classroom.
To Inform
To Entertain
A History of Christmas Trees
All About Kwanzaa
The Talking Menorah
TEC43058
Synonyms
Flying on Ice
Copy each word.
For each word, list two or more synonyms.
fast
happy
short
cold
best
glide
TEC43058
Paragraph
A Man With a Dream
Copy a topic sentence.
Write a paragraph.
Martin Luther King Jr. was a brave man.
Dr. King was an important leader.
Like Dr. King, I look for peaceful solutions to problems.
TEC43058
Transition words
Thawing Out
Describe how you get warm on a cold day.
Use words like first, next, then, and finally.
TEC43058

How to use Copy and cut out the cards. Use them as center or free-time activities.

Symmetry, congruency
Right for the Weather
Which items have symmetry? How do you know?
Which items are congruent? How do you know?
TEC43058
Two-digit subtraction, no regrouping
Home, Sweet Home
Write 8 or more subtraction problems.
Use the numbers on the gumdrops.
Put the larger number on top!
75
89
54
43
10
TEC43058
Expanded form
Growing Numbers
Use the digits on the poinsettia to write ten different numbers.
Then write each number in expanded form.
9
6
4
1
3
1,349 = 1,000 + 300 + 40 + 9
TEC43058
Properties
Winter Warm-Up
Copy each mug.
Write three or more examples in each.
Commutative Property
8 + 9 = 17 and 9 + 8 = 17
Associative Property
5 + (4 + 6) = (5 + 4) + 6
5 + 10 = 15 and 9 + 6 = 15
TEC43058

SWEETEN SKILLS PRACTICE With THE GINGERBREAD MAN!

You Can't Break Me...

After reading aloud a version of *The Gingerbread Man*, ask students what *indestructible* means. Lead them to understand that it means that something can't be destroyed; then ask how the gingerbread man could have dressed or what he might have done to be indestructible. Next, give each child a copy of the small pattern on page 231 and have him decorate it to reflect what he thinks an indestructible gingerbread man looks like. Instruct the student to glue the pattern to the top of a sheet of paper and rewrite the story so that the gingerbread man continues living to this day. Bind the stories in a class book titled "You Can't Break Me!"

Theresa Cress, Bellingrath Hills Elementary, Greenwell Springs, LA

YOU CAN'T BREAK ME!

Glyph Key

Who is your favorite character?
gingerbread man = yellow buttons
cow = purple buttons
threshers = orange buttons
fox = green buttons

Do you think *you* could catch the gingerbread man?
yes = round, black eyes
no = round, white eyes

What's your favorite gingerbread treat?
cookie = right leg cut off
house = left leg cut off
neither = no legs cut off

Are you a boy or a girl?
boy = white icing
girl = pink icing

New and Improved

Students make personalized gingerbread men projects and display data with this decorative glyph activity. Have each child cut out a copy of the large pattern from page 231; then post the glyph key shown. Instruct each student to refer to the key to add details to her pattern before coloring it brown. Display the completed projects and a copy of the key on a board titled "New and Improved." Use the projects to ask questions such as "How many students think they could catch the gingerbread man?" and "Do more boys like the gingerbread man or the fox?"

Laura Mihalenko, Harry S. Truman Elementary, Parlin, NJ

That's "Sense-sational"!

Here's an activity that's just right for practicing sensory details! Have each child decorate a copy of the large pattern on page 231. Then have him write a description of his masterpiece, telling what it looks like, what it might sound like if it talked, what it feels like, what it smells like, and what it might taste like. Post each gingerbread pattern on the board and write a different number near each one. Invite each child to read his description aloud and challenge his classmates to guess which gingerbread man he's describing.

Elizabeth Ullinger, Cranston, RI

7

8

tip

For a delicious twist, provide mini marshmallows and mini chocolate candies for students to glue to their patterns.

Gingerbread Man Patterns

Use with the ideas on page 230.

TEC43058
TEC43058

Celebrate the Season!

Earth-Friendly Valentines

Letter writing

Instead of exchanging valentines with every classmate, invite each student to create a single valentine for the entire class using recycled materials. First, provide students with printed materials, such as old newspapers, magazines, catalogs, or advertising flyers. Instruct each child to cut out words or phrases to use in a message of friendship. Next, have the student cut out a heart from a piece of construction paper and write the greeting "Dear Class," as shown. Direct her to prepare a message to the class, gluing the cutout words and phrases where needed. Display the completed valentines on a bulletin board titled "From the Heart."

Karen Slattery, Dunrankin Drive Public School, Mississauga, Ontario, Canada

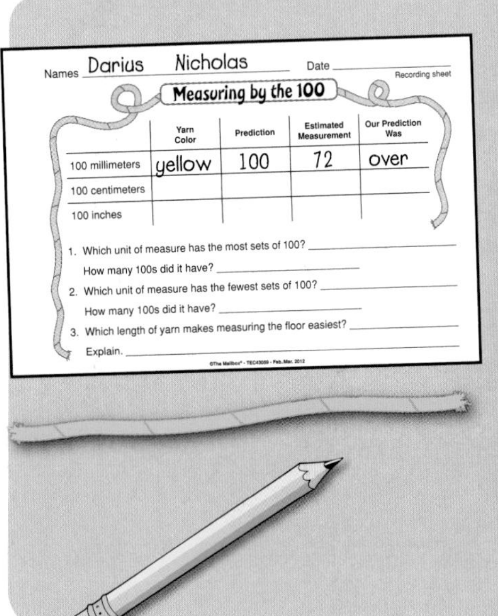

Names Darius Nicholas Date ______ Recording sheet

Measuring by the 100

	Yarn Color	Prediction	Estimated Measurement	Our Prediction Was
100 millimeters	yellow	100	72	over
100 centimeters				
100 inches				

1. Which unit of measure has the most sets of 100? ______
   How many 100s did it have? ______
2. Which unit of measure has the fewest sets of 100? ______
   How many 100s did it have? ______
3. Which length of yarn makes measuring the floor easiest? ______
   Explain. ______

©The Mailbox® • TEC43059 • Feb./Mar. 2012

How Big Is 100?

Measurement

Here's a 100th Day partner activity that will help students compare customary and metric units of length. In advance, cut three lengths of yarn: one 100 millimeters long, one 100 centimeters long, and one 100 inches long. Use a different color for each length. To begin, the duo determines which color yarn measures 100 millimeters and writes that color on a copy of page 233. Then the students predict and record how many 100-millimeter lengths it will take to measure the length of the classroom floor. The pair measures the floor to the nearest 100 millimeters, writes the measurement on the recording sheet, and evaluates its prediction as *over* or *under* the recorded measurement. The duo repeats the steps for each of the remaining yarn pieces. When the chart is complete, the students answer the questions at the bottom of the recording sheet.

Tomekia Darrisaw, Diamond Lakes Elementary, Hephzibah, GA

Valuable Contributors

Historic figures

Students will flip for these supersize commemorative coins! First, list on the board seasonal observances, such as Presidents' Day, Black History Month (February), and National Women's History Month (March). Then identify important people connected with each observance. Next, direct each student to choose one of these figures and research details about his or her life. If desired, have the child record her findings on a copy of the planning sheet at the bottom of page 233. Direct the child to draw pictures related to the figure on both sides of a paper plate. Instruct the student to flatten the edges of his plate before writing important dates, titles, and other details along its outer edge. Finally, have the child color the plate so it looks like a coin.

Stephanie Brachtenbach, Harmony Elementary, Overland Park, KS

Check out the seasonal practice sheets on pages 234–237!

Names ______________________ Date ______________

Recording sheet

Measuring by the 100

	Yarn Color	Prediction	Estimated Measurement	Our Prediction Was
100 millimeters				
100 centimeters				
100 inches				

1. Which unit of measure has the most sets of 100? ______________

   How many 100s did it have? ______________

2. Which unit of measure has the fewest sets of 100? ______________

   How many 100s did it have? ______________

3. Which length of yarn makes measuring the floor easiest? ______________

   Explain. ______________

Name ______________________ Date ______________

Planning page

Getting to Know...

Who? ______________

When did he or she live? ______________

____

Why was he or she important? ______________

____

____

When do we honor this person? ______________

Note to the teacher: Use the recording sheet with "How Big Is 100?" on page 232 and the planning page with "Valuable Contributors" on page 232.

Name ______________________ Date ______________

R-controlled vowels

Sending All His Love

Read each word.
Write it on the matching cage.

bear
word
soar
door
turkey
chair
shirt
board
four
square
fair
turtle
beware
north
corn
there
dessert
winter

vowel sound like *bird*

______
______
______
______
______
______

vowel sound like *care*

______
______
______
______
______
______

vowel sound like *more*

______
______
______
______
______
______

Bonus: Write another word on each list.

Name ______________________ Date ______________

Reading comprehension

A Seat for Change

On the first of December in 1955,
Rosa Parks left her job at the tailor shop.
She found a seat in the middle of the bus
And sat down to ride to her stop.

Later, as a white man looked for a seat on the bus,
the driver told Mrs. Parks to move to the back.
In Alabama, the law said she should go
Because, you see, Rosa was black.

When Rosa wouldn't change her seat, they took her to jail.
She was scared, but our heroine knew she was right.
Rosa's bravery helped blacks everywhere—
She was a leader for civil rights.

Read the poem. Respond.

1. Did the author write the poem to *entertain*, *inform*, or *persuade*? ______________

   Explain. ______________________________

   ____

2. What is the main idea of the poem? (Circle below.)

   a. Rosa Parks rode a bus home from work.

   b. Rosa Parks lived in Alabama.

   c. Rosa Parks was a leader because she stood up for her beliefs.

3. Circle the proper nouns in the poem. Use the code.

   name of a person = red   name of a month = blue   name of a state = yellow

4. What is a **heroine**? ______________________________

   Why does the author call Rosa Parks a heroine? ______________

   ____

Bonus: Do you think "A Seat for Change" is a good title for this poem? Why or why not?

Name ______________________ Date ______________

Organizing data

Follow the Rainbow!

red
orange
yellow
green
blue
indigo
violet

Question: Which color do you like best?

Survey your classmates.
Use tally marks.

Write a title and label the graph.
Then use your survey results to complete the graph.

____

R														
O														
Y														
G														
B														
I														
V														

____

Use your data to complete each sentence.

1. Most students chose the color ______________.
2. ______________ was the least popular color.
3. ______________ was chosen more than ______________.
4. Fewer people chose ______________ than ______________.
5. ______________ people chose the same color I like best.

Bonus: Write a sentence to tell what your data reveals about the color indigo.

Name ______________________ Date ______________

Marvelous March

Pick and Practice Skill Review

Pick ______ activities to do.
When you finish an activity, color its number.

1 For each word, write two different sentences to show two different meanings.

march
fly
top

2 March is National Women's History Month. Describe a woman you look up to and tell why you admire her.

3 March 17 is St. Patrick's Day. Write a list of five or more verbs that describe actions that a leprechaun might do.

4 "March comes in like a lion and goes out like a lamb," or so they say. What do you think this proverb means? Do you think it will be true for this March? Why or why not?

5 Other than a pot of gold, what would you like to find at the end of a rainbow? Make a list of ten or more items, but use only compound words!

6 Pretend you are hunting for four-leaf clovers outside your school. Is it *impossible*, *unlikely*, *possible*, or *likely* that you will find one? Explain.

7 Half the foods you eat should be fruits and vegetables. Draw a plate and divide it in half. On one half, list all the green fruits and vegetables you can think of.

8 March can be a great time to fly a kite! Draw and color a kite. Then measure and label its sides.

9 March 20 is the first day of spring. Make a schedule of all the things you would like to do on this day. Include start and stop times.

How to use: Program the student directions on a copy of this page with the number of activities to be completed. Then copy the page for each student.

Language Arts Activity Cards

How to use Copy and cut out the cards. Use them as center or free-time activities.

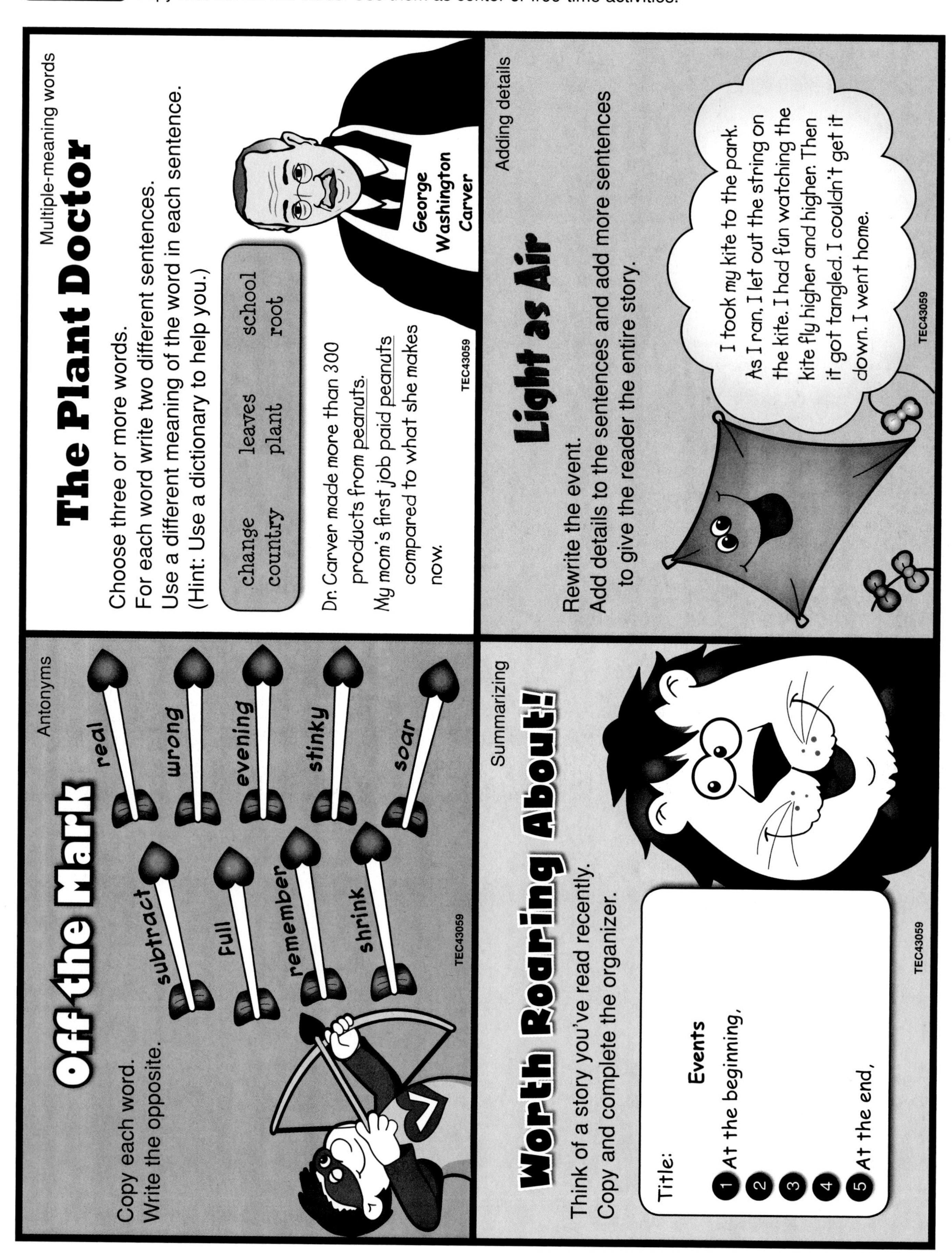

Antonyms

Off the Mark

Copy each word.
Write the opposite.

subtract
full
remember
shrink
real
wrong
evening
stinky
soar

TEC43059

Multiple-meaning words

The Plant Doctor

Choose three or more words.
For each word write two different sentences.
Use a different meaning of the word in each sentence.
(Hint: Use a dictionary to help you.)

change	leaves	school
country	plant	root

Dr. Carver made more than 300 products from <u>peanuts</u>.
My mom's first job paid <u>peanuts</u> compared to what she makes now.

George
Washington
Carver

TEC43059

Summarizing

Worth Roaring About!

Think of a story you've read recently.
Copy and complete the organizer.

Title:

Events

1. At the beginning,
2.
3.
4.
5. At the end,

TEC43059

Adding details

Light as Air

Rewrite the event.
Add details to the sentences and add more sentences to give the reader the entire story.

I took my kite to the park. As I ran, I let out the string on the kite. I had fun watching the kite fly higher and higher. Then it got tangled. I couldn't get it down. I went home.

TEC43059

Math Activity Cards

How to use Copy and cut out the cards. Use them as center or free-time activities.

Slides, flips, turns
Head Over Heels
For each heart, draw and label the slide (translation), flip (reflection), and turn (rotation).
A.
B.
C.
TEC43059
Fractions of a group
Tooth Fairy Treasures
For each set, write a fraction to describe each kind of tooth. Then circle the larger fraction.
A.
B.
C.
D.
= molars
= bicuspids
TEC43059
Multiplication facts
Lucky Numbers
For each four-leaf clover, write and solve 4 multiplication problems.
Use the bold number in each problem.
A. 1 4 3 6 8
B. 2 0 5 3 9
C. 5 3 7 7 8
1 x 3 =
TEC43059
Skip-counting by four
Leaping Ahead
2012 is a leap year. This means February has 29 days instead of 28.
Since a leap year occurs every four years, in which years will the next five leap years occur? Explain how you found your answers.
TEC43059

Love Connections!

3 Valentine's Day Read-Alouds for Making Connections

1 *Roses Are Pink, Your Feet Really Stink*

by Diane deGroat

Gilbert's teacher assigns the task of writing a poem for each classmate, but Gilbert gets stuck when writing for Lewis and Margaret. As a result, these two classmates get their feelings hurt and Gilbert has to find a way to make things right.

Have each child fold a large paper heart in half and then unfold it. Instruct the child to write about one of the three characters' feelings or actions on the left side of the heart. Then have her write a connection to those feelings or actions on the right side. Punch two holes in each child's project and feed a length of yarn through the holes to connect them; then tape one end to a heart labeled with the title and author's name.

Roses Are Pink,
Your Feet Really Stink
Diane deGroat
Gilbert hurt Lewis's and Margaret's feelings. He wrote a nice poem to each one to show he was sorry.
One time, I saw my mom was upset. I wrote her a silly poem. It made her smile.

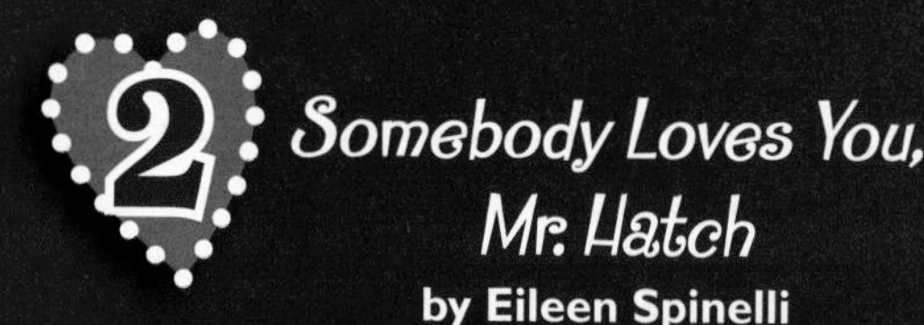

SOMEBODY LOVES YOU, MR. HATCH
Story by Eileen Spinelli
Paul Yalo
A Valuable Classmate and Friend
Ms. Burant's Class
St. John Vianney School
Brookfield, WI

2 *Somebody Loves You, Mr. Hatch*

by Eileen Spinelli

Normally Mr. Hatch keeps to himself. Then one day he receives an unexpected love note in the mail.

After sharing the story, put students into small groups. Give one child in each group an envelope labeled like the one shown. Invite the student to reflect on the story and share a connection he made to it. Then direct the child to pass it to another child in his group to do the same. Students continue in this manner until everyone has spoken.

3 *The Day It Rained Hearts*

by Felicia Bond

In this short story, Cornelia Augusta carefully chooses which hearts to give to each of her friends.

Discuss these actions as well as other actions from the story students can relate to. Then have each child write a connection to the story on a heart-shaped cutout, adding a smiley face if he listed a text-to-self connection, a book for text-to-text, or a globe for text-to-world. If desired, post the hearts on a display so they look like they are falling from a cloud in the sky.

Cornelia Augusta made her friends feel special by making each one a special card. I like to make homemade cards for my friends too.
The Day It Rained Hearts
Felicia Bond

Michelle Bayless, Croughton, England; Carolyn Burant, St. John Vianney School Brookfield, WI; Cynthia Wicks, Eastwood Elementary, Roseburg, OR

HOORAY FOR Presidents' Day

☆ Where Do They Call Home? ☆

Displaying data

How do the states compare when it comes to the number of presidents born in each one? This activity gives students the answer! First, have each child complete a copy of page 242. Then direct him to graph the data on a large sheet of construction paper. Lead students in a discussion of the states represented, the state where the most presidents were born, and which states are not included. **To extend the activity**, also give each child a copy of a United States map. Have him locate each state listed on page 242 and write within the state outline the number of presidents born there.

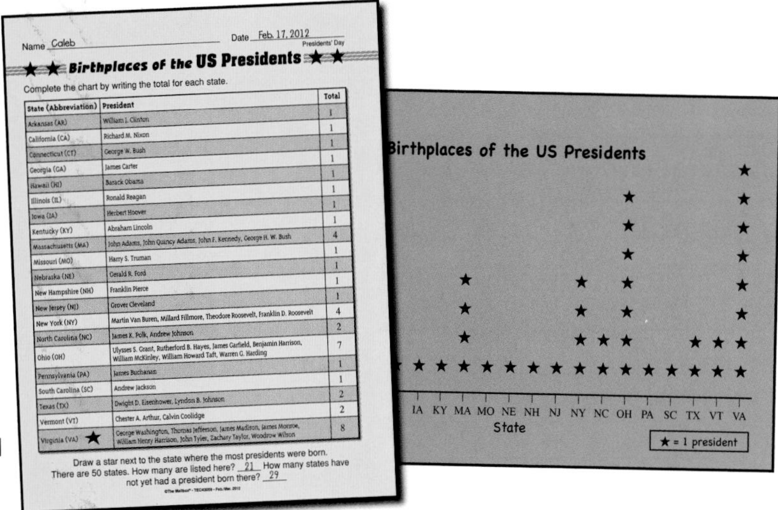

Name Caleb   Date Feb. 17, 2012

Presidents' Day

★★ Birthplaces of the US Presidents ★★

Complete the chart by writing the total for each state.

State (Abbreviation)	President	Total
Arkansas (AR)	William J. Clinton	1
California (CA)	Richard M. Nixon	1
Connecticut (CT)	George W. Bush	1
Georgia (GA)	James Carter	1
Hawaii (HI)	Barack Obama	1
Illinois (IL)	Ronald Reagan	1
Iowa (IA)	Herbert Hoover	1
Kentucky (KY)	Abraham Lincoln	1
Massachusetts (MA)	John Adams, John Quincy Adams, John F. Kennedy, George H. W. Bush	4
Missouri (MO)	Harry S. Truman	1
Nebraska (NE)	Gerald R. Ford	1
New Hampshire (NH)	Franklin Pierce	1
New Jersey (NJ)	Grover Cleveland	1
New York (NY)	Martin Van Buren, Millard Fillmore, Theodore Roosevelt, Franklin D. Roosevelt	4
North Carolina (NC)	James K. Polk, Andrew Johnson	2
Ohio (OH)	Ulysses S. Grant, Rutherford B. Hayes, James Garfield, Benjamin Harrison, William McKinley, William Howard Taft, Warren G. Harding	7
Pennsylvania (PA)	James Buchanan	1
South Carolina (SC)	Andrew Jackson	1
Texas (TX)	Dwight D. Eisenhower, Lyndon B. Johnson	2
Vermont (VT)	Chester A. Arthur, Calvin Coolidge	2
Virginia (VA) ★	George Washington, Thomas Jefferson, James Madison, James Monroe, William Henry Harrison, John Tyler, Zachary Taylor, Woodrow Wilson	8

Draw a star next to the state where the most presidents were born.
There are 50 states. How many are listed here? 21 How many states have not yet had a president born there? 29

Birthplaces of the US Presidents
IA KY MA MO NE NH NJ NY NC OH PA SC TX VT VA
State
★ = 1 president

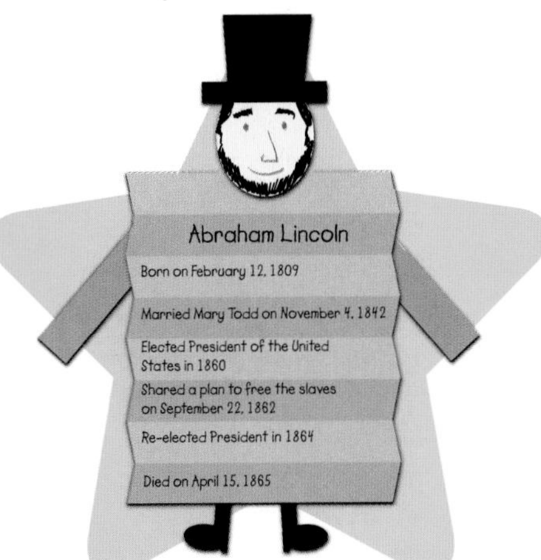

Abraham Lincoln
Born on February 12, 1809
Married Mary Todd on November 4, 1842
Elected President of the United States in 1860
Shared a plan to free the slaves on September 22, 1862
Re-elected President in 1864
Died on April 15, 1865

☆ Lovable Leaders ☆

Sequencing events, timeline

Perfect for any president, these low-prep projects are positively precious! To make one, accordion-fold a sheet of paper eight times and then unfold it. Cut an oval from flesh-colored construction paper and add facial details to match the president. Glue the oval to the top section of the folded paper and write the president's name in the second section. In each remaining section, write one important event from the president's life. Glue on construction paper arms and feet; then use crayons to add other details to complete the project. **To vary the activity**, have each student list fun facts about the president instead.

☆ Presidential Math Prompts ☆

- Abraham Lincoln was the tallest president. He stood 6 feet, 4 inches tall. What was Lincoln's height in inches? *(76 inches)*
- It took Washington three days to travel about 90 miles from New York City to Philadelphia. If he traveled the same distance each day, about how many miles did he cover in one day? Explain how you found your answer. *(30 miles; Explanations will vary.)*
- President Lincoln's portrait is on the US penny and five-dollar bill. President Washington's portrait is on the one-dollar bill and the standard quarter. If you had one of each bill and coin, which president would be worth more? *(Lincoln)* What is the total value of the two coins and the two bills? *($6.26)*
- When a president takes the oath of office, he gives a speech. George Washington's speech for his second oath of office was 135 words long. William Henry Harrison's speech was 8,445 words long. How many more words was Harrison's speech than Washington's speech? *(8,310 words)*

Name ______________________ Date ______________

Birthplaces of the US Presidents

Complete the chart by writing the total for each state.

State (Abbreviation)	President	Total
Arkansas (AR)	William J. Clinton	
California (CA)	Richard M. Nixon	
Connecticut (CT)	George W. Bush	
Georgia (GA)	James Carter	
Hawaii (HI)	Barack Obama	
Illinois (IL)	Ronald Reagan	
Iowa (IA)	Herbert Hoover	
Kentucky (KY)	Abraham Lincoln	
Massachusetts (MA)	John Adams, John Quincy Adams, John F. Kennedy, George H. W. Bush	
Missouri (MO)	Harry S. Truman	
Nebraska (NE)	Gerald R. Ford	
New Hampshire (NH)	Franklin Pierce	
New Jersey (NJ)	Grover Cleveland	
New York (NY)	Martin Van Buren, Millard Fillmore, Theodore Roosevelt, Franklin D. Roosevelt	
North Carolina (NC)	James K. Polk, Andrew Johnson	
Ohio (OH)	Ulysses S. Grant, Rutherford B. Hayes, James Garfield, Benjamin Harrison, William McKinley, William Howard Taft, Warren G. Harding	
Pennsylvania (PA)	James Buchanan	
South Carolina (SC)	Andrew Jackson	
Texas (TX)	Dwight D. Eisenhower, Lyndon B. Johnson	
Vermont (VT)	Chester A. Arthur, Calvin Coolidge	
Virginia (VA)	George Washington, Thomas Jefferson, James Madison, James Monroe, William Henry Harrison, John Tyler, Zachary Taylor, Woodrow Wilson	

Draw a star next to the state where the most presidents were born.
There are 50 states. How many are listed here? _____ How many states have not yet had a president born there? _____

 Note to the teacher: Use with "Where Do They Call Home?" on page 241.

Wonderful Work, Ladies!

National Women's History Month

Use this partner game to introduce students to important American women. Instruct each duo to study a copy of the list below. Then direct the students to draw a tic-tac-toe grid on a sheet of paper and write a different name from the list in each section. To play, read aloud the contribution of one woman below. Students review their lists and their boards, and if they have the name of the matching woman, they circle it. Continue in this manner until a duo has three spaces in a row circled. Those students call out, "Wonderful work, ladies!" and then read aloud the names circled in the row. If time allows, direct students to create a new board and play again.

- ☐ **Jane Addams** She helped people in need. She also worked to help women get the right to vote.
- ☐ **Clara Barton** She was a nurse during the Civil War. She started the American Red Cross.
- ☐ **Elizabeth Blackwell** She was the first woman in the US to earn a degree to be a doctor. She also opened a hospital for the poor in New York City.
- ☐ **Marie Curie** She was a scientist and the first woman to win a Nobel Prize.
- ☐ **Amelia Earhart** She was the first woman to fly a plane across the Atlantic Ocean alone.
- ☐ **Mae Jemison** She was the first African American woman to travel in space.
- ☐ **Helen Keller** Blind and deaf, she wrote books, spoke to groups, and raised funds to support disabled people.
- ☐ **Ellen Ochoa** She was the first Hispanic woman to travel in space.
- ☐ **Sandra Day O'Connor** She was the first woman to serve on the US Supreme Court.
- ☐ **Rosa Parks** When she refused to give up her bus seat, she started a movement for equality for black Americans.
- ☐ **Sally Ride** She was the first American woman to travel in space.
- ☐ **Nellie Tayloe Ross** She was the first female governor of a US state.
- ☐ **Mother Teresa** She was a nun who helped the poor. She won the Nobel Peace Prize for her work.
- ☐ **Harriet Tubman** She was a nurse and a spy in the Civil War. She served as a "conductor" of the Underground Railroad and helped nearly 800 slaves get to freedom.

Celebrate the Season!

Shake, Shake, Shake
Observing sound

These centers are "eggs-actly" what your students need to identify, compare, and sort a variety of sounds. To prepare, copy the activity cards on page 245; then follow the steps below. Instruct a student to follow the directions on each activity card to complete each activity.

Activity One: Use a permanent marker to number eight plastic eggs 1–8. Fill pairs of eggs with different household objects, such as rice, buttons, beans, coins, and hardware. Place the eggs in a basket labeled "Activity One" and set it out with a copy of the "Activity One" card from page 245 and a supply of paper.

Activity Two: Use a permanent marker to draw a dot on the deepest half of six different-colored plastic eggs. Fill the eggs with varying quantities of rice, filling only the half with the dot and being careful not to overfill the eggs. Store the eggs in a sanitized egg carton labeled "Activity Two" and set the carton out with a copy of the "Activity Two" card from page 245 and a supply of paper.

Activity Two
Scrambled Eggs

1. One at a time, remove each egg from the carton. Gently shake it. Listen for the sound differences among the eggs.
2. Shake each egg again. Guess which egg is filled with the least amount of rice. Place that egg first in the egg carton.
3. Order the remaining five eggs from the least amount filled to the greatest.
4. On a sheet of paper, draw the eggs as shown below. Color the eggs to match the order in the carton.
5. Open each egg by carefully holding the half of the egg with the dot in one hand and removing the other half with your other hand. Set the half of the egg with rice back in the carton. Write about your findings. Explain how you ordered the eggs.

I (did / did not
greatest.
Explain the ste

Elizabeth Searls Almy, Greensboro, NC

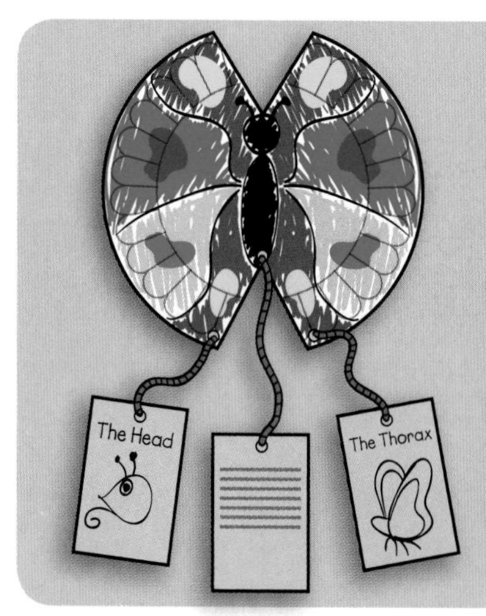
The Head
The Thorax

Wings and Things
Research skills, insects

Attract students to nonfiction books with this magnificent mobile. After a child reads about an interesting creature, have him write three facts about the insect on separate index cards and then illustrate each fact on the other side of each card. To make the mobile, the student colors and cuts a paper plate so it resembles the insect he studied. He punches a hole in the plate and one in a card. The student feeds a length of yarn through each hole and ties the ends; then he repeats the steps with the other two cards. Display the mobiles and watch as interest in nonfiction books takes flight!

Jennifer Stakes, Norfolk, VA

In Full Bloom
Similes

Reduce and reuse the scrap papers from your classroom recycling container to get students' figurative-language skills blossoming. First, a student cuts a medium-size flower shape from a piece of paper. She tears different-colored construction paper scraps into small pieces and glues the pieces so they resemble a mosaic in the center of the cutout. Then she cuts out two green leaves and writes on one leaf "Waiting for a flower to bloom is [like/as]..." and completes the simile on the other leaf. The student posts her project as part of a display titled "Worth the Wait."

Waiting for a flower to bloom is like...
...waiting for the sun to rise.
Tamara

Teresa Vilfer-Snyder, Fredericktown, OH

Turn to pages 246–248 for **seasonal practice sheets.**

Activity One
I'm All Ears

1. Fold a sheet of paper in fourths and then unfold it. Label each section with these sentence starters.

My prediction: ______________________

____

The sound reminds me of ______________________

____

Inside the eggs are ______________________

____

2. Select an egg. Shake it gently. Listen to the sound it makes. Set it aside.
3. Choose a different egg and shake it. Compare its sound to the first egg. Do the sounds match?
   - If yes, write the eggs' numbers on one section of your paper. Guess what the sound is and record your prediction. Also write what the sound reminds you of. Set the pair aside.
   - If the sounds do not match, select a different egg until a match is made.
4. Repeat Steps 2–3 until all four pairs of eggs are matched.
5. Carefully look inside each egg. Record your findings.

TEC43060

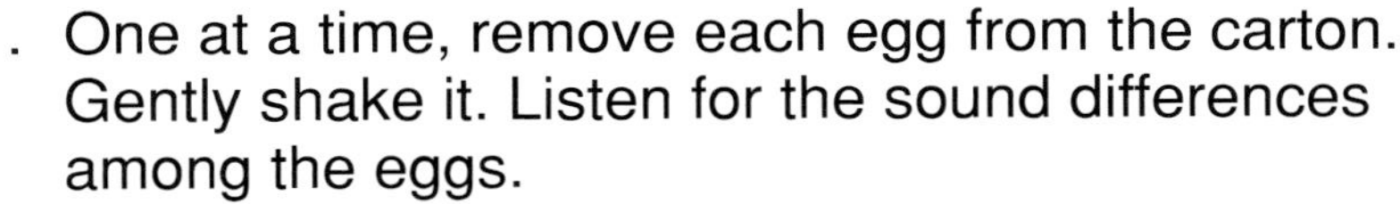

Activity Two
Scrambled Eggs

1. One at a time, remove each egg from the carton. Gently shake it. Listen for the sound differences among the eggs.
2. Shake each egg again. Guess which egg is filled with the least amount of rice. Place that egg first in the egg carton.
3. Order the remaining five eggs from the least amount filled to the greatest.
4. On a sheet of paper, draw the eggs as shown below. Color the eggs to match the order in the carton.
5. Open each egg by carefully holding the half of the egg with the dot in one hand and removing the other half with your other hand. Set the half of the egg with rice back in the carton. Write about your findings. Explain how you ordered the eggs.

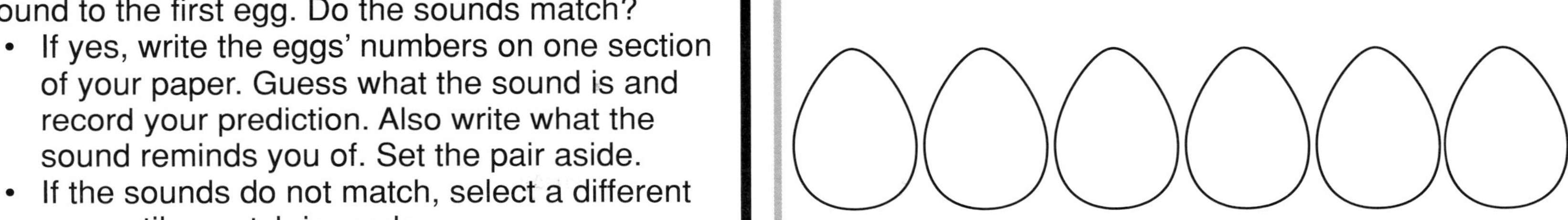

I (did / did not) order the eggs from least to greatest.
Explain the steps you took to order the eggs.

TEC43060

Name ______________________________ Date ______________

End marks

Signs of Spring

Read each sentence.
Write the missing end mark.
Cross out a matching end mark on the wall.

1. Spring is in the air
2. What are the signs of spring
3. Look at all those amazing flowers blooming
4. Do the days last longer
5. Hooray, it's getting warmer
6. Birds return to their homes
7. Tilly's home is not as she left it
8. Wow, Tilly's house is a mess
9. What happened while she was gone
10. She has some chores to do
11. Where should Tilly start
12. Should she sweep or dust first
13. Whew, spring cleaning is hard work
14. Tilly is a busy bird
15. Oh, how her home will sparkle

. ? . ? .
? ! ! ! ?
! . ? . !

Bonus: Write a sentence that tells when to use a question mark.
Write a sentence that tells when to use an exclamation mark.

Name ______________________ Date ______________

Compare and contrast

Play Ball!

Read each character's description.
Then answer each question about the bears.

Coach Bruno is fair and cheers for his players. He gives each player a turn on the field. Coach Bruno teaches his team the rules and how to be good athletes.

Bart loves baseball. He is the best batter on the team. Bart is confident and fast. Each time Bart is at bat, the other team gets a real workout. Bart just loves baseball.

Belle is the best pitcher. She tends to be shy around others, but Belle does not look shy on the mound. She throws the best curveball in the league.

Bud would rather watch baseball than play it. He is fair and honest. This makes him a great scorekeeper. Bud sits on the bench and cheers for the team. He loves this game!

How are the bears alike?

1. Bart and Belle ______________________

2. Coach Bruno and Bud ______________________

3. Bart and Bud ______________________

How are the bears different?

4. Coach Bruno and Belle ______________________

5. Belle and Bud ______________________

6. Bart and Belle ______________________

Bonus: Write two sentences. Explain which bear is most like you and which bear is least like you.

Name ________________________________ Date ________________

Multiplication and division fact families

Painting by Numbers

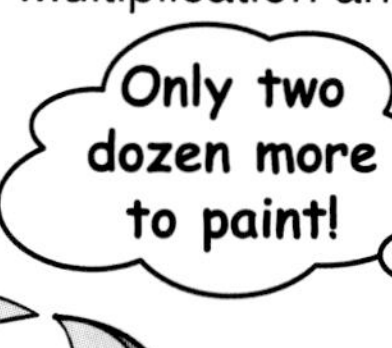

Only two dozen more to paint!

Color each set of eggs that make a fact family.
Write the fact families on the lines below.

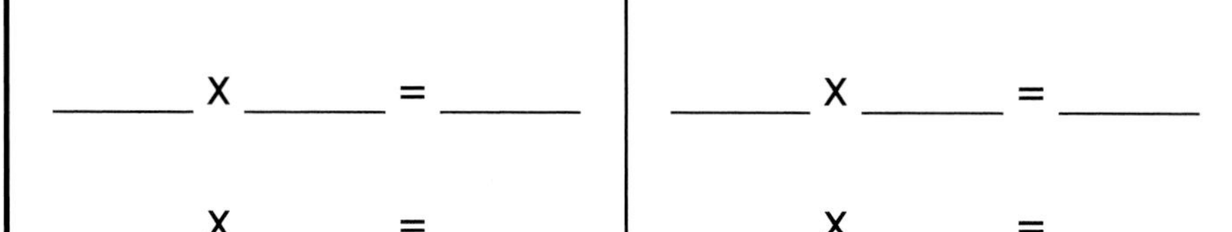

____ x ____ = ____ ____ x ____ = ____ ____ ÷ ____ = ____ ____ ÷ ____ = ____	____ x ____ = ____ ____ x ____ = ____ ____ ÷ ____ = ____ ____ ÷ ____ = ____
____ x ____ = ____ ____ x ____ = ____ ____ ÷ ____ = ____ ____ ÷ ____ = ____	____ x ____ = ____ ____ x ____ = ____ ____ ÷ ____ = ____ ____ ÷ ____ = ____
____ x ____ = ____ ____ x ____ = ____ ____ ÷ ____ = ____ ____ ÷ ____ = ____	____ x ____ = ____ ____ x ____ = ____ ____ ÷ ____ = ____ ____ ÷ ____ = ____

9
4
36
6
24
5
6
3
18
3
21
7

2
15
7
8
40
5
56
8
7

6
2
12

Bonus: For each uncolored set of eggs, change one number to make a fact family. Write the fact family.

How to use Copy and cut out the cards. Use them as center or free-time activities.

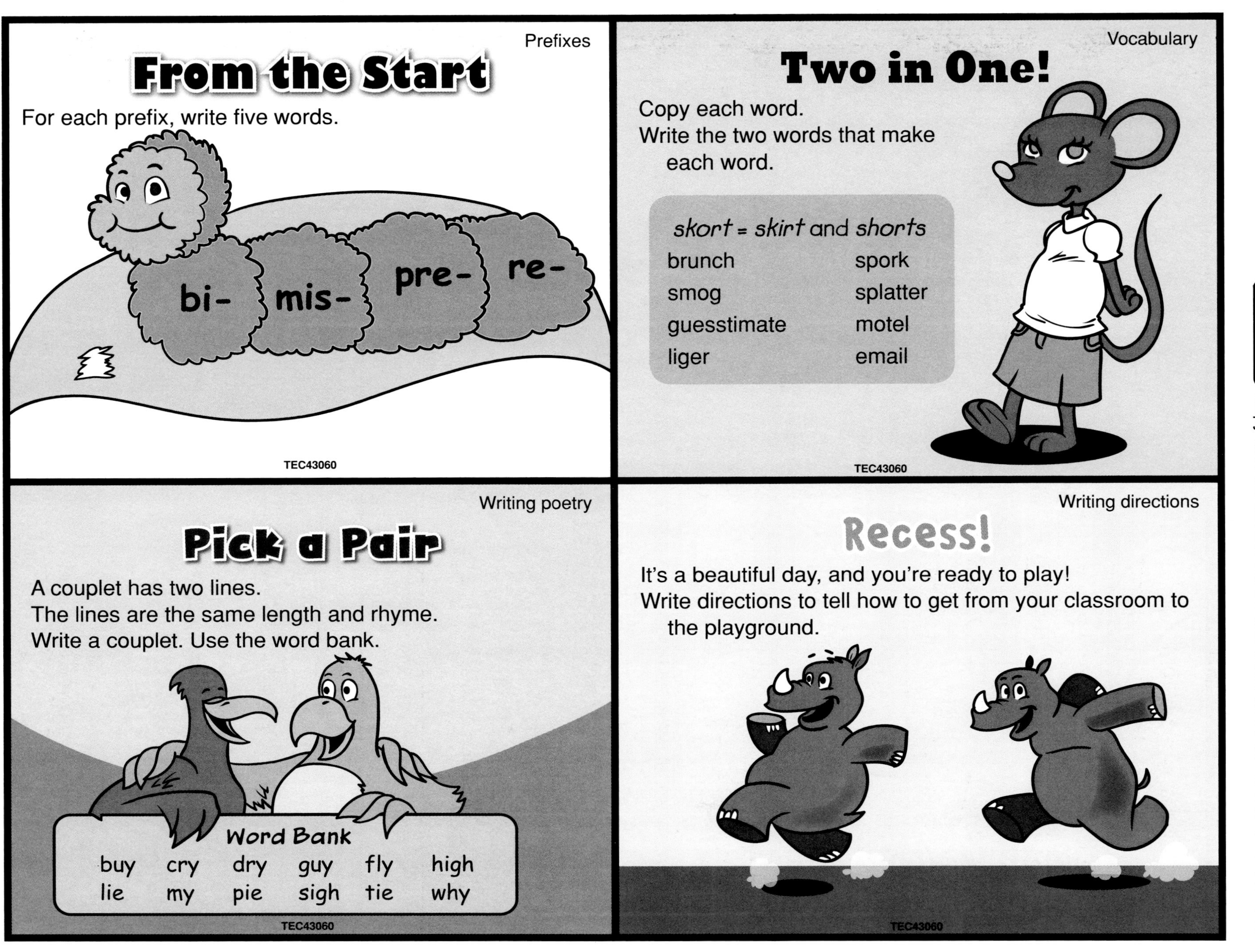
Prefixes
From the Start
For each prefix, write five words.
bi-
mis-
pre-
re-
TEC43060
Vocabulary
Two in One!
Copy each word.
Write the two words that make each word.
skort = skirt and shorts
brunch
smog
guesstimate
liger
spork
splatter
motel
email
TEC43060
Writing poetry
Pick a Pair
A couplet has two lines.
The lines are the same length and rhyme.
Write a couplet. Use the word bank.
Word Bank
buy cry dry guy fly high
lie my pie sigh tie why
TEC43060
Writing directions
Recess!
It's a beautiful day, and you're ready to play!
Write directions to tell how to get from your classroom to the playground.
TEC43060

Math Activity Cards

How to use Copy and cut out the cards. Use them as center or free-time activities.

Patterns
Splish, Splash
For each rule, write a matching pattern.
A. Add 7.
B. Subtract 4.
C. Add 10.
D. Subtract 5.
TEC43060
Multiplication readiness
Jelly Bean Jumble
Redraw each set three or more times.
Make as many arrays as you can.
A.
B.
C.
TEC43060
Data
For the Earth
Use the data to make a bar graph.
Pounds Recycled
plastic 卌 I
paper 卌 卌 卌 卌 卌
glass 卌 I
cans 卌 卌 II
TEC43060
Perimeter
Big Plans
Write the steps to find the perimeter of the seed packet.
Nature's Best
Carrots
TEC43060

Here's to Mom!

Heartfelt Ideas for Mother's Day

Forever Bouquet

Here's a practical way to send a bunch of flowers home with each student. Purchase one bouquet of colorful flowers and photograph each child holding it. After printing the photos, have each student glue his print to a folded sheet of construction paper. Direct the child to write a message to his mother or other female loved one on the cover and the inside flap of the card.

Jane Walsh, Sweetwater Elementary
Lithia Springs, GA

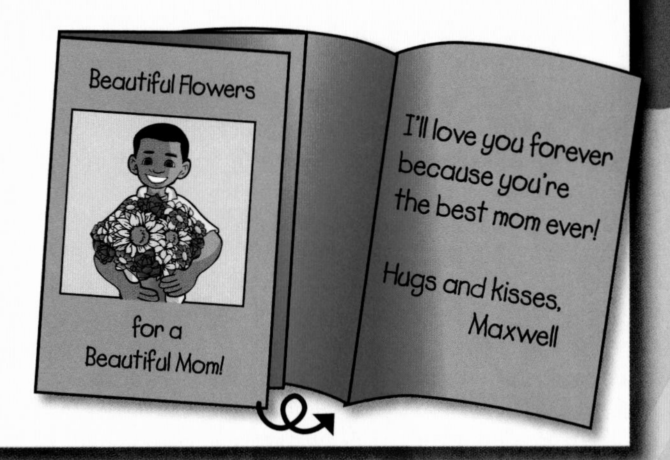
Beautiful Flowers
for a
Beautiful Mom!
I'll love you forever
because you're
the best mom ever!
Hugs and kisses,
Maxwell

From the Kitchen of Ava to Mom
Recipe for My Mom
Ingredients:
2 cups kindness
5 cups intelligence
1 cup laughter
1 cup bravery
10 cups patience
Mix the ingredients in a large bowl. Spread the mixture in a short pan. Bake at 350° for 20 minutes, but don't let her burn! Allow another 20 minutes of quiet time before removing Mom from the pan. (She'll still be warm and sweet when you do!)

Recipe for Love

What's not to love about this recipe card holder? It's cute, practical, and comes straight from the heart! To make one, a child uses craft glue to cover a two-inch binder clip with a 2" x 3⅛" piece of decorative paper. Then she adds embellishments, such as stickers, decorative buttons, and ribbon. While the glue dries, she writes on an index card a recipe titled "My Mom." Finally, the student inserts the recipe card between the wire loops. **As an alternative,** insert a photo of the child instead of the recipe card!

Laurie Eriksen, Trinity Lutheran School, Delray Beach, FL

Come Into Bloom

This simple project makes a big impression! To start, a child cuts a vase shape from a piece of construction paper and glues it to a sheet of tagboard. Next, the child uses a brown marker to draw several stems from the vase. He glues white beans to each stem and then adds the message shown. Finally, the student signs his name.

Lou Smeja, Emerson School, Elmhurst, IL

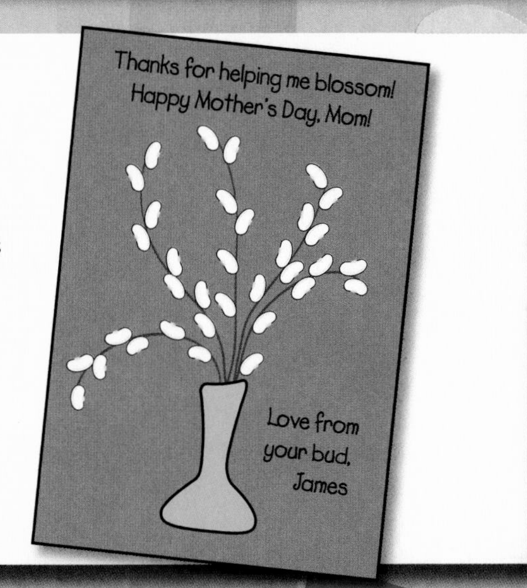
Thanks for helping me blossom!
Happy Mother's Day, Mom!
Love from
your bud,
James

Take Learning Outdoors

With spring's warmer temperatures, now is the perfect time to move fun practice activities from the classroom to the schoolyard.

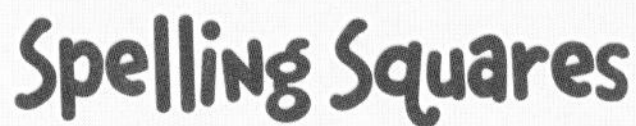

Spelling Squares

Get your spelling practice moving with this variation of hopscotch. In advance, choose ten letters that are widely found in your spelling list and plan the placement of each letter on a paper hopscotch grid. Pair students and give a piece of sidewalk chalk to each child. Have each duo draw a hopscotch grid on the pavement to look like yours, placing each letter in its designated square. To start, a student hops from side to side or diagonally to land on the squares to spell a word. As she hops, the student calls out each letter of the word while her partner records the spelling on the pavement. Then her partner takes his turn. **As an alternative**, invite students to create an original hopscotch board for another pair of students to use.

Tiffany Gammaro
Temple Beth Sholom Schools
Sarasota, FL

Find the Math Facts

This egg hunt equals one thing—fun! In advance, use a permanent marker to number a set of plastic eggs from 1 to 15. Write math problems on strips of paper and place one paper strip inside each egg. Then hide the eggs around the schoolyard. To play, each student takes outside a notebook or a sheet of paper and a clipboard and numbers his paper from 1 to 15. He searches for an egg and, when he finds one, he opens the egg, copies the math problem next to the corresponding number on his paper, and solves the equation. Then the child puts the paper strip back inside the egg and continues his search for the remaining eggs.

Lisa Compher, Westtown Thornbury Elementary, West Chester, PA

Race to Review

To review facts or vocabulary with the whole class, arrange four hula hoops on the ground in the center of an open area as shown and divide the class into four teams. Assign one hula hoop to each team and have each team stand at least three feet away from its hoop. Then place two different-colored balls in front of each team, designating one color as true and the other color as false. To begin play, call out a true-false review question and direct each team to collaborate to find the answer. As soon as a team decides on a response, one student (runner) picks up the appropriate ball and runs with it to her team's hula hoop. She sets the ball down inside the hoop and stands alongside it. When each team has a ball inside its hoop, give the correct answer. Guide each runner to return her ball to her team and select the next runner. Continue the activity until all team members have at least one turn to run.

adapted from an idea from Colleen Dabney, Williamsburg, VA

Celebrate the Season!

Keep in Touch
Friendly letter writing

Here's a fun way for students to practice correspondence skills this summer. Give each student a letter-size envelope. Direct him to write your home address and his return address on the front of the envelope. Then give each child a blank sheet of paper. Have him fold his paper and place it inside the envelope but not seal it. Put a postage stamp on each envelope. Invite students to use the materials to write and mail you a letter about their summer reading or activities.

Vickie Dent, Plaza Heights Christian Academy, Blue Springs, MO

James Smith
123 Main Street
Blue Springs, MO 00000
Ms. Dent

tip

Send the unsealed envelopes home with each child's report card to make sure they aren't misplaced.

SM

What a Super Man!
Similes

These greeting cards will be a super hit on Father's Day! In advance, copy the superhero emblem patterns from page 254 on tagboard and cut them out. To begin, give each student a sheet of red and yellow construction paper. Have her fold the red and yellow papers in half and trace the templates as shown. Then have the child cut out the patterns while keeping the folds intact, unfold the patterns, and glue each part on a half sheet of blue paper as shown. Next, she brainstorms a simile about a super male loved one, such as *My dad is as brave as a lion, My uncle is as smart as a dolphin,* or *My grandfather is strong as a locomotive*. The child writes her simile on the back of the blue paper before adding her own personal Father's Day greeting.

Amy Butler Barsanti, Pines Elementary, Plymouth, NC

Thirsting for Knowledge
Vocabulary

Use this refreshingly cool idea to review vocabulary terms with the whole class. First, make student copies of the gameboard on page 254. Write on the board a list of 12 vocabulary terms and have each child program the ice cubes with any eight words from the list. Then call out a definition. If the child has the matching term written on his gameboard, direct him to circle it. If he does not, he does nothing. Continue calling out definitions until one student circles all eight words on his gameboard and calls out, "Quenched!" Check that the student's words match the definitions that were called and, if desired, reward him with a small prize.

Name Cristian
Date June 6, 2012
Vocabulary review
Q U E N C H E D
right angle
obtuse angle
acute angle
parallel
perpendicular
intersecting
line
ray

Superhero Emblem Patterns

Use with "What a Super Man!" on page 253.

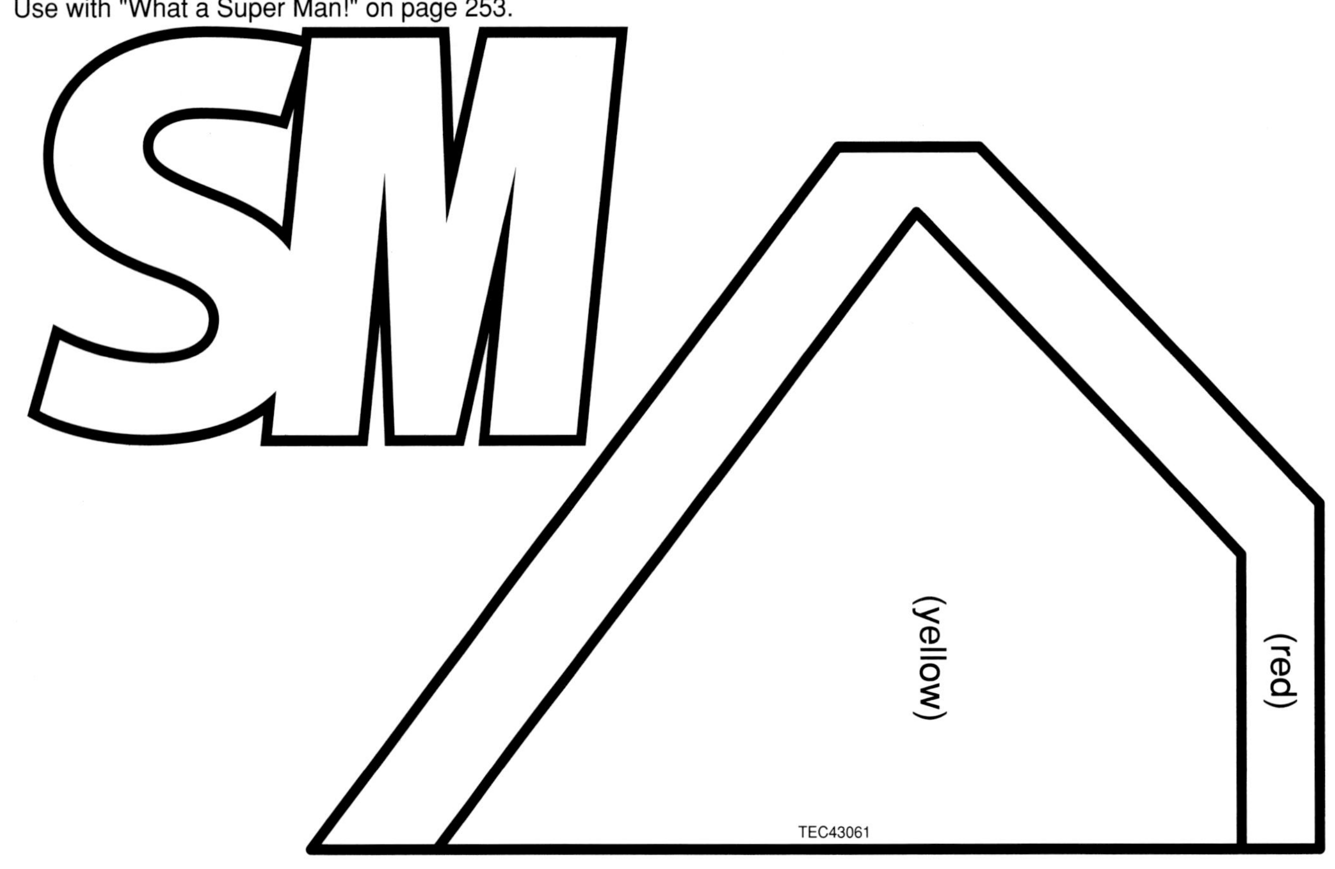
SM
(yellow)
(red)
TEC43061

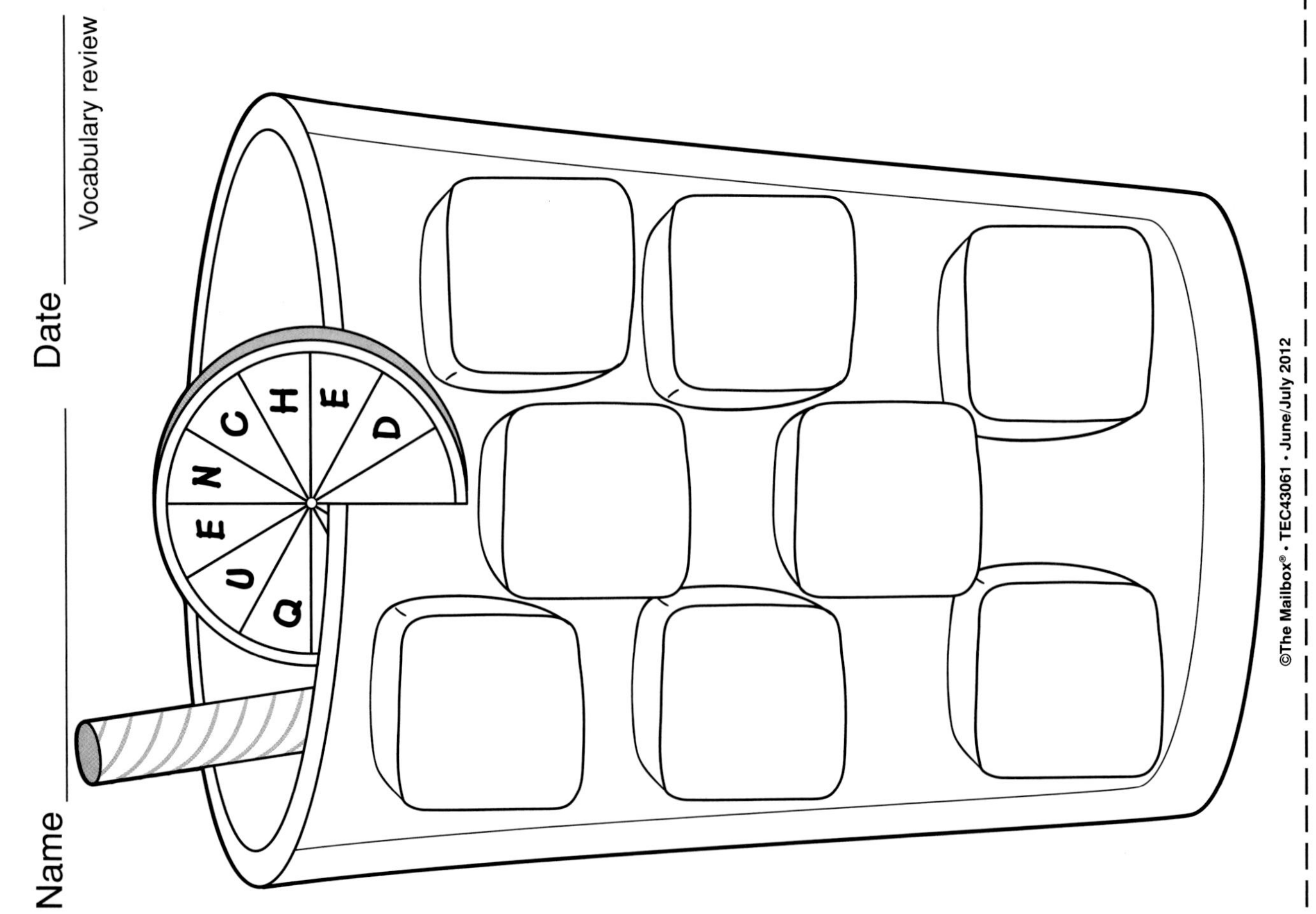
Name
Date
Vocabulary review
QUENCHED

Note to the teacher: Use with "Thirsting for Knowledge" on page 253.

Name ______________________ Date ______________

Conducting research

"Fin-tastic" Facts

Use a nonfiction resource to draw a picture of a shark. Color the shark tooth next to the name of the shark you chose. Then use the resource to answer the questions below.

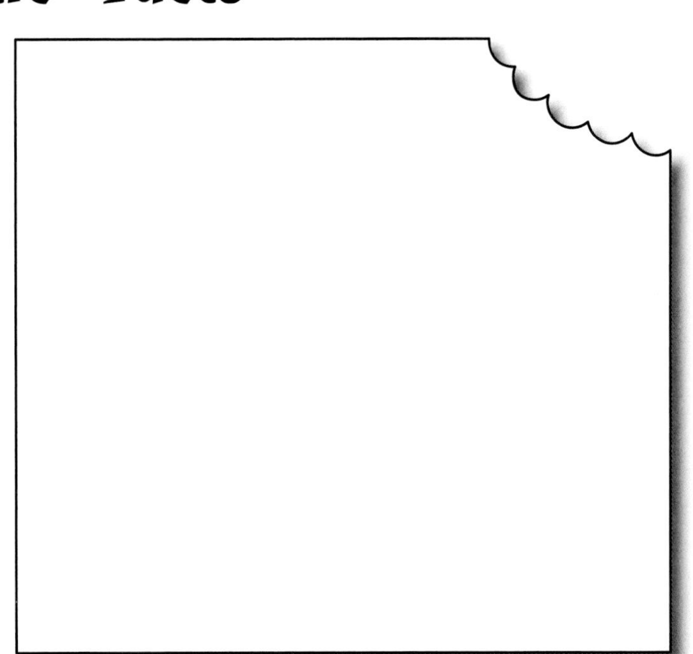

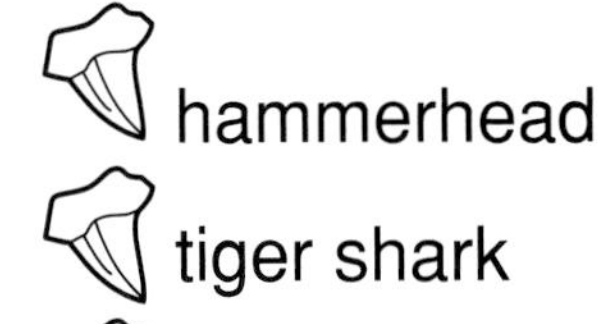

hammerhead

tiger shark

great white shark

other ______________________

nurse shark

goblin shark

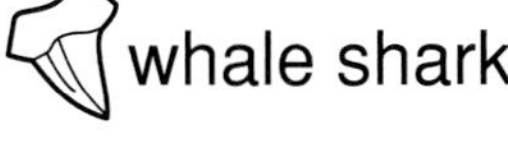

whale shark

1. What kind of animal is a shark? ______________________
2. How big does the shark get? ______________________
3. Where does the shark live? ______________________
4. What does the shark eat? ______________________

I just love
sinking my teeth
into shark facts!

5. List three interesting facts about the shark.

____

____

____

6. What source did you use to find your information?

____

Bonus: Write a paragraph about the shark you chose using the information above.

Name ______________________ Date ______________

Division

Catch a Wave

Divide.
Cross out each matching quotient as you use it.

A. $6\overline{)168}$	B. $8\overline{)904}$	C. $7\overline{)322}$	D. $3\overline{)57}$	E. $8\overline{)96}$	F. $7\overline{)28}$	G. $4\overline{)52}$
H. $5\overline{)45}$	I. $9\overline{)261}$	J. $6\overline{)84}$	K. $4\overline{)64}$	L. $9\overline{)441}$	M. $7\overline{)182}$	N. $3\overline{)60}$
O. $2\overline{)550}$	P. $5\overline{)735}$	Q. $6\overline{)264}$	R. $2\overline{)34}$			

4 8 9 14 19 5 12 16 28 13 20 29 46 75 17 26 44 49 64 113 147 275

Bonus: Write two division problems using the remaining numbers on the surfboard.

Language Arts Activity Cards

How to use Copy and cut out the cards. Use them as center or free-time activities.

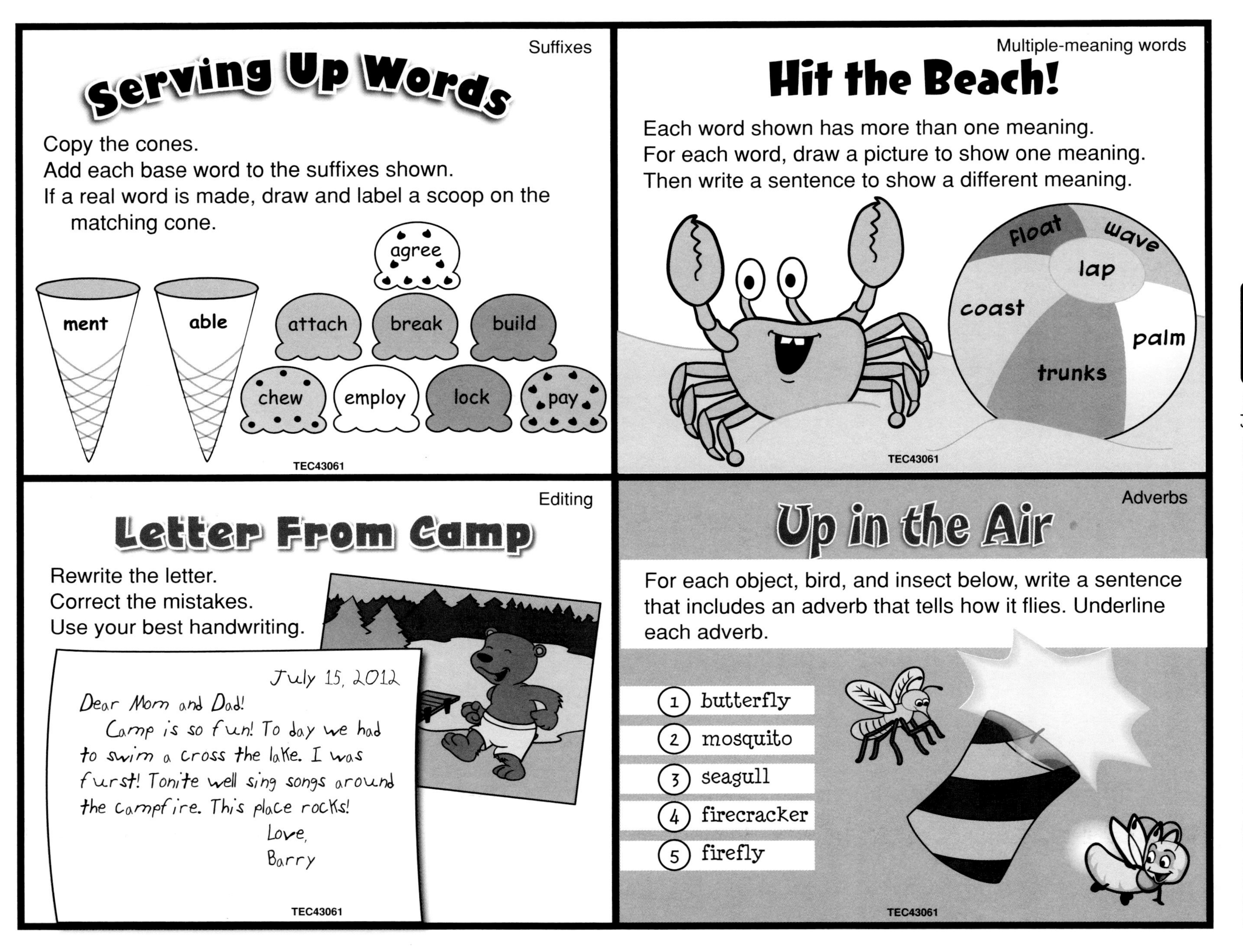
Suffixes
Serving Up Words
Copy the cones.
Add each base word to the suffixes shown.
If a real word is made, draw and label a scoop on the matching cone.
ment
able
agree
attach
break
build
chew
employ
lock
pay
TEC43061
Multiple-meaning words
Hit the Beach!
Each word shown has more than one meaning.
For each word, draw a picture to show one meaning.
Then write a sentence to show a different meaning.
float
wave
lap
coast
palm
trunks
TEC43061
Editing
Letter From Camp
Rewrite the letter.
Correct the mistakes.
Use your best handwriting.
July 15, 2012
Dear Mom and Dad!
Camp is so fun! To day we had
to swim a cross the lake. I was
furst! Tonite well sing songs around
the campfire. This place rocks!
Love,
Barry
TEC43061
Adverbs
Up in the Air
For each object, bird, and insect below, write a sentence that includes an adverb that tells how it flies. Underline each adverb.
1 butterfly
2 mosquito
3 seagull
4 firecracker
5 firefly
TEC43061

Math Activity Cards

How to use Copy and cut out the cards. Use them as center or free-time activities.

Number sense
So Many Shells
Write ten numbers that each have up to four digits.
Draw a picture to match each number.
Use the code.
Code
= ones
= tens
= hundreds
= thousands
401 =
TEC43061
Coins and bills
Souvenir Shopping
Write or draw two different ways a shopper could pay for each item.
A. $0.89
B. $1.25
C. $2.00
D. $1.63
I ♥ Sandy Beach
E. $0.45
TEC43061
Solid shapes
Bird at Work
Sully Seagull builds sand castles.
Today he used two cylinder molds, one rectangular prism mold, and two cube molds.
Draw a picture to show what his sand castle might look like.
Label each shape.
TEC43061
Problem solving
Wally Wakeboarder
For his next contest, Wally wants to show one trick followed by two grabs.
What might Wally show? Show all the trios you can.
Tricks
body slide
no-hander
Grabs
indy
roast beef
seatbelt
TEC43061

Beach-Bound!

Activities Your Students Are "Shore" to Love

Toss and Tell

Prefixes and suffixes

Students will have a ball with this indoor game! In advance, purchase two inexpensive beach balls. Use a permanent marker to label one with prefixes and suffixes and label the other with base words. To play, have students sit in a large circle. Toss each ball to a different student and have each child name the word or word part her right thumb is on. Guide the first child to tell the meaning of the combined word and affix, and instruct the other student to use the word in a sentence. Then have the students toss the balls to two other classmates. Continue until each child has had a chance to catch a ball.

Stephanie Brachtenbach, Harmony Elementary, Overland Park, KS

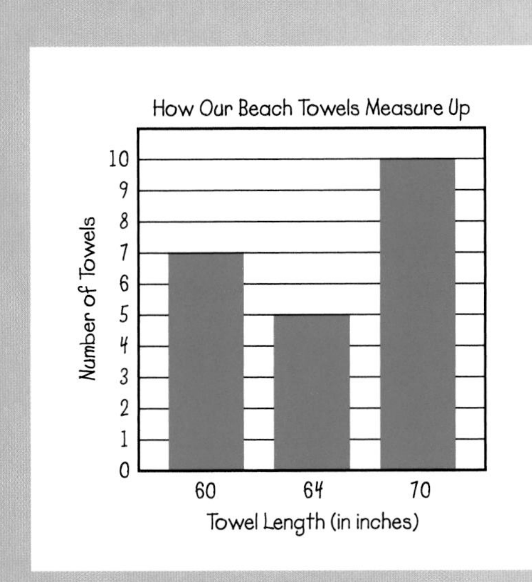
How Our Beach Towels Measure Up
Number of Towels
0
1
2
3
4
5
6
7
8
9
10
60
64
70
Towel Length (in inches)

Get Geared Up

Measuring, displaying data

Invite students to bring beach towels to class. Throughout the day, have students lay their towels flat, measure their lengths, and record the lengths on a class chart. Later, review the data with the class and have each student create a graph that displays the results. **As an alternative,** have each child show his towel to the class. Make a tally chart to reflect the appearances of the towels (with categories such as stripes, cartoon characters, scenes, or solids) and record a tally on the chart for each towel. Have students use the data to create their graphs.

Stars in the Sand

Writing an imaginative narrative

Use these stunning sea stars to kick-start students' writing! To prepare, put uncooked rice in a resealable plastic bag and add food coloring. Shake the bag to distribute the color; then spread out the rice and allow it to dry. Next, have each child trace a sea star template (pattern on page 260) onto a piece of tagboard and cut out the shape. He covers the star with liquid glue and then adds rice. While the glue dries, the student writes a story about finding the sea star on a beach. If desired, post the projects and stories on a display titled "Stars in the Sand."

Susie Kapuan, Orchard Park, NY

Check out the **practice sheet** on page 262.

A Day at the Beach

Writing with descriptive details

Prepare for some fun in the sun with this "sun-sational" center. In advance, label each of four plastic sand shovels with a different sense, excluding sight. Place the shovels in a sand pail and then spread a beach towel on the floor. Put the sand pail and a pair of silly sunglasses on top of the towel. A child puts on the sunglasses and then chooses a shovel. Pretending she is at the beach, she writes on a copy of the organizer from page 261 the sense listed on the shovel and then lists related observations. She repeats with each of the remaining shovels, returns them to the pail, and removes the sunglasses. Then the student returns to her seat to write a descriptive paragraph about the beach.

Michelle Bayless, Croughton, England

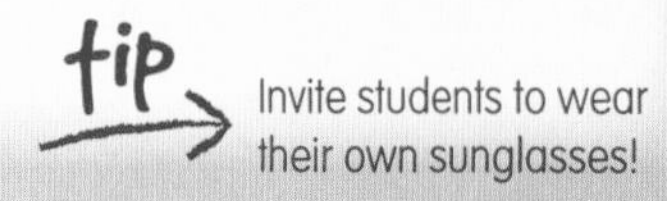
tip
Invite students to wear their own sunglasses!

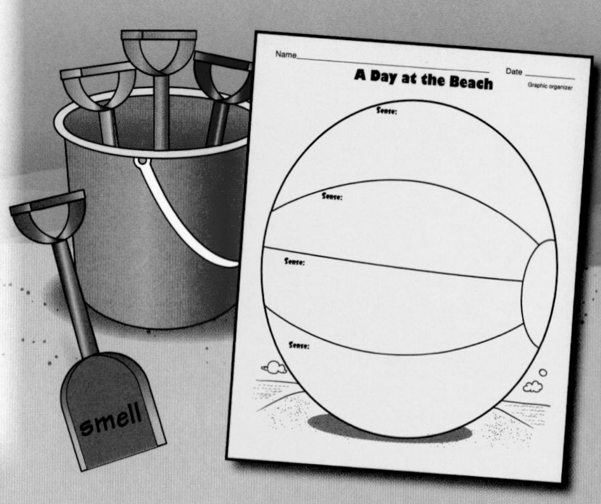
smell
A Day at the Beach

At the Shore
seagull
sea star
jellyfish
sea urchin
crab
sea turtle

Dive In!

Researching

What lives near the shore? Challenge students to use reference materials to find out. Then have each child draw and label on white paper pictures of animal life found near the seashore. Next, instruct each student to color his diagram with crayons, leaving the water areas white. Finally, have the child use diluted blue paint to paint the water areas of the diagram. When the paint is dry, invite each student to share his diagram with a partner.

Susie Kapaun, Orchard Park, NY

Sea Star Pattern

Use with "Stars in the Sand" on page 259.

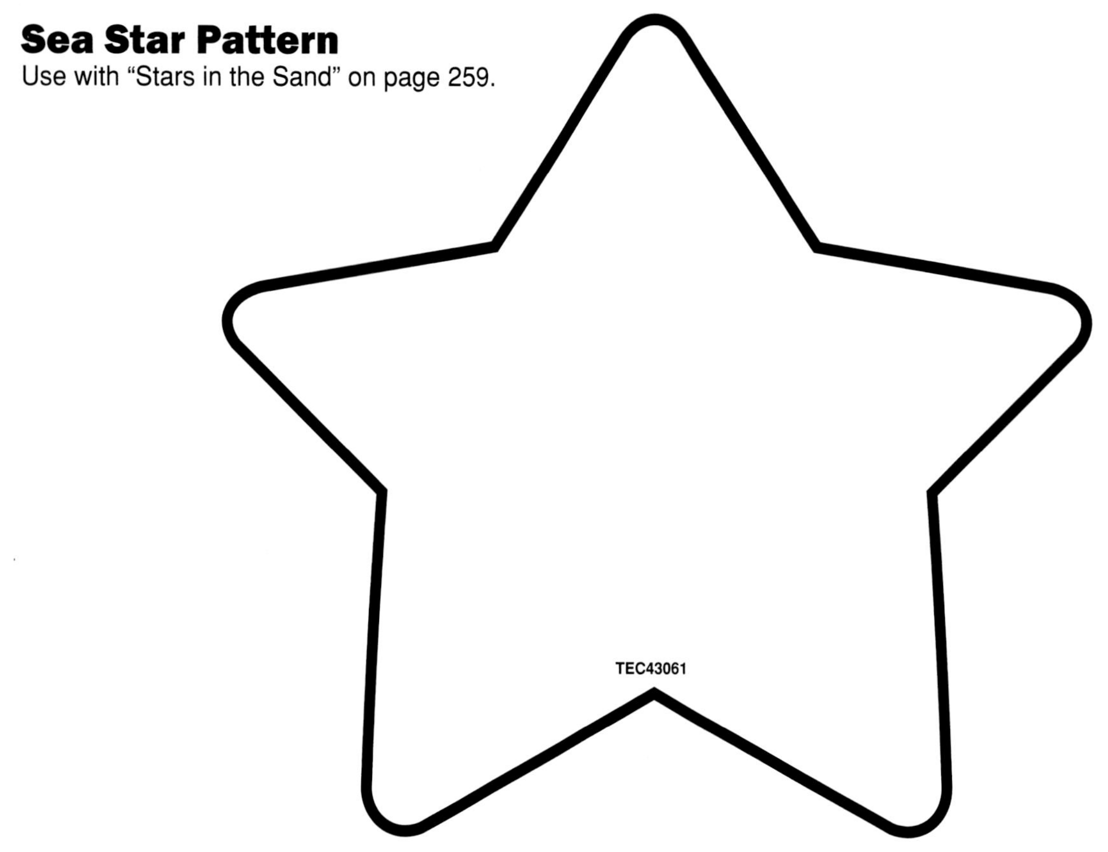
TEC43061

Name____________________ Date ____________

Graphic organizer

A Day at the Beach

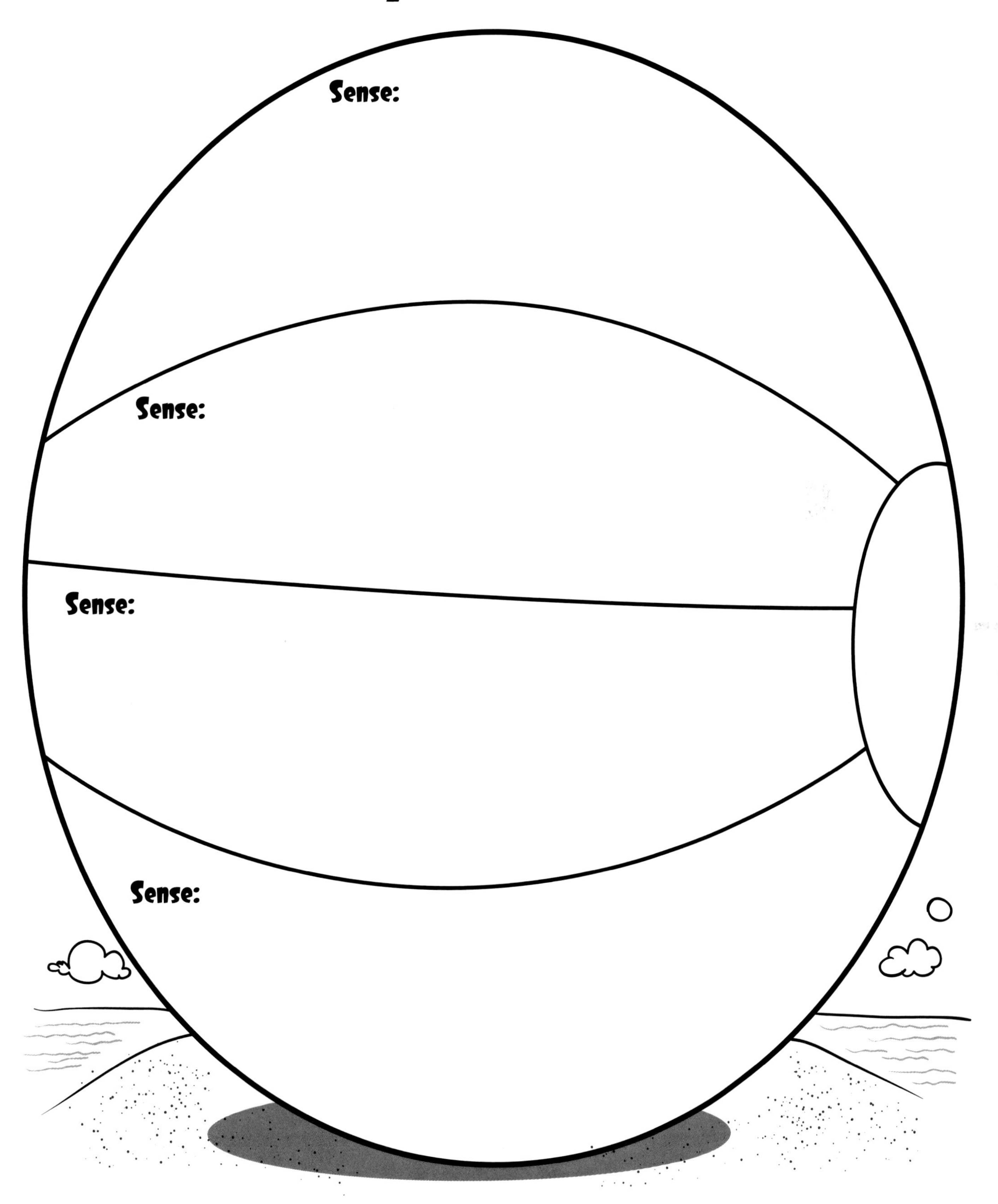

Sense:
Sense:
Sense:
Sense:

Note to the teacher: Use with "A Day at the Beach" on page 260.

Name ____________________ Date ____________

Fiction: comprehension, vocabulary

Arm Wrestling

Read.

Arm Wrestling

Ollie was the wrestling champ
And proudly wore his crown.
Each time he faced **opponents**,
He quickly pinned them down.

He didn't win his **bouts** by wit
Or due to good-luck charms.
He was the wrestling **champion**
Because he had eight arms!

Respond.

1. Write *ou* or *ow* to complete each word.

   pr__ __dly cr__ __n

   d__ __n b__ __ts

2. Write the meaning of each word. Use a dictionary to help.

   bout ____________________

   opponent ____________________

   champion ____________________

3. Which words from the poem tell that Ollie is an octopus? ____________________

4. Underline the line in the poem that tells how Ollie defeated his opponents.

5. Look at the first stanza. Based on what you learned from reading the poem, why would Ollie wear a crown? ____________________

Bonus: How does having eight arms help Ollie be a good wrestler?

Arts & Crafts

Arts & Crafts

Which Witch?

After students make this project, have each child write a detailed description of his creation. (Since everyone is using the same colors, very specific details will be needed!) Display the projects; then provide time for each student to read his description and have his classmates guess which witch is his.

Tina Lilly, Weisenberg Elementary, Kutztown, PA

Materials for each student:

- orange paper, cut into long strips in a paper shredder
- green and black paper
- yellow paper scrap
- black marker
- scissors
- glue
- tape

Steps:

1. Cut a head shape from green paper. Also cut out the side view of a nose.
2. Cut a slit in the middle of the head that is as long as the side of the nose. Slide the nose through the slit. Bend the end back and tape it to the back of the head.
3. Cut a hat from black paper.
4. Glue orange paper (hair) to the head. Then glue on the hat.
5. Cut a smile from yellow paper. Glue the smile to the head.
6. Use the markers to add other facial details.

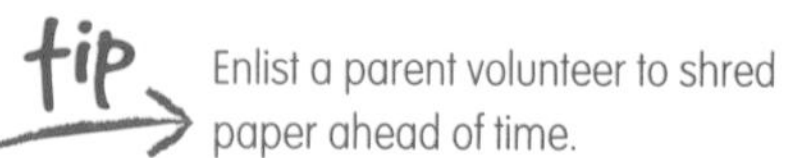
tip

Enlist a parent volunteer to shred paper ahead of time.

Cornucopia of Thanks

Celebrate this season of thankfulness with a personalized craft!

Amy Barsanti, Pines Elementary, Plymouth, NC

Materials for each student:

- tagboard copy of the cornucopia pattern on page 269
- copy of the key on page 269
- brown paint
- paintbrush
- pom-poms (red, pink, orange, yellow, green, blue, purple, brown, black, white)
- glue
- scissors

Steps:

1. Cut out the cornucopia pattern.
2. Paint the cutout brown.
3. When the paint is dry, use the key to gather pom-poms.
4. Glue the pom-poms to the opening of the cornucopia.

Arts & Crafts

Mini Shadow Box

This personalized holiday gift will be a treasured keepsake for years to come!

Amy Barsanti, Pines Elementary, Plymouth, NC

TELEVISION
Pizza
Robots

Materials for each student:

student photo
empty CD case
glitter glue
catalogs and magazines
4¾" paper square
scissors
glue

Steps:

1. Write your name and the date on one side of the paper square. Turn it over.
2. Glue your photo to the middle of the paper square.
3. Outline your photo with glitter glue.
4. Cut from the catalogs and magazines pictures or names of things you like.
5. Glue the cutouts to the paper square.
6. Place the paper square inside the CD case and close it.

O Christmas Tree

Give every child a chance to trim a tree with this adorable project!

Colleen Gregory, Washington Elementary, Minot, ND

Materials for each student:

6 sanitized egg carton cups
tinsel garland
buttons, beads, or stickers
8" x 10" tagboard
liquid glue

Steps:

1. Arrange the cups on the tagboard to make an evergreen tree shape.
2. Glue the cups to the tagboard.
3. Lay garland between the cups and around the tree shape.
4. Glue the garland to the tagboard.
5. Glue buttons or beads to each cup or attach stickers to each cup.

tip: Ask parents to donate worn garland rather than buying it new.

Arts & Crafts

Here's a Heart

Perfect for a Valentine's Day party activity or simply as a following-directions task, these adorable lollipop holders make sweet treats for your students!

Amy Barsanti, Pines Elementary, Plymouth, NC

Materials for each student:

2 clean, empty juice pouches
lollipop
ribbon (about 12")
scissors
hole puncher
liquid glue

Steps:

1. Stack the juice pouches and fold them in half.
2. Starting at the fold, cut half a heart shape. Unfold.
3. Stack the hearts and punch holes around the perimeter as shown.
4. Starting on one side of the heart, feed one end of the ribbon through the hole and knot it.
5. Lace the rest of the ribbon through the holes until you reach the other side of the heart. Tie another knot.
6. Place the lollipop through the heart so the stick extends through the bottom.

tip To clean the pouches, simply snip off the top and bottom sealed edges, wash them with dish detergent, and hang them to dry.

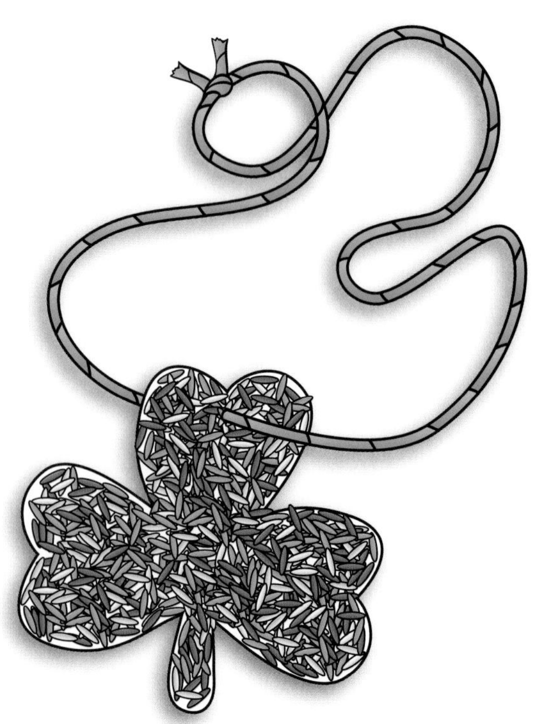

Preparing and Wearing of the Green

Have students work in small groups to make colored rice. For each group, simply put white rice in a resealable plastic bag and have students add green food coloring. Instruct them to seal the bag and shake it before spreading the rice on newspaper to dry. Then have each student follow the directions below to make his own St. Patrick's Day shamrock necklace.

Materials for each student:

green rice
shamrock template (page 270)
sheet of tagboard
3' length green yarn
scissors
hole puncher
liquid glue

Steps:

1. Trace the shamrock template onto the sheet of tagboard.
2. Cut out the shamrock.
3. Hole-punch the shamrock.
4. Cover one side of the shamrock with glue.
5. Cover the glue with rice.
6. When the glue is dry, feed the yarn through the hole. Tie the ends together.

Arts & Crafts

"Sun-sational" Friends

After each child creates this year-end project, provide time for students to autograph each one. Just watch everyone beam with enthusiasm!

Materials for each student:
2 sheets of yellow construction paper
sheet of orange construction paper
marker
scissors
glue

Steps:

1. Cut a six-inch circle from one sheet of yellow construction paper.
2. Trace your hand three times on the other sheet of yellow construction paper and three times on the orange construction paper.
3. Cut out each tracing.
4. Glue the palm of each hand cutout along the outer edge of the yellow circle (sun).
5. Turn the sun over. Draw sunglasses and a smiley face in the center.

Courtney Bartlett, Sunnyview Primary School, Knoxville, TN

Corbin
Brenden
Landon
Eesha
Aiden
Daekwon
Gracie
Robert
Matthew
Madison
Wyatt
Abbey
Wesley
Ms. Bartlett
Ava
Naddia
Diego
Jabrielle
Taj
Violet
Haashim
Aubrey
Calvin

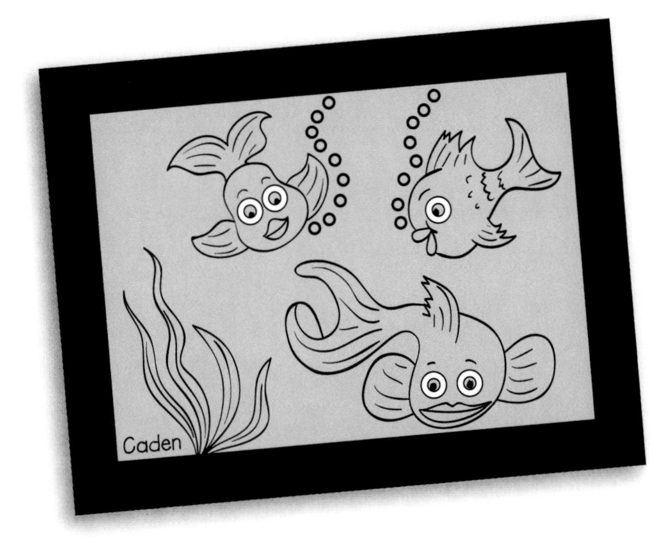
Caden

Something Fishy

Here's a quick drawing project for students to dive into!

Materials for each student:
6" x 9" sheet of light blue construction paper
9" x 12" sheet of black paper
self-adhesive hole reinforcers
fine-tip black marker
glue

Steps:

1. To make a pair of fish eyes, place two hole reinforcers side by side on the blue paper. (Use one hole reinforcer for a side view.)
2. Use a pencil to sketch the body of a fish around the reinforcers.
3. Trace over the sketch with a fine-tip black marker.
4. Repeat Steps 1–3 as desired to make more fish.
5. Add details to the fish and the background.
6. Glue the blue paper atop the black paper.

Colleen Dabney, Williamsburg, VA

Art in Action

What You Need

- large aluminum foil square
- small tagboard square
- scrap paper
- liquid glue
- scissors

1. Cut the foil in three places.

2. Scrunch the top left and right sections to make arms.

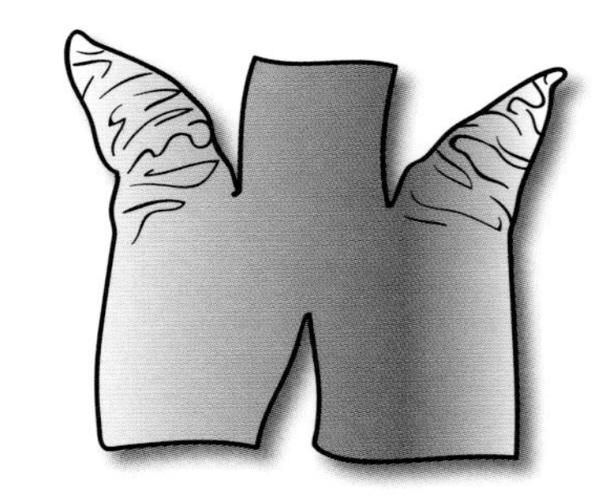

3. Mold a head from the middle section.

4. Wrinkle the bottom two halves to make legs.

5. Continue molding until your sculpture shows something you enjoy doing in summer.

6. Make a prop from scrap paper. Glue.

GLUE

7. Glue the sculpture to the tagboard.

Step-by-step craft: Make a copy of page 267 for your files. Remove this activity card and put it in a plastic page protector for durability. Then put the activity card and the needed materials at a center.

Cornucopia Pattern and Key

Use with "Cornucopia of Thanks" on page 264.

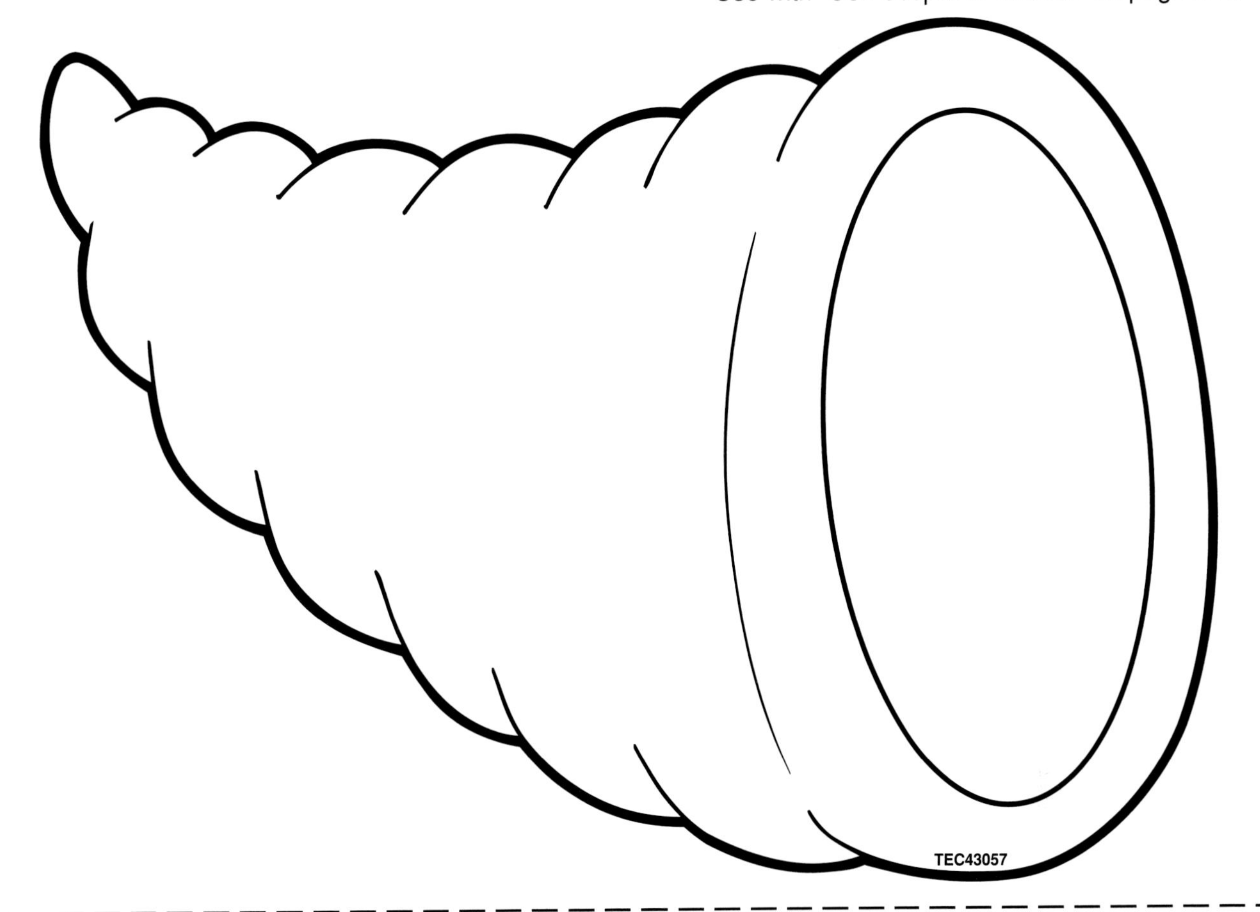
TEC43057

Key

I am thankful for…

good friends = brown

my home = white

my clothes = pink

my sister or sisters = red

my brother or brothers = green

my dog = orange

my cat = blue

another pet = yellow

sports = purple

music = black

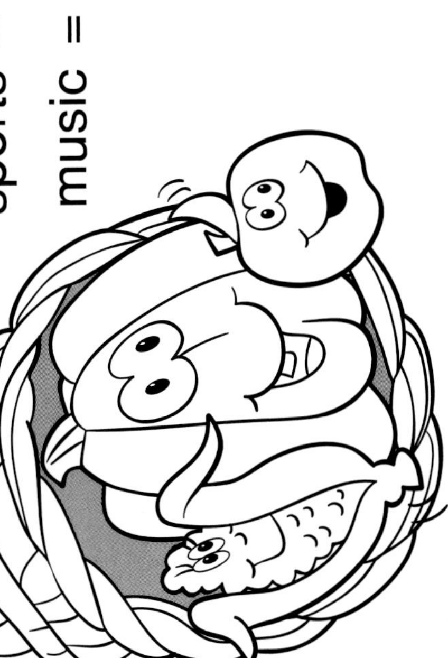

Shamrock Patterns

Use with "Preparing and Wearing of the Green" on page 266.

©The Mailbox®
©The Mailbox®

Displays That Do More Than Decorate

Ms. Spurck
Emily
Diego
Trent

Our Cooperation Train

Invite students to get on board and take a trip into a cooperative school year. Explain that the class is like a train, working together as one unit and stopping at various stations (classroom, cafeteria, art room, etc.) during the day. Tell students that cooperation is the key to having a successful trip each day. Next, instruct each child to personalize a passenger car pattern from page 277 and cut it out. Finally, write your name on a train engine cutout, post it in an easy-to-see location, and then display the passenger cars beside it.

Madeline M. Spurck, Neil A. Armstrong Elementary, Richton Park, IL

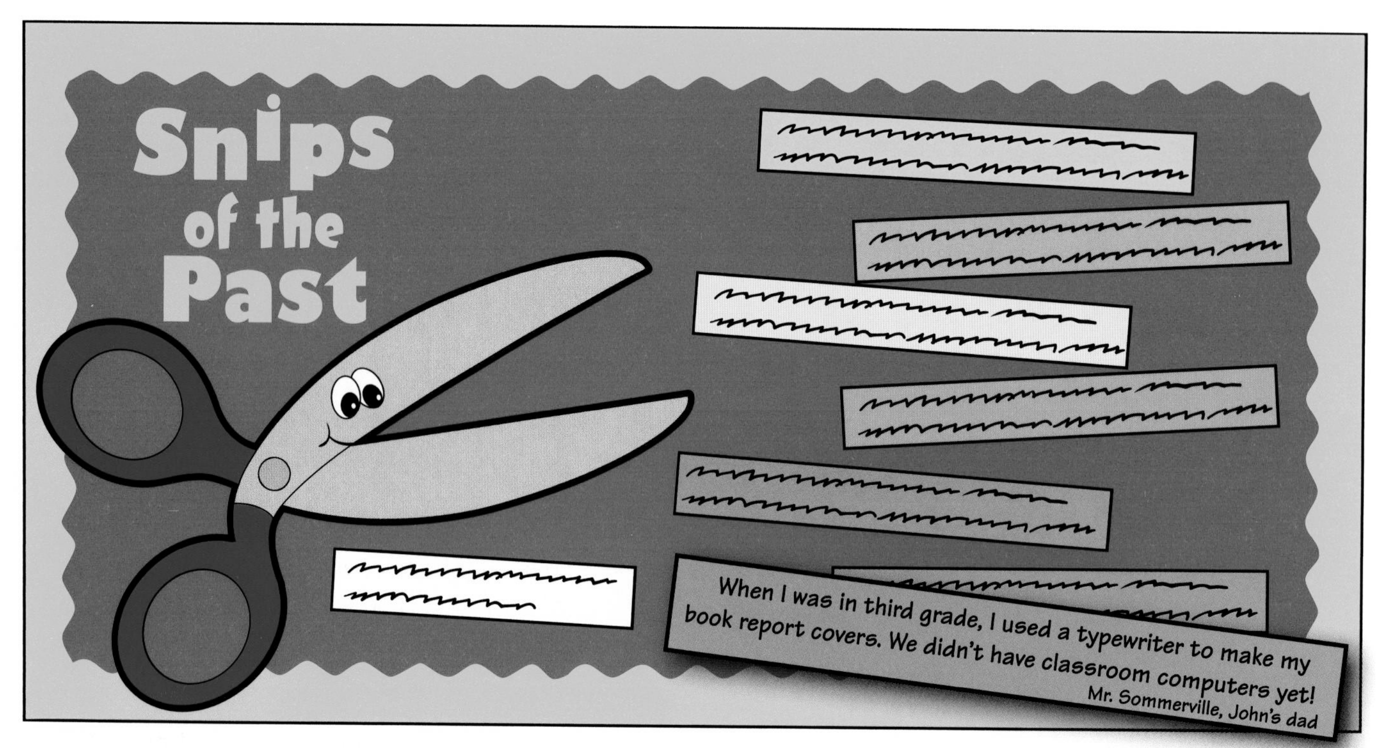
Snips of the Past
When I was in third grade, I used a typewriter to make my book report covers. We didn't have classroom computers yet!
Mr. Sommerville, John's dad

Connect with parents and have them help you decorate a display at the same time! Post an enlarged copy of the scissors pattern from page 277. Set a supply of colorful scrap paper strips near the display. At back-to-school night, invite each parent to write on a paper a memory from when he was in the grade level you teach. Post the papers; then use the entries to prompt a discussion of time and change with students.

Corrie Brubaker, Providence School, Waynesboro, PA

DISPLAYS That Do More Than Decorate

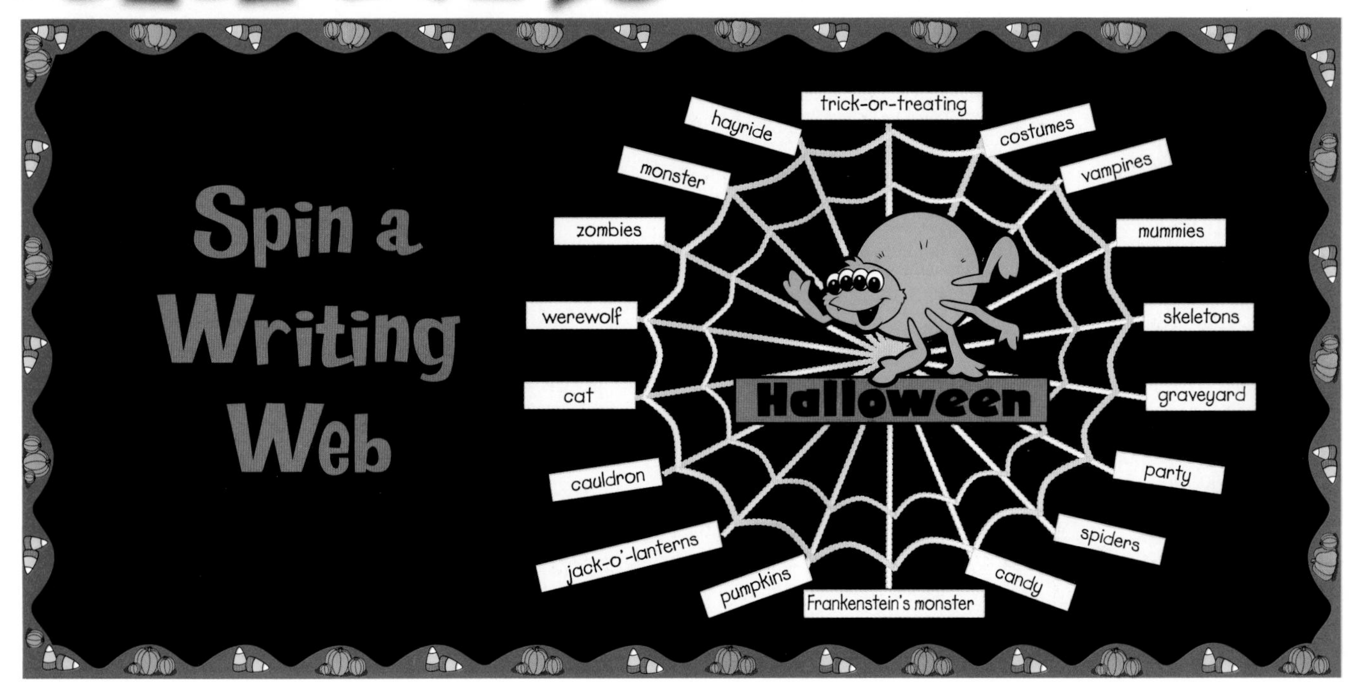

Spin a Writing Web
trick-or-treating
hayride
costumes
monster
vampires
zombies
mummies
werewolf
skeletons
cat
Halloween
graveyard
cauldron
party
spiders
jack-o'-lanterns
candy
pumpkins
Frankenstein's monster

Use glitter glue to make a large spiderweb. (Include one thread point for each student.) Then color and cut out a copy of the spider pattern on page 278. In the middle of the web, place the spider and a paper strip programmed with a seasonal topic. Give each child a paper strip and direct him to write a related term. Staple the terms around the web. Then instruct students to use a term or terms from the web to plan and write an imaginary narrative. If desired, post students' completed work around the web.

Rebecca Pratt, Northville Central School, Northville, NY

On Target
Capitalize proper nouns.

Cut five paper circles and layer them to make a target as shown. Post the target and copy the arrow patterns on page 278. **To use the board during writing instruction**, program the arrows with different editing conventions. At the start of each writing project, post a different arrow on the target. As each student proofreads and edits a classmate's work, have her focus on editing for that convention only. **To use the board for classroom management**, label an arrow with a behavior or goal you'd like students to strive for (walking quietly in the hall, 100 percent of the class turning in homework, etc.). Post the arrow on the outer circle of the target. Each time your students accomplish the goal, move the arrow toward the center. When the arrow reaches the middle circle, award a class prize. Then move the arrow to the outer circle and begin again, or replace it with a newly labeled arrow.

Jennifer Giegler, Rosa Taylor Elementary, Macon, GA

DISPLAYS That Do More Than Decorate

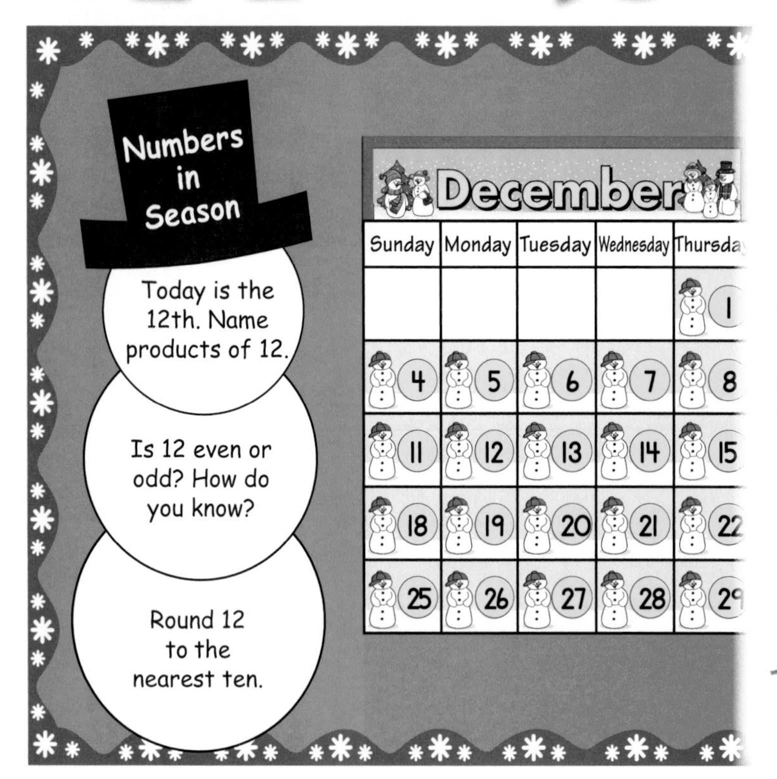
Numbers in Season
December
Sunday
Monday
Tuesday
Wednesday
Today is the 12th. Name products of 12.
Is 12 even or odd? How do you know?
Round 12 to the nearest ten.

Cut three large circles from white paper and laminate them. Then cut a top hat shape from black paper and use a white colored pencil to label it as shown. Post the shapes as a snowman near your classroom calendar. Each day, use a dry-erase marker to write on each circle a different question about the date or the number of days students have been in school. Refer to the questions to guide a class discussion or direct students to write each response in their math journals. **To vary the display for spring,** use the circles as eggs and post them on a labeled paper nest.

Barbara Hennigan, Northern Elementary, Greensboro, NC

tip If you don't have a calendar display, post the snowman on your board next to where you've written the date.

Toast to the New Year
In 2012, I look forward to reading harder books! I also can't wait for baseball season to start this spring, and I hope to play soccer in the fall. I think 2012 will be great!
Sam

Toast the new year with this student-friendly display. Instruct each child to write on a copy of the toast pattern (page 279) a description of what he's looking forward to in 2012. Then direct each child to lightly color and cut out his pattern. Post the cutouts around an enlarged copy of the toaster pattern (page 279) and add the title shown.

Tara Durning, Mother Teresa Academy, Clifton Park, NY

DISPLAYS That Do More Than Decorate

Words Worth Millions
Word Bank of America
Part of Speech
verb
admit
word
Use this word when you want to tell someone you did something.
A word you can trust
Cristian
treasurer
Valuable Vocabulary
Estrella
Wyatt
Lian
Skye
Abby
Pilar
Antwan
Cole
Jamil
Phoebe

Bring value to your students' vocabulary banks! After discussing with students the difference between ordinary words and words that bring value to their reading, set out several cutout copies of the dollar bill pattern from page 280. When a child comes across a valuable word in her reading, she uses a marker to write the word on a cutout and explains when to use the word in a sentence. Then she writes the word's part of speech on the left side of the bill and signs her name on the "treasurer" line. Finally, the student posts the cutout for others to reference.

tip Copy the dollar bill pattern on green paper.

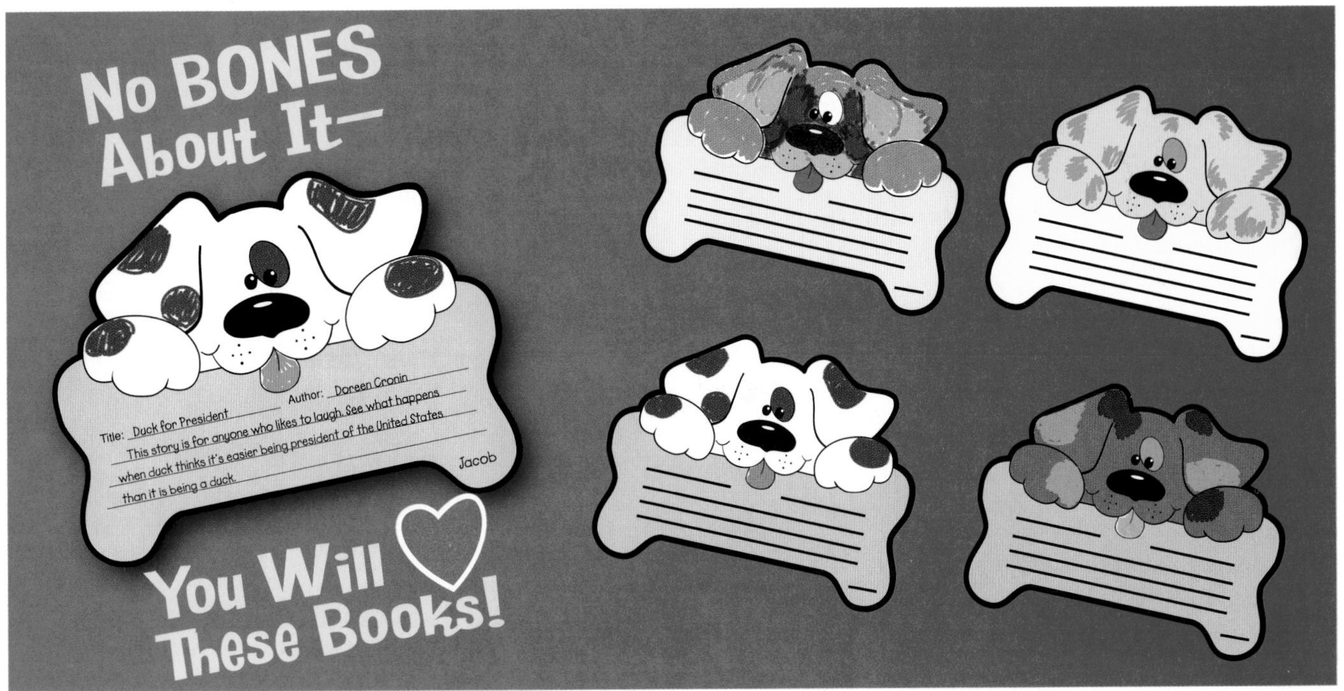

No BONES About It—
Title: Duck for President
Author: Doreen Cronin
This story is for anyone who likes to laugh. See what happens when duck thinks it's easier being president of the United States than it is being a duck.
Jacob
You Will ♥ These Books!

Share student book recommendations with this irresistible display. After a child reads a book he enjoys, invite him to color and cut out a copy of the dog and bone pattern on page 281. The student writes the book's title and author's name; then he writes a reason his classmates should read the book. Post the cutout on a display titled as shown.

adapted from an idea by Betsy Liebmann, Gotham Avenue School, Elmont, NY

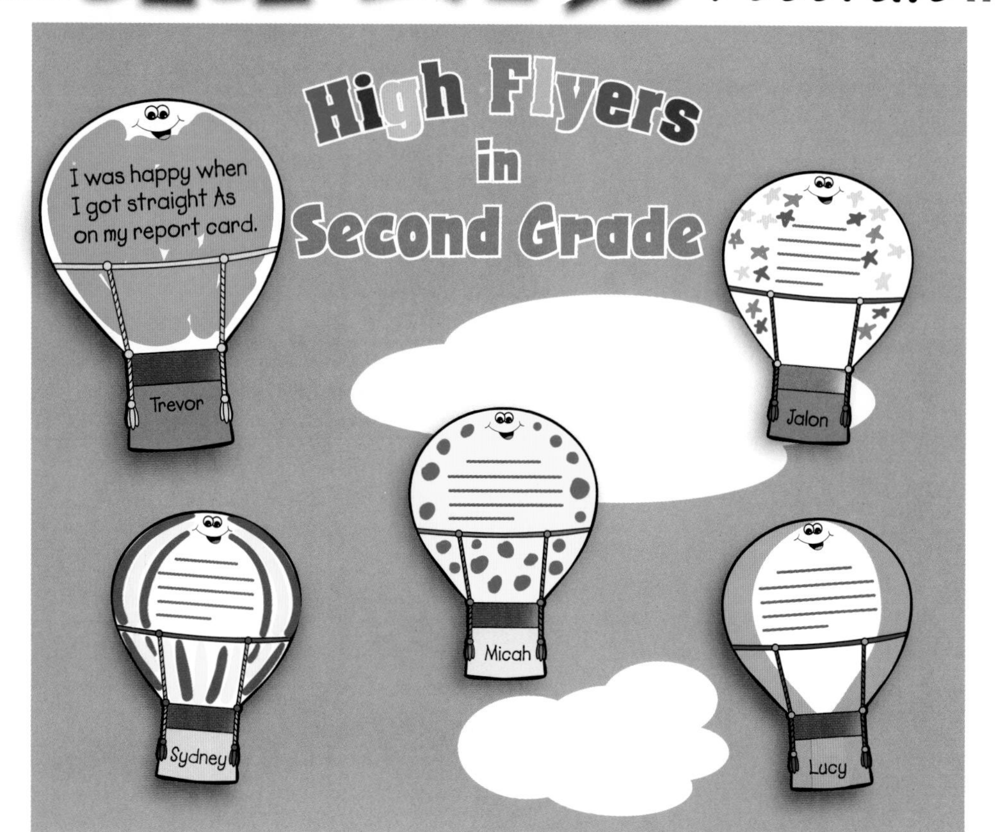
High Flyers in Second Grade
I was happy when I got straight As on my report card.
Trevor
Jalon
Micah
Sydney
Lucy

Use this soaring good display to highlight students' achievements from the school year. Give each student a copy of the hot-air balloon from page 282. Have him write on the pattern a description of his favorite accomplishment from the school year. Then instruct him to color the pattern and cut it out. Post the balloons on a display with a title similar to the one shown. Students' pride will surely soar when they see all their successes!

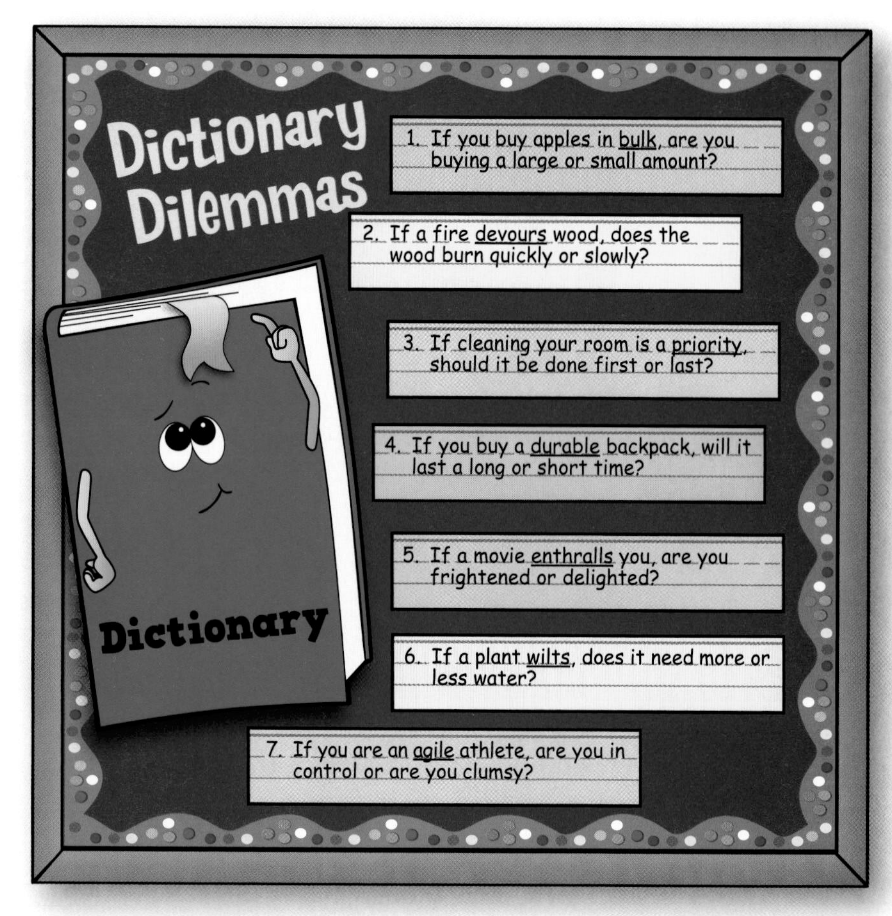
Dictionary Dilemmas
1. If you buy apples in bulk, are you buying a large or small amount?
2. If a fire devours wood, does the wood burn quickly or slowly?
3. If cleaning your room is a priority, should it be done first or last?
4. If you buy a durable backpack, will it last a long or short time?
5. If a movie enthralls you, are you frightened or delighted?
6. If a plant wilts, does it need more or less water?
7. If you are an agile athlete, are you in control or are you clumsy?
Dictionary

Students practice dictionary skills with this easy-to-update vocabulary display. First, copy and cut out the dictionary pattern from page 282. Next, program a set of sentence strips with questions like the ones shown. Post the pattern and the strips on an accessible bulletin board; then place paper and a dictionary nearby. A student uses the dictionary to answer each question, writing on a sheet of paper her response and the dictionary page number where she found the word. Periodically, post a new set of questions.

Lou Smeja, Emerson School, Elmhurst, IL

Passenger Car Pattern

Use with "Our Cooperation Train" on page 272.

TEC43056

Scissors Pattern

Use with "Snips of the Past" on page 272.

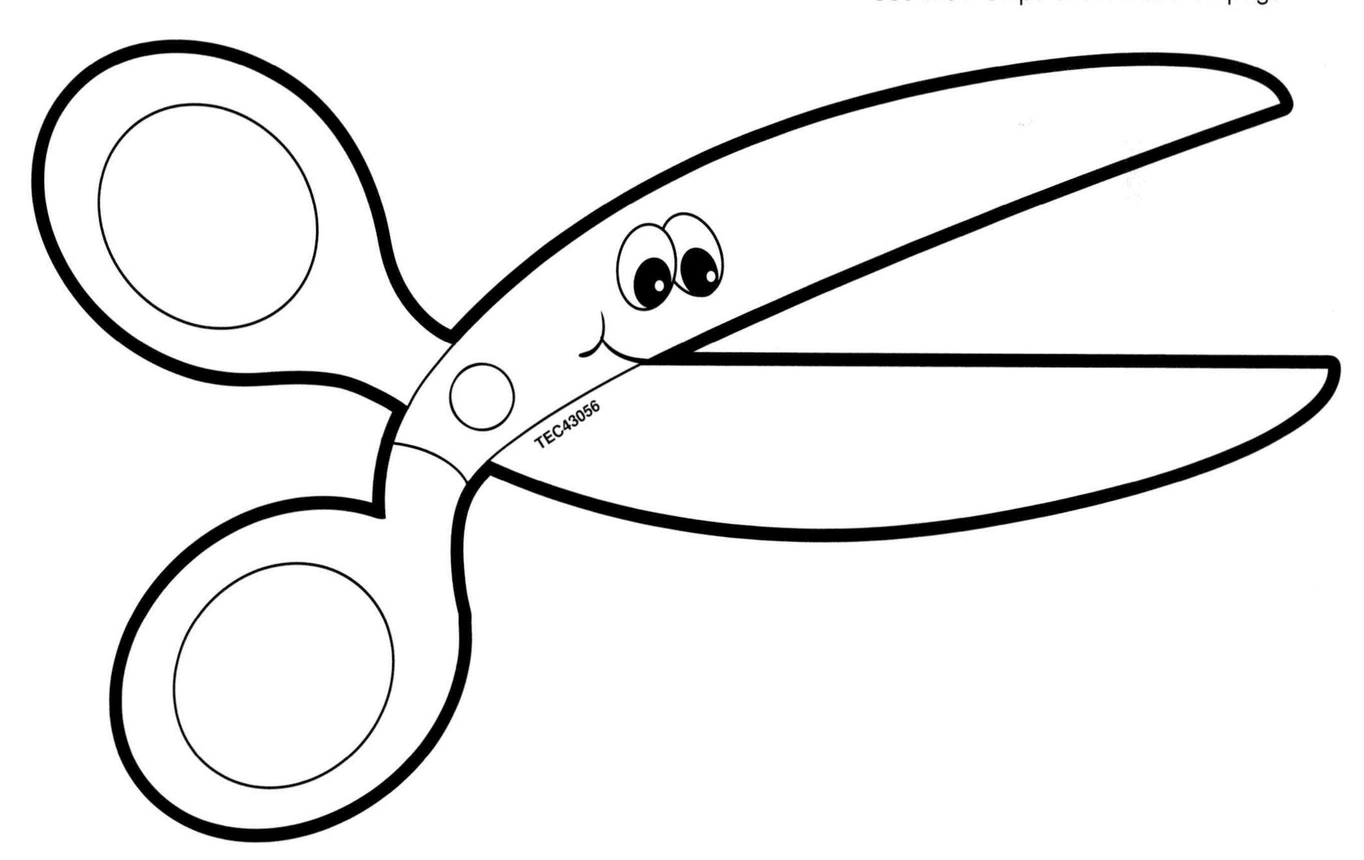
TEC43056

Spider Pattern

Use with "Spin a Writing Web" on page 273.

TEC43057

Arrow Patterns

Use with "On Target" on page 273.

TEC43057

TEC43057

Toast and
Toaster Patterns
Use with "Toast to the New
Year" on page 274.
TEC43058
TEC43058

Dollar Bill Pattern

Use with "Words Worth Millions" on page 275.

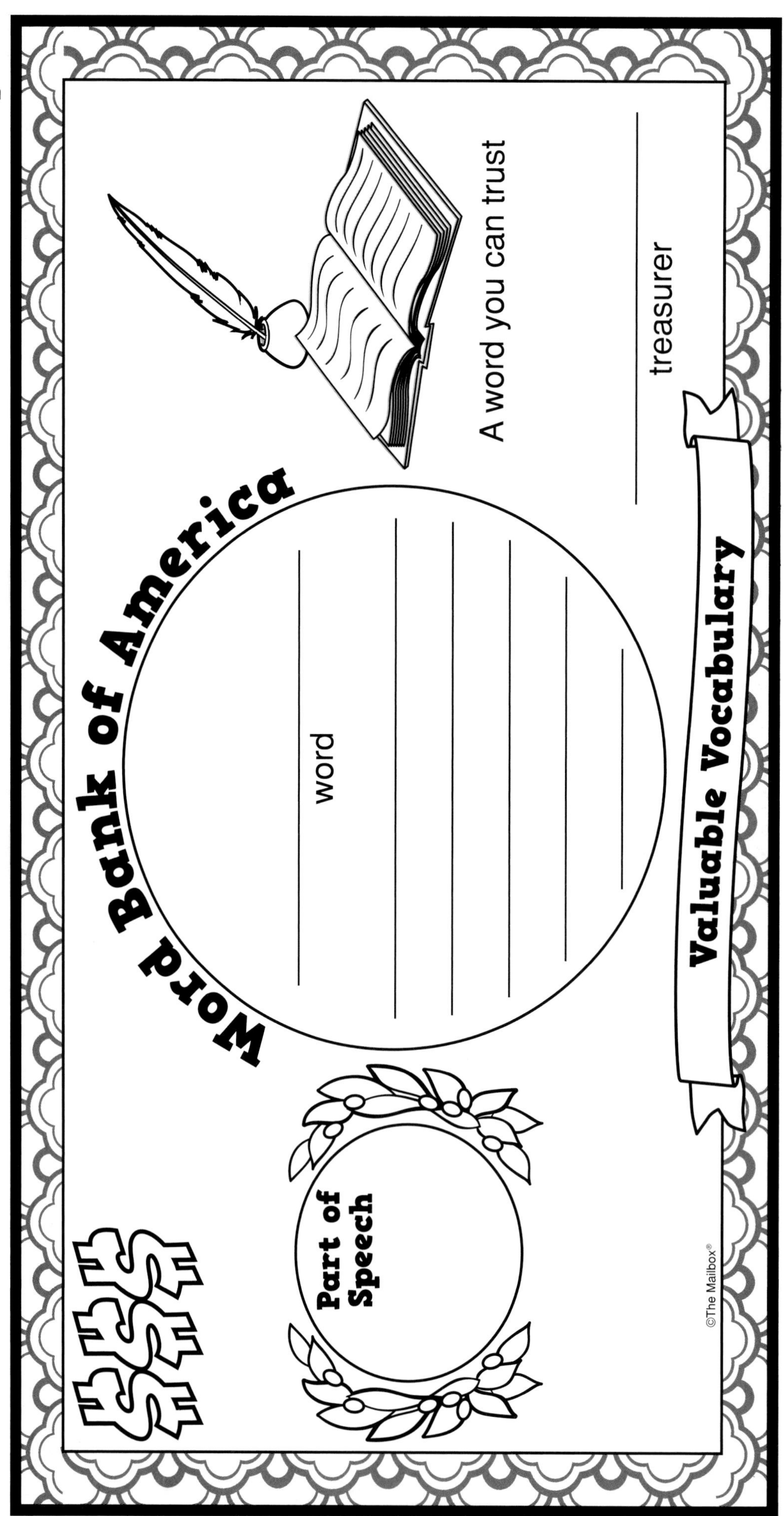

Word Bank of America
word
A word you can trust
treasurer
Valuable Vocabulary
Part of Speech
©The Mailbox®

Dog and Bone Pattern

Use with "No Bones About It—You Will ♥ These Books!" on page 275.

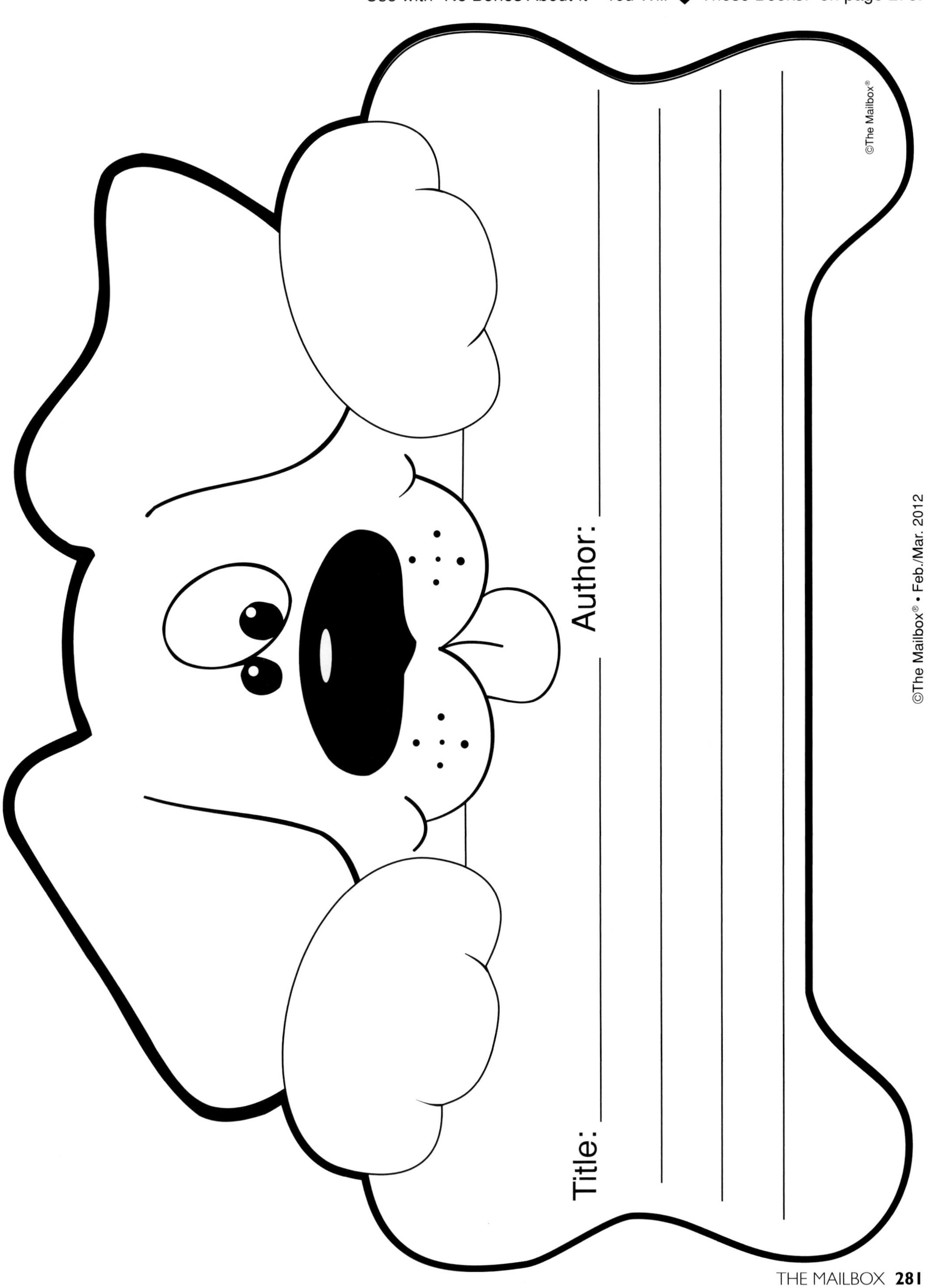
©The Mailbox®
Title:
Author:

Hot-Air Balloon Pattern

Use with "High Flyers in Second Grade" on page 276.

Dictionary Pattern

Use with "Dictionary Dilemmas" on page 276.

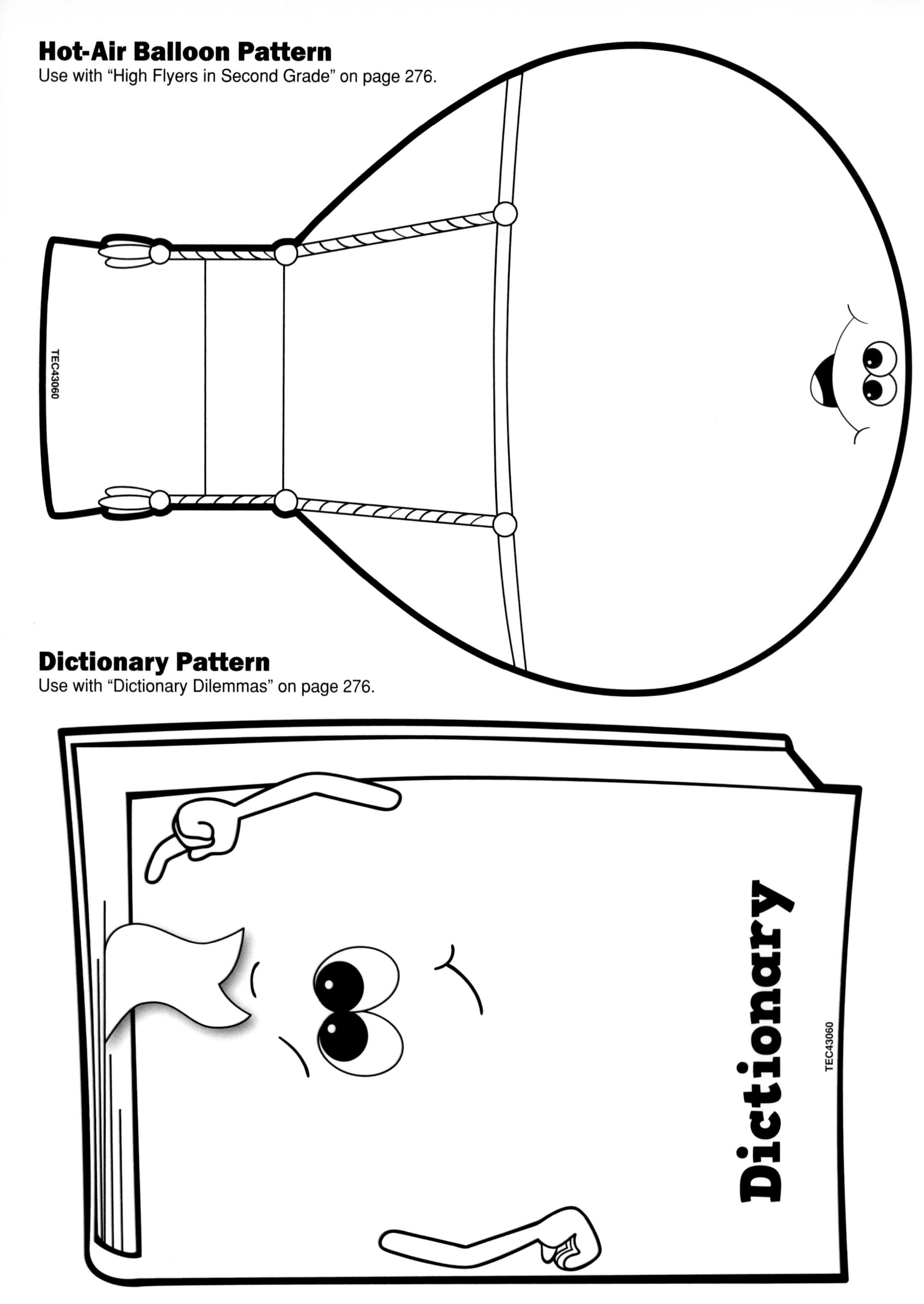
TEC43060
TEC43060
Dictionary

Management Tips & Timesavers

The Homework Bag

Help students stay on top of makeup work when they are out for a few days. Use fabric paint to label a plain canvas bag with your name and other desired decorations. When a student is out for a prolonged absence, simply place any needed books and paperwork inside the bag. If desired, add a note and a small treat; then make arrangements for the child to get the bag. When the student is ready to start her homework, everything is contained! Plus she can return the work to school in the same bag.

Barb Krohn, New Prague Primary, New Prague, MN

Ms. Krohn's Homework Bag
We miss you!
We're not the same without you!
Please hurry back!

MANAGEMENT TIPS AND TIMESAVERS

Going, Going, Gone!

Encourage good behavior with a weekly auction! Throughout the week, monitor students' behavior and present a ticket to a child when he exhibits good behavior. Direct the child to write his name on the ticket and store it in a safe place. On Friday, have students take out their tickets. Then guide each child to make an auction paddle by writing an assigned number on an index card and then taping the card to a craft stick. Review the auction process with students; then choose a classroom job and start the bidding. As each job is sold, have the winning child pay by putting his tickets in a bucket. When all the jobs are auctioned off, instruct students to store their paddles and remaining tickets so they can be used the following week.

Suzette Pfanstiel, Forest Park Elementary, O'Fallon, MO

14
Jack
Jack
Jack
Jack
Jack

Overflowing With Organization

Looking for a **handy way to organize** the ideas you've clipped from your issues of *The Mailbox®* magazine? Try this! Sort the ideas by topic and then glue each set onto a different file folder. Laminate the folders for durability; then tuck skill-related reproducibles and patterns inside each one. Store the folders with your other lesson-planning materials.

Lisa Davidson, Glencoe Elementary, Portland, OR

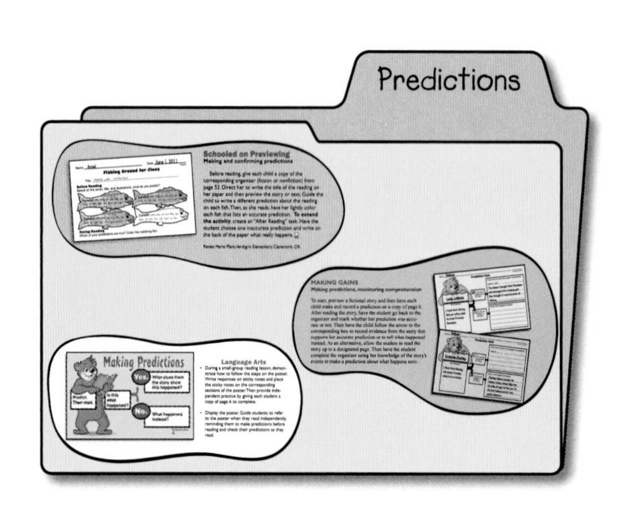
Predictions
Making Predictions

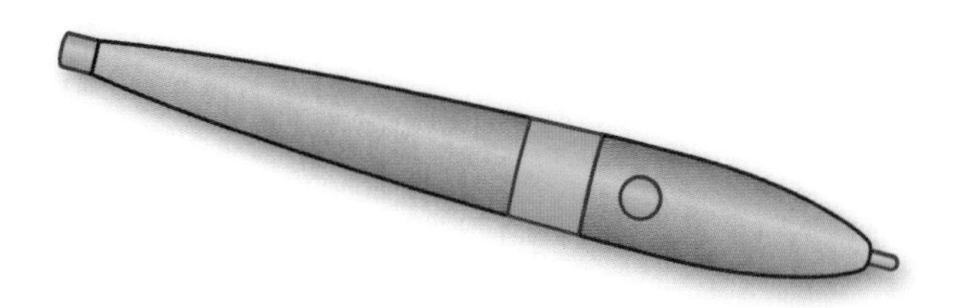

Pass the Pen

Use this simple routine to **review homework**. First, project a copy of the assignment onto the board. Next, pass a dry-erase marker or interactive whiteboard pen to a student and have him complete the first item. Then invite the child to choose another student who is quiet and focused and have him pass the pen to her. Students stay involved as they wait for their chance to use the pen.

Virginia Garcia, Deatsville, AL

Scheduling Technology

Here's a quick and easy way to keep track of **which students have visited a classroom computer** each week. Record your class list and, next to each child's name, write the first letter of each weekday, as shown. Photocopy the form onto colored paper and display it near the classroom computers. When a child visits a computer, he simply circles the matching day. A quick glance at the form shows which students have been to the computer that week.

Janeen Beresh, Ritzman CLC Elementary, Akron, OH

Sylvia	M	T	W	T	F
Lilly	M	T	W	T	F
Asher	M	T	W	T	F
Deonne	M	T	W	T	F
Alvin	M	T	W	T	F

MANAGEMENT TIPS
AND
TIMESAVERS

Assigning Teams

Looking for a new way to **divide the class into teams** for games or projects? Assign a different sequential number to each child. Before the game starts, direct students to line up in order. Then give a direction such as "Students with odd numbers, step to the right" or "Students with numbers less than 12, sit on the floor." Not only does this easy process sort students into groups, it provides a quick review of basic math skills!

Crystal Reinertson, Ballard East Elementary, Cambridge, IA

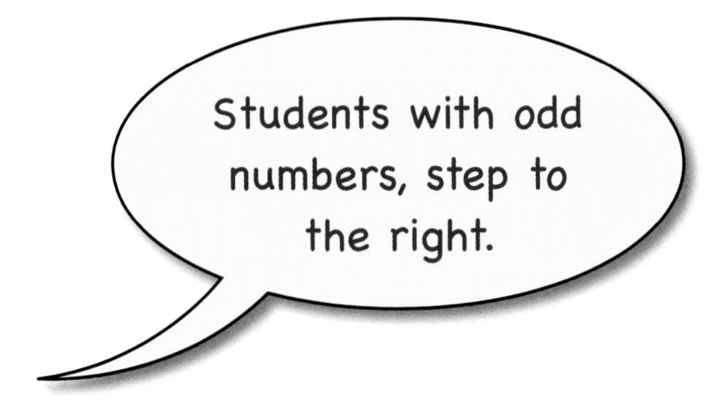
Students with odd numbers, step to the right.

Stick to Cool Behavior!

Expect a blizzard of good conduct when you give your **behavior system** a seasonal theme. Enlarge one of the cards from page 289 and display it near a bag of cotton balls. Explain to students that each time they display good behavior—such as making a positive choice, following classroom rules, or receiving a compliment from another staff member—you will glue a cotton ball to the picture. When the white areas of the picture are covered, reward students with a prize, such as an extra recess or a class game.

Carolyn Burant, St. John Vianney School, Brookfield, WI

Stick to Cool
Behavior!

We're Number One!

A sporty foam hand makes a great **hallway behavior** reminder. Before you leave the classroom, don the foam hand and hold the finger up to your lips in an exaggerated "Shhhh" signal. Explain to students that the hand is a reminder to walk quietly. In the hallway, keep the foam hand raised as you lead the class to its destination. Go, quiet class!

Stacey St. Peter, Gesner Street Elementary
Oromocto, New Brunswick, Canada

Fridge Facts Make School Cool!

Fridge Facts

Week of February 13-17, 2012

Math Facts or Vocabulary to Know

7 x 0 = 0	7 x 4 = 28	7 x 8 = 56
7 x 1 = 7	7 x 5 = 35	7 x 9 = 63
7 x 2 = 14	7 x 6 = 42	7 x 10 = 70
7 x 3 = 21	7 x 7 = 49	

Spelling Words

one	they're	scent
won	where	sent
there	wear	your
their	cent	you're

Reading
- studying facts and opinions
- Donavan's Word Jar

Science
studying rocks and soil

Social Studies
learning about cardinal directions

Important dates and events:
Valentine's Day party—Tuesday, Feb. 14
multiplication quiz—Friday, Feb. 17

Use this cool form to encourage **home-school communication**. Each week, make a copy of the reproducible on page 290 and program it with the appropriate information. Direct each child to take a copy home, share it with his family, and post it on his refrigerator. If desired, instruct students to return the paper with a parent or guardian's signature at the end of the week.

Kim Minafo, Apex, NC

MANAGEMENT TIPS
AND
TIMESAVERS

An Exercise in Creativity

Manage recess time and offer students a chance to exercise their creativity by having them invent their own games. Give each small group an assortment of equipment such as jump ropes, cones, hula hoops, bean-bags, and balls. Challenge the group to use the items to create a game. Guide them to develop rules and a name for their game. When the games are prepared, designate a day for each group to lead the class in playing its game.

Jennifer Otter, Oak Ridge, NC

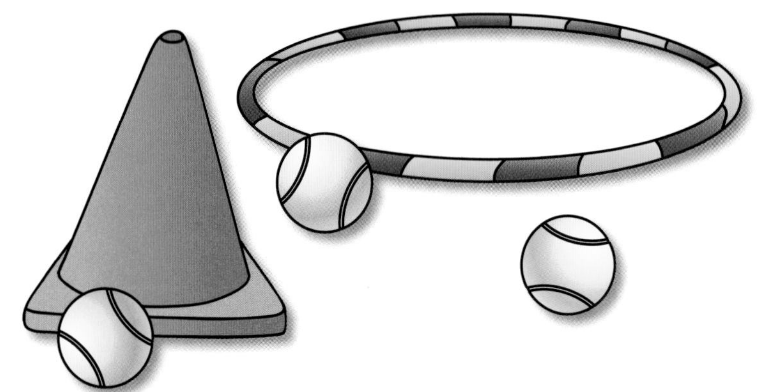

Speed-Cleaning Pit Stop

Keep the **classroom neat and tidy** by directing students to perform routine maintenance checks. Divide the class into small pit crews and assign one shared area of the room to each crew. At your signal, direct the crews to work quickly and quietly to straighten their assigned areas.

Elizabeth Searls Almy, Greensboro, NC

Need Homework Help?

Empower students to ask for **homework help** without feeling embarrassed. Post a laminated homework chart in a designated area of the classroom. Periodically write on the chart the name of a homework assignment and the number of each problem. Before students take the assignment home, instruct each child to draw a star next to the problem(s) he does not understand as he completes it. Then, when he returns to class with the assignment, have him use a dry-erase marker to draw a star next to the problem(s) on the chart that he wants reviewed.

Jennifer Otter, Oak Ridge, NC

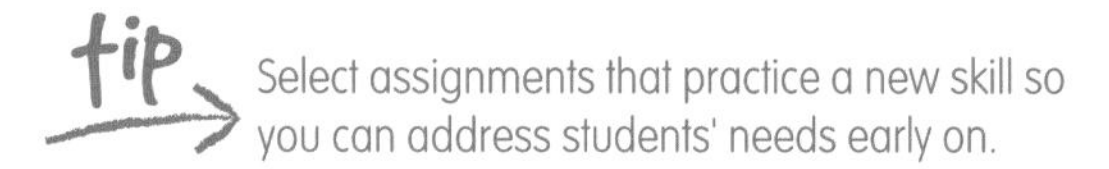
tip
Select assignments that practice a new skill so you can address students' needs early on.

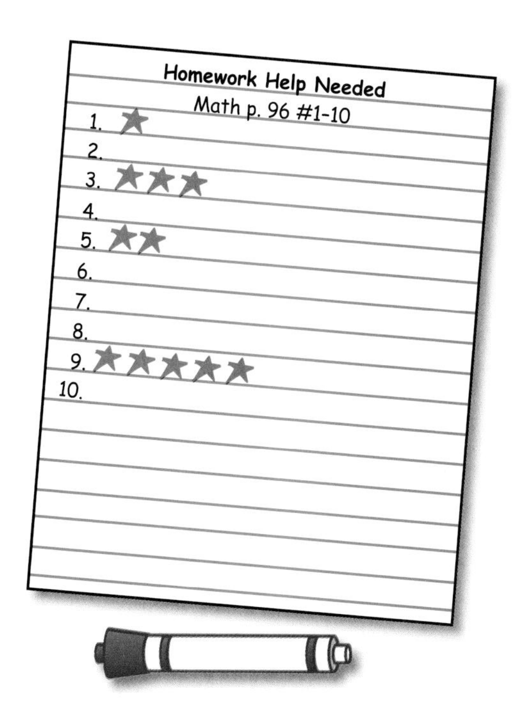
Homework Help Needed
Math p. 96 #1-10
1.
2.
3.
4.
5.
6.
7.
8.
9.
10.

Actions Speak Louder

Put a positive spin on this familiar **behavior management** tactic. When students become too chatty or lose focus during a lesson, simply stop teaching and write the names of students who are exhibiting acceptable behavior. After the class settles down, give them a specific reason you chose these students, such as that they were listening and quiet, sitting properly, or working independently. Repeat the strategy as needed, giving a different reason for writing the names each time.

Ann Fisher, Toledo, OH

MANAGEMENT TIPS
AND
TIMESAVERS

Clip It!

Unfinished worksheets no longer get lost or forgotten with this attractive solution. Give each student a magnetic clip for her desk and have her attach any unfinished work to her clip. Not only will she know where to find the paper to finish it, but it's easy to estimate how many students need to complete an assignment.

Barbara Brewster, A. E. Burling Elementary, Pennsauken, NJ

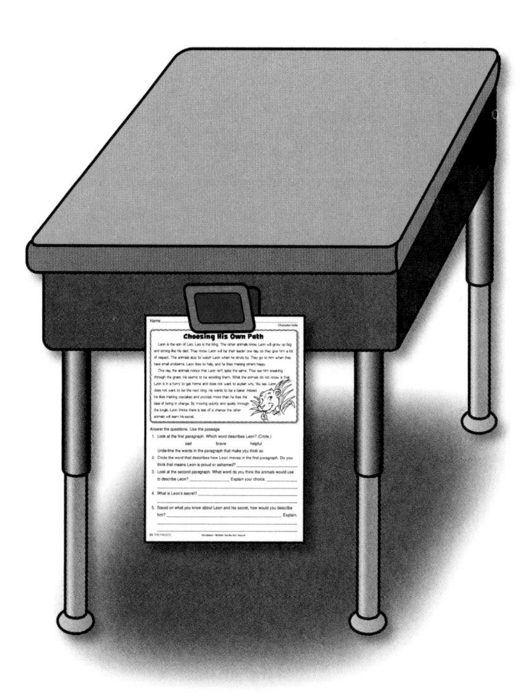

Passing the Time

Here's a great way to fill students' **free time during those last few days of school**. Set up four to five game stations with familiar card and board games. Divide the class into small groups and set a timer for ten minutes. Have each group play a game until students hear the timer. After the timer goes off, have the groups rotate to a different game station and then reset the timer. Students spend their final days at school having a little fun with their classmates.

Laura Johnson, South Decatur Elementary, Greensburg, IN

MANAGEMENT TIPS
AND
TIMESAVERS

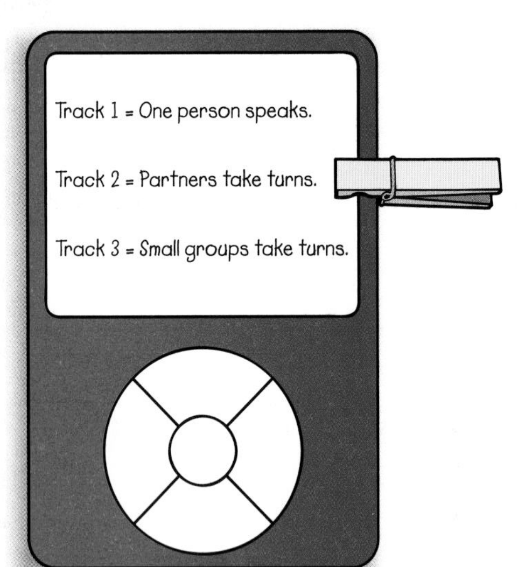
Track 1 = One person speaks.
Track 2 = Partners take turns.
Track 3 = Small groups take turns.

Stay on Track

Remind students about the **appropriate times for listening and speaking** during class with this simple-to-make poster. Draw on poster board a portable music player device like the one shown. Label the settings "Track 1," "Track 2," and "Track 3." Place a clothespin next to the track that indicates how students should behave during a particular time of the day. Refer to the poster anytime students need to be redirected.

Colleen Dabney, Williamsburg, VA

Behavior Bucks

These auction dollars will **keep students motivated** as the school year winds down. Gather classroom items you are willing to auction off, such as leftover rewards and prizes that won't be stored for next year, posters, books, and slightly used games. Next, make a supply of auction bucks, like the ones shown. Show students the bucks and explain the criteria for earning the classroom currency, such as completing homework, staying on task, listening, and following directions. Also give students a preview of the auction items in order to build interest and enthusiasm. During the last week of school, hold an auction where the highest bidder exchanges his auction bucks for an item of his choice. Not only is this a great way to keep students engaged, but it also helps you eliminate items you no longer need.

Teresa Vilfer-Snyder, Fredericktown, OH

Auction
Dollar

Use with "Stick to Cool Behavior!" on page 285.

Stick to COOL
Behavior!
TEC43058
Ho! Ho! Ho!
Stick to Happy
Holiday Behavior!
TEC43058

Fridge Facts

Week of ______________________________

Math Facts or Vocabulary to Know

Spelling Words

Reading

Science

Social Studies

Important dates and events:

 Note to the teacher: Use with "Fridge Facts Make School Cool!" on page 286.

Our Readers Write

Our Readers WRITE...

(and EMAIL and BLOG and TWEET and POST)

Seeds of Success

To show parents I care about my students, I use this simple but meaningful approach. In advance, I gather a class supply of seed packets and attach a label, as shown, to each one. On Parent Night, I read aloud *Mrs. Spitzer's Garden* by Edith Pattou. Next, I explain my expectations of, as well as my commitment to, my students as I distribute the labeled seed packets. Throughout the year, I send small notes or emails thanking each parent for nurturing his child's growth and education. Then, at the end of the school year, I give each student and his family a real flower that represents how much he has grown and blossomed. ***Deb Brun, Myron J. Francis Elementary, Rumford, RI***

Let's partner together to nurture the seeds of today so our children can bloom into the flowers of tomorrow!

"I LOVE your magazine. I have been using it in my classroom since 1990."—*Cajsa Howland Sheen via Facebook*

"Great teaching ideas! My students love them all!"—*Jennifer Marcinkus Chumbley via Facebook*

Read All About It!

I encourage my students and their parents to read my newsletter by using a trivia question. The question may be about something mentioned in the newsletter, or it may be a more detailed response about something we have been studying in class. I encourage each parent to read the newsletter with his child to answer the question; then they both sign off on the trivia question, and the child returns the related form to school. For each correct response, I provide a small reward. This idea keeps everyone in my classroom on top of the latest news! ***Stephanie McHugh, Bristol Bay Elementary, Yorkville, IL***

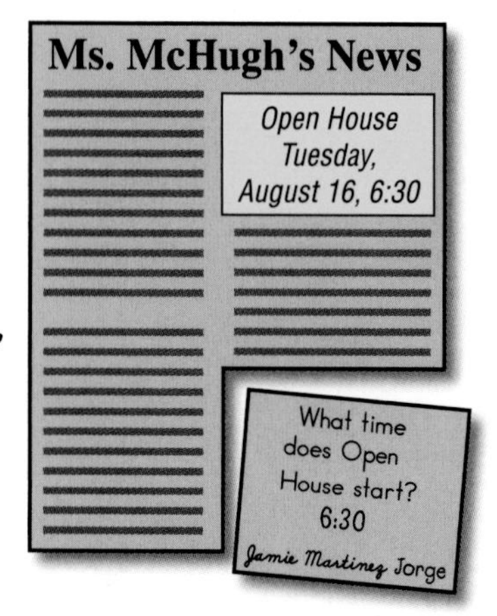
Ms. McHugh's News
Open House Tuesday, August 16, 6:30
What time does Open House start?
6:30
Jamie Martinez Jorge

Cost and Space Savers

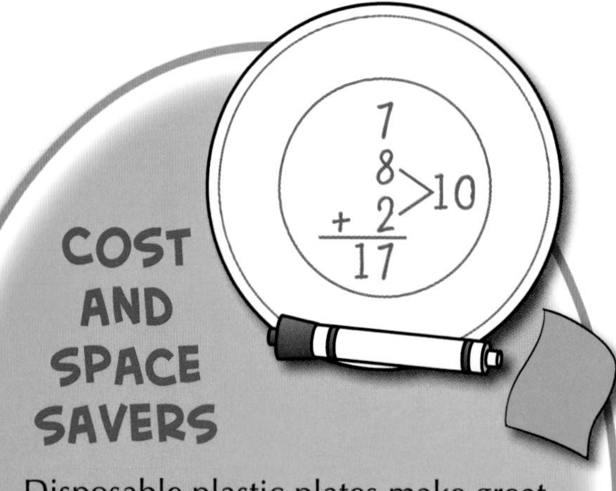
7
8
+ 2
>10
17

Disposable plastic plates make great individual dry-erase boards! During guided instruction, I give each child a plate, a felt square (eraser), and a dry-erase marker. When the activity is over, I stack the plates with a felt square on top of each one. The plates take up very little storage space and there's no wasted paper! ***Nan Duffer, P. W. Moore Elementary, Elizabeth City, NC***

The MAILBOX® BLOG

"Thank you for the wonderful ideas that you provide every month! I look forward to my new edition like it's Christmas morning!"—*Rolanda Staley, Aiken, SC, via The Mailbox® Blog*

Our Readers WRITE...

(and EMAIL and BLOG and TWEET and POST)

"I love *The Mailbox* magazine. It has enhanced my classrooms since the 1980s."—*Lisa Parks Reed via Facebook*

Roll a Name!

When it's time to choose a child to be the line leader, answer a question, or complete a classroom chore, I use the 26-sided die from my Scattergories game. At the beginning of the year, I assign a letter of the alphabet to each child. Then, when I need a child's help or response, I roll the die, call out the letter that is rolled, and have the assigned student perform the task. ***Brett Bielewicz, Franklin Regional School District, Murrysville, PA***

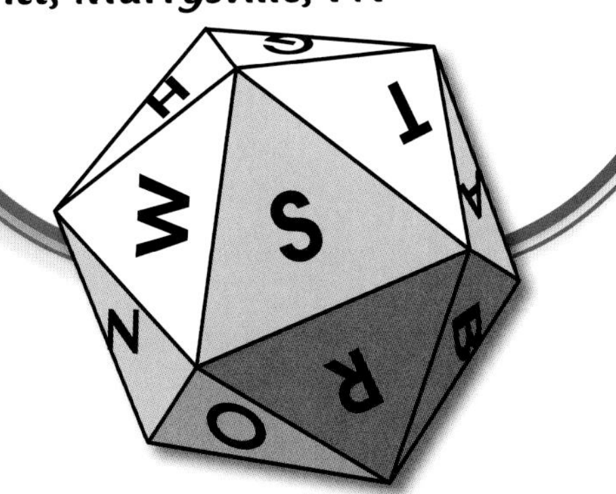

Organized Fun

Spin a Fraction!
Comparing fractions

I've found the perfect way to store games in a small, compact space—I use coffee containers! I place the game pieces for each game in a different container. If a game requires a spinner, I duplicate a copy of the spinner base, resize it to fit the can's lid, and hole-punch its center. Next, I hole-punch the lid and glue the spinner base on it. I use a brass fastener to secure a paper clip (spinner arrow) to the lid. Finally, I label the outside of each can with the game's title and skill. Everything needed to play the game is in one place! *Nicholas Sveum, Edgerton WI*

The MAILBOX BLOG

"Thank you for the ideas I have gotten from *The Mailbox* magazine over the years. My fellow teachers think I am so smart—even when I tell them my idea is from *The Mailbox*."—*Linda Jones, Austin, TX, via The Mailbox Blog*

WRITE AND REVIEW

It only takes a few minutes for my students to reinforce objectives, skills, and essential vocabulary with this activity. At the end of each lesson, I set a timer for one minute; then each child writes an explanation of something from the lesson he feels is important to remember. When time is up, each student finds a partner and I again set the timer for one minute. One child explains what he has written to his partner. The timer is reset; then the other student in the duo explains what she has written. Finally, each child returns to his desk to write about the idea his partner shared with him. ***Mialynn Didomenico, Oakwood Elementary, Norfolk VA***

Oct. 18, 2011

I think it is important to remember that every sentence must have a noun and verb. If one is missing, a sentence is incomplete.

Tara thinks it is important to remember that the noun and verb in a sentence are often called the subject and the predicate.

Our Readers WRITE...

(and EMAIL and BLOG and TWEET and POST)

Tap, Tap, I Agree

Here's an easy tip that lets more of my students share a response. Sometimes one of my students will give the answer or opinion that other students are waiting to share. When this happens, students who have the same response tap their fingers on their heads. This simple action encourages those students to participate without calling out or repeating answers. ***Kristen Merrell, Lee's Summit Elementary, Lee's Summit, MO***

"***The Mailbox*** **is an excellent resource for my teaching plans. Thank you for helping me find great ideas to implement in my lessons each and every week."—*Cathy Jo McCall via Facebook***

No-Cost Cards

I collect holiday greeting cards, recycle them, and present them to my students the following school year. For each card, I cut off the front flap, turn it over, and sign my name. Then I punch two holes in the card and thread ribbon through the holes. I tie a candy cane to each card and present one card to each student. I use the same technique for birthday cards, tying a colorful birthday pencil to the card instead of a candy cane. *Jean Wright, Meadows Elementary, Terre Haute, IN*

Happy holidays!
Ms. Wright

Calvin

Science Test

Grade B
Your child is encouraged to correct this test for an improved grade. Each corrected item will be worth 2 points. Please return the corrected test by 1/20/12. New grade ____

Extra Learning

To make student tests more than an assessment tool, I allow students to make corrections. I prepare a batch of printed labels like the one shown and stick one on each test. After I grade the tests, I fill in each blank with the corresponding information and then send the papers home. Students are motivated to improve their grades, and their learning is reinforced when they correct their own errors. *Jen Woodmansee Barnett, Buckey Valley East Elementary, Ashley, OH*

The MAILBOX BLOG

"I totally love *The Mailbox* website and magazines!" —*Karen Lesmerises, Allenstown, NH, via The Mailbox Blog*

Our Readers WRITE...

(and EMAIL and BLOG and TWEET and POST)

"I love the various types of activities in *The Mailbox* magazine. It's really a pleasure to have it!"—*Rola Abou Dargham via Facebook*

TAKING TIME OUT

If you made reducing stress one of your New Year's resolutions, then this is the tip for you! My grade-level teammates and I found one day and time during school hours when we can all get together. During that time, we eat a themed lunch made by a pair of teammates. While we eat, school talk is off limits! Instead, it's a time to discuss families, vacations, recipes, and other fun topics. These weekly get-togethers are a great way to build a stronger team bond.
Adell Chase, Halethorpe, MD

The "Their" Song

Singing this fun song gives students a simple spelling reminder!

The "Their" Song
(sung to the tune of "Old MacDonald Had a Farm")

If it is theirs, we spell the word
E-I, E-I, R.
It's not the same as "over there."
E-I, E-I, R.
Think, "That's their cat," and "That's their dog,"
"That's their hen," and "That's their hog."
When you write and mean "It belongs to them,"
Write *E-I, E-I, R!*

Jane Anderson-Eacueo, Helen Mae Sauter Elementary, Gardner, MA

Salami Means Stop!

When I want my students' attention, I say, "SALAMI!" My students know this acronym stands for "Stop and Look at Me Immediately," and they respond accordingly. It really works! ***Rina Walter, Flushing, NY***

Stop
And
Look
At
Me
Immediately

WELCOME TO OUR ROOM!

To welcome a new class member, I invite each of my students to introduce himself to the child. Next, I assign a buddy who takes the new student on a campus tour while I prepare the new student's desk. In addition to his textbooks and supplies, I tuck a snack, a colorful pencil, and a few stickers into a gift bag and place it on his desk. This simple routine always makes new students feel welcome!
Renee Silliman, Spring Shadows Elementary, Houston, TX

The
MAILBOX
BLOG

I have made many games and activities from ideas in *The Mailbox*. I love this magazine!"—*Cindy MacDonald, Raynham, MA, via The Mailbox Blog*

Our Readers WRITE...

(and EMAIL and BLOG and TWEET and POST)

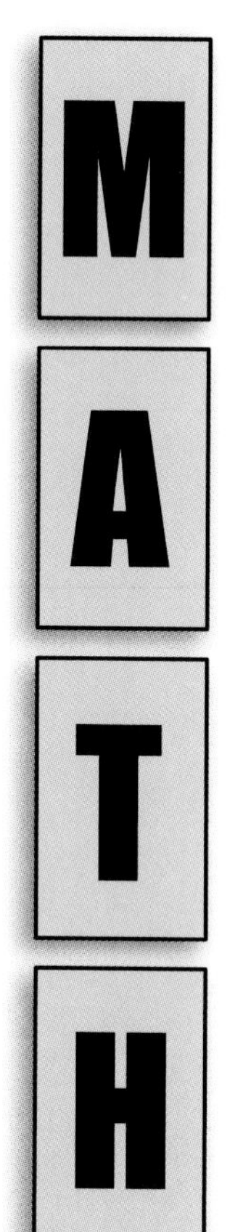
M
A
T
H

No More Tangled Letters!

Storing die-cut letters for bulletin boards became much easier for me when I started gluing each individual letter on a rectangular piece of paper. Not only do my bulletin boards look neat, the letters don't get tangled when I store them, allowing me to reuse them year after year. ***Stephanie Woodward, Berlin Memorial School, Berlin, MA***

"I love the new layout of *The Mailbox* magazine. It's easy to find what you need, and the latest tweets and messages from Facebook get published. I can't wait to use it!"—*Nicole DeVincenzo via Facebook*

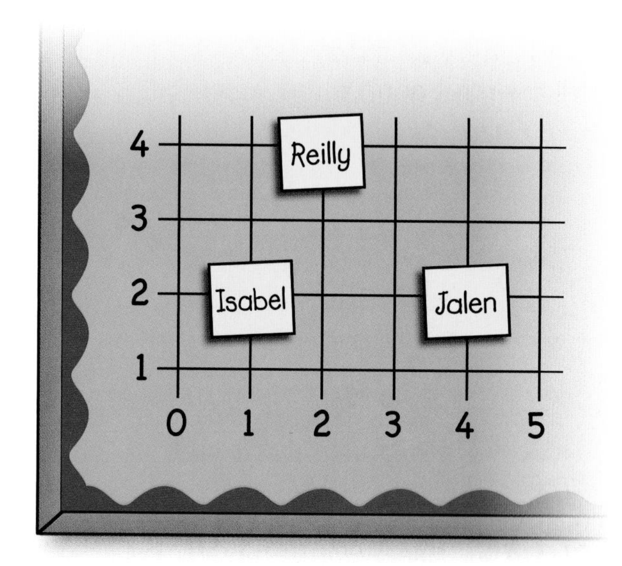
Reilly
Isabel
Jalen
4
3
2
1
0
1
2
3
4
5

A POETIC REMINDER

To help my students remember how to organize narrative writing, I teach them this rhyme. ***Karen Almond, Royston Elementary, Royston, GA***

A bold **beginning** is the way to start,
A meaty **middle** for the next part.
An exciting **end** makes a work of art.
My job is done; I'm so smart!

Coordinating a Classroom

I display a grid with numerical coordinates and use it for various management needs. I write each child's name on a small sticky note. About once a week, I plot each student's name in a different place on the grid. When I want to call on a student to answer a question, to assign partners, or to choose a classroom helper, I announce the child's coordinate pairs. ***Ashley Isaacson, Codington Elementary, Wilmington, NC***

The MAILBOX BLOG

"Thanks so much for striving to make learning fun!"—*Sarah Chestnut via The Mailbox Blog*

Our Readers WRITE...

(and EMAIL and BLOG and TWEET and POST)

The MAILBOX® BLOG

"I love this magazine. I have used it most of my 28 years of teaching and will continue to use it until I retire! Thank you for all the wonderful 'tools' you have given me over the years!"—*Lisa Reed via The Mailbox Blog*

Finding Files

Saving all my paperwork on a thumb-drive helps me find files in a jiffy. Anytime I come across a really great worksheet, I scan it to my computer. Then I save the file with a dual-purpose name, such as *February Addition Review*. This way I can easily search for the worksheet based on the month or the skill even if I don't recall the file's exact name. *Stephanie Woodward, Berlin Memorial School, Berlin, MA*

ANECDOTAL RECORDS

For a quick and easy way to write anecdotal records, I use a clipboard and sticky notes. I simply arrange short stacks of sticky notes on a clipboard. As I walk around the classroom, I jot down student observations. Then I transfer each student's note to a designated sheet I have stored in a three-ring binder. The notes come in handy as I plan report cards or when I need some quick examples of each student's work during conferences. *Lynn Sanders, Sope Creek Elementary, Marietta, GA*

Team Building

When I want to review math skills, I play a basketball game with my students. First, I group my class into teams and give each team a small dry-erase board, dry-erase marker, and eraser. To play, I call out a math problem. The first team to show the correct answer on its dry-erase board wins a point. Then each team member gets to throw a soft foam ball into an unused trash can to earn additional points. What a great way for students to see that working as a team pays off! *Malinda Pryor, Pine Ridge Elementary, Ellerslie, GA*

The MAILBOX®
BLOG

"Thank you, *Mailbox*. I have subscribed to this magazine for more than a decade, and I love how it has continued to evolve with the changes in education."—*Theresa Clevenstine via The Mailbox Blog*

CHEERING THEM ON

Before standardized testing begins at my school, classes at other grade levels that are not testing adopt a classroom that will be testing. Students make motivational posters and write letters of encouragement for the students in their adopted class. Since students love giving encouragement as much as they love receiving it, everyone benefits! ***Tara Kicklighter, Bunnell Elementary, Bunnell, FL***

Shoot for the Stars!
You Are One Smart Cookie!
A+

Our Readers WRITE...

(and EMAIL and BLOG and TWEET and POST)

Rainbow Review

For a fun skills check-up, I gather six sheets of construction paper—each representing a different color of the rainbow—and write a review question on each sheet. Then I post the papers around the room. Next, I have each student draw on a blank sheet of paper a large rainbow with the matching colors. On my signal, I direct my students to drift through the room as quietly as clouds, searching for each review question. Each child records his answers above the matching color on his rainbow. *Colleen Dabney, Williamsburg, VA*

What body system includes the nose, mouth, and lungs?

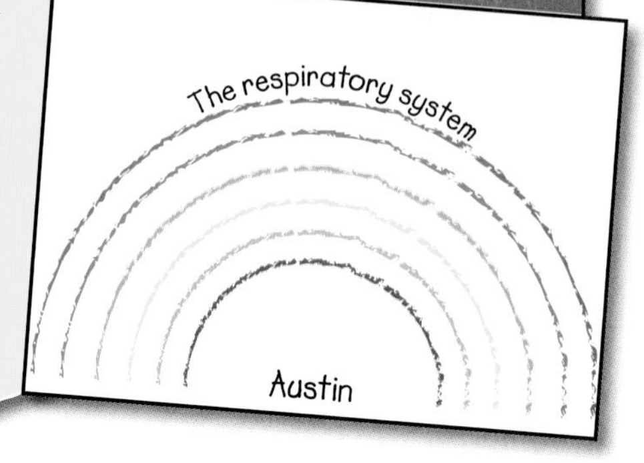
The respiratory system
Austin

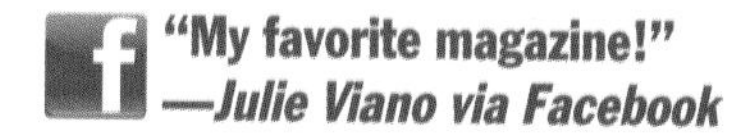
"My favorite magazine!"
—Julie Viano via Facebook

The MAILBOX BLOG

"I really love reading all the tips and ideas from my fellow teachers. *The Mailbox* magazines are great!"
—Linda Stoffan, Rio Rancho, NM, via The Mailbox Blog

Get Organized

I found an inexpensive way to create supply organizers for my classroom. I hot-glue several empty cleaning wipe containers together in the form of a pyramid. Then I fill each storage unit with items such as pencils, scissors, paintbrushes, and markers! The organizers can easily fit on most surfaces, and they're portable. *Barbara Duran, Rockwall, TX*

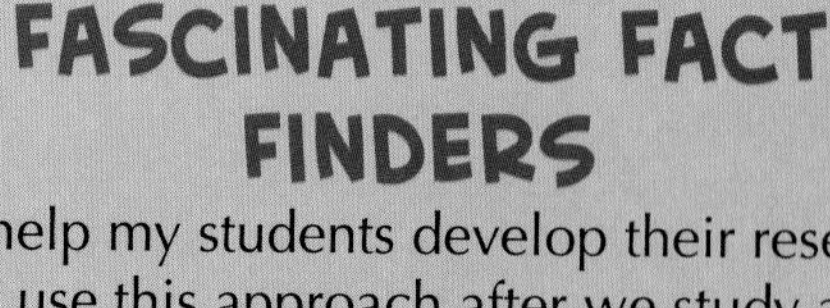
FASCINATING FACT FINDERS

To help my students develop their research skills, I use this approach after we study a topic. During our media center time, I guide students to use nonfiction books, reference materials, and the Internet to research additional interesting facts about the subject. When we return to our classroom, students share their findings aloud and then add their papers to a binder titled "Super Cool Facts." I store the binder in our classroom library for easy access to this new information. ***Christa Burnette, Patrick Springs Primary School, Patrick Springs, VA***

Super Cool Facts

Our Readers WRITE...

(and EMAIL and BLOG and TWEET and POST)

Add a Little Speck

Who needs a lot of materials to spark students' creative thinking? Not me! I give each student a sheet of white paper and have her choose a colored pom-pom. Next, I tell each child to glue the pom-pom any place on the paper. After the pom-pom is set in place, I have her draw a picture or design around the pom-pom. Then I provide time for students to share their unique creations. *Margaret Cromwell, Georgetown, TX*

LUCKY PENCIL

To build my students' test-taking confidence, I give each of them a special pencil. I write "You're a Star!" on a construction paper star cutout. Then I cut several pieces of thin ribbon streamers and attach the ribbon and star cutout to a brand-new pencil. Students love having a lucky charm in their grasps. ***Colleen Dabney, Williamsburg, VA***

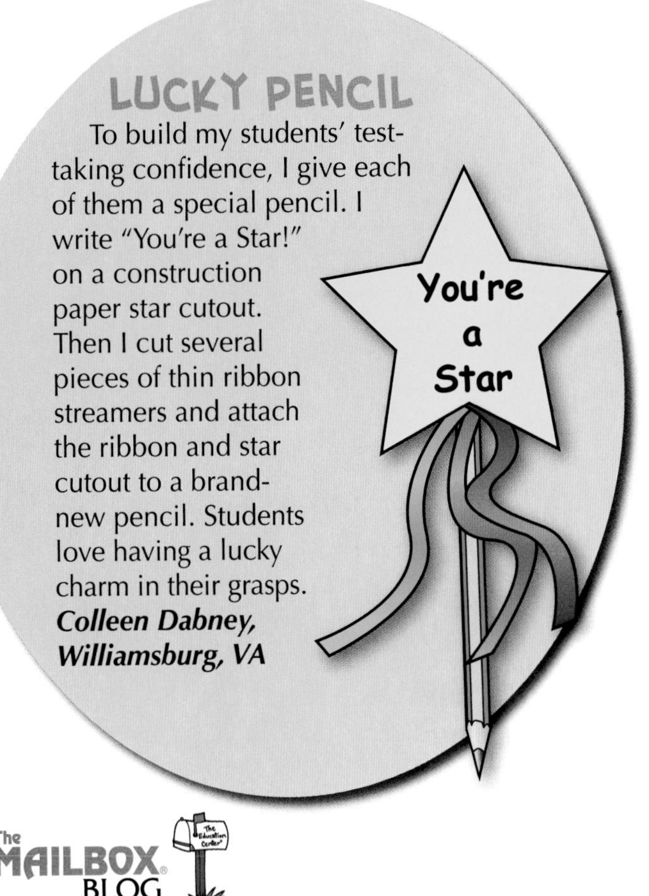

You're
a
Star

The MAILBOX BLOG

"I love *The Mailbox*. The activities are so colorful and creative."—*Nancy C. Allen, Glen Allen, VA*

Morning Mix-Up

During my daily morning meeting, I conduct a memory exercise to help my students enhance their observation skills. I select one student to stand in a corner of the room with his back to the class. Then I quietly tap the shoulders of five students and they exchange seats. Once the five students are seated, I have the student in the corner turn around and face the class. He guesses the five students who have changed their seats and, in turn, each student confirms his guess. *Tracy Smith, Petersham Center School, Petersham, MA*

"Love *The Mailbox*. It's been a big part of my classroom for many years!"—*Lynn McMinds Harrell via Facebook*

Boundless Borders

Instead of using traditional borders for my math displays, I use flash cards and trivia game cards that I find at flea markets and garage sales. Not only are the cards decorative, they also serve as an interactive visual aid for my students. I refer to the cards during warm-up sessions and sometimes use them as a giant gameboard. *Nicholas Sveum, Edgerton Elementary, Edgerton, WI*

Our Readers WRITE...

(and EMAIL and BLOG and TWEET and POST)

HOOKED ON ORGANIZATION

With very little storage space in my room, I needed a simple way to store my tons of bulletin board borders. My solution? I bought inexpensive metal shower hooks and punched one hole at the end of each border strip. I placed three or four sets of borders on each shower hook and hung the hooks in my classroom closet. Now, whenever I need a certain border set, I can easily see the ones I want and can access them quickly! ***Dana Gilberston, Elton Hills Elementary, Rochester, MN***

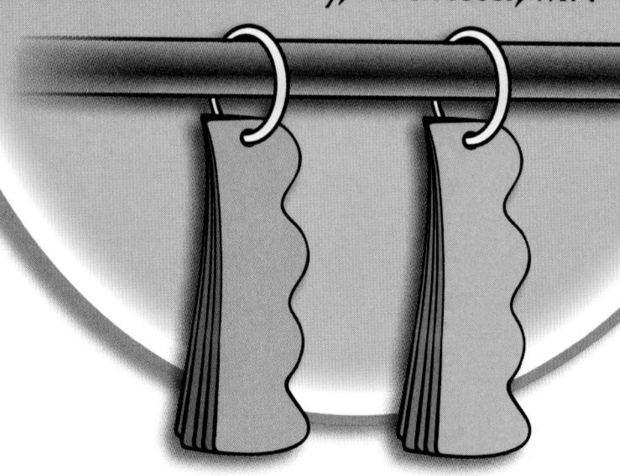

Book Bags

To help my students transport library books and projects home safely and neatly, I purchase various recyclable shopping bags and label each bag with a luggage tag. On each luggage tag, I write a number and my teacher information. Anytime a child borrows a bag, I simply jot down her name and the bag's number to keep a record of the bag's whereabouts. The bags are versatile, and my students can easily carry home their belongings! *Lori Kessel, Quest Elementary, Melbourne, FL*

The MAILBOX BLOG

"When I open my mailbox and find the next issue of *The Mailbox* magazine, it's like receiving a gift in the mail. Thanks for sharing."—*Cindy Macdonald via The Mailbox Blog*

Keeping an Inventory

Restocking classroom supplies and getting learning activities ready for next year's class has been easy for me ever since I started keeping an inventory notebook. Throughout the school year, I keep a notebook handy so I can record my ideas for pocket charts, games, and activities. I also jot down any supplies that need to be replenished or replaced by next year. When it's time for my school break, I review my notebook and use the summer to get the things I need for another successful year! *Jessica Hines, Rivercrest Elementary, Bogata, TX*

"I love everything about *The Mailbox*. It is just full of practical ideas from real teachers. It is very easy to read the magazine the night you get it in the mail and implement something new the next day." —*Jami Brabson Welden via Facebook*

Familiar Faces

When I receive my class list for the upcoming school year, I find each student's picture in our school yearbook and photocopy it. I cut out each picture, glue them in alphabetical order on a sheet of paper, and write each child's name next to the photo. On the day of open house, I review my students' photos and names. When I meet the children for the first time, I am able to greet them by their names! ***Karen Gilbert, Hudson Elementary, Hudson, NC***

Alexa B.

Baz C.

Lucy C.

Jack G.

Sam H.

PROBLEM SOLVED

Q&A Problem Solved!

Your Solutions to Classroom Challenges

I reinforce our classroom rules with this interactive idea. I write the rules on a large piece of bulletin board paper. Then I have each child sign his name on the paper and use tempera paint to put his handprint near his signature. I display the project at student height. As students arrive each morning, I ask them to high-five their handprints to show they agree to follow the rules that day.

Carrie McClaine, Columbus City Schools, Columbus, OH

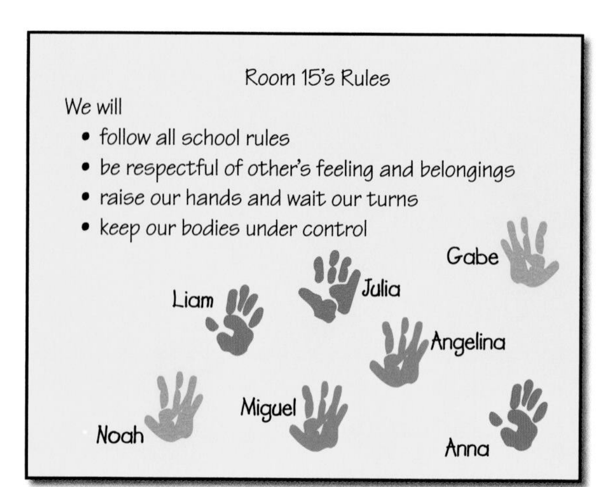

Room 15's Rules
We will
• follow all school rules
• be respectful of other's feeling and belongings
• raise our hands and wait our turns
• keep our bodies under control
Gabe
Julia
Liam
Angelina
Miguel
Noah
Anna

How do you teach students your *classroom rules?*

At the beginning of the year, my class and I read *Lilly's Purple Plastic Purse* by Kevin Henkes. We discuss the fact that Lilly doesn't follow the rules and talk about why rules are important. Then we brainstorm rules for our class. I tell students that we can add a new rule if the need arises during the year.

Barbara Duran
Dorris A. Jones Elementary, Rockwall, TX

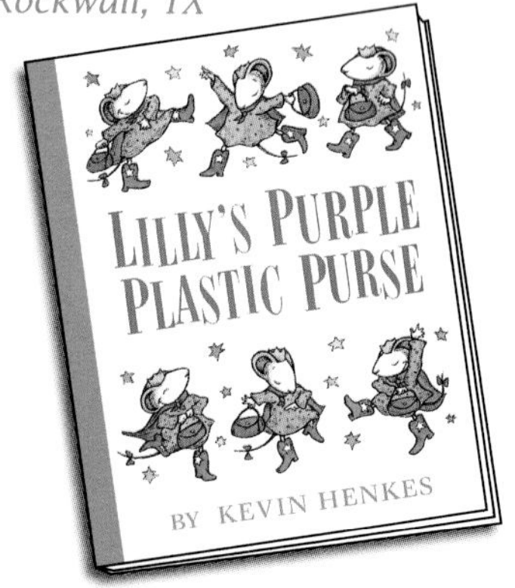

Lilly's Purple Plastic Purse
by Kevin Henkes

I make sure my students understand that the way they behave at home isn't necessarily the same as the way they should behave at school. I use myself as an example and explain that, at home, I might borrow my daughter's jacket without asking, but, at my job, I would never borrow something without asking. Anytime students need a reminder of how to behave, I tell them to speak or act like they're at their jobs. Discipline problems are few and far between in my class.

Amy Barsanti, Pines Elementary, Plymouth, NC

What's your biggest classroom-management challenge? Visitors to TheMailbox.com chose "fostering student responsibility," "establishing expectations and consequences," and "monitoring behavior" as their biggest hurdles.

It's your turn! We're always looking for your tips, tricks, ideas, and suggestions. Go to TheMailbox.com to share!

Q&A Problem Solved!

Your Solutions to Classroom Challenges

For each child, I attach an **incentive chart** to a paper pocket. When a student displays good behavior, I place a token in his pocket. At the end of the day, the tokens are exchanged for ministickers to put on the chart. When a child earns ten stickers, he receives a homework pass. When he earns 20 stickers, he receives a certificate and a prize from my prize box.

Vicki Giuffre, Roosevelt Elementary, North Arlington, NJ

Earning My Stripes!
Terrance

How do you *encourage positive behavior?*

A **coordinate grid** doubles as a learning tool and a reward chart! First, I draw and label a grid on chart paper. Next, I use a permanent marker to write different rewards on the backs of laminated paper cutouts. Then I tape the cutouts onto the grid. When a student earns a reward, I have her name a coordinate where a cutout is placed. She removes the cutout and reveals the reward. I keep the cutouts in a stack until the board is empty; then I put the cutouts in new locations on the grid.

Mary Burgess
Howell Valley Elementary
West Plains, MO

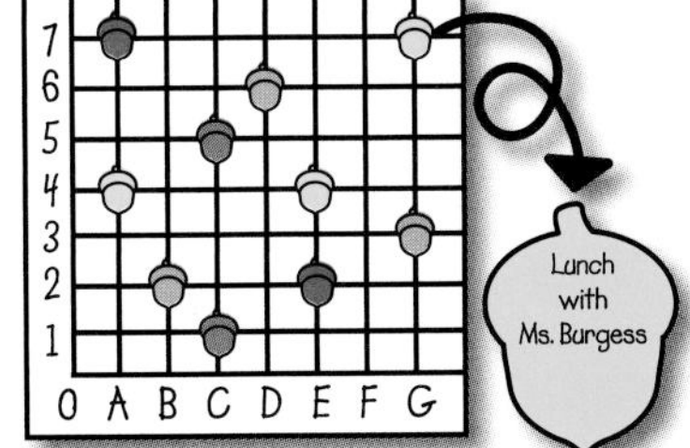
7
6
5
4
3
2
1
0 A B C D E F G
Lunch with Ms. Burgess

To reinforce money skills and encourage good behavior, I gather **play coins and bills**. I also have each child decorate a clean soup can and place it on his desk. As students arrive, I place three pennies in each child's can. He earns more money throughout the day when he shows good choices. However, if he participates in unsafe behaviors, he pays a penny fine. Each afternoon, I provide time to exchange ten pennies for a dime and, when needed, exchange dimes into dollars. Every Friday, I open a class store where students can spend their money on small items such as pencils, crayons, or erasers.

Janice Sutherland, Louisiana Schnell Elementary, Placerville, CA

I add a little **mystery** to my reward system! I label each of three paper lunch bags with a different number and place a different prize in each bag. During the week, a student who shows positive behavior earns a ticket. She writes her name on the ticket and places it in our class ticket jar. On Friday, I draw a ticket, invite the child to choose a bag, and reveal her prize. I continue drawing tickets until all the prizes are awarded. The jar is emptied and we start over the next week!

Melissa Patrick, Northlake Christian School, Covington, LA

You can't direct the wind, but you can adjust the sails.
—Anonymous

It's your turn! We're always looking for your tips, tricks, ideas, and suggestions. Go to TheMailbox.com to share!

Problem Solved!

Your Solutions to Classroom Challenges

I display a dry-erase calendar on the board and write work and homework for each day. I also keep a folder below the calendar to store any undistributed practice sheets. When a student returns from an absence, it is his responsibility to check the calendar, find any related practice sheets in the folder, and complete the work by an assigned due date.

Renee Silliman, Spring Shadows Elementary, Houston, TX

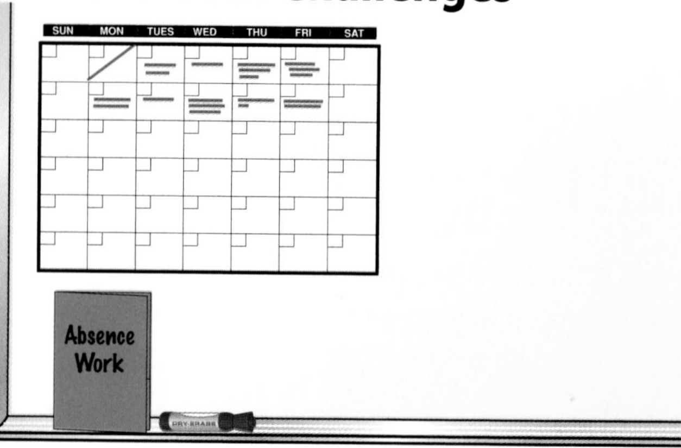
SUN MON TUES WED THU FRI SAT
Absence Work

tip

At the end of each day, pull out the practice sheets, paper-clip them together, and place a sticky note with the date on the top copy. Then return the stack to the folder.

How do you *manage work for absent students?*

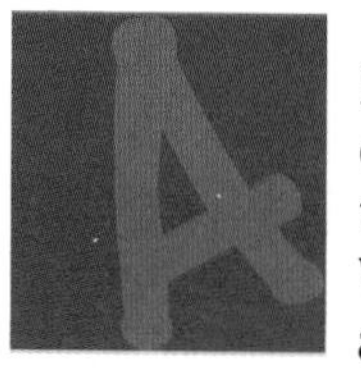

In advance, I make several copies of a chart like the one shown. When a student is absent I have a responsible student collect the child's work and fill in the chart. I also direct her to write the child's name on any handouts. At the end of the day, the student stacks the papers and places the chart on top. When the absent child returns to school, he knows what assignments were completed in class and what was assigned for homework.

Satina Smith, Timber Drive Elementary Garner, NC

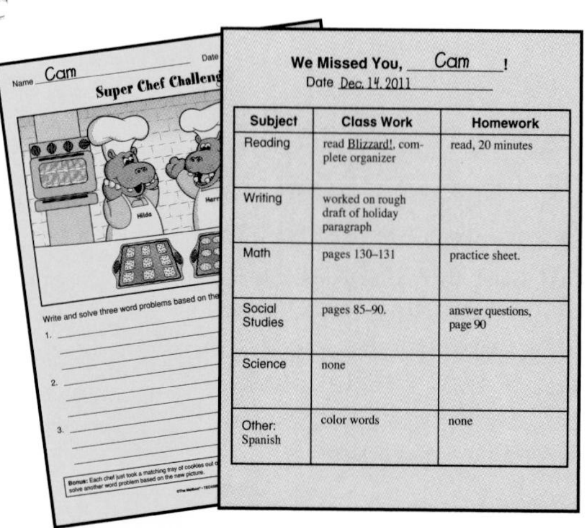

We Missed You, Cam!
Date Dec. 14, 2011

Subject	Class Work	Homework
Reading	read Blizzard!, complete organizer	read, 20 minutes
Writing	worked on rough draft of holiday paragraph	
Math	pages 130–131	practice sheet.
Social Studies	pages 85–90.	answer questions, page 90
Science	none	
Other: Spanish	color words	none

Sometimes students need information from lessons that can't be found in a book or on a practice page. To make sure students who were absent don't miss these tips and reminders, I assign a child to serve as my absence ambassador. This child explains to a returning student what was missed while she was out, shares any tips he learned from that day, and provides assistance with work when needed.

Janet Boyce, Cokato, MN

Twenty-three percent of students don't miss any school days; nearly six percent miss 11 or more days.
—*US Department of Health and Human Services*

It's your turn! We're always looking for your tips, tricks, ideas, and suggestions. Go to TheMailbox.com to share!

Q&A Problem Solved!

Your Solutions to Classroom Challenges

To keep all **student awards and recognition certificates** organized before Awards Day, I gather a supply of large manila envelopes. I write each student's name and the name of each certificate he will receive on the outside of the envelope. Then I place the students' certificates inside their individual envelopes. On Awards Day, I have a quick and easy way to announce each child's award and, in turn, the envelopes keep my students from misplacing their certificates.

Courtney Bartlett, Sunnyview Primary, Knoxville, TN

Aaron
Honor Roll
Perfect Attendance
Perfect Attendance
3rd Grade Honor Roll
Aaron Clarkson

How do you keep up with *year-end paperwork*?

My grade-level partners and I have had great success with trading our individual **students' cumulative folders**. After completing our folders, we trade them with another teacher. When it comes to checking for mistakes or missing folder items, we find it's easier to see errors on the students' folders when they are not our own.

Virginia Zeletzki
The Villages, FL

I prepare for the **end-of-year paperwork** rush by standing a large manila envelope in each student's hanging file folder. As I receive test score reports, complete report cards, and sort student portfolio items, I file them inside each child's envelope. When it's time to send home these items, I simply seal the envelopes and hand them to my students.

Sue Walker, Blowing Rock Elementary
Blowing Rock, NC

According to a poll from The Mailbox.com, 40% of second- and third-grade teachers haven't seen their desks in weeks. The culprit? Paperwork!

It's your turn! We're always looking for your tips, tricks, ideas, and suggestions. Go to TheMailbox.com to share!

Answer Keys

Page 38
Order will vary.

Teddy y sounds like long e			Ty y sounds like long i
baby	apply	July	apply
candy	baby	my	butterfly
daisy	butterfly	party	cry
fuzzy	candy	pry	pry
happy	cry	reply	July
party	daisy	shy	my
sloppy	fuzzy	sloppy	reply
very	happy	very	shy

Teddy wins the contest.

Bonus: Answers will vary.

Page 39

Sir Oddalot is a very strange knight. You might even say he lives in his own world. He knocks with his toes, not his knuckles. He also turns knobs with his knees instead of his hands, and he keeps a watch around his ankle, not his wrist. When he wraps gifts, he ties knots instead of bows in the ribbons. "What a wreck," his royal highness, the king, says.

However, Sir Oddalot knows how to rescue a princess and wrestle a dragon. He even has a knack for writing poetry. Sir Oddalot is wrong about many things, but he's right when it really matters.

Order of the words will vary.

Silent *k*	Silent *w*
knight	wrist
knocks	wraps
knuckles	wreck
knobs	wrestle
knees	writing
knots	wrong
knows	
knack	

Bonus: Words will vary.

Page 40
1. Who's as tired as I am? Who is
2. I can't wait to get some rest. cannot
3. I didn't think I would be so tired from flying around all night. did not
4. I could've sprained a wing from all that flying! could have
5. Note to self—don't overdo it again! do not
6. At least finding food wasn't a problem. was not
7. The bugs weren't able to hide from me. were not
8. I'm so full! I am
9. I must've eaten over 100 bugs. must have
10. You couldn't pay me to eat another one. could not
11. I'll need to brush my teeth soon. I will
12. Now, where's my toothpaste? where is

It had "bat" breath.

Bonus: Answers will vary.

Page 41
1. runners
2. tip, midbody, tail
3. poles
4. buckles; In the "boots" entry, *usually fastened by buckles* should be circled.
5. If a skier falls, they release the boot from the ski.
6. basket
7. in alphabetical order
8. after *poles* and before *skis*

Bonus: no; The book's title is *Ready to Ski* and all the terms relate to skiing.

Page 42

1. week	5. berry	9. pour	13. no
2. Sunday	6. pair	10. knew	14. too
3. wear	7. red	11. whole	15. nose
4. cellar	8. hours	12. sighed	16. scent

Bonus: Sentences will vary.

Page 43

1. uneven	7. cheerful
2. colorful	8. reheat
3. dreamer	9. thankful
4. restart	10. reuse
5. uncover	11. teacher
6. skater	12. unharmed

Word Bank

reheat	reuse
skater	unharmed
colorful	dreamer
teacher	restart
uncover	uneven
thankful	cheerful

Bonus: The prefix *re-* can mean again or back. The suffix *-er* can mean one that does or is.

Page 44

1. S	7. S
2. S	8. M
3. M	9. S
4. M	10. M
5. S	11. M
6. M	12. S

Bonus: 1. as easy as pie 2. as stinky as rotten eggs 3. the soap is a bouquet of roses 4. time is money 5. as light as a feather 6. paws are wrinkled raisins 7. as cold as ice 8. dog is a trooper 9. as white as snow 10. He is a fluffy pile of cotton 11. washing was a breeze 12. run like the wind

Page 46

1. D	6. I
2. F	7. G
3. B	8. C
4. J	9. H
5. A	10. E

Bonus: Sentences will vary.

Page 47
1. Penny and Parker yawn and stretch.
2. Grandma Pearl
3. Answers will vary but may include the following: Who yawns and stretches with Penny? Who tidies the nests? Who does Grandma Pearl watch first?
4. eggplants
5. Answers will vary but may include the following: What happens after Parker and Penny finish the chores? What do the younger family members like to do when the chores are done?
6. Answers will vary but may include the following: What does Grandma Pearl do after a day of working? What does Grandma Pearl do on a freshly made nest?

Bonus: Answers will vary.

Page 48
Explanations will vary.
1. friendly, funny
2. caring, selfless
3. serious, shy
4. confident, pesky

Bonus: Answers will vary.

Page 49
1. helpful, Leon likes to help
2. struts proud
3. Words will vary but should reflect that the animals see Leon sneaking around and avoiding them.
4. Leon does not want to be king. He wants to be a baker.
5. Descriptions and explanations will vary.

Page 50
1. It is one of the seven continents.
2. It is cold and dry. It is covered by snow and ice.
3. The maps show where Antarctica is located compared to the other continents. They also show what bodies of water are around Antarctica.
4. Weddell Sea, Ross Sea
5. krill, whales, seals, penguins; They all live in or near the seas around Antarctica.

Bonus: Answers will vary but should include the cold conditions and lack of resources.

Page 51

4 Within minutes of trapping the bug, an air-tight seal forms and the bug cannot get out.
5 The trap squeezes the insect, and digestion begins.
6 After five to 12 days the plant has digested the bug. Its exoskeleton is all that is left.
3 The leaf snaps shut in less than a second, and the bug is trapped.
7 Now the plant is finished eating. The leaf reopens.
1 First, a small bug smells the plant's sweet nectar. It lands on the plant's leaf.
2 The bug touches stiff hairs on the plant's leaf called trigger hairs.
8 Finally, any leftover parts of the bug blow away or get washed away by rain.

Bonus: Answers will vary.

Page 52

1. When is the moon heaviest? It is heaviest when it is full. How are false teeth like stars? They both come out at night.
2. Answers will vary but may include *backpack, blacktop, bookend, bookmark, bookshelf, carpool, chalkboard, classmates, classroom, desktop, doorway, hallway, handwriting, homework, inside, keyboard, lunchroom, notebook, outside, overhead, playground, restroom, textbook, whiteboard, workbook,* and *worksheets.*

3–4. Answers will vary.

5. Answers will vary but may include *apple, carrot, grapefruit, kiwi, orange, popcorn, pretzels, raisins, smoothie,* and *yogurt.*
6. dog, fish, snake, bird
7. Oatmeal, Texas; Toast, North Carolina; Buttermilk, Kansas; Milkwater, Arizona; Cheeseville, Wisconsin.
8. Answers will vary.

Page 53

1. Answers will vary but may include the following: they are both one-syllable words, they are both seasons, both are verbs, both are nouns, each word has one vowel, each word has an even number of letters, *fall* has four letters and *spring* has six letters, *fall* has three tall letters and *spring* has no tall letters.
2. Answers will vary.
3. Possible nouns include *branch, bush, food, ground, oxygen, pigment, plant, stem, sun,* and *vein.*

4, 5. Answers will vary.

6. Answers will vary but may include *entreat, mistreat, pretreat, retreat, treatable, treated, treater, treatment,* and *untreated.*
7. Answer will vary but may include the following:
   brave: *bold, courageous, fearless, gutsy, heroic, heroical; chicken, coward, cowardly, fainthearted, fearful, gutless, spineless, spiritless, uncourageous, unheroic, weakhearted, yellow*
   dangerous: *hazardous, risky, serious, threatening, unhealthy, unsafe; harmless, nonhazardous, nonthreatening, safe, unthreatening*
   friendly: *buddy-buddy, chummy, neighborly, warm, warmhearted; unfriendly*
   wicked: *dark, evil, rotten, unlawful, wrong; decent, good, honest, right*
8. What kind of cat goes bowling? An alley cat

Page 54

1. Answers will vary.
2. Possible sorts include the following: hard *g* words and soft *g* words, one-syllable words and two-syllable words, words that start with *g* and words that do not start with *g.*
3. I ate a taco at the game.
   We got mom's car fixed.
   Meg loves winter!
   He speaks Spanish at home.
   This ticket will admit ten friends to the show.
4. Answers will vary. Possible similarities include the following: they are all one-syllable words; they are all spelled with *oo*; they all have four or five letters; *oo* are the second and third letters. Possible differences include the following: some are nouns and some are verbs; some have four letters and some have five; *oo* does not make the same sound every time.
5. *blow, flow, grow, meow, plow, show, snow,* and *stow*
6. Answers will vary.
7. 7 d. in a wk. = 7 days in a week
   26 l. in the a. = 26 letters in the alphabet
   an h. has 60 m. = an hour has 60 minutes
   100 p. is the same amount as 1 d. = 100 pennies is the same amount as 1 dollar
   2 rhyming l. in a c. = 2 rhyming lines in a couplet
8. Answers will vary.

Page 55

Answers for 1, 3, 5, 6, and 8 will vary.

2. A cat
4. Answers will vary. Possible answers include: *go, hang, hint, hit, is, sang, sat, saw, show, shot, sing, sit, swat, swing, swig, tag, tan, wag, was, wash, win,* and *won*
7. Answers will vary. Possible answers include *crosswind, tailwind, whirlwind, windbreaker, windblown, windburn, windchill, windjammer, windmill, windpipe, windshield, windsock, windstorm,* and *woodwind.*

Page 56

Answers for 3, 4, and 6–8 will vary.

1. Answers will vary.

A. never	D. full	G. add
B. lead	E. south	H. false
C. smile	F. answer	I. dry

2. A. beetle B. A bee comes after it.
5. Explanations will vary but should reveal that each word shows one set but there are several parts in each set. These are collective nouns.

Page 57

Answers for 1–3, 5, and 6 will vary.

4. call
   able
   math
   play
7. a s k
   i l l
   d o t
   u s e
   w h o
8. Answers will vary but may include *remelt, remelted, remelting, overmelt, melted, melting, meltable, unmeltable, unmelted, overmelted,* and *overmelting.*

Page 92

(S) The best band in town
(P) is my friend Baldie
(P) perform every Saturday morning
(P) is the lead singer
(P) pounds his drums
(S) The guitar player
(S) They
(S) Bertie
(S) Their shows
(S) Bertie's brother Blaze
(P) is called The Early Birds
(P) are always sold out

Order may vary.

1. The best band in town is called The Early Birds.
2. They perform every Saturday morning.
3. Their shows are always sold out.
4. Bertie is the lead singer or Bertie pounds his drums.
5. Bertie's brother Blaze pounds his drums or Bertie's Brother Blaze is the lead singer.
6. The guitar player is my friend Baldie.

Bonus: Answers will vary.

Page 93

1. **?** (red)
2. **.** (blue)
3. **?** (red)
4. **!** (yellow)
5. **.** (blue)
6. **?** (red)
7. **!** (yellow, green)
8. **!** (yellow)
9. **.** (blue)
10. **?** (red)
11. **!** (green, yellow)
12. **.** (blue)
13. **!** (green)
14. **.** (blue)
15. **?** (red)

Page 94

Down
1. are
2. treat
3. gives
4. need
6. helps
9. slithers
10. crawls
11. knows
12. is

Across
5. work
7. care
8. mending
10. checks
13. rolls

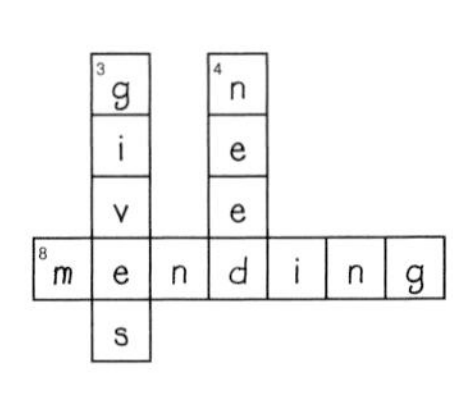

Bonus: Sentences will vary.

Page 96

1. the (red)
2. united states (green)
3. april (yellow)
4. jamz (blue)
5. manny (blue)
6. billy (blue)
7. next (red)
8. friday (yellow)
9. tickets (red)
10. main street (green)
11. new york (green)
12. do (red)
13. saturday (yellow)
14. boston (green)
15. the (red)

Bonus: Answers will vary.

Page 97

1. **?**
2. **.**
3. **?**
4. **.**
5. **.**
6. **?**
7. **!**
8. **.**
9. **.** or **!**
10. **.**
11. **?**
12. **.** or **!**
13. **.**
14. **.** or **!**
15. **!**

Bonus: Sentences will vary.

Page 98

A.
1. family
2. feather
3. fish
4. flash
5. fun

B.
1. pals
2. penny
3. pizza
4. pony
5. pretzel

C.
1. ribbon
2. rides
3. right
4. ring
5. ripe

D.
1. cake
2. camera
3. candy
4. caps
5. carnival

Bonus: Answers will vary.

Page 99

1. moving
2. taking
3. coming
4. arrived
5. taped
6. placed
7. stopped
8. hugged
9. leaving
10. scrubbed
11. riding
12. driving

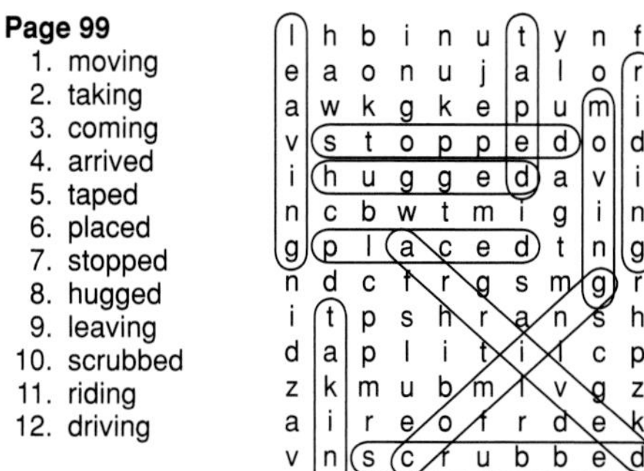
l h b i n u t y n f
e a o n u j a l o r
a w k g k e p u m i
v s t o p p e d o d
i h u g g e d a v i
n c b w t m i g i n
g p l a c e d t n g
n d c f r g s m g r
i t p s h r a n s h
d a p l i t i l c p
z k m u b m l v g z
a i r e o f r d e k
v n s c f u b b e d
r g e d r i v i n g

Bonus: Drop the silent *e* and, if the word has a short-vowel sound, double the ending consonant before adding the ending. If it has a long-vowel sound, add the ending after dropping the silent *e*.

Page 100

Order may vary.
A. flower, flowers; cape, capes; basket, baskets
B. lunch, lunches; dish, dishes; glass, glasses
C. berry, berries; lady, ladies; story, stories
D. wolf, wolves; scarf, scarves; loaf, loaves

Bonus: Answers will vary.

Page 123

Answers for 2, 3, 6, and 8 will vary.
1. Order may vary.
   A. 2 or 8.
   B. 3 or 11
4. Order may vary but should include six different possibilities.
5. 20 + 9
   635
   1000 + 600 + 90 + 7
   8,091
   4,503
7. A. 18
   B. 10
   C. 9
   D. 5
   E. 22

Page 124

2, 4–8. Answers will vary.
1. A. 18, 21: add 3
   B. 20, 25: add 5
3. 90 500 6
   8 60 80
   1 300 100

876, 680, 574, 401, 392, 321, 269, 188, 138

Page 125

1, 4, 6, 7. Answers will vary.

2. A. 33 > 17
   B. 48 > 22
   C. 63 < 71
   D. 44 < 59
   E. 27 < 68
   F. 35 < 53
   G. 48 > 44
   H. 10 < 39

3. 8 + 4 = 12
   4 + 8 = 12
   12 – 8 = 4
   12 – 4 = 8

   5 + 6 = 11
   6 + 5 = 11
   11 – 5 = 6
   11 – 6 = 5

   7 + 3 = 10
   3 + 7 = 10
   10 – 7 = 3
   10 – 3 = 7

   6 + 3 = 9
   3 + 6 = 9
   9 – 6 = 3
   9 – 3 = 6

5. A. Answers will vary.
   B.

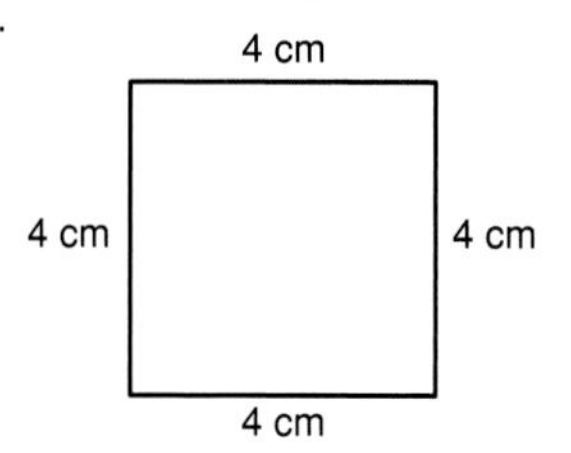
4 cm
4 cm
4 cm
4 cm

8. Patrick—dog
   Sarah—fish
   Charlie—cat
   Explanations will vary.

Page 126

1.

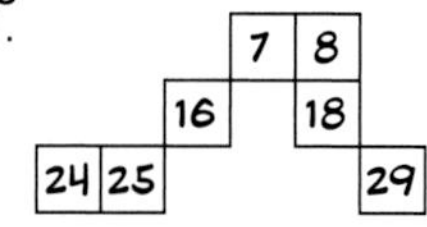
7
8
16
18
24
25
29

2. Answers will vary.
3. Possible answers include 104 < 140 or 140 > 104, 256 > 140 or 140 < 256, 308 > 140 or 140 < 308, 104 < 197 or 197 > 104, 256 > 197 or 197 < 256, 308 > 197 or 197 < 308, 104 < 380 or 380 > 104, 256 < 380 or 380 > 256, 308 < 380 or 380 > 308.
4. Saturday; The hens lay four more eggs each day.
5. Answers will vary but should include information about using the inverse operation.
6. A. 80, 79 B. 190, 193 C. 20, 19
7. A. The tens weren't regrouped. $88.90 + $29.07 = $117.97
   B. The numbers were added instead of multiplied. 6 x 3 = 18
8. Each pie takes ten minutes to eat, so it should take 100 minutes to eat ten pies.

Page 127

Answers for 1, 3, 7, and 8 will vary.
2. A. yes B. no C. yes
4. Take away the *s*.
5. yes, yes
6. 58 = 60, 100; 143 = 140, 100; 216 = 220, 200

Page 128

Answers for 2, 4, and 6 will vary.
1. A. 7 B. 8; Explanations will vary.
3. A. 246 B. 256, 236 C. 346, 146
5. 6, x, =
7. A. 1:05 B. 2:17 C. 3:29; The time increases by one hour and 12 minutes each time.
8. 4 + 4 + 4 = 12, 3 x 4 = 12, 12 ÷ 3 = 4 or 12 ÷ 4 = 3

Page 129

549	**4 tens** M	4 ones N	4 hundreds O
73	3 hundreds K	**3 ones** L	3 tens M
3,592	5 ones Y	5 thousands Z	**5 hundreds** A
8,601	8 hundreds L	8 tens M	**8 thousands** N
6,395	9 hundreds N	**9 tens** O	9 thousands P
102	1 ten A	1 thousand B	**1 hundred** C
427	**7 ones** E	7 hundreds F	7 tens G
9,570	9 tens G	9 hundreds H	**9 thousands** I
2,441	4 thousands J	**4 hundreds** K	4 tens L
706	**7 hundreds** R	7 tens S	7 ones T
1,059	**1 thousand** U	1 hundred V	1 ten W
4,928	2 hundreds B	2 ones C	**2 tens** D

40 M
700 R
3 L
9,000 I
7 E
20 D
90 O
400 K
500 A
1,000 U
100 C
8,000 N
"MOCK-ARONI"

Page 130

A. 24 > 15 63 < 84
15, 24, 63, 84

B. 88 > 79 70 > 69
88, 79, 70, 69

C. 81 > 62 25 < 52
25, 52, 62, 81

D. 54 > 52 46 < 53
54, 53, 52, 46

E. 121 < 143 152 > 135
121, 135, 143, 152

F. 260 < 268 321 > 123
321, 268, 260, 123

G. 119 < 125 132 > 126
119, 125, 126, 132

H. 307 < 319 311 < 314
319, 314, 311, 307

Page 131

A: 36 + 12 = 48; 36 − 12 = 24	B: 64 + 13 = 77; 64 − 13 = 51	C: 82 + 10 = 92; 82 − 10 = 72	D: 53 + 32 = 85; 53 − 32 = 21
E: 56 + 43 = 99; 56 − 43 = 13	F: 74 + 24 = 98; 74 − 24 = 50	G: 45 + 12 = 57; 45 − 12 = 33	H: 47 + 31 = 78; 47 − 31 = 16
I: 35 + 31 = 66; 35 − 31 = 4	J: 63 + 21 = 84; 63 − 21 = 42		

Bonus: Answers will vary but should indicate that the order of numbers in an addition problem does not affect the answer. In a subtraction problem, the larger number must be first.

Page 132

Rock colors will vary.

1. 13 + 16 = **29**; ○20 ○40 ●30	2. 21 + 68 = **89**; ○80 ●90 ○70	3. 56 + 22 = **78**; ●80 ○70 ○60
4. 33 + 21 = **54**; ○30 ○60 ●50	5. 12 + 55 = **67**; ○80 ●70 ○60	6. 37 + 32 = **69**; ●70 ○60 ○80
7. 43 − 22 = **21**; ●20 ○10 ○30	8. 19 − 12 = **7**; ●10 ○20 ○30	9. 67 − 31 = **36**; ○20 ●40 ○50
10. 75 − 31 = **44**; ●50 ○30 ○40	11. 88 − 26 = **62**; ○80 ○70 ●60	12. 57 − 22 = **35**; ○20 ○30 ●40

Bonus: Answers will vary.

Page 133

A. 12:30 B. 1:10 C. 1:50 D. 2:30 E. 3:10

F. 5:35 G. 5:50 H. 6:05 I. 6:20 J. 6:35

K. 8:20 L. 8:30 M. 8:40 N. 8:50 O. 9:00

Bonus: A–E, goldfish; F–J, guppies; K–O, bettas

Page 134

A. 6:37 B. 7:02
C. 10:29 D. 8:41
E. 3:23 F. 4:55
G. 9:52 H. 1:36
I. 2:15 J. 12:09
K. 11:49 L. 5:11
Bonus: The clock should show 6:45.

Page 135

"What's the Scoop?"

1. 11:00; Explanations will vary.
2. Answers will vary.

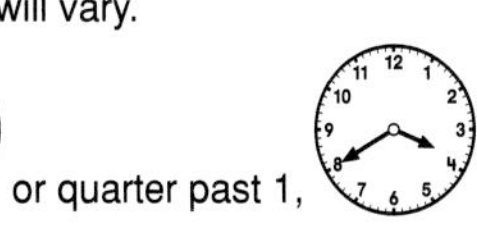

or quarter past 1, or twenty minutes before four, or five minutes before six

3. PM; Explanations will vary.

"Gone Fishing!"
Explanations will vary.

1. ruler
2. yes
3. Fish A

Page 136

Answers for A, D, and F–I will vary.
B. 1 centimeter
C. 10 yards
E. 3½ years
J. 99 inches

Page 137

1. $6.80
2. $2.25
3. $3.20
4. $3.50
5. $4.67
6. $3.25
7. $3.49
8. $4.70

Bonus: $2.12

Page 138

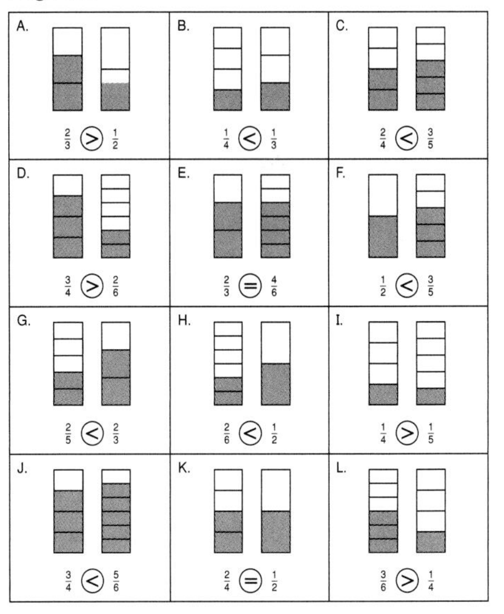
A. 2/3 > 1/2
B. 1/4 < 1/3
C. 2/4 < 3/5
D. 3/4 > 2/6
E. 2/3 = 4/6
F. 1/2 < 3/5
G. 2/5 < 2/3
H. 2/6 < 1/2
I. 1/4 > 1/5
J. 3/4 < 5/6
K. 2/4 = 1/2
L. 3/6 > 1/4

Bonus: Answers will vary.

Page 139

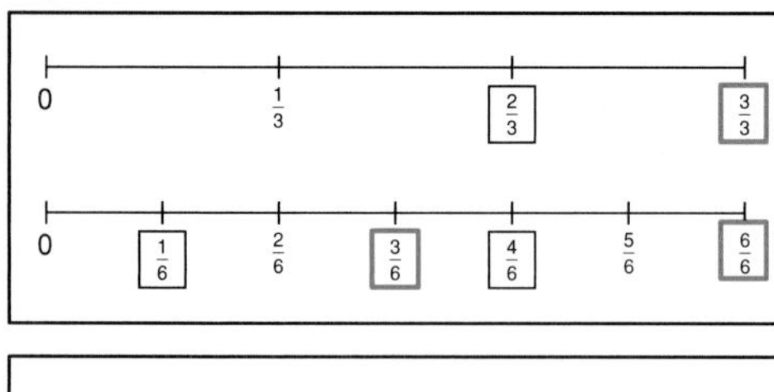

0
1/3
2/3
3/3
0
1/6
2/6
3/6
4/6
5/6
6/6

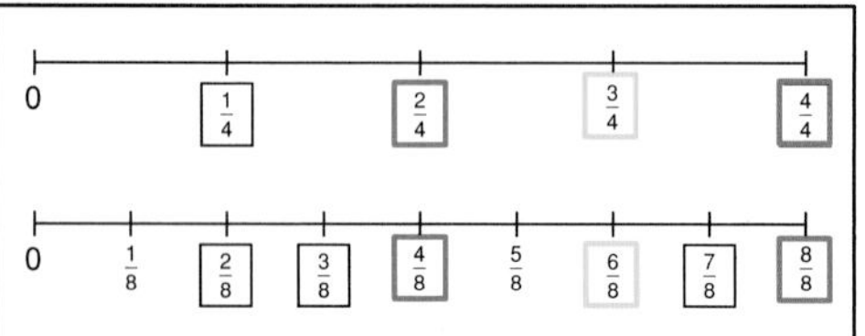

0
1/4
2/4
3/4
4/4
0
1/8
2/8
3/8
4/8
5/8
6/8
7/8
8/8

Bonus: ¼; Explanations will vary.

Page 140
1, 4, 5, 6, 7, 8, 10, 12, 13, 15, 18, 19, and 20 should be colored.

THE WIZARD OF JAWS

Bonus: 1, 4, 5, and 13 should be circled.

Page 141

1. false	7. false
2. true	8. true
3. false	9. false
4. false	10. true
5. true	11. true
6. false	12. false

Bonus: The cup should show five red balls.

Page 142

(A) 120	(B) 160	(D) 90	(E) 360	(G) 350
(H) 240	(I) 200	(M) 320	(N) 140	(R) 180
(T) 150	(U) 210	(V) 80	(Y) 300	

HE ATE EVERYTHING THAT BUGGED HIM.

Bonus: Answers will vary but should indicate that all problems require multiplying by zero in the ones column and zero times any number equals zero.

Page 154
1. yellow
2. plumage
3. facial disk; it reflects sound to the owl's ear openings.
4. feathers; They can provide camouflage and their position shows the owl's mood.
5. claws; They help the owl carry prey.
6. cutting and tearing meat

Bonus: Answers will vary.

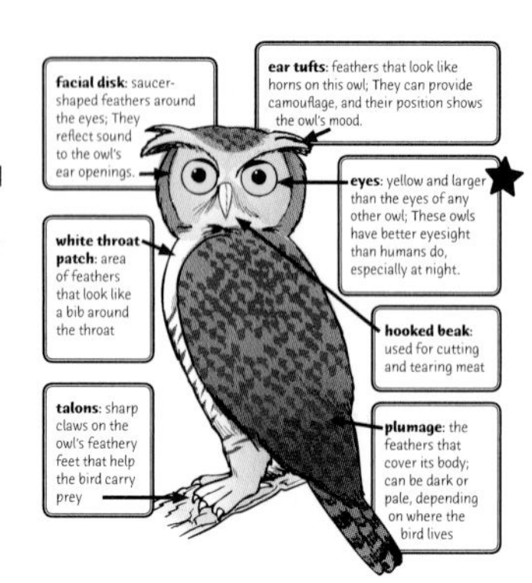

facial disk: saucer-shaped feathers around the eyes; They reflect sound to the owl's ear openings.
ear tufts: feathers that look like horns on this owl; They can provide camouflage, and their position shows the owl's mood.
eyes: yellow and larger than the eyes of any other owl; These owls have better eyesight than humans do, especially at night.
white throat patch: area of feathers that look like a bib around the throat
hooked beak: used for cutting and tearing meat
talons: sharp claws on the owl's feathery feet that help the bird carry prey
plumage: the feathers that cover its body; can be dark or pale, depending on where the bird lives

Page 163
1. between August 25 and October 31, 1451, in Genoa, Italy.
2. to sail west to reach the Indies
3. Spain
4. *Niña, Pinta, Santa Maria*
5. 90
6. 1492
7. Atlantic
8. October 11 or 12, 1492
9. West Indies
10. October

Bonus: October 10, 2011

Page 190
A. 3; 8; 8 + 8 + 8 = 24; 24; 3 x 8 = 24
B. 8; 5; 5 + 5 + 5 + 5 + 5 + 5 + 5 + 5 = 40; 40; 8 x 5 = 40; 40
C. 5; 3; 3 + 3 + 3 + 3 + 3 =15; 15; 5 x 3 = 15; 15
D. 6; 4; 4 + 4 + 4 + 4 + 4 + 4 = 24; 24; 6 x 4 = 24; 24
E. 7; 6; 6 + 6 + 6 + 6 + 6 + 6 + 6 = 42; 7 x 6 = 42; 42
F. 4; 10; 10 + 10 + 10 + 10 = 40; 40; 4 x 10 = 40; 40 or 8; 5; 5 + 5 + 5 + 5 + 5 + 5 + 5 + 5 = 40; 40; 8 x 5 = 40; 40

Page 202

A. 53	I. 69
B. 99	J. 215
C. 23	K. 162
D. 146	L. 85
E. 67	M. 15
F. 38	N. 45
G. 268	O. 127
H. 82	

Bonus: Order may vary. 59 = 5 tens, 9 ones; 74 = 7 tens, 4 ones; 283 = 2 hundreds, 8 tens, 3 ones

Page 203
"Write On!"
Answers will vary. Possible answers include the following:
ban, can, fan, man, pan, ran, tan, van
bed, beg, bet
ham, hem, him, hum
bob, bog, bop, cod, cog, con, cop, cot, dog, dot, fog, gob, god, got, hog, hop, hot, job, jog, jot, lob, log, lop, lot, nod, not, pod, pop, pot, rob, rod, rot, sob, sod, sop, top, tot
pad, pan, pat, peg, pen, pep, pet, pig, pin, pip, pit, pod, pop, pot, pub, pug, pun, pup
bluff, fluff, gruff, snuff, stuff
champ, chant, chats, check, chefs, chess, chest, chick, chimp, chips, chomp, chops, chuck, chump, chunk
brick, check, click, clock, cluck, crock, flack, fleck, flick, knack, knock, pluck, prick, quick, shack, shock, shuck, slack, slick, smack, smock, snack, snuck, speck, track, trick, truck, whack, wreck

"Word Parts"
Answers will vary. Possible answers include *bashful, brightly, cheerful, coldly, eventful, evenly, fearful, firmly, graceful, gladly, houseful, hotly, playful, proudly, respectful, rudely, thankful,* and *truly.*

"Clued In"
1. PE
2. music
3. art

Page 204
"Fact Factories"

A. 16	I. 4
B. 10	J. 10
C. 2	K. 18
D. 12	L. 6
E. 9	M. 10
F. 7	N. 1
G. 3	O. 10
H. 10	

Page 213

Things Seen at the Patch		
Object	**Tally Marks**	**Total**
pumpkins	~~IIII~~ ~~IIII~~ II	12
gourds	~~IIII~~ I	6
spiders	~~IIII~~ III	8
owls	III	3
tractors	II	2

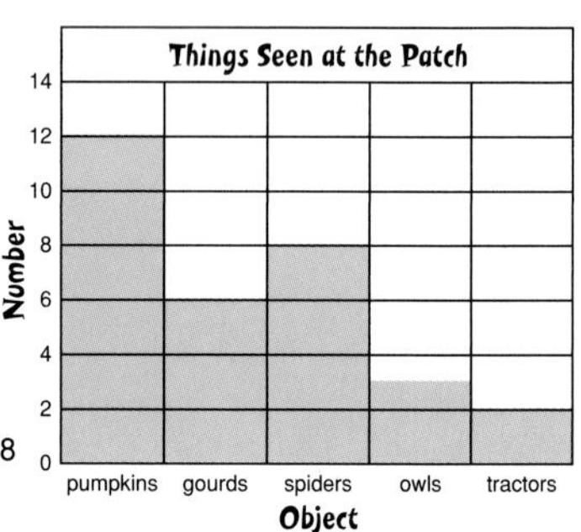

Things Seen at the Patch
Number
0
2
4
6
8
10
12
14
pumpkins
gourds
spiders
owls
tractors
Object

A. pumpkins	E. 18; 12 + 6 = 18
B. tractors	F. 6; ~~IIII~~ I
C. 11	G. 2
D. 5	H. 31

Bonus: Answers will vary.

Page 214

A. 37¢
B. 65¢ C. 36¢
D. 37¢ E. 62¢
F. 53¢ G. 91¢
H. Sour Skulls
I. gummy worms
J. Goblin Gum
K. candy corn
L. raisins
M. Monster Choco Bar
N. candy corn
O. gummy worms and lollipop

Bonus: 53¢, 62¢, 65¢, 91¢

Page 215

Answers will vary.

Thanksgiving Day in the US	Both	Thanksgiving Day in Canada
The first Thanksgiving took place in 1621. In 1863, President Lincoln made the last Thursday in November a day for all Americans to give thanks. It is now held on the fourth Thursday in November. In 2011, Thanksgiving will be on November 24.	People at the first Thanksgiving were from England. People will enjoy turkey, time with family, and parades on this day.	The first Thanksgiving took place in 1578. For many years, this holiday was held on the last Monday in October. It is now held on the second Monday in October. In 2011, Thanksgiving will be on October 10.

Page 216

"More, More, More!"

(fatter)
(thinner)
(rounder)
beautifuller
(older)
(smaller)
(fancier)
oranger
(bigger)
(longer)
carefuller
(smoother)

Page 217

"Spread Your Wings"

6 + 7 = 13, 13 – 7 = 6 or 13 – 6 = 7; 14 – 9 = 5, 5 + 9 = 14; 15 – 8 = 7, 7 + 8 = 15; 16 – 7 = 9, 9 + 7 = 16; 8 + 4 = 12, 12 – 4 = 8 or 12 – 8 = 4

"Turkey Trot"

6,052: six thousand fifty-two; 6,000 + 50 + 2
981: nine hundred eighty-one; 900 + 80 + 1
2,743: two thousand seven hundred forty-three; 2,000 + 700 + 40 + 3
135: one hundred thirty-five; 100 + 30 + 5
9,428: nine thousand four hundred twenty-eight; 9,000 + 400 + 20 + 8

"Big Jack"

Explanations will vary; 3,900

Page 225

1 are
2 was
3 has
4 am
5 were
6 is
7 has
8 are
9 was
10 is
11 is
12 have

2. were
3. have
5. was
8. is
11. are
12. has

Bonus: Sentences will vary.

Page 226

1. 7:20
2. 1:45
3. 3:25
4. 10:50
5. 2:50
6. 4:35
7. 3:45
8. 10:15
9. 8:55
10. 2:05
11. 6:15
12. 8:30
13. 12:15
14. 8:15
15. 5:30

Bonus: 2 hours, 45 minutes; Explanations will vary.

Page 227

4 A. Martin marries (coretta) (scott) in 1953.
10 B. Martin Luther King Jr. dies on (april) 4, 1968, in (memphis), Tennessee.
8 C. (in) 1964, King accepts the Nobel Peace Prize.
3 D. (in) 1948, (martin) becomes a minister.
1 E. Martin is born on (january) 15, 1929.
5 F. In 1954, Martin is a pastor in (montgomery), (alabama).
7 G. Martin gives his "I Have a Dream" speech on (august) 28, 1963.
2 H. Martin goes to Morehouse College in Atlanta, (georgia) in 1944.
9 I. Dr. (king) organizes peaceful protests in 1965.
6 J. In 1955, King meets (rosa) (parks) and begins the bus boycotts.

Bonus: Sentences will vary.

Page 229

"Right for the Weather"

The hat, the coat, and the skis have symmetry.
The mittens, boots, and skis are congruent.

"Home Sweet Home"

Order will vary. Possible answers include 89 – 75 = 14, 89 – 54 = 35, 89 – 43 = 46, 89 – 10 = 79, 75 – 54 = 21, 75 – 43 = 32, 75 – 10 = 65, 54 – 43 = 11, 54 – 10 = 44, 43 – 10 = 33.

"Growing Numbers"

Answers will vary but should include two or more of the digits 1, 3, 4, 6, and 9.

Page 234

Order of words will vary.

vowel sound like *bird*	vowel sound like *care*	vowel sound like *more*
dessert	bear	soar
turkey	chair	four
shirt	fair	corn
turtle	beware	door
winter	square	board
word	there	north

Bonus: Answers will vary.

Page 235

1. inform; Explanations will vary.
2. c
3. Rosa, Mrs. Parks (red); December (blue); Alabama (yellow)
4. a woman who is admired for her achievements; Explanations will vary.

Bonus: Answers will vary.

Page 238

"Off the Mark"

Order and antonyms may vary.
real: fake, phony, unreal
subtract: add
wrong: correct, right
full: bare, empty
evening: dawn, morning
remember: forget, unlearn
shrink: expand, swell
stinky: perfumed, sweet
soar: dip, dive, fall

Page 239
"Head Over Heels"

A. slide, flip, turn
B. slide, flip, turn
C. slide, flip, turn

"Tooth Fairy Treasures"

A. 2/6 molars, (4/6) bicuspids
B. (5/8) molars, 3/8 bicuspids
C. (3/4) molars, 1/4 bicuspids
D. 1/3 molars, (2/3) bicuspids

"Lucky Numbers"
Order of problems and order of factors in problems will vary.
A. 1 x 3 = 3, 4 x 3 = 12, 6 x 3 = 18, 8 x 3 = 24
B. 2 x 5 = 10, 0 x 5 = 0, 3 x 5 = 15, 9 x 5 = 45
C. 5 x 7 = 35, 3 x 7 = 21, 7 x 7 = 49, 8 x 7 = 56

"Leaping Ahead"
2016, 2020, 2024, 2028, 2032; Explanations will vary.

Page 246

1. **.**	6. **.**	11. **?**
2. **?**	7. **.**	12. **?**
3. **!**	8. **!**	13. **!**
4. **?**	9. **?**	14. **.**
5. **!**	10. **.**	15. **!**

Bonus: Sentences will vary.

Page 247
Sentences will vary.

1. Bart and Belle are good players on the team.
2. Coach Bruno and Bud cheer for the players, and both are fair.
3. Bart and Bud love baseball.
4. Belle plays baseball. Coach Bruno teaches how to play baseball.
5. Belle plays the game on the field. Bud sits on the bench and watches the game.
6. Bart is the best batter. Belle is the best pitcher.

Bonus: Sentences will vary.

Page 248
Order will vary.

9 x 4 = 36 4 x 9 = 36 36 ÷ 4 = 9 36 ÷ 9 = 4		8 x 5 = 40 5 x 8 = 40 40 ÷ 8 = 5 40 ÷ 5 = 8
3 x 7 = 21 7 x 3 = 21 21 ÷ 7 = 3 21 ÷ 3 = 7		8 x 7 = 56 7 x 8 = 56 56 ÷ 8 = 7 56 ÷ 7 = 8
6 x 3 = 18 3 x 6 = 18 18 ÷ 6 = 3 18 ÷ 3 = 6		6 x 2 = 12 2 x 6 = 12 12 ÷ 6 = 2 12 ÷ 2 = 6
Bonus: 6 x 4 = 24 4 x 6 = 24 24 ÷ 6 = 4 24 ÷ 4 = 6	or	6 x 5 = 30 5 x 6 = 30 30 ÷ 6 = 5 30 ÷ 5 = 6
2 x 7 = 14 7 x 2 = 14 14 ÷ 2 = 7 14 ÷ 7 = 2		

Page 249
"Two in One"
brunch, *breakfast* and *lunch*; *smog*, *smoke* and *fog*; *guesstimate*, *guess* and *estimate*; *liger*, *lion* and *tiger*; *spork*, *spoon* and *fork*; *splatter*, *splash* and *spatter*; *motel*, *motor* and *hotel*; *email*, *electronic* and *mail*

Page 250
"Jelly Bean Jumble"
Arrays will vary but should represent three or more of the following arrangements:
A. 12 rows of one, one row of 12, two rows of six, six rows of two, three rows of four, four rows of three
B. six rows of one, one row of six, two rows of three, three rows of two
C. four rows of one, one row of four, two rows of two

Page 256

A. 28	B. 113	C. 46	D. 19	E. 12	F. 4	G. 13
H. 9	I. 29	J. 14	K. 16	L. 49	M. 26	N. 20
O. 275	P. 147	Q. 44	R. 17			

Bonus: $\begin{array}{r}15\\5\overline{)75}\end{array}$ $\begin{array}{r}8\\8\overline{)64}\end{array}$

Page 257
"Serving Up Words"
Order may vary.

agreeable, attachable, breakable, buildable, chewable, employable, lockable, payable

agreement, attachment, employment, payment

"Letter From Camp"

July 15, 2012

Dear Mom and Dad,
Camp is so fun! Today we had to swim across the lake. I was first! Tonight we'll sing songs around the campfire. This place rocks!

Love,
Barry

Page 258
"Wally Wakeboarder"
Order may vary. Possible trios are body slide, indy, roast beef; body slide, roast beef, seatbelt; body slide, indy, seatbelt; no-hander, indy, roast beef; no-hander, indy, seatbelt; no-hander, roast beef, seatbelt.

Page 262

1. proudly, crown, down, bouts
2. bout: an athletic match, opponent: one that takes the opposite position (in a contest), champion: a winner of first prize
3. he had eight arms
4. He quickly pinned them down.
5. He was the wrestling champion.

Bonus: Answers will vary.

INDEX